LAB MANUAL

Networking
Fundamentals
Fourth Edition

Ola Jobi • Richard M. Roberts • Chuck Easttom

Publisher
The Goodheart-Willcox Company, Inc.
Tinley Park, IL
www.g-w.com

Copyright © 2024
by
The Goodheart-Willcox Company, Inc.

All rights reserved. No part of this work may be reproduced, stored, or transmitted
in any form or by any electronic or mechanical means, including information storage
and retrieval systems, without the prior written permission of
The Goodheart-Willcox Company, Inc.

ISBN 978-1-68584-604-6

1 2 3 4 5 6 7 8 9 – 24 – 28 27 26 25 24 23

The Goodheart-Willcox Company, Inc. Brand Disclaimer: Brand names, company names, and illustrations for products and services included in this text are provided for educational purposes only and do not represent or imply endorsement or recommendation by the author or the publisher.

The Goodheart-Willcox Company, Inc. Safety Notice: The reader is expressly advised to carefully read, understand, and apply all safety precautions and warnings described in this book or that might also be indicated in undertaking the activities and exercises described herein to minimize risk of personal injury or injury to others. Common sense and good judgment should also be exercised and applied to help avoid all potential hazards. The reader should always refer to the appropriate manufacturer's technical information, directions, and recommendations; then proceed with care to follow specific equipment operating instructions. The reader should understand these notices and cautions are not exhaustive.

The publisher makes no warranty or representation whatsoever, either expressed or implied, including but not limited to equipment, procedures, and applications described or referred to herein, their quality, performance, merchantability, or fitness for a particular purpose. The publisher assumes no responsibility for any changes, errors, or omissions in this book. The publisher specifically disclaims any liability whatsoever, including any direct, indirect, incidental, consequential, special, or exemplary damages resulting, in whole or in part, from the reader's use or reliance upon the information, instructions, procedures, warnings, cautions, applications, or other matter contained in this book. The publisher assumes no responsibility for the activities of the reader.

The Goodheart-Willcox Company, Inc. Internet Disclaimer: The Internet resources and listings in this Goodheart-Willcox Publisher product are provided solely as a convenience to you. These resources and listings were reviewed at the time of publication to provide you with accurate, safe, and appropriate information. Goodheart-Willcox Publisher has no control over the referenced websites and, due to the dynamic nature of the Internet, is not responsible or liable for the content, products, or performance of links to other websites or resources. Goodheart-Willcox Publisher makes no representation, either expressed or implied, regarding the content of these websites, and such references do not constitute an endorsement or recommendation of the information or content presented. It is your responsibility to take all protective measures to guard against inappropriate content, viruses, or other destructive elements.

Image Credits. asharkyu/Shutterstock.com.

Introduction

This *Lab Manual* complements the *Networking Fundamentals* textbook and classroom-related studies. The laboratory activities in this manual are designed with the novice or entry-level student in mind as well as the new professional. The activities provide the valuable skills needed to obtain or retain a job in the networking environment.

Laboratory activities should be an essential part of your training because they link the concepts and related knowledge presented in the *Networking Fundamentals* textbook to on-the-job performance. A network technician cannot be trained simply through textbooks, lectures, and demonstrations.

Many of the laboratory activities are designed to use minimal equipment. Whenever possible, you should perform the laboratory activities at home to reinforce what you have learned in class or to catch up if you fall behind. Check with your instructor to determine which activities you can perform at home. Some activities may be beyond your scope of expertise at that given time and may result in disastrous consequences to your home computer.

It is strongly advised that serious students of networking technology build or buy two computers to connect as a simple network. The computers do not need to be expensive, especially the workstation. Check with your instructor for some suggestions about setting up a home network.

In most lab settings, the equipment is used by more than one student. Your instructor may wish you to make a restore point before every laboratory activity on the computer you are using. Always leave the computer in working order for the next student to use.

The typical networking fundamentals student is assumed to have basic knowledge of standard desktop operating systems obtained through a CompTIA A+ type of classroom instruction or by completing relevant coursework. Since not all students will have completed a CompTIA A+ course, many key topics are presented in this manual that should have been covered or mastered during the study of computer service and repair. Some critical topics, such as installing a network adapter card, setting up a peer-to-peer network, and installing network shares, are included in this *Lab Manual* to ensure that students have the required basic skills necessary to complete the course.

Using This Manual

Each laboratory activity begins with a number of learning outcomes. These are the goals you should accomplish while working through the activity. In addition to the outcomes, each laboratory activity contains an *Introduction* section, which presents a brief description of the activity and, in some cases, an overview of the required theory.

Following the *Introduction* is an *Equipment and Materials* list. The list provides general guidelines for the material required for the activity. Check the *Equipment and Materials* list before beginning the activity to see what software and equipment is needed.

The *Procedure* section provides step-by-step instructions for completing the activity. You should read through the entire laboratory activity, including the *Procedure* section, before beginning an activity. If you have any questions about the requirements or procedures involved with the activity, ask your instructor for help. Some laboratory activities require you to enter information in the *Equipment and Materials* list or *Procedure* section. These are not test questions, but simply opportunities to record information about the computer you are using. Often, this information will be required in later steps in the activity.

These labs were developed using Windows 10. Since there are multiple versions of Windows 10 available, there may be some differences in file paths, titles, and visual appearance. If you happen to encounter a difference between what is listed in this manual and what you experience as you perform the activity, consult with your instructor.

The final part of each laboratory activity is the *Review Questions*. The *Review Questions* are designed to reinforce the concepts critical to each lesson and to closely match the CompTIA Network+ certification objectives. Not all questions can be answered simply by reading through the laboratory activity. Some questions require you to deduce the answer using the knowledge you have gained from working through the exercise. Other questions require you to consult outside sources. Such questions force you to use your new knowledge, and thus, reinforce the new knowledge. You should complete all review questions and then routinely review the questions to better prepare for Network+ certification exam and classroom exams.

Be sure to read any Notes or Warnings that you encounter. Such features may alert you to an act that may damage your computer or yourself. Losing all of your data is the most common danger you will encounter with computers, but you may also encounter some dangerous voltages. Those repairs should be left to special technicians. Consult the following general safety procedures before performing any laboratory activity.

General Safety Procedures

1. Before opening a computer's case, turn off all power to the PC and accessories and unplug the power cord from the outlet.

2. Before working on the computer, discharge static electricity by touching an unpainted, metallic surface. Paint is an insulator and may prevent a static discharge from the body.

3. Do not touch pin connectors on chips or other components. Pins can be easily bent. Additionally, when a person touches something, the oils in the person's skin leave a residue, which can hinder a low-voltage electrical connection.

4. Leave components in their antistatic bags until needed. When you are done with the parts, return them to the antistatic bags. Do not leave parts on work surfaces or on the PC case.

5. Do not touch connection pins or the conductive edge of any electronic component, such as network interface cards.

Never unplug or connect any device while power is applied to the PC. Unplugging a device, such as the hard disk drive or network adapter card, while power is applied can seriously damage the device.

Contents

CHAPTER 1
Introduction to Networking

Laboratory Activity 1 Introduction to the CompTIA Network+ Examination Objectives 1

CHAPTER 2
Network Media—Copper Core Cable

Laboratory Activity 2 Making a Crossover Cable . . . 5
Laboratory Activity 3 Viewing Network Connection Status and Properties (Part I) . . . 7
Laboratory Activity 4 Navigating Windows 10 . . . 13
Laboratory Activity 5 Viewing Network Connection Status and Properties (Part II) 17
Laboratory Activity 6 Network and Sharing Center 21
Laboratory Activity 7 Connecting Two Computers Using a Crossover Cable . . . 27
Laboratory Activity 8 Testing Internet Connection Speeds 29

CHAPTER 3
Fiber-Optic Cable

Laboratory Activity 9 Installing and Configuring a PCI Network Adapter . . . 33
Laboratory Activity 10 Creating a Windows 10 Peer-to-Peer Network 41
Laboratory Activity 11 HomeGroup 45
Laboratory Activity 12 Exploring Network Adapter Configuration Settings 51

CHAPTER 4
Wireless Technology

Laboratory Activity 13 Configuring and Troubleshooting Wireless Connections . . . 59

Laboratory Activity 14 Wireless Throughput vs. Distance 67

CHAPTER 5
Digital Encoding and Data Transmission

Laboratory Activity 15 Wireshark Network Protocol Analyzer 71
Laboratory Activity 16 Wireshark OSI Model Exploration 79

CHAPTER 6
Network Operating Systems and Network Communications

Laboratory Activity 17 Observing ARP, LLMNR, and NBNS with Wireshark 83
Laboratory Activity 18 Observing Background Communication with Wireshark 89
Laboratory Activity 19 Observing Ping with Wireshark 93

CHAPTER 7
Microsoft Network Operating Systems

Laboratory Activity 20 Installing Windows Server 2022 95
Laboratory Activity 21 Configuring Windows Server 2022 Roles 103
Laboratory Activity 22 Creating a Shared Folder in Windows Server 2022 109
Laboratory Activity 23 Adding the File Server Role to Windows Server 2022 117
Laboratory Activity 24 Adding a Group in Windows Server 2022 125
Laboratory Activity 25 Joining a Domain . . . 129
Laboratory Activity 26 Adding the Print Services Role to Windows Server 2022 133
Laboratory Activity 27 Observing Share Transactions with Wireshark 137

CHAPTER 8
UNIX/Linux Operating Systems

Laboratory Activity 28 Installing Ubuntu Linux . . .143
Laboratory Activity 29 Adding
 a New User in Ubuntu. 149
Laboratory Activity 30 Introduction to KDE
 Terminal Konsole. 153
Laboratory Activity 31 Exploring
 the Linux File System 161
Laboratory Activity 32 Introduction to Samba. . .169

CHAPTER 9
Introduction to Servers

Laboratory Activity 33 Inspecting and
 Defragmenting Partitions. 177
Laboratory Activity 34 Using the Disk
 Management Utility. 183
Laboratory Activity 35 Installing
 a RAID System 189

CHAPTER 10
TCP/IP Fundamentals

Laboratory Activity 36 Configuring
 a DHCP Server. 193
Laboratory Activity 37 Observing APIPA. . . . 205
Laboratory Activity 38 Configuring an
 Alternate IPv4 Address 207
Laboratory Activity 39 Configuring ICS 211
Laboratory Activity 40 Observing DHCP
 Commands with Wireshark. 219
Laboratory Activity 41 Observing ICS
 Activity with Wireshark. 223

CHAPTER 11
Subnetting

Laboratory Activity 42 Using Microsoft
 Calculator for Binary Conversion 225
Laboratory Activity 43 Observing the Effects
 of an IPv4 Subnet Mask 229

CHAPTER 12
Additional Transmission Modalities

Laboratory Activity 44 Route Print Command. . . 233
Laboratory Activity 45 Performing a System
 Backup and Restore 239

CHAPTER 13
Web Servers and Services

Laboratory Activity 46 Creating a Web
 Page Using HTML 245
Laboratory Activity 47 Creating
 an Intranet Web Page. 249
Laboratory Activity 48 Observing E-Mail
 Activity with Wireshark. 253
Laboratory Activity 49 Configuring FTP 257
Laboratory Activity 50 Observing FTP
 Activity with Wireshark. 263
Laboratory Activity 51 Observing HTTP
 Activity with Wireshark. 265

CHAPTER 14
Remote Access and Long-Distance Communications

Laboratory Activity 52 Creating a Virtual
 Private Network Connection 269
Laboratory Activity 53 Observing VPN
 Activity with Wireshark. 279
Laboratory Activity 54 Microsoft Quick Assist . . .285
Laboratory Activity 55 Using the Tracert
 and Pathping Commands. 291

CHAPTER 15
Network Security

Laboratory Activity 56 Observing the TCP/IP
 Three-Way Handshake 295
Laboratory Activity 57 Wireless Encryption. . . 299
Laboratory Activity 58 NTFS
 Encrypting File System 305
Laboratory Activity 59 Configuring a Firewall . . .309

Laboratory Activity 60 Digital Certificates. . . .317
Laboratory Activity 61 SANS Organization. . . .325
Laboratory Activity 62 TCP/IP Filtering. 327

CHAPTER 16
Cloud Computing

Laboratory Activity 63 Downloading and
　　　　　Installing an Antivirus Program 333
Laboratory Activity 64 Obtaining
　　　　　Malware Information 335

CHAPTER 17
Fundamentals of Troubleshooting a Network

Laboratory Activity 65 Reset Menu Options . . .337
Laboratory Activity 66 Windows 10
　　　　　Recovery Environment 339
Laboratory Activity 67 Create a
　　　　　Recovery Drive 343
Laboratory Activity 68 System
　　　　　Configuration Utility 349
Laboratory Activity 69 Using the
　　　　　Nbtstat Command. 353
Laboratory Activity 70 System Information . . .359
Laboratory Activity 71 Online Help
　　　　　for Network Problems. 363

CHAPTER 18
Designing and Installing a New Network

Laboratory Activity 72 Establishing a Baseline. . .367

CHAPTER 19
Network+ Certification Exam Preparation

Laboratory Activity 73 Creating a CompTIA
　　　　　Network+ Certification Study Guide 373

CHAPTER 20
Employment in the Field of Networking Technology

Laboratory Activity 74 Writing a Résumé 375
Laboratory Activity 75
　　　　　Conducting a Job Search 377

Name _____ Date _____ Class _____

Introduction to the CompTIA Network+ Examination Objectives

Outcomes
After completing this laboratory activity, you will be able to:
- Use the Internet to locate and download the Network+ examination objectives.
- Identify required knowledge associated with the Network+ certification exam.

Introduction
The CompTIA organization provides a blueprint of the areas or objectives tested for on the CompTIA Network+ certification exam. This laboratory activity will familiarize you with these objectives. Becoming familiar with the Network+ examination objectives will help you concentrate on the required knowledge associated with the exam as you proceed through this course.

The Network+ examination objectives are revised periodically. While every effort has been made to keep the course content up-to-date, it is recommended that you check the CompTIA website (www.comptia.org) periodically throughout this course for additional changes.

However, do not lose focus on the intent of this networking fundamentals course. You are not in this course simply to pass the CompTIA Network+ certification exam. You are in this course to learn networking fundamentals. You can prepare for the Network+ certification exam by memorizing facts and figures, but memorization of facts and figures will not prepare you to be a successful network technician. To be a successful network technician, you need a combination of textbook readings, classroom lecture and discussion, lab activities, and, most importantly, a desire to learn the subject. The laboratory activities can provide you with a wealth of experiences that cannot be obtained through textbook readings and classroom lectures.

Equipment and Materials
- PC with Internet access

NOTE
This laboratory activity may be performed at home.

Procedure

1. _____ Report to your assigned workstation for this activity.

2. _____ Boot the PC and access the CompTIA website at www.comptia.org. (Note that the website domain address ends in .org, not .com.)

3. _____ Navigate the website until you locate the **Certifications** link. At the time of this writing, the **Certifications** link is near the center of the home page, as shown in the following image.

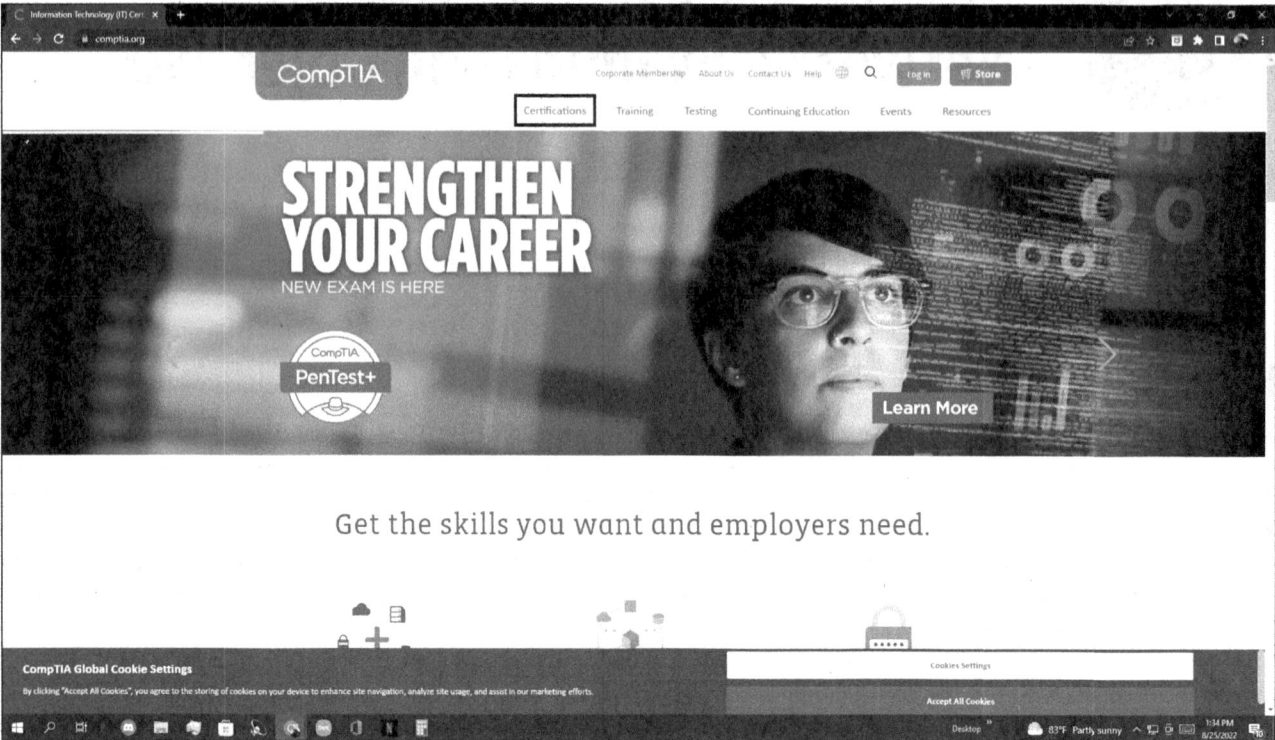

Goodheart-Willcox Publisher

4. _____ Once you have found the **Certifications** link, click the link to navigate to the certification objectives download page. On the Certification page, hover over the **Certifications** tab and then click the **Network+** link, shown in the following image.

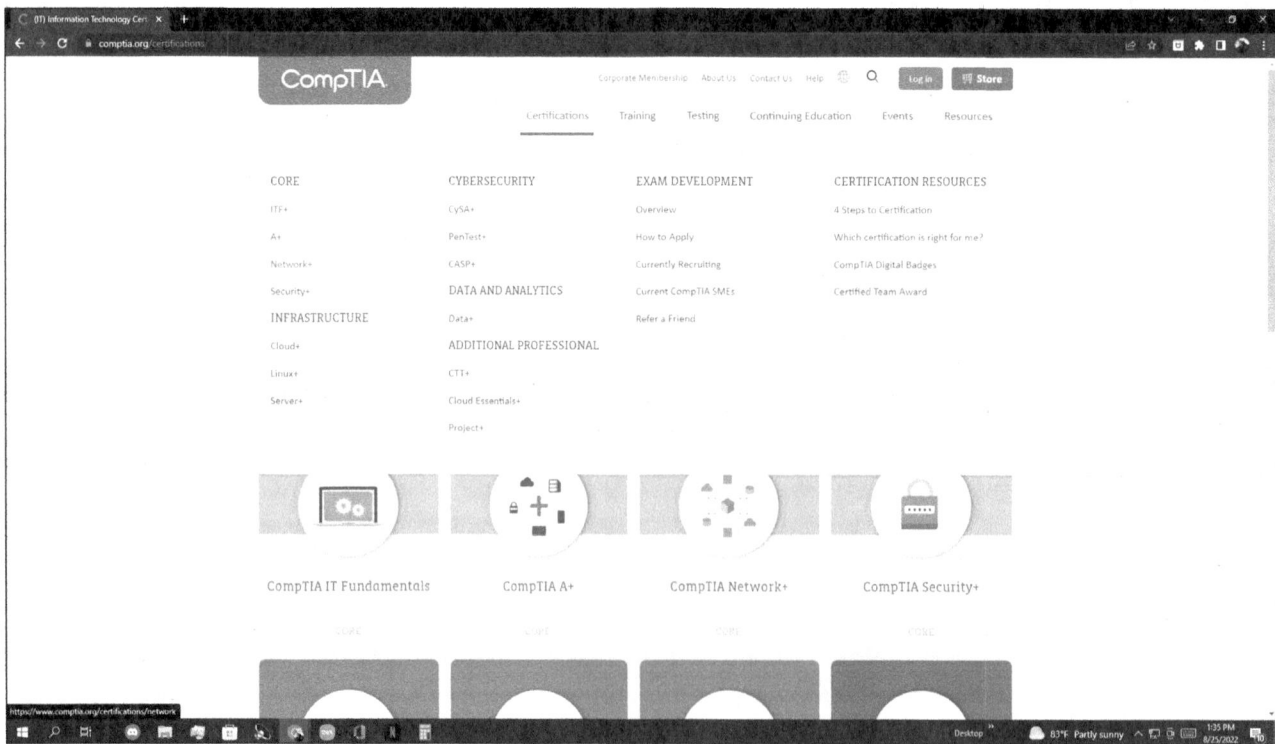

Goodheart-Willcox Publisher

Name _____

Scroll down the page to complete the registration form under the **Get Practice Questions and Exam Objectives** label. You will have to register before you can download the certification objectives. Registration requires a valid e-mail address, your name, and country before being allowed to download a PDF of the test objectives. You may be presented with several variations of the test objectives. Be sure to download the very latest version. Currently, the latest version is N10-008. Also, be aware that CompTIA provides a short set of sample test questions so that you will have an idea of the difficulty level of the questions and insight of what to expect on the test. If you have difficulty locating the certification objectives download page, you can conduct an online search using the phrase CompTIA Network+ objectives.

5. _____ After you have completed the download, look at the objectives and fill in the domain areas and the percentage that each domain represents in the following chart.

CompTIA Network+ Certification Domain Areas	Percent of Examination
Total	**100%**

(Based on N10-008 objectives)

6. _____ Scan through the Domain 1.0 contents, and note the many acronyms listed in the objectives. There are hundreds of acronyms used in the network-technology industry. The last few pages of the Network+ examination objectives list the common acronyms associated with the test. Scan the last few pages of the objectives to see how the acronyms are presented.

7. _____ Scan Domain 2.0 through Domain 5.0. You will see more acronyms.

8. _____ Look through the entire list of Network+ examination objectives to see if you can locate which network operating system will be covered. See if you can locate operating system terms such as Novell, Microsoft, and Linux.

Did you see any of these terms within the testing objectives? Yes _____ No _____

You should not have located any terms specific to the three major operating systems. The Network+ certification exam is vender neutral, which means it does not align specifically with any one vender's network operating system. As you progress through the course, you will become familiar with the various operating systems, and you will see that the terminology is very similar, especially the acronyms used. The test measures basic networking technology, not vender-specific, operating-system knowledge. Vender-specific certifications are more advanced than the Network+ certification, but mastering networking fundamentals is a must before mastering vender-specific skills.

9. _____ Keep a copy of the CompTIA Network+ certification exam objectives in your notebook for reference. As you progress through this course, check off items listed in the objectives as you learn them. By the time you finish the course, you should have covered each and every objective.

10. _____ Use your copy of the Network+ examination objectives to answer the review questions.

Review Questions

1. What is the purpose of the test?

2. How many layers in the OSI model are listed in Domain 1.1?

3. List the network types described in Domain 1.2.

4. What is the main topic in the first section of Domain 4.0?

5. What do the two acronyms "Mbps" and "MBps" represent?

Name _____ Date _____ Class _____

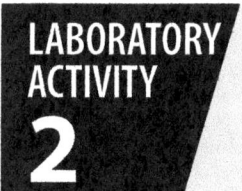

Making a Crossover Cable

Outcomes

After completing this laboratory activity, you will be able to:
- Construct an Ethernet crossover cable.
- Differentiate a crossover cable from a straight-through cable.
- Recall where a crossover cable might be used.

Introduction

In this laboratory activity, you will make an Ethernet crossover cable from two RJ-45 connectors and a one three-foot length of Category 5e cable. Crossover cables are typically used for connecting two workstations together without the use of a hub. They are also used for connecting some network equipment together that do not have a cable select feature, such as hubs. A cable select feature allows the equipment to establish a specific connection port automatically for use with either a straight-through cable or a crossover cable.

The crossover cable is made by reversing pin connections 1, 2, 3, and 6 at one end of the cable. Look at the following wire map.

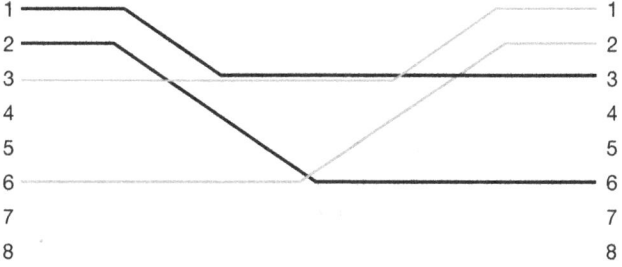

Goodheart-Willcox Publisher

The wire map indicates that pin 1 connects to pin 3 and pin 2 connects to pin 6. A crossover cable can be made easily by wiring an RJ-45 connector at one end of the cable following the 568A standard and wiring the RJ-45 connector at the other end of the cable following the 568B standard.

	568A		568B
Pin #	**Color**	**Pin #**	**Color**
1	Green striped	1	Orange striped
2	Green	2	Orange
3	Orange striped	3	Green striped
4	Blue	4	Blue
5	Blue striped	5	Blue striped
6	Orange	6	Green
7	Brown striped	7	Brown striped
8	Brown	8	Brown

Goodheart-Willcox Publisher

Equipment and Materials

- Two or more RJ-45 connectors (Additional connectors may be required for mistakes.)
- Standard RJ-45 crimping tool
- UTP cable stripper (Some crimping tools incorporate a striping tool as part of the assembly.)
- 3-foot length of Category 5e UTP cable
- Cable tester
- Paper and pencil or pen to make drawing of the cable assembly color code

Procedure

1. _____ Gather all required materials and report to your assigned workstation.
2. _____ Make a chart representing the color sequence for each end of the cable based on the 568A and 568B standards. Ensure the instructor has approved the chart before you proceed.
3. _____ Remove approximately 1 1/2" to 2" of outer jacket from one end of the UTP cable.
4. _____ Arrange the conductors into the 568A color-code sequence. Trim the conductors so that approximately 1/2" protrudes from the outer jacket.
5. _____ Carefully insert the conductors into the RJ-45 connector and then crimp the connector.
6. _____ Repeat steps 3 through 5 using the 568B color-code sequence instead of the 568A color-code sequence.
7. _____ Test the cable using a standard cable test tool. If required, set the tool to test for a crossover cable.
8. _____ Have your instructor check your project.
9. _____ Clean up your workstation and then return all materials and equipment to their proper storage areas.
10. _____ Answer the review questions.

> **NOTE**
> Save this cable. It will be used in a later laboratory activity to connect two workstations.

Review Questions

1. Where would you use a crossover cable?

   _____

   _____

   _____

2. How does a crossover cable differ from a straight-through cable?

   _____

   _____

3. Which pin assignments are changed for a crossover cable?

   _____

Name _____ Date _____ Class _____

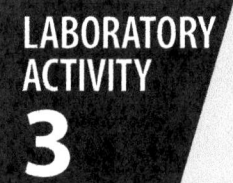

Viewing Network Connection Status and Properties (Part I)

LABORATORY ACTIVITY 3

Outcomes

After completing this laboratory activity, you will be able to:
- Check the network connection status in Windows 10.
- Evaluate information about the network adapter configuration in Windows 10.
- Carry out a diagnostic test of the network connection using Windows 10.
- Compare and contrast network status dialog box options for Windows 10.
- Summarize how to enable or disable featured items in the **Local Area Connection Dialog** box.

Introduction

In this laboratory activity, you will explore the **Local Area Connection Status** dialog box similar to the one in the following screen capture.

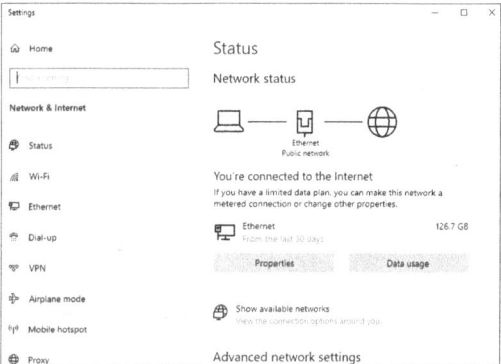

Goodheart-Willcox Publisher

The **Local Area Connection Status** dialog box is very similar in Windows operating systems. This dialog box is where you would go to quickly inspect the status of the network connection and verify that network packets are being sent and received. Be sure to practice accessing this dialog box and the features presented in this lab activity.

Equipment and Materials

- Windows 10 computer connected to a network

Procedure

1. _____ Report to your assigned workstation.
2. _____ Boot the computer and verify it is in working order.

3. ____ Open the **Network and Sharing Center**. To do this, navigate to **Start>Control Panel>Network and Internet>Network and Sharing Center**, as shown in the following image.

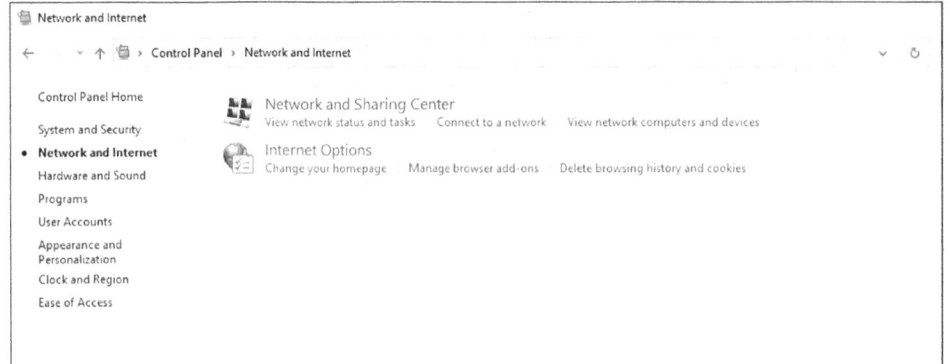

Goodheart-Willcox Publisher

Alternatively, you could open the **Start** menu, type *net* into the **Search** box, and then select **Network and Sharing Center** from the generated search list. You can also access the **Network and Sharing Center** by right-clicking the **Network** icon in the notification area of the taskbar and selecting **Open Network and Sharing Center**.

Goodheart-Willcox Publisher

As you can see, there are many different ways to access the Network and Sharing Center. Practice each method before moving to step 4.

4. ____ Select **Change adapter settings** on the left so you can see the various adapters.

Goodheart-Willcox Publisher

8 Networking Fundamentals Lab Manual

Name _____

You will see several adapters. At a minimum, you will see one wireless and one wired. Right click on the adapter that is currently being used and select **Properties**. You will then see the following:

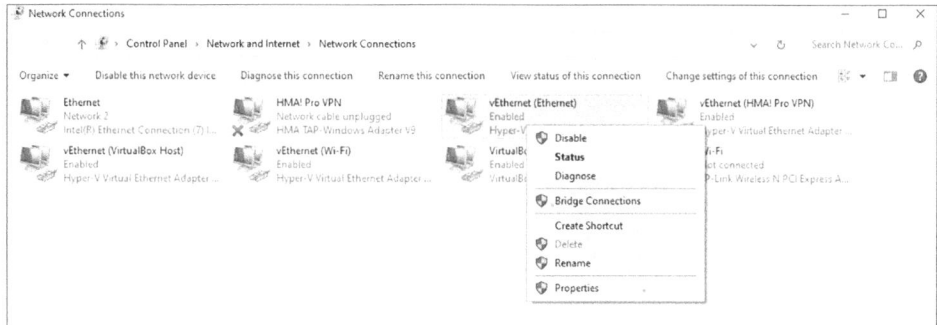

Goodheart-Willcox Publisher

This will bring you to the **Properties** screen.

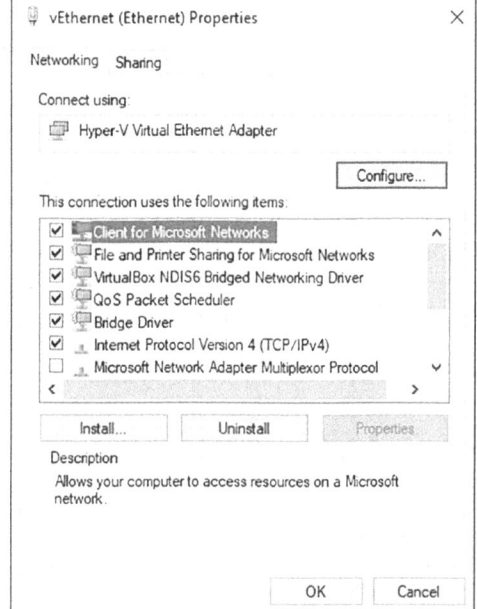

Goodheart-Willcox Publisher

You will use the **Properties** screen later to set both IPv4 and IPv6 properties, so it is essential you can locate it. If you wish to see the activity going on with a given adapter, then when you right click the adapter, select **Status**.

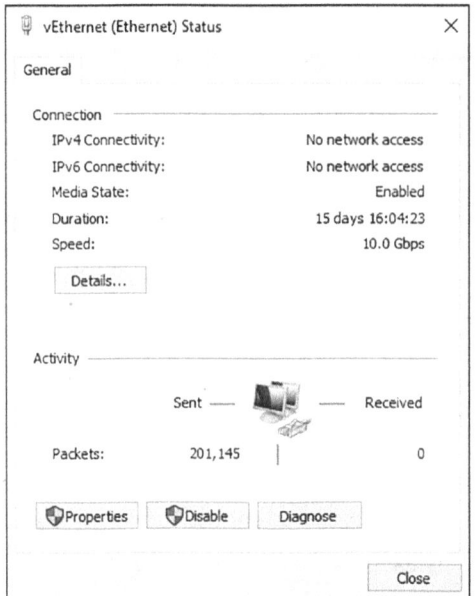

Goodheart-Willcox Publisher

Note that if you click **Properties** from this screen, it will also take you to the properties screen shown previously. The **Status** screen will show speed, media state, and packets sent and received, all interesting information when troubleshooting your network. You can also click the **Diagnose** button or right click on the adapter and choose **Diagnose** (rather than **Status** or **Properties**).

5. _____ Click the **Diagnose** button for practice. The operating system will complete a set of automatic diagnostic tests on the connection to see if there is a problem and then will recommend a course of action. Since the connection is working, there will not be a recommendation.

The diagnostic dialog box allows you to try suggested repairs, view detailed information, or explore additional options.

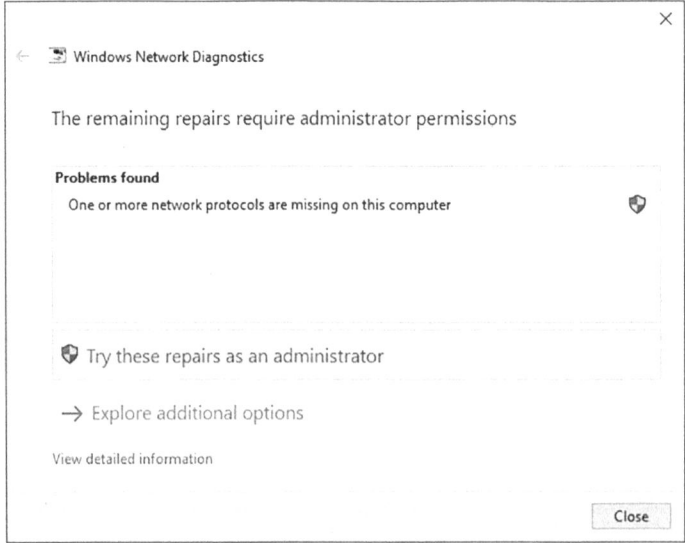

Goodheart-Willcox Publisher

6. _____ Close the diagnostic dialog box for the appropriate operating system to return to the **Properties** window for your particular adapter dialog box.

Name _____

7. _____ Select IPv4 and note what you see. You can also click on the **Advanced** button to see more settings, such as DNS settings.

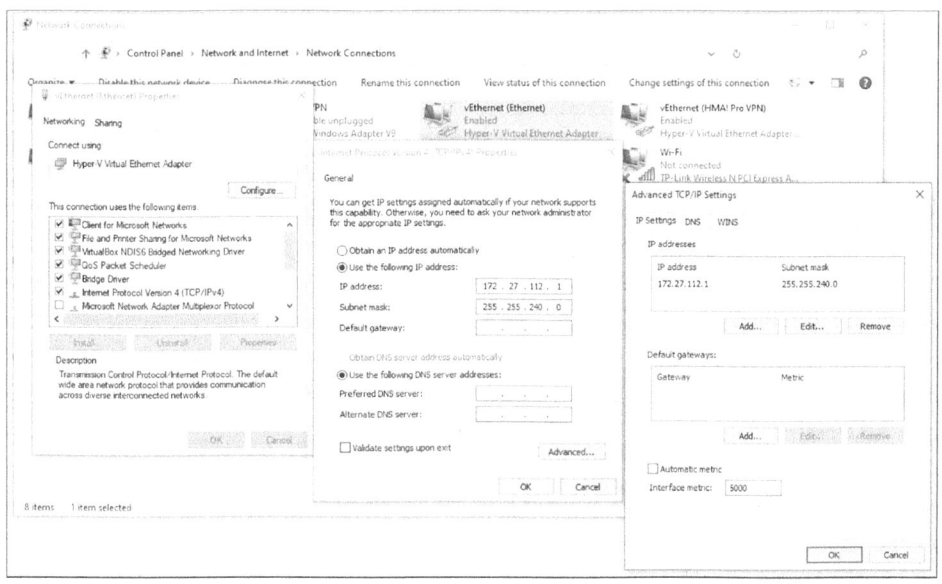

Goodheart-Willcox Publisher

8. _____ Write the information that is revealed about your computer's network connection in the space provided. Do *not* use the information from the screen capture.

Connection-specific DNS Suffix:

_____

Description:

_____

Physical Address:

_____

DHCP Enabled (Yes or No?):

_____

IPv4 Address:

_____

IPv4 Subnet Mask:

_____

Lease Obtained:

_____

Lease Expires:

_____

IPv4 Default Gateway:

_____

IPv4 DHCP Server:

_____

IPv4 DNS Servers:

_____

_____

IPv4 WINS Server:

_____

NetBIOS over TCP/IP Enabled (Yes or No?):

_____

Link-local IPv6 Address:

_____

IPv6 Default Gateway:

_____

IPv6 DNS Server:

_____

In most cases, the WINS Server field will be blank because there will most likely not be a WINS server in your network. Also, the IPv6 Default Gateway and IPv6 DNS Server will most likely be blank if there is no IPv6 gateway or DNS server.

You will learn more about these configuration properties as you progress through the textbook and additional lab activities. For now, be sure you know how to access the various network information dialog boxes. You will be using them frequently during your study of networking fundamentals.

9. _____ You can now close the various properties windows you have opened.

10. _____ Complete the review questions, and then return the computer to its original order. Return all materials to their proper storage area.

Review Questions

1. Which option would you select in Windows 10 **Network and Sharing Center** to view the status of the network adapter?

   _____

2. What items of information are immediately displayed in the **Local Area Connection Status** dialog box for Windows 10?

   _____

   _____

3. Which button in the Windows 10 **Local Area Connection Status** dialog box would you select to see detailed information about the network adapter?

   _____

4. How do you enable or disable IPv4 and IPv6 protocols in the **Local Area Connection Properties** dialog box?

   _____

Name _____ Date _____ Class _____

Navigating Windows 10

Outcomes

After completing this laboratory activity, you will be able to:
- Navigate Windows 10.
- Start and shut down Windows 10.

Introduction

The release of Windows 10 incorporated numerous changes from both Windows 7 and Windows 8. This laboratory activity is important because it provides you with the information necessary to navigate the Windows 10 operating system efficiently. This lab activity does not require an in-depth understanding of the operating system. You will simply learn to use the keyboard or the mouse to navigate your way around the Windows 10 operating system.

On a separate sheet of paper, record your assigned username, password, the number or name of your assigned workstation, and your assigned server. You will most likely need to record the server name if there is more than one server for students to access. The default server specified in the logon box could be different than the server used for the Networking Fundamentals class, or there may not be any server specified at all. Your instructor will provide you with all pertinent information.

The following screen capture displays the login screen for Windows 10. **Test1** is the user account created during installation. The textbox is for you to enter your password associated with the user account. Notice the word **Password** in grey inside the text field. The notification area provides information such as network connectivity. This area also provides users with power options and Ease of Access options.

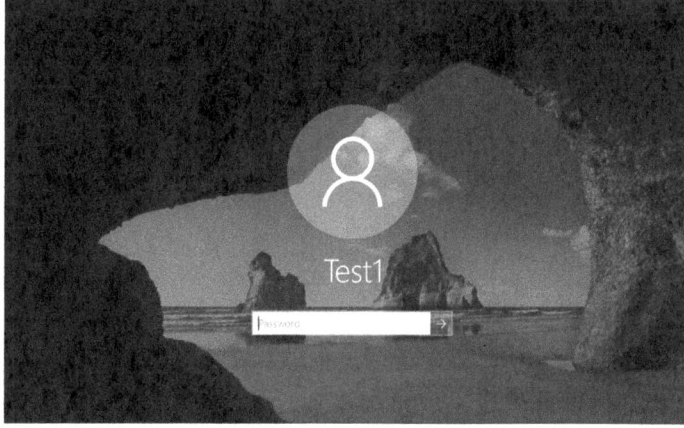

Goodheart-Willcox Publisher

The Windows 10 Start menu is visually different from previous versions of Windows. However, the function is still the same. It allows easy access to different tools, as shown in the following screen capture.

Goodheart-Willcox Publisher

Important tools to be able to access and use in Windows 10 include the Start Menu, Search feature, Task View button, Taskbar, and Notification Area.
- **Start Menu**. Provides access to applications. Selecting the Windows button opens the alphabetical list of all installed applications.
- **Search**. Allows users to search their computer or the web if they have an Internet connection.
- **Task View**. Enables users to create or delete virtual desktops.
- **Taskbar**. Provides access to the Start menu, pinned applications, and the Notification Area.
- **Notification Area**. Informs the user of important information or statuses, such as network connectivity, new e-mails, and antimalware alerts.

As with previous Windows operating systems, shortcuts for system functions are available through key combinations. These key combinations all incorporate the [Windows] key found on the keyboard. For example, [Windows][D] will take display the desktop, [Windows][S] will open the Windows search feature, [Windows][E] will open the File Explorer window, [Windows][L] will lock the computer, and pressing the [Windows] key by itself will open the **Start** menu.

Equipment and Materials
- Assigned computer with Windows 10 installed. The computer must be installed as part of a network or have a direct connection to the Internet for the lab activity to work correctly.
- The following information from your instructor:

Username:

Password:

Workstation number or name:

Server name:

Name _____

Procedure

1. _____ Report to your assigned workstation for this activity.

2. _____ Boot the computer and look for the logon screen. Depending on its configuration on the network, there may or may not be a logon screen. If there is, use your assigned user name and password to log on to the network.

3. _____ Navigate to **Start>Settings**.

4. _____ Record the names of five icons in the **Windows Settings** menu:

   _____

   _____

   _____

   _____

   _____

5. _____ Locate the Notification Area, and mouse over the icons. Record three of the icons in the Notification Area.

   _____

   _____

   _____

6. _____ Locate the search box on the Taskbar. Type file, and press [Enter]. Record the name of the window that opened.

   _____

7. _____ Answer the following review questions. When you have finished the review questions, shut down your workstation and return all materials to their proper storage area.

Review Questions

1. What is the purpose of the Notification Area?

   _____

   _____

2. Where do you find the pinned applications icons?

   _____

3. What is the shortcut key to open the **Start** menu?

   _____

4. What key combination locks the computer?

   _____

5. What key combination opens the File Explorer window?

   _____

Notes

Name _____ Date _____ Class _____

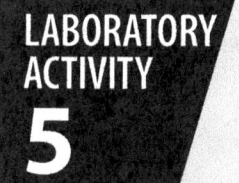

Viewing Network Connection Status and Properties (Part II)

Outcomes

After completing this laboratory activity, you will be able to:
- Check the status of a network connection in Windows 10.
- Check the properties of a network connection in Windows 10.
- Recall the values associated with the status of a network connection.
- Recall the values associated with the properties of a network connection.

Introduction

In this laboratory activity, you will view the status dialog box and properties dialog box associated with a particular network connection. You will need to access these locations throughout the course and throughout your career as a network technician or administrator. The purpose of this laboratory activity is to show you the location of and general features associated with these dialog boxes in Windows 10. You will use them often to inspect and modify the network connection. You will need to practice locating, opening, and viewing the contents until you are confident that you will be able to locate these items in future laboratory activities and on the job.

To view the network connections associated with the workstation, click **Start>Settings>Network & Internet**. A window similar to the following will display.

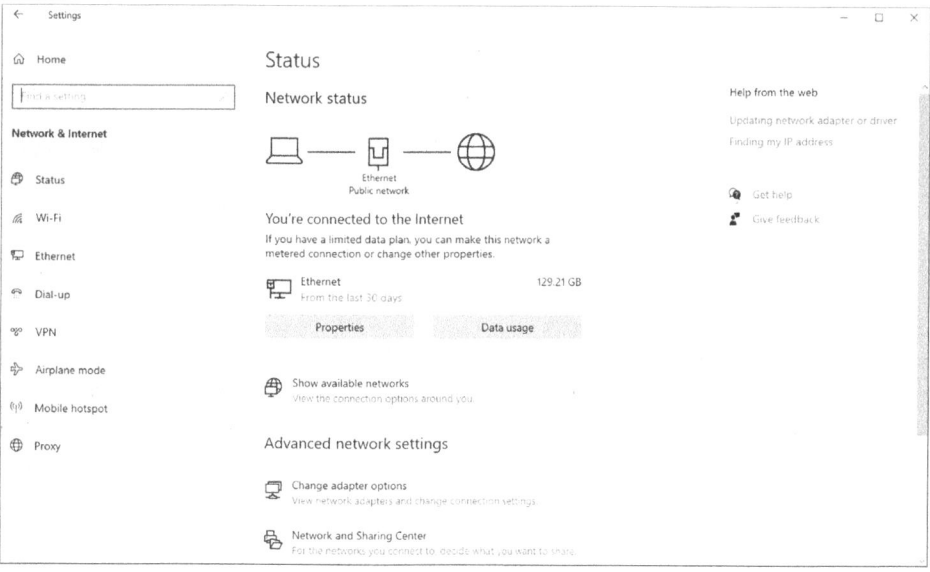

Goodheart-Willcox Publisher

> **NOTE**
> As you have seen in previous labs, there is often more than one way to access the features in Windows.

The **Network & Internet** window displays current network status. It also provides a list of common network administrative options on the left-hand side of the window, as shown in the previous image. You can also access **Properties**, **Data usage**, and **Advanced network settings**.

These options shown on the left will vary depending on your network connections, but a typical list includes **Status**, **Wi-Fi**, **Ethernet**, **Dial-up**, **VPN**, **Airplane mode**, **Mobile hotspot**, and **Proxy**. When one of these menu options is selected, details for it will display in the window. For example, selecting the **Status** option will show the current network status and allow the user to show available networks, view network properties, join a HomeGroup, troubleshoot connections, change adapter options, and view or change Windows Firewall, among other options. Additional administrative activities within the **Network & Internet** menu include enable Airplane Mode, change connection properties, establish a new dial-up or VPN connection, view data usage, and configure a proxy server for Ethernet or Wi-Fi connections.

While in the **Network & Internet** window, select **Ethernet>Change adapter options**.

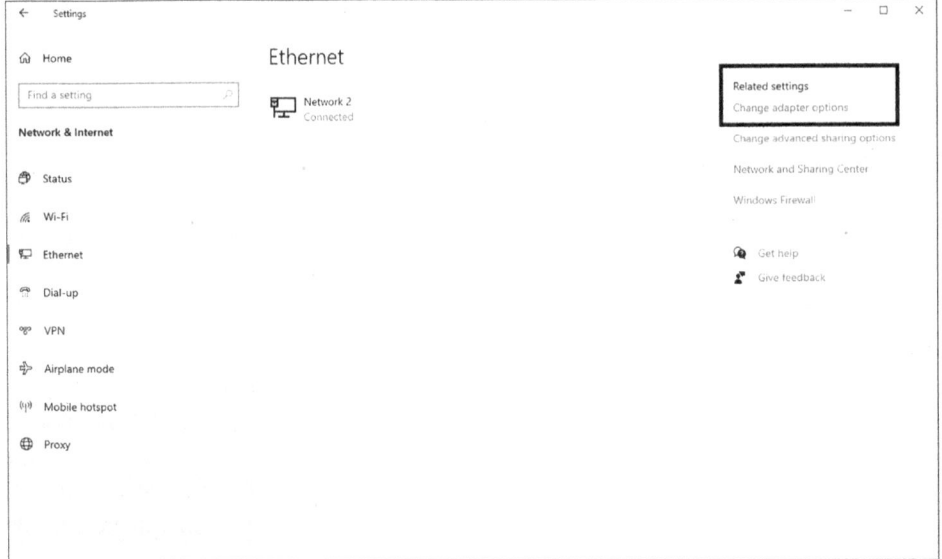

Goodheart-Willcox Publisher

This will take you to a screen we have seen before, in Laboratory Activity 3. This screen shows you all available network connections.

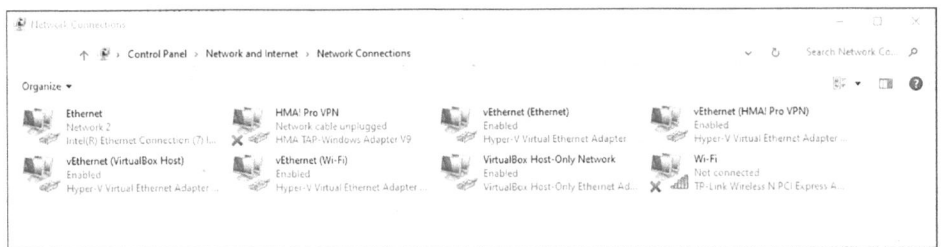

Goodheart-Willcox Publisher

Administrators typically rename connections so that their function can be easily identified. For example, a workstation could have a telephone modem, a LAN connection through a network adapter, and a wireless connection using a wireless network adapter. The default names would be confusing and difficult to determine for which connection each is used. The connections can be renamed for easy identification. To rename a connection, right-click the connection and then select **Rename** from the shortcut menu.

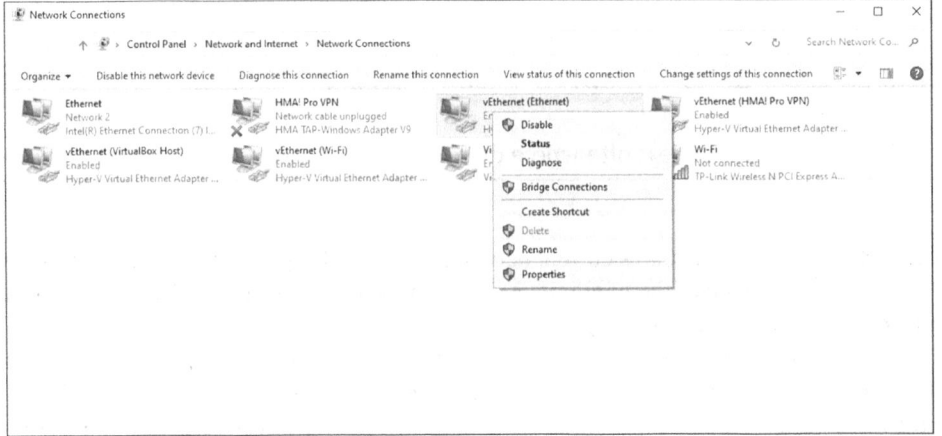

Goodheart-Willcox Publisher

Name _____

Two other important shortcut menu options available are **Status** and **Properties**. These were explored in Laboratory Activity 3.

Equipment and Materials

- Windows 10 computer connected to a network

Procedure

1. _____ Report to your assigned workstation.

2. _____ Boot the computer and verify that it is in working order.

3. _____ Navigate to **Start>Settings>Network & Internet**.

4. _____ Select the **Ethernet>Change adapter options** to open the **Network Connections** window. Right-click on the **Ethernet** connection and select **Properties** from the shortcut menu. The **Ethernet Properties** window should display.

> **NOTE**
> A network connection must exist for a network connection to display in the **Network Connections** window.

5. _____ Close all windows and disconnect the network cable.

6. _____ Navigate to and open the **Network Connections** window. You should no longer see an Ethernet connection.

7. _____ Close the **Network Connections** window and then reconnect the network cable.

8. _____ Re-open the **Network Connections** window. The Ethernet connection should display.

9. _____ Access the **Ethernet Status** dialog box by right-clicking the network connection and selecting **Status** from the shortcut menu. Inspect the information available. What information is displayed? Use the space provided to describe the information.

_____

_____

_____

10. _____ Select the **Details** button. What additional information is displayed? Summarize the information in the space provided.

_____

_____

_____

11. _____ Close the **Network Connection Details** dialog box.

12. _____ Select the **Diagnose** button from the **Ethernet Status** dialog box and then observe the activity.

13. _____ Close the **Windows Network Diagnostics** dialog box.

14. _____ Right-click the Ethernet connection and select **Properties** from the shortcut menu. You should see a list of items such as **Client for Microsoft Networks**, **File and Printer Sharing for Microsoft Networks**, and **Internet Protocol (TCP/IP)**.

15. _____ Open the **Internet Protocol Version 4 (TCP/IPv4) Properties** dialog box by selecting the **Internet Protocol Version 4 (TCP/IPv4)** option and then clicking the **Properties** button.

16. _____ Summarize the information found in the **Internet Protocol Version 4 (TCP/IPv4) Properties** dialog box.

17. _____ Practice alternative methods for locating and opening the **Network Connections** window and the dialog boxes presented in this laboratory activity until you feel confident that you can open or locate them in the future.

18. _____ Answer the review questions, and shut down the workstation.

Review Questions

1. How is the **Network Connections** window accessed in Windows 10?

2. Which dialog box provides a feature to troubleshoot a connection?

3. What information does the **Ethernet Status** dialog box provide?

4. What additional information is revealed in the **Network Status** dialog box after the **Details** button is selected?

5. What would be a reason for a network connection not displaying in the **Network Connections** window?

Name _____ Date _____ Class _____

Network and Sharing Center

Outcomes

After completing this laboratory activity, you will be able to:
- Use the Network and Sharing Center.
- Recall the various options available through the Network and Sharing Center.
- Differentiate between the Windows 7 and Windows 10 Network and Sharing Center.

Introduction

In this laboratory activity, you will explore the Network and Sharing Center of the Windows 10 operating system. As a network technician, you will constantly be required to inspect and modify network configurations. Because the task is so common, you need to be extremely familiar with the Network and Sharing Center.

The Network and Sharing Center was first introduced as part of the Windows Vista operating system and became a standard feature in later versions of Windows. The Network and Sharing Center is similar in function in all workstation Windows operating systems. It provides a centralized dialog box to handle the most common networking configuration options and networking status. The following is a screen capture of the Network and Sharing Center in Windows 10.

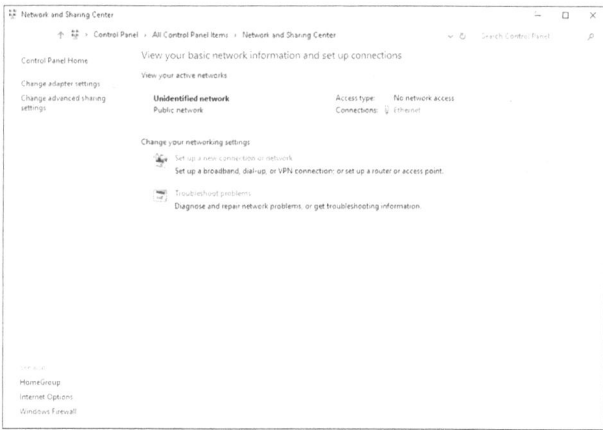

Goodheart-Willcox Publisher

Compared to Windows 7, there are some subtle differences in the presentation of options. Microsoft often changes the location of various configuration options whenever they design a new operating system.

Equipment and Materials
- Windows 10 computer preferably connected to a network workgroup

Procedure

1. _____ Report to your assigned workstation.

2. _____ Boot to Windows 10 and verify that the computer is in working order.

3. _____ Open the Network and Sharing Center by typing **network** into the **Search** box located off the **Start** menu.

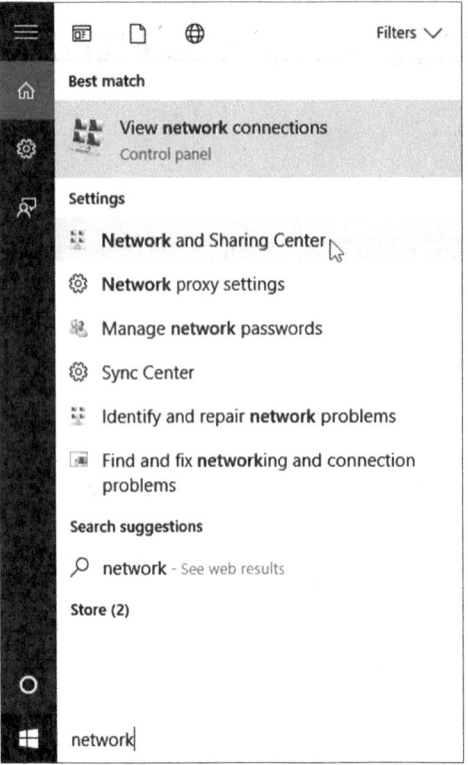

Goodheart-Willcox Publisher

The search results are different for Windows 10 when compared to Windows 7. Network and Sharing Center may not be listed as the best match, as shown in the above screen. This is because the search results generate more network-related results of various programs, such as **View network connections**, **Network proxy settings**, and **Manage network passwords**. The search results in Windows 10 also include web results. Click on the **Network and Sharing Center** link.

> **NOTE**
> The Network and Sharing Center can be accessed in Windows 10 by right-clicking the networking icon in the notification area.

4. _____ Close the Network and Sharing Center. Open it once more by navigating to **Start>All apps>Windows System>Control Panel>Network & Internet>Network & Sharing Center**.

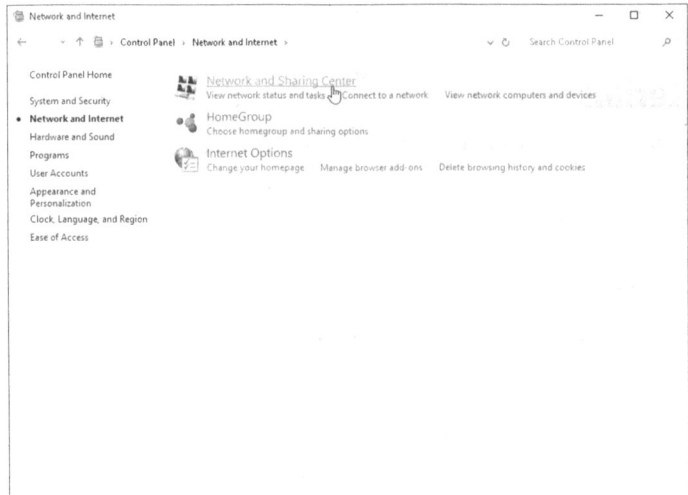

Goodheart-Willcox Publisher

Name _____

5. _____ The graphic for the Network and Sharing Center map is different from those in Windows Vista and Windows 7 but similar to Windows 8.1.

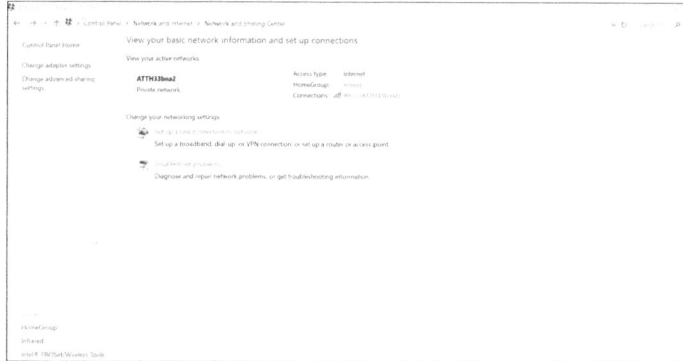

Goodheart-Willcox Publisher

6. _____ Look at the **View your available networks** section in the Network and Sharing Center. Notice that there is a link beside the **Connections** property named **Ethernet**. This link opens the **Ethernet Status** dialog box.

7. _____ Click the **Ethernet** link that is next to the **Connections** property. The **Ethernet** dialog box will display similar to the following.

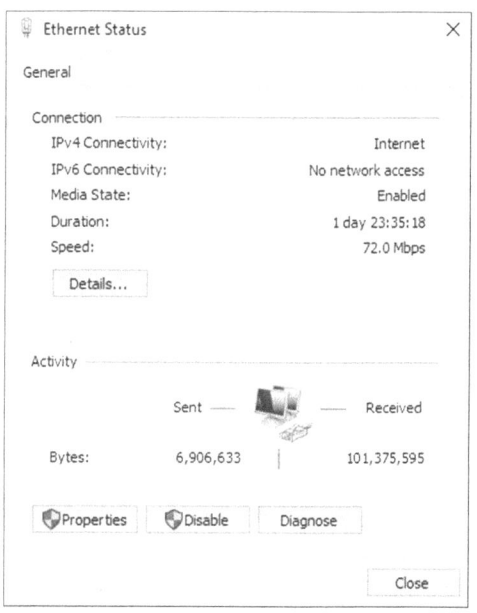

Goodheart-Willcox Publisher

8. _____ Close the **Ethernet Status** dialog box to return to the Network and Sharing Center.

9. _____ Click the **HomeGroup** link in the **See also** section. You will see a dialog box similar to the following.

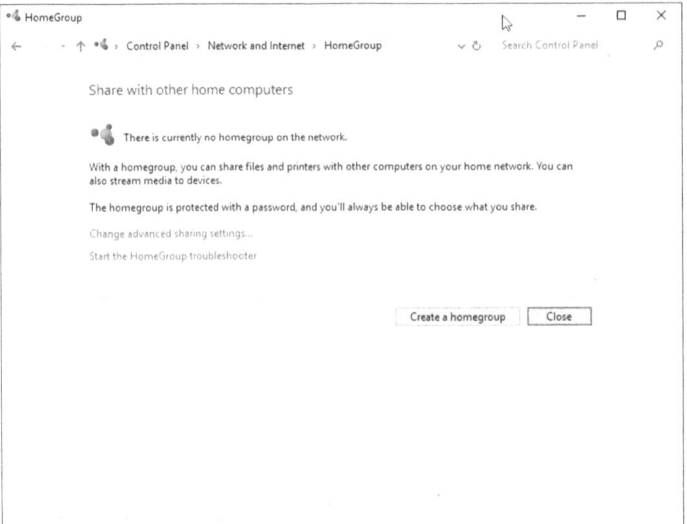

Goodheart-Willcox Publisher

There will be more about the HomeGroup feature in a later lab activity. For now, take a few seconds to look at the options briefly. When finished, use the arrow at the top left to return to the Network and Sharing Center.

10. _____ Now, look at the section labeled **Change your networking settings**. This section is different in Windows 10 from Windows 7.

11. _____ In the **Change your networking settings** section, click **Set up a new connection or network option**. The **Set Up a Connection or Network** dialog box will open, similar to the following.

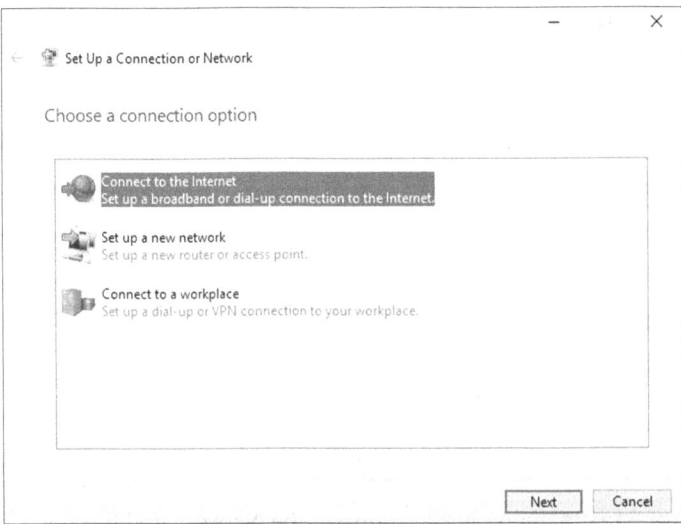

Goodheart-Willcox Publisher

This dialog box is similar to the **Set up a connection or network** dialog box in Windows 7. There will be more about these featured options in later lab activities. Simply take a few seconds to briefly look at the available options and then click **Cancel** to return to the Network and Sharing Center.

Name _____

12. _____ In the Network and Sharing Center **Change your networking settings** section, you only have two options: **Setup a new connection or network** and **Troubleshoot problems**. Select the **Troubleshoot problems** option. A dialog box similar to the following will display.

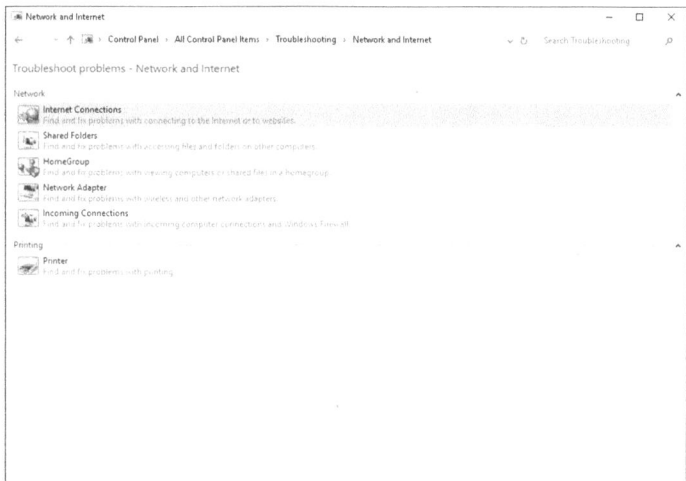

Goodheart-Willcox Publisher

This menu is similar to the one in Windows 7; it allows you to target a problem area specifically and guides you through the troubleshooting process with a wizard. Return to the Network and Sharing Center by clicking the arrow icon in the upper-left corner of the screen.

13. _____ On the left side of the Network and Sharing Center under **Control Panel Home**, click **Change advanced sharing settings**. A dialog box similar to the following will display.

Goodheart-Willcox Publisher

This is another menu that was largely unchanged from Windows 7. The **Advanced sharing settings** dialog box contains options to configure Network Discovery, file and printer sharing, HomeGroup connections, and more. The advanced sharing settings will be explored in greater detail in a later lab activity. For now, just take a few seconds to look at the various options available. Many of the options from Windows 7 were retained in the development of Windows 10 but were relocated.

14. _____ Return the computer to its original condition and then answer the review questions.

Review Questions

1. What is the correct path for accessing the Network and Sharing Center through Control Panel in Windows 10?

2. How can you access the Network and Sharing Center through the taskbar in Windows 10?

3. What can you type into the **Search** box located on the **Start** menu to access the Network and Sharing Center in Windows operating systems?

4. Which operating system introduced the HomeGroup feature?

Name _____ Date _____ Class _____

Connecting Two Computers Using a Crossover Cable

LABORATORY ACTIVITY 7

Outcomes

After completing this laboratory activity, you will be able to:
- Use a crossover cable to connect two workstations.
- Identify the IPv4 APIPA address range.
- Summarize the purpose for using APIPA.
- Check if the DHCP service has failed.

Introduction

In this laboratory activity, you will connect two workstations using a crossover cable and running the same operating system. This is a very easy task because Windows 10 automatically detects a network connection and then assigns an IPv4 address and an IPv6 address automatically. The IPv4 address will be a special type of IPv4 address known as an *Automatic Private IP Address (APIPA)*. The APIPA address is automatically generated by the host computer when it is configured to receive a DHCP address but fails to receive a DHCP-assigned IPv4 address. The two most common reasons for failure are that a connection to the DHCP service device has failed or the DHCP service device has failed.

A workstation must be assigned an IP address to be able to communicate with other computers on an Ethernet network. When you connect two computers together using a crossover cable, you will have eliminated the DHCP server. Each computer will automatically generate a random IPv4 address in the range from 169.254.0.1 to 169.254.255.254 with a subnet mask of 255.255.000.000.

The IPv4 address is divided into four sets of numbers separated by a period. When an APIPA is assigned, the first two sets of numbers are always 169.254. This is a good way to tell if the DHCP service has failed when troubleshooting a network problem.

> **NOTE**
> You may not need a crossover cable if both computers are equipped with a Gigabit Ethernet network adapter. The Gigabit Ethernet standard requires that the network card be capable of automatically switching the transmit and receive cable pairs at the connection. This feature, called *Auto-MDIX*, automatically negotiates the connection, thus eliminating the need for a crossover cable.

Equipment and Materials

- Two workstations running Windows 10
- Crossover cable (You may be able to use a straight-through cable if both computers are using a network adapter with Auto-MDIX capabilities. Most Gigabit Ethernet network adapters have the Auto-MDIX feature.)

> **NOTE**
> With instructor approval, this lab may be performed with another student, each using one of the two required workstations.

Procedure

1. _____ Report to your assigned workstation(s).
2. _____ Boot the computers and verify they are in working order.
3. _____ Shut down the two computers and disconnect them from any existing network system.
4. _____ Plug one end of the crossover cable into the network adapter port on each computer.
5. _____ Reboot each computer and wait while the two computers detect each other.

6. _____ At one of the two computers, open the Network and Sharing Center. When the Network and Sharing Center opens, you should see an unidentified network in the map area, similar to the following screen capture.

   If using Windows 10, there will be a red *X* to indicate a lack of Internet connection. In Windows 10, the name for the crossover cable network is "Unidentified network."

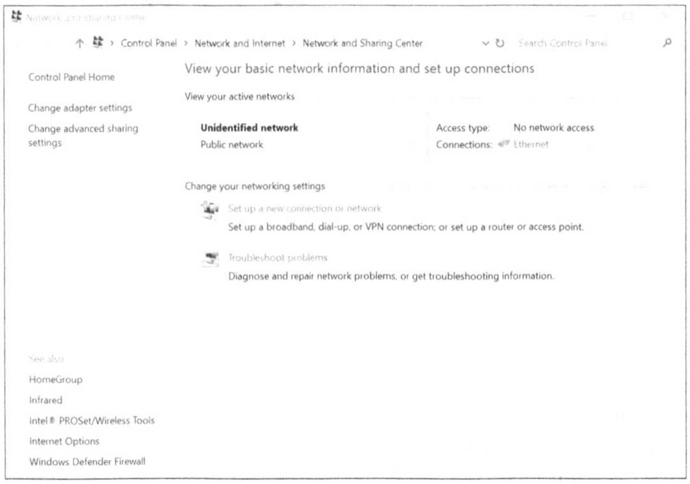

   Goodheart-Willcox Publisher

7. _____ Open the **Local Area Connection Status** (**Ethernet** link on Windows 10) dialog box and then click the **Details** button to inspect the assigned IPv4 address. Record the assigned IPv4 address in the space provided below.

   _____

8. _____ Shut down both computers. Disconnect the crossover cable. If the computers were part of a network, reconnect both computers.

9. _____ Reboot both computers and verify they are working correctly. If they are part of a network, inspect the assigned IPv4 address once more.

10. _____ Return all materials to the proper storage areas and then answer the review questions.

Review Questions

1. What does the acronym APIPA represent?

   _____

2. What is the numeric value for the first two numerical octets of an APIPA address?

   _____

3. What is the entire range of IPv4 addresses used for APIPA?

   _____

4. What is the subnet mask equal to for APIPA?

   _____

5. What must you do if you cannot generate a map of the two crossover cable connected computers?

   _____

   _____

6. What are the two most common reasons for DHCP failure?

   _____

   _____

Testing Internet Connection Speeds

Outcomes

After completing this laboratory activity, you will be able to:
- Check Internet download speed using the McAfee Internet Connection Speedometer utility.
- Give examples of factors that affect advertised access/download speeds.

Introduction

In this laboratory activity, you will test the speed of your Internet connection with the Speedtest by Ookla utility. This is a free utility that can be run directly from the Speedtest website: http://www.speedtest.net. You can enter the URL into your browser directly, or you can conduct a search using the key words **Ookla** and **speed test**. These words will produce many hits because this utility is popular, free, and easily accessible.

After accessing the Ookla Speedtest utility, you will see a screen similar to the following.

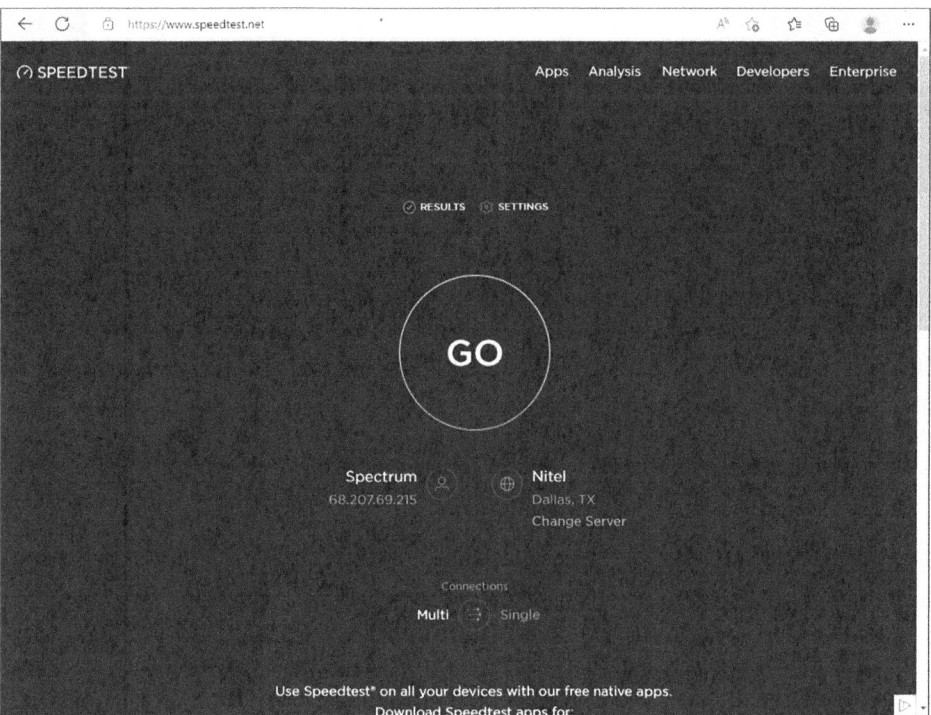

Goodheart-Willcox Publisher

To test the speed of your Internet connection, select **Go**.

Your Internet connection speed will be indicated on the animated speedometer. The speedometer indicates the speed for the total number of packets received from the destination, measured in Megabits per second (Mbps). Both your download and upload speeds are measured and are displayed after the test is completed, as shown in the following figure.

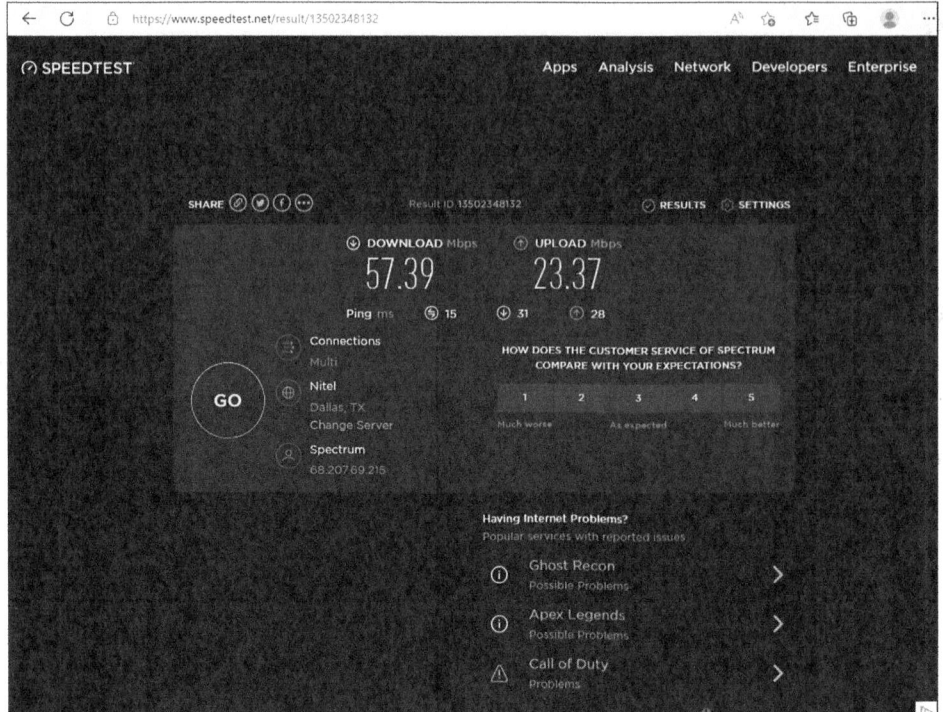

Goodheart-Willcox Publisher

A high amount of traffic on the network (local and Internet) can slow transmission. Transmission over the Internet may be forced to take a longer, alternate route because of congestion or downed routers. Control messages sent to and from the destination and source can also slow transmission. For example, after several blocks of data are received, a message is sent to the source verifying the data was received. Since most Internet connections are half-duplex, the download sequence must stop in order to send an acknowledgment that the data sent so far has been received. A half-duplex system can only transmit in one direction at a time; therefore, the source and destination must take turns transmitting.

Data encapsulation also affects speed. A single block of data transmitted across the network contains the desired data plus information such as the IP address, MAC address, and assorted information required by the protocol to function properly. The desired data accounts for only a portion of the entire block of data. You will learn more about data encapsulation in later laboratory activities.

Another factor that affects speed is the operating system's browser cache. A copy of a frequently accessed web page is stored in a cache so that it can be instantly displayed the next time the page is requested. Proxy servers cache web pages to reduce network traffic, and many ISP providers run proxy servers to provide faster access.

Equipment and Materials
- Computer with Internet access

> **NOTE**
> If you have a different type of Internet access than your school, you may want to perform this laboratory activity from your home and compare the results with that obtained at school. For example, if your school has a T1 line and you have DSL, run this laboratory activity from your school and then at home and compare the results.

Name _____

Procedure

1. _____ Report to your assigned workstation.

2. _____ Boot the computer and verify it is in working order.

3. _____ Access the Internet and conduct a search using the key words **Ookla** and **speed test**. The search will generate many hits. Alternatively, navigate to the following URL: http://www.speedtest.net.

4. _____ Run the Ookla Speedtest and complete the following chart.

Test #	Speed in Mbps
1	
2	
3	
4	
5	
Average	

5. _____ After running five tests, calculate and record the average speed. To calculate the average speed, add the five speeds together and divide by five.

6. _____ Based on the average speed recorded in the chart, calculate how long it would take to download a 500 MB file.

_____

7. _____ Navigate to the **Help** link at the bottom of the Ookla Speedtest page. The **Help** page provides answers to multiple questions.

8. _____ Answer the review questions before disconnecting from the Internet and shutting down the computer.

Review Questions

1. What speed is suggested by Ookla for online gaming?

_____

2. Based on the information on the Ookla website, how much time is estimated to be needed to transfer a 1GB file at 1,000 Mbps?

_____

3. Why do results of each test vary?

_____

_____

_____

_____

_____

4. Why might someone not be able to find servers in their area?

   _____

   _____

5. What port is used by Ookla Speedtest?

   _____

Name _____ Date _____ Class _____

Installing and Configuring a PCI Network Adapter

Outcomes
After completing this laboratory activity, you will be able to:
- Carry out proper procedures for installing and configuring a PCI network adapter card.
- Give examples of common problems associated with installing a network adapter card.
- Use Device Manager to confirm the proper installation of the network adapter card.
- Carry out proper procedures to disable or uninstall a network adapter card for troubleshooting purposes.
- Use the **Controller Properties** dialog box to identify system resources assigned to the network adapter card.

Introduction
In this laboratory activity, you will install a PCI network adapter card. A network adapter card is commonly referred to as a *NIC*. While most network adapter cards are automatically configured through plug-and-play technology, there are many times when technician intervention is required. This most commonly happens when the network card and the operating system are from two different eras. For example, when installing a dated network adapter into a computer running the latest operating system, a driver may need to be installed manually.

You should check the Microsoft hardware compatibility list (HCL) prior to purchasing a network adapter. Purchase a card that is on the list. Cards not on the HCL may present a problem during installation. When using a network adapter not previously tested and approved by Microsoft, a warning message may appear. The message will inform you that the drivers are not digitally signed and will advise you not to install the card. You may ignore the warning and continue with the installation process. Most times, the network adapter will install properly, but you will most likely need to supply the driver disk during the installation process.

All network adapters require driver software. When a plug-and-play network adapter is detected by the operating system, the driver is typically automatically installed and no further intervention is required from the technician. Occasionally, a network adapter driver must be installed manually. When such an instance occurs, the next step in the installation process can vary depending on how much information about the network adapter was identified by the operating system. For example, the device may be identified as a network adapter, but the network driver software must be supplied by the technician. Alternatively, the hardware device may not be identified by type of device, so the network technician may need to identify the device as a network adapter and manually install the drivers. The operating system may not detect the new device at all. In such a case, the technician will need to start the process from the **Add a device** wizard.

Device Manager can be used to view the status of a hardware device installed in the computer. From Device Manager, the technician can uninstall, disable, scan for property changes, or update the network adapter driver. Device Manager can also be used to view the system resource assignments of hardware devices. Network adapters use three system resources: Interrupt Request (IRQ), I/O port, and RAM memory. Some network adapters also use Direct Memory Access (DMA). Device Manager usually detects conflicts between devices using the same system resource.

The Windows 10 operating systems install the TCP/IP protocol by default when a network adapter is installed. To verify that the TCP/IP protocol is installed, issue the **ping** command at the command prompt. If TCP/IP is not installed, you will not be able to use the **ping** command.

> **NOTE**
> When installing a network adapter into a computer that has a network port built into the motherboard, the motherboard network port usually needs to be disabled to prevent a conflict with the additional network adapter. The network port can be disabled through Device Manager.

Equipment and Materials

- Computer running Windows 10
- Patch cable
- PCI Ethernet network adapter card and driver disc
- Manufacturer's instructions for installing the network card and the device driver CD or DVD (Your instructor may require you to download a copy of the installation instructions and drivers for the network adapter card from the manufacturer's website.)
- Hub
- Screwdriver to match expansion slot screw
- Antistatic wrist strap

Procedure

1. _____ Gather all required materials and report to your assigned workstation.

2. _____ Familiarize yourself with the manufacturer's installation instructions.

3. _____ Boot the computer and verify it is in working order.

4. _____ Shut down the computer and unplug the power cord. Follow antistatic procedures as defined by your instructor.

5. _____ Remove the computer case cover and check for an available PCI slot. Remove the slot cover associated with the chosen PCI slot. A small screw at the top of the slot cover typically retains the slot cover. Some slot covers do not use a screw to hold it in place. Slot covers without a screw usually must be bent back and forth several times to break free of the metal frame. Some computer cases use a simple latching mechanism to retain the slot cover. Check carefully before proceeding with the removal. If you are in doubt as to how to remove the slot cover, ask your instructor.

6. _____ Position the network adapter over the PCI slot and then insert the card by applying firm, even pressure along the top edge of the card. Do *not* rock the card excessively. Note, the card may be *keyed*. This means the card will only lock into place in one position. Check the card for notches or tabs and ensure they line up with the appropriate cutouts in the PCI slot before inserting.

7. _____ After the card has been fully inserted into the PCI slot, use the screw or appropriate mechanism to mount the card.

8. _____ Plug the power cord back into the wall outlet and boot the computer. The network adapter may or may not be automatically detected and configured. If it is not automatically detected and configured, you will need to configure the card manually. You will be prompted to identify the hardware device or to install the driver, or both. When prompted for installing the driver, click the **Have Disk** button.

> **NOTE**
> Be sure to read each screen carefully. Most installation problems are caused by failure to read the information presented.

9. _____ After the driver has been installed, open Device Manager to check the status of the network adapter. You can access Device Manager by right-clicking **My Computer** or **Computer** and selecting **Manage** from the shortcut menu. In Windows 10, navigate to **Start>All apps>Windows System>Control Panel>Hardware and Sound>Devices and Printers>Device Manager**.

Name _____

In the Device Manager list, you should see **Network adapters**. Expand the **Network adapters** heading by clicking the arrow icon next to it. Clicking the arrow expands the device type network adapters and shows all of the network adapters installed in the computer.

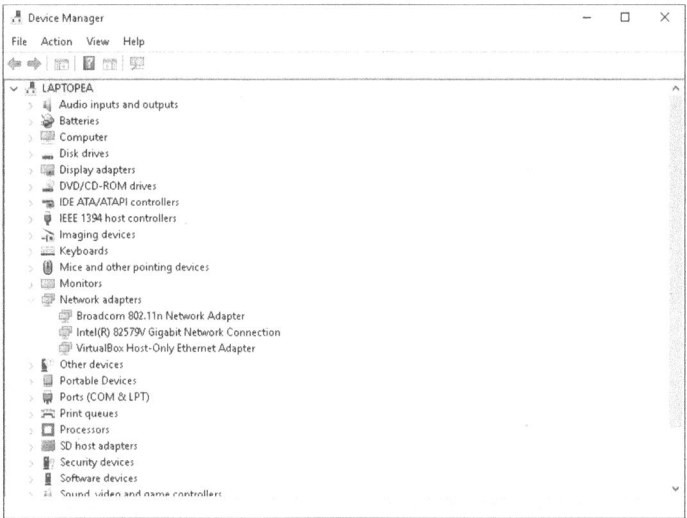

Goodheart-Willcox Publisher

In the previous screen capture, three network adapters are identified. All are in working order. No problems are indicated. Device Manager indicates a hardware device problem by inserting a symbol over the device icon. A yellow exclamation point over the device icon means the computer cannot communicate with the device. A black arrow is less serious than the exclamation point. Most often, it means the device is disabled. A red X is similar to a black arrow. It means the device needs to be reactivated.

10. _____ Right-click the network adapter entry. A shortcut menu will appear with the following commands: **Update Driver Software**, **Disable**, **Uninstall**, **Scan for hardware changes**, and **Properties**.

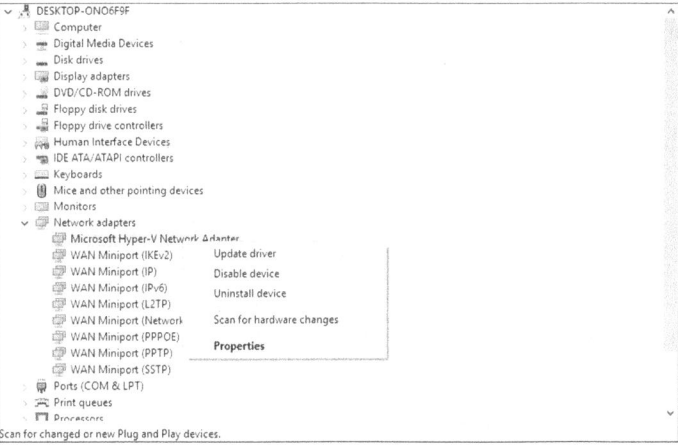

Goodheart-Willcox Publisher

11. _____ Select **Disable** from the shortcut menu. You may be prompted with a dialog box to confirm your desire to disable the device. Click **Yes**. Notice the effect on the appearance of the device. What symbol appeared over the network adapter to indicate that it is disabled? Record the answer in the space provided.

_____

12. _____ Re-enable the network adapter by right-clicking the network adapter entry and selecting **Enable** from the shortcut menu. The **Enable** option replaces the **Disable** option in the shortcut menu after the **Disable** command is selected.

13. _____ Right-click the network adapter entry and select the **Uninstall** option.

> **NOTE**
> After uninstalling the network adapter using Device Manager, some versions of Windows will automatically detect and install the network device again. If the network adapter is no longer viewable in Device Manager, select **Action>Scan for hardware changes**.

14. _____ After the network adapter has been reinstalled, open Device Manager and select the network adapter once more. Right-click the network adapter entry and select **Properties** from the shortcut menu. A dialog box similar to the following will display. Notice that the **Device status** box indicates the network adapter is working properly.

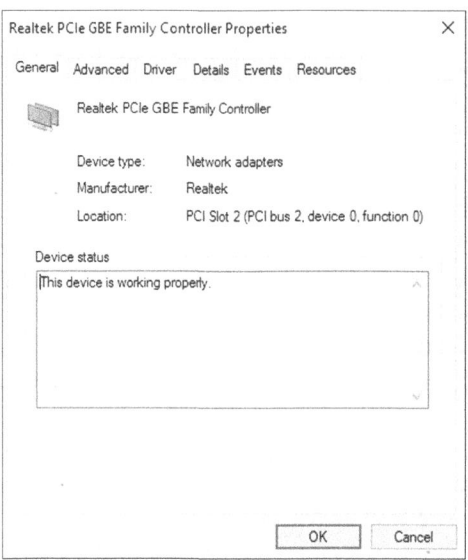

Goodheart-Willcox Publisher

15. _____ Select the **Advanced** tab. This area of the dialog box will allow you to change various properties for the network adapter card.

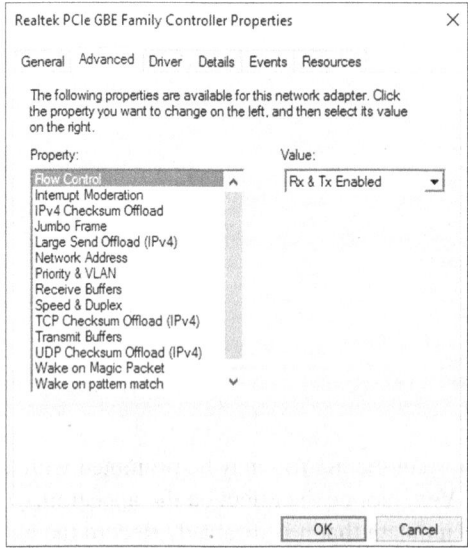

Goodheart-Willcox Publisher

> **NOTE**
> Available tabs in a VM environment include **General, Advanced, Driver, Details,** and **Events**.

Name _____

16. _____ Select the **Driver** tab. From this location, you can view driver details, update the driver, roll back the driver, and uninstall the driver. The **Driver Details** button reveals information about the manufacturer, where the driver is located, and if the driver was digitally signed. A digitally signed driver means Microsoft has approved the driver. The Roll Back Driver feature removes the last installed driver for the card. You would normally use this option in place of using the System Restore feature, which rolls back all changes to the computer since the last restore point was created. Rolling back all changes since the last restore point was created can undo many changes that you wish to retain. The Roll Back Driver feature is the best choice for uninstalling a driver.

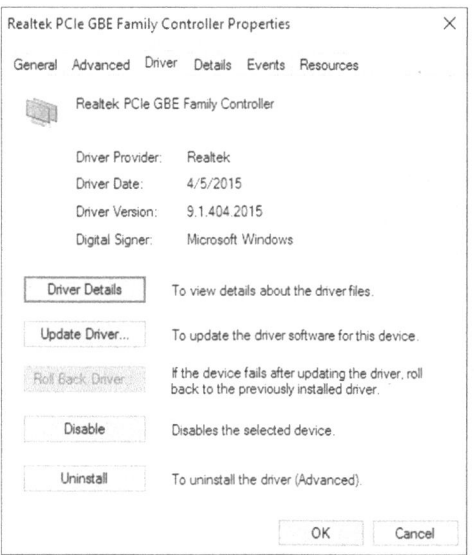

Goodheart-Willcox Publisher

17. _____ Select the **Resources** tab. A dialog box similar to the following will appear and will display system resources assigned to the network adapter.

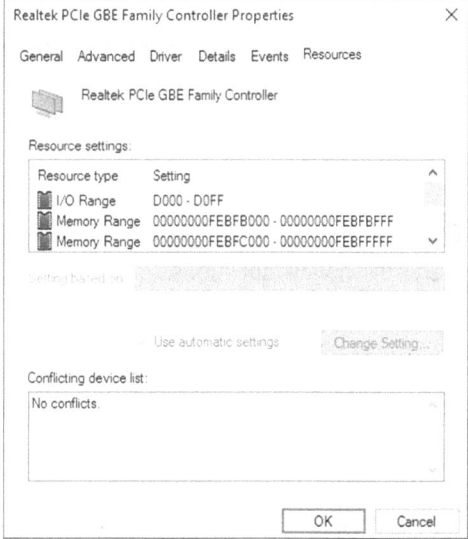

Goodheart-Willcox Publisher

Copyright Goodheart-Willcox Co., Inc.
May not be reproduced or posted to a publicly accessible website.

Laboratory Activity 9   Installing and Configuring a PCI Network Adapter   37

18. _____ Record in the spaces provided the resources assigned to your network adapter.

I/O range:

_____

Memory range:

_____

IRQ:

_____

19. _____ Select the **Power Management** tab. This area of the dialog box displays several options related to power saving features available for the network adapter. Typically, you will not need to access this tab or the other tabs mentioned in this laboratory activity. Also, be aware that the type of information as well as the appearance of the information presented in a dialog box can change by card manufacturer. Manufacturers have access to Windows programming information. They often change the way a dialog box appears to match the capabilities of their network adapters.

Goodheart-Willcox Publisher

20. _____ Practice accessing and opening the menu items and dialog boxes presented in this laboratory activity. After you have practiced, answer the review questions.

21. _____ Return all materials to their proper storage area.

Review Questions

1. What does the acronym HCL represent?

_____

2. What does the acronym NIC represent?

_____

3. What symbol is used to indicate a device is disabled in Device Manager?

_____

_____

Name _____

4. What symbol is used to indicate a problem with a device in Device Manager?

   _____
   _____

5. What three system resources are assigned to a network adapter?

   _____
   _____

6. List four options that are available from the **Driver** tab.

   _____
   _____

7. Why is the Roll Back Driver feature the preferred way to remove a network adapter driver rather than using the System Restore feature?

   _____
   _____
   _____

Notes

Name _____ Date _____ Class _____

Creating a Windows 10 Peer-to-Peer Network

Outcomes

After completing this laboratory activity, you will be able to:
- Carry out proper procedures for configuring a simple peer-to-peer network.
- Understand Windows 10 basic networking configuration settings.
- Use the **net view** command to view local area network computers.

Introduction

In this laboratory activity, you will join two or more computers together as a peer-to-peer network. It is amazingly simple to connect computers together as a peer-to-peer network when using the same operating system for all computers.

The first time you connect a Windows 10 computer to a network, you will see a dialog box that will ask you to identify the network location. This usually takes place during the installation of the operating system. You will be asked to identify a home, public, or work location (domain). Any time after that, the computer will typically automatically configure itself as part of a peer-to-peer network. In this lab, you will simply connect a computer to a hub or switch using an Ethernet cable. The computer will automatically detect other computers and devices in the peer-to-peer network.

A hub or a switch may be used as the center connection of the peer-to-peer network. The main difference between a hub and a switch is a switch can limit network traffic by allowing packets to travel through the switch to only the designated computer.

Setting up Internet access is optional and not required for a peer-to-peer network. If you are going to set up a peer-to-peer network with Internet access, it is advisable to use a router as the center connection.

Running the Network Setup Wizard is only necessary for wireless adapters, not for a wired peer-to-peer network. A computer wired to a peer-to-peer network will automatically detect the other network devices and automatically configure the computer as part of the network.

Testing the Network Connection

Testing the network is easy. If you can view other computers, then you have successfully networked the computer(s). This does not mean that you have created sharing between the computers. You have simply created a network.

To see all devices connected in Windows 10, navigate to **Start>All apps>Windows System>Control Panel>Network and Internet>View network computers and devices**. You should see a screen similar to one of the following.

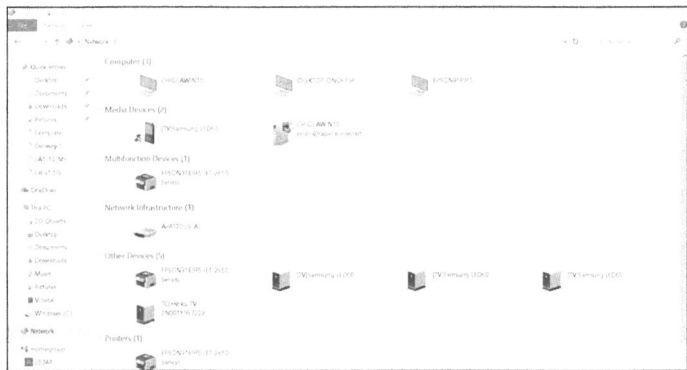

Goodheart-Willcox Publisher

If you do not see the other computers and network devices, check if the Network Discovery feature has been enabled. Be aware that some software programs, such as antivirus suites, may block the network discovery process, thus not allowing you to view other computers.

You can use the command prompt to view other computers and devices on the local area network or the peer-to-peer network. Simply open the command prompt and then enter the command **net view**. You will generate a list of devices that are presently connected and running on the local network. Look at the screen capture of the results of issuing the **net view** command. Note that the command consists of two words: *net* and *view*.

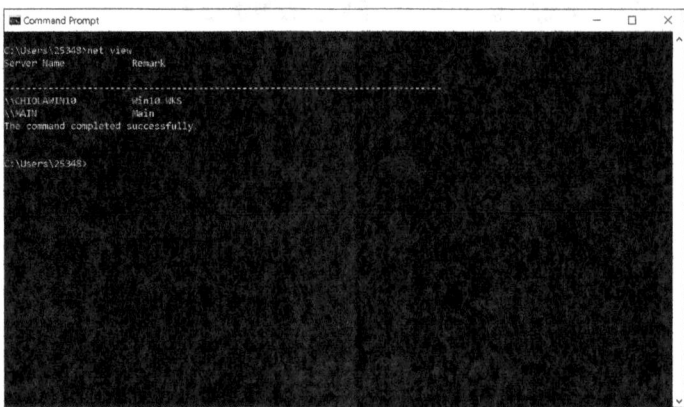

Goodheart-Willcox Publisher

Set Network Location Dialog Box

Windows 10 has a dialog box called **Set Network Location**, which automatically changes the configuration of the Windows Firewall and shared files and devices. Look at the following screen capture of the Windows 10 Set Network Location dialog box.

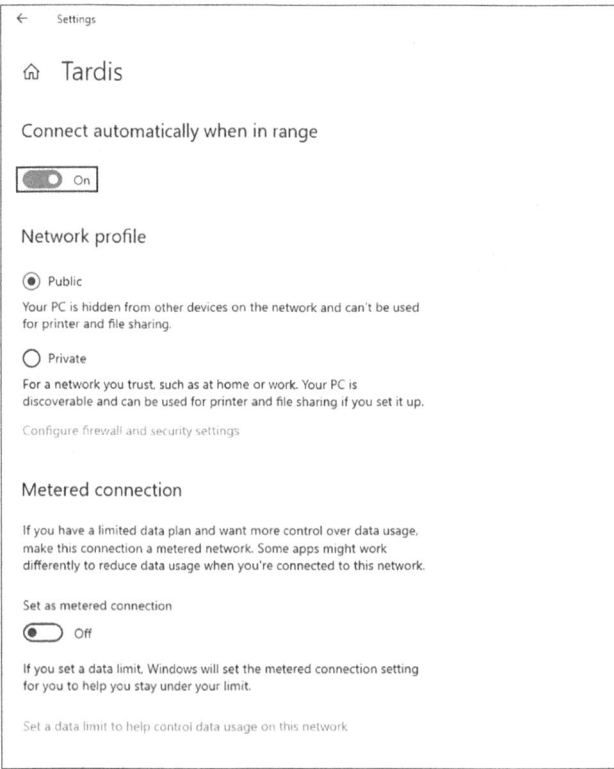

Goodheart-Willcox Publisher

Windows 10 has private and public networks. A short description accompanies each location type. The network location providing the highest level of security is **Public** or **Public network**. Windows 10 location settings varied slightly. Location settings only feature **Public** or **Private** as options, but **Public** is still the option with the highest level of security.

By default as a security measure, the Network Discovery feature and file sharing are not enabled. The theory is that if you cannot see a computer, you will not attempt to access the computer.

Name _____

Check the Microsoft docs website for additional information on networking in a Windows environment: http://docs.microsoft.com. You can also learn more through **Start>Help and Support** in Windows 10. Enter the term networking into the **Windows Help and Support** dialog box to generate a long list of networking topics that cover networking basics. In Windows 10, you can navigate to **Start>All apps>Get Help**. You should take time to review the topics available in Windows 10.

> **NOTE**
> When using lab computers that are used by multiple students, the default settings are often changed by other students. Never make assumptions about the network, network devices, or computer configuration.

Equipment and Materials

- Two computers running Windows 10
- Two Cat 5, Cat 5e, or Cat 6 Ethernet cables
- Hub or switch

> **NOTE**
> You can perform this lab activity with another student, each using one of the two required computers.

Procedure

1. _____ Gather the required materials and report to your assigned workstations.

2. _____ Boot the computers and verify they are in working order.

3. _____ After checking each computer, power them off.

4. _____ Connect each computer to the hub or switch using the Ethernet cables.

5. _____ Boot each computer and look at the hub or switch LED associated with each cable. The LED should be blinking to indicate network activity.

6. _____ To view all computers and network devices in Windows 7, select **Start>User Name>Network**. In Windows 10, navigate to **Start>All apps>Windows System>Control Panel>Network and Sharing Center>View network computers and devices**. You should see both computers listed by assigned computer name. If you cannot see the other computer, check that the Network Discovery feature has been enabled.

   In Windows 10, navigate to Control Panel and select **Network and Internet>Network and Sharing Center>Change advanced sharing settings>Turn on network discovery**.

> **NOTE**
> The two Windows 10 computers do not need to be part of the same workgroup to be viewable.

7. _____ If you still cannot view the other computer, call your instructor for assistance. If you can view the other computer, call your instructor to inspect your lab activity as completed.

8. _____ Open the command prompt by entering cmd into the **Start>Search** dialog. Use the **net view** command to view the other computer. Using the command prompt is an alternative way to view the local area network computers.

9. _____ Answer the review questions and return all materials to their proper storage areas.

Review Questions

1. What feature must be enabled in order to see other computers and network devices?

2. Which network location option has the highest level of security?

3. Which network location does not allow the HomeGroup feature to be enabled?

4. What is the default setting for the Network Discovery feature and file sharing?

5. What command issued from the command prompt will display a list of local area network computers?

Name _____ Date _____ Class _____

HomeGroup

Outcomes

After completing this laboratory activity, you will be able to:
- Use the Network and Sharing Center to create a HomeGroup.
- Use the Network and Sharing Center to join a computer to a HomeGroup.
- Use a computer to access resources on another member of the HomeGroup.
- Use the **HomeGroup** dialog box to remove a computer from a HomeGroup.
- Use the **HomeGroup** dialog box to recover a HomeGroup password.

Introduction

In this laboratory activity, you will explore the Windows HomeGroup feature for sharing resources on a home or small network. HomeGroup was first introduced in Windows 7. Microsoft designed the HomeGroup feature to make it as easy as possible for the average computer user to create a peer-to-peer network automatically. The concept of workgroups and domains proved to be too difficult for the average computer user to comprehend. The HomeGroup feature is designed especially for home networking and is not intended for corporate applications found in a domain environment. The HomeGroup feature has been designed to easily and safely share pictures, videos, music, documents, and printers in a home network.

A HomeGroup is automatically created when you install Windows 10 on a computer. To participate in a HomeGroup, all computers must be running Windows 7 or later. Any version of Windows 10 can join a HomeGroup.

Shared items in a HomeGroup are referred to as *libraries*. Only members of the same HomeGroup can view the contents of the libraries. If a computer is a member of a HomeGroup, it will be identified in the Network and Sharing Center. Look at the following partial screen capture.

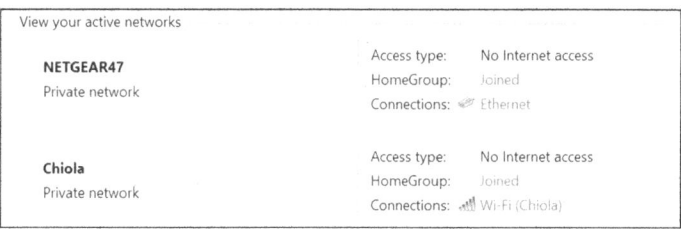

Goodheart-Willcox Publisher

You can see that each computer has "joined" a HomeGroup as indicated in the Network and Sharing Center.

Windows 10 changed the organization of the HomeGroup feature. Instead of seeing a **Ready to create** link, users will have to navigate to the Network and Sharing Center and click the **HomeGroup** button from the **See also** options in the bottom-left corner of the window, as shown in the following screen capture.

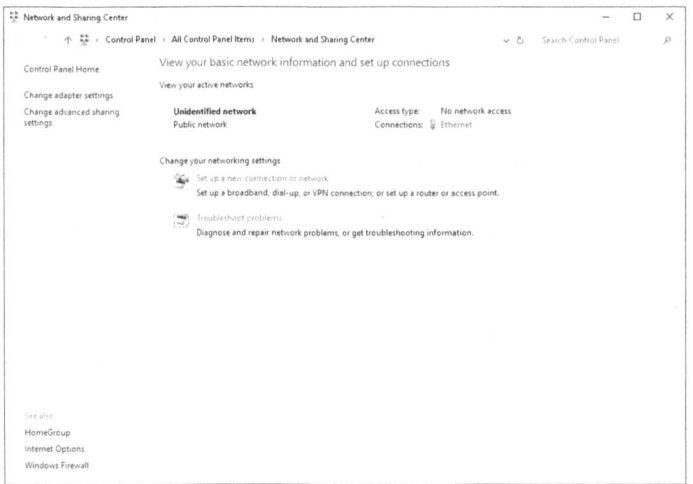

Goodheart-Willcox Publisher

You can modify the HomeGroup configuration through the **HomeGroup** dialog box, which will appear similar to the one in the following screen capture.

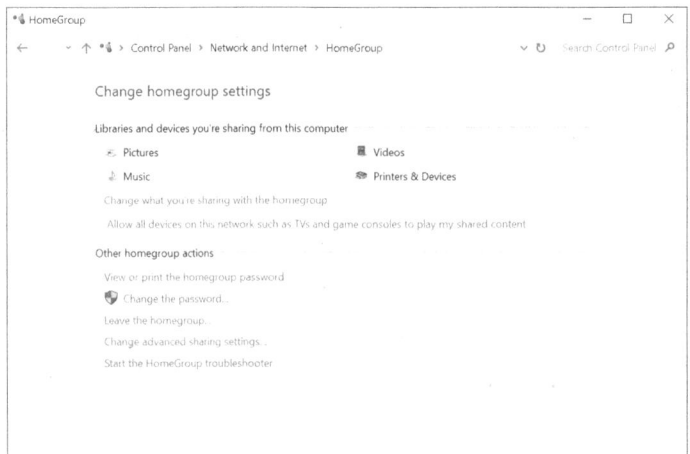

Goodheart-Willcox Publisher

You select which items or libraries to share, such as pictures, music, videos, and documents. You can select the option to share your printer also. Pay particular attention to the options at the bottom of the screen in the **Other HomeGroup actions** section. The options listed here allow you to accomplish the most common tasks associated with HomeGroup. For example, if you forget what the password is, you can view a copy of the password here.

Equipment and Materials

- Two networked Windows 10 computers

> **NOTE**
> You may perform this lab activity with a partner, each person using their own assigned networked computer.

Name _____

Procedure

1. _____ Gather the required materials and report to your assigned workstations.

2. _____ Boot the computers and verify they are in working order.

3. _____ Open the Network and Sharing Center to see if the computer is part of a HomeGroup. If the computer is not part of a HomeGroup, go to step 4 in the lab activity. If the computer is part of a HomeGroup, go to step 10.

4. _____ In the Windows 10 Network and Sharing Center, select the **Ready to create** link to start the HomeGroup wizard. In Windows 10, select the HomeGroup link from the **See also** options in the bottom-left corner of the window.

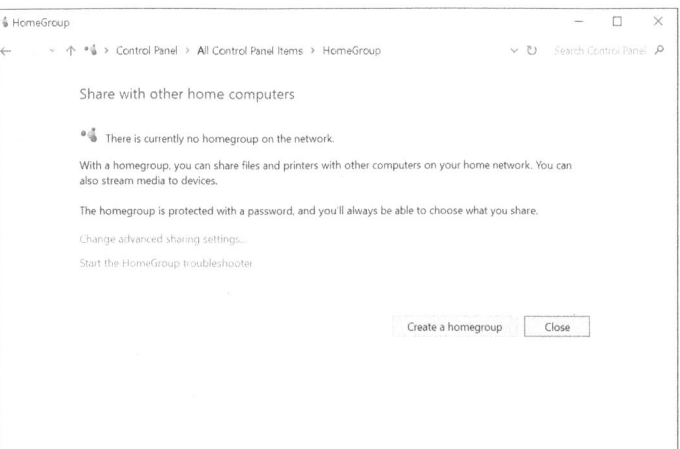

Goodheart-Willcox Publisher

Notice that there are links to allow you to perform routine tasks such as changing the advanced sharing settings. There is also a HomeGroup troubleshooter. Click the **Create a homegroup** button.

5. _____ The next dialog box to appear is similar to the following.

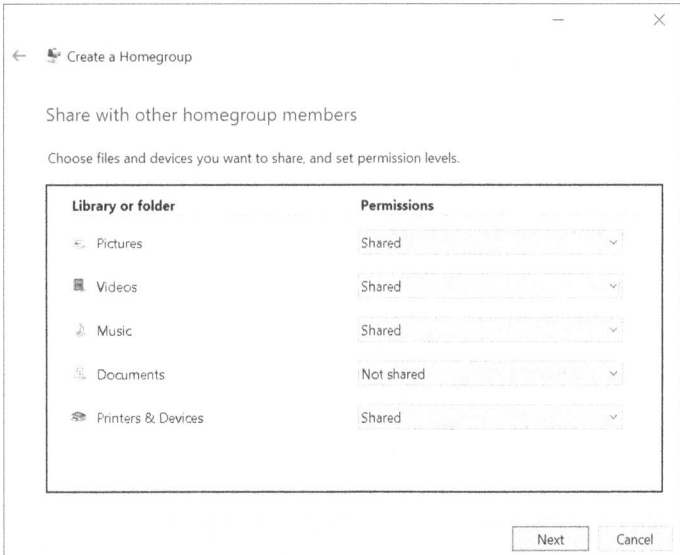

Goodheart-Willcox Publisher

You can select which items or libraries you wish to share with other users. By default, all items except **Documents** are automatically set to be shared. You can leave the default settings for this exercise. Click **Next** to continue.

6. _____ The next dialog box presents the HomeGroup password.

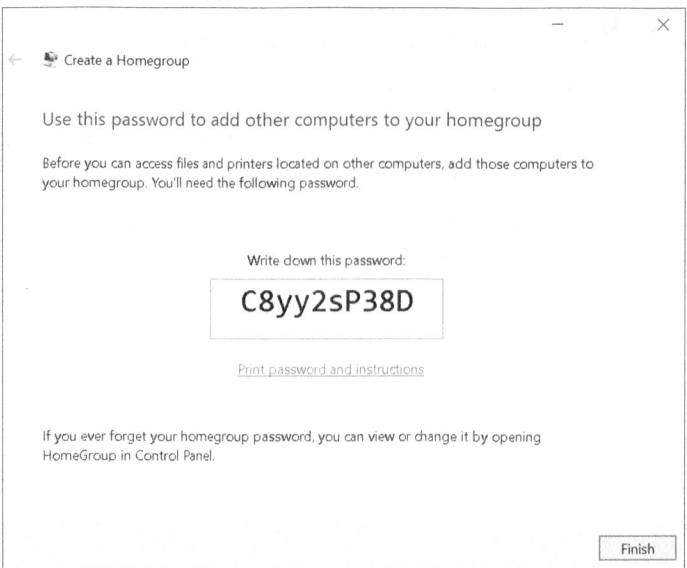

Goodheart-Willcox Publisher

The password is automatically generated by the wizard. You can also create your own password by simply typing the desired password into the text box. You will use the HomeGroup password for each computer in the HomeGroup. The password must match at each computer to be able to access resources in the HomeGroup.

Notice that the password generated by the wizard follows the general guidelines for a secure password. The general guideline for secure passwords is the password should contain numbers and characters of the alphabet, both uppercase and lowercase letters. The password should also not be any word that would match a word in a dictionary. This is an example of a password that would be virtually impossible to guess.

Record the password in the space provided so that you can use it later on another computer.

7. _____ Click **Finish**. You have successfully created a HomeGroup.

8. _____ Open the Network and Sharing Center to verify that you have joined the HomeGroup as indicated by the word *Joined* beside the **HomeGroup** label.

9. _____ Close the Network and Sharing Center.

10. _____ Access **Start>Computer**. You should see the **HomeGroup** icon listed on the left side of the screen and a list of libraries being shared by HomeGroup. Right-click the **HomeGroup** icon. A shortcut menu will appear that includes the following options:

    Change the HomeGroup settings.

    View the HomeGroup password.

    Start the HomeGroup troubleshooter.

11. _____ Take a few minutes to explore these three options. Look for and explore the links **How do I share additional libraries?** and **How do I exclude files and folders?**

12. _____ Notify your instructor that you have finished so they can check your lab activity.

Name _____

Review Questions

1. Why was HomeGroup developed?

   _____

   _____

   _____

2. Which operating system first introduced the HomeGroup feature?

   _____

   _____

3. What resources are shared? List five.

   _____

   _____

4. Which resource is not shared by default?

   _____

5. Can you share additional resources using HomeGroup?

   _____

6. What is another name for the shared resources in HomeGroup?

   _____

Notes

Name _____ Date _____ Class _____

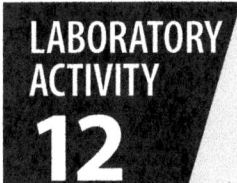

Exploring Network Adapter Configuration Settings

Outcomes

After completing this laboratory activity, you will be able to:
- Recall the purpose of typical network adapter settings.
- Recall the purpose of a DHCP server.
- Recall the purpose of a DNS server.
- Recall the purpose of a WINS server.

Introduction

In this laboratory activity, you will explore various settings for the configuration of network adapters. An in-depth understanding of a vast array of networking topics is required to fully understand the purpose, function, and effect of these settings. The purpose of this laboratory activity, however, is only to familiarize you with the various options available and where they are located. As you progress though this course, you will gain an in-depth understanding of the networking topics mentioned in this lab.

The network-adapter configuration settings can be accessed through **the Local Area Connection Properties** dialog box. This dialog box contains information specific to the network adapter configured for the local area network. From Network and Sharing Center, you can select the **Ethernet** link, then select **Properties**.

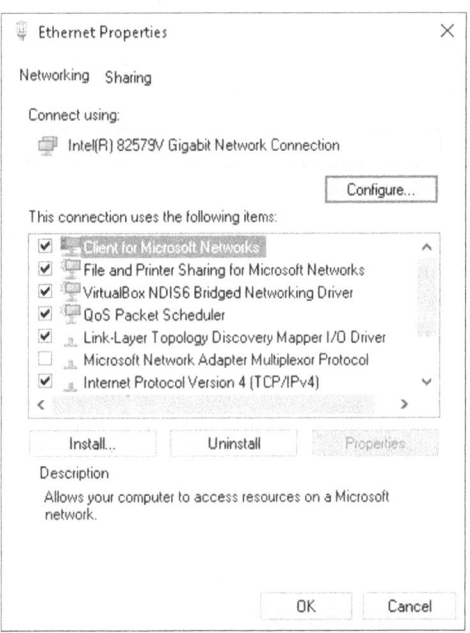

Goodheart-Willcox Publisher

Configurations specific to the TCP/IP protocol can be accessed by highlighting **Internet Protocol Version 4 (TCP/IPv4)** and clicking the **Properties** button. The **Internet Protocol Version 4 (TCP/IPv4) Properties** dialog box will display.

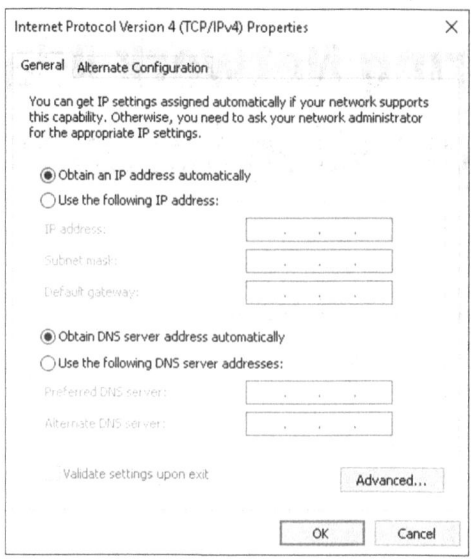

Goodheart-Willcox Publisher

Through this dialog box, an entire set of options are made available for managing the TCP/IP properties, such as the method of IP address assignment, DNS settings, and WINS settings. We will briefly explore the meanings of these settings as you work through the lab. These settings will be revisited in later laboratory activities. At that time, you will gain a deeper understanding of the networking technology related to each setting.

Equipment and Materials

- Windows 10 workstation connected to an Ethernet network

Procedure

1. _____ Report to your assigned workstation.

2. _____ Boot the computer and verify it is in working order.

3. _____ Access the network adapter properties from Network and Sharing Center. Select **Local Area Connection>Properties**. The **Local Area Connection Properties** dialog box will display. In Windows 10, navigate to Network and Sharing Center, and select **Ethernet>Properties**, which will display the **Ethernet Properties** dialog box.

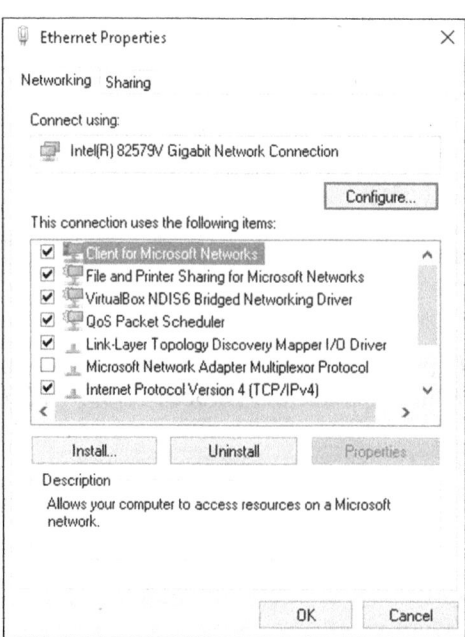

Goodheart-Willcox Publisher

52   Networking Fundamentals Lab Manual

Name _____

Notice that the network adapter for the LAN connection is identified in the **Connect using:** text box. Record the name or model number identified in your display in the space provided.

_____

4. _____ Click **Configure**. Notice that the dialog box displayed allows you to change the network card configuration. Explore the various tabs and note in the space provided the various items under each tab that can be changed. Note, depending on your operating system, some tabs may not match the following headings.

General:

_____

Advanced:

_____

Driver:

_____

Resources:

_____

Details:

_____

Events:

_____

Power Management:

_____

Click **Cancel** to exit the network card's configuration dialog box. You will be returned to the network-adapter status window. Select **Properties** again.

5. _____ Look at the items displayed in the **This connection uses the following items** text box. This is a list of installed services and protocols, for example, Client for Microsoft Networks, File and Printer Sharing for Microsoft Networks, QoS Packet Scheduler, and Internet Protocol (TCP/IP). A check mark entered in the box on left of the item indicates the item is enabled. Removing the check mark only disables the item. It does not remove it. Use the information in the **Ethernet Properties** dialog box to answer the following questions.

What client is installed?

_____

Is File and Printer Sharing for Microsoft Networks enabled?

_____

What protocols are configured for the network adapter (i.e., NetBEUI, TCP/IP, and IPX/SPX)?

_____

6. _____ Notice the three buttons directly below this text box: **Install**, **Uninstall**, and **Properties**. These buttons are used to make changes to the installed services and protocols. For example, to view the properties of the Internet Protocol (TCP/IP), you would first select Internet Protocol (TCP/IP) and then click the **Properties** button.

Not all buttons are enabled for each of the items. A shaded button indicates that the function is not available for the selected property. Highlight each item in the **This connection uses the following items** text box and observe the buttons.

7. _____ Disable the TCP/IP protocol. To do this, simply click the box to the left of the Internet Protocol (TCP/IP) entry.

8. _____ Attempt to uninstall the TCP/IP protocol. What happened?

_____

9. _____ Re-enable the TCP/IP protocol.

10. _____ Click the **Advanced** button. The **Advanced TCP/IP Settings** dialog box provides you with access to the Windows 10 TCP/IP settings, as shown in the following screen capture.

Goodheart-Willcox Publisher

11. _____ Turn your attention to the **IP addresses** box in the **IP Settings** tab. Is DHCP enabled?

_____

12. _____ Click **Cancel** to exit the **Advanced TCP/IP Settings** dialog box.

13. _____ Access the **Internet Protocol TCP/IP Properties** dialog box by highlighting the **Internet Protocol (TCP/IP)** entry and selecting **Properties**.

The **General** tab of the **Internet Protocol Version 4 (TCP/IPv4) Properties** dialog box contains options for the way the network adapter is to obtain TCP/IP settings. During the installation of the Windows operating system, the network adapter is configured for **Obtain an IP address automatically**. This means that the network adapter is configured to accept TCP/IP settings, such as an IP address, subnet mask, and default gateway address, automatically from a Dynamic Host Configuration Protocol (DHCP) server. This method of obtaining TCP/IP settings is called *dynamic IP addressing*. A DHCP server can be any server that provides the DHCP service. You will learn about the DHCP service later in this course. An administrator can also enter an IP address, subnet mask, and gateway address manually in the text boxes provided. This is called *static IP addressing*.

Name _____

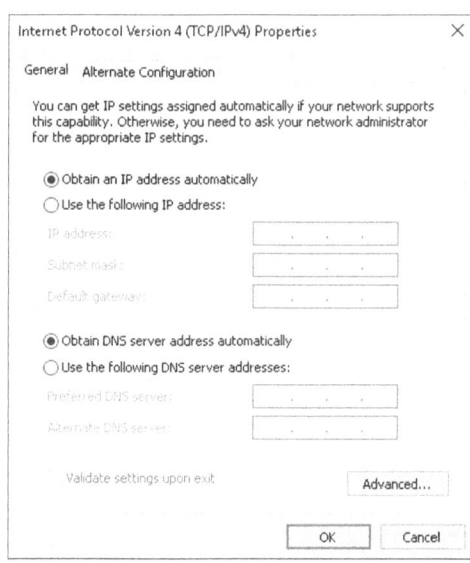

Goodheart-Willcox Publisher

14. _____ Look at the dialog box on your display. Is the network adapter configured to obtain an IP address dynamically or statically?

_____

15. _____ Click the **Alternate Configuration** tab. The first option, **Automatic private IP address**, allows Microsoft to use the Automatic Private IP Addressing (APIPA) service to automatically assign an IP address to a network adapter if the device fails to connect to a DHCP server. APIPA assigns a Class B network IP address, 169.254.xxx.xxx, so the device can continue to communicate with other devices on the LAN. The APIPA assignment cannot be used to communicate across the Internet. Once the DHCP service is restored, the APIPA assigned IP address is discarded and the DHCP server assigns an IP address. APIPA and IP address classes are covered later in this course.

The **User configured** dialog box allows a different TCP/IP configuration to be set up for the network adapter. This is useful if the computer is a laptop that will be used at home and at work, since both locations typically require different TCP/IP settings. Configuring an alternate IP address is covered in a later laboratory activity.

16. _____ Click the **General** tab and then click the **Advanced** button. The **Advanced TCP/IP Settings** dialog box will display. Look at the three tabs available at the top of the dialog box: **IP Settings**, **DNS**, and **WINS**.

Goodheart-Willcox Publisher

Laboratory Activity 12   Exploring Network Adapter Configuration Settings   55

From the **IP Settings** tab, multihoming can be configured for the computer. When a computer is configured as a multihomed device, it is configured with two or more IP addresses to communicate with two or more subnets at the same time. This is not the same as Alternate Configuration presented earlier, which is used to connect to two or more networks, but not at the same time. It is accomplished by manually adding a static IP address by clicking the **Add** button, which will prompt the TCP/IP Address dialog box, as shown in the following screen capture.

Goodheart-Willcox Publisher

17. _____ Now, select the **DNS** tab. The **DNS** dialog box is used for configuring how the workstation will resolve the assigned computer name (host name) to an IP address. The Internet network system uses IP addresses to locate destinations, not host names or URLs. A Domain Name Service (DNS) server is used to resolve host and domain names to IP addresses. The IP addresses of DNS servers that the workstation is to consult are entered in the **DNS Server Addresses, in order of use** text box. The DNS dialog box does not normally need to be configured when the network adapter has been configured for DHCP (dynamic IP addressing) because the DHCP server provides the required DNS server information.

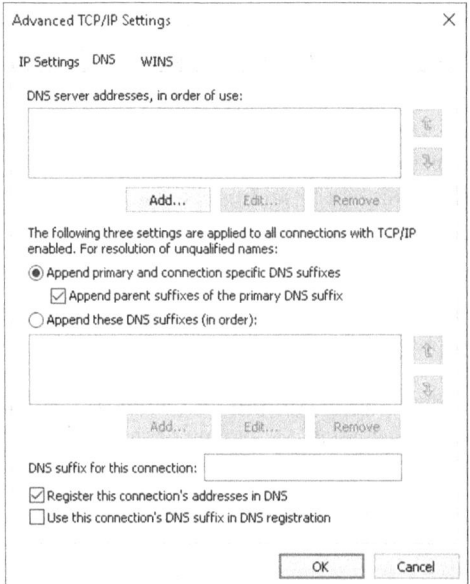

Goodheart-Willcox Publisher

Look at the **DNS Server Addresses, in order of use** text box in your display. What address(es) has been entered for the DNS server? (If the network adapter has been configured to receive TCP/IP information dynamically, the DNS address section will be blank.)

_____

18. _____ Look through the rest of the options in the **DNS** tab. Notice that they reference a *DNS suffix*. The DNS suffix is part of the Fully Qualified Domain Name (FQDN). An FDQN is the name of the computer (host name) appended to the front of a domain name in which the workstation is installed. For example, an FQDN for a workstation called Client1 installed in a domain called RMRoberts.com would be Client1.RMRoberts.com. The DNS suffix would be RMRoberts.com. There will be much more about DNS, FQDNs, and domains later in this course.

56   Networking Fundamentals Lab Manual

Name _____

19. _____ Click the **WINS** tab. The Windows Internet Naming Service (WINS) is used to resolve NetBIOS names to IP addresses. A NetBIOS name is the name given to a computer during the Windows operating system installation process. The **WINS addresses, in order of use** text box is used to list the IP addresses of the WINS servers the workstation is to consult.

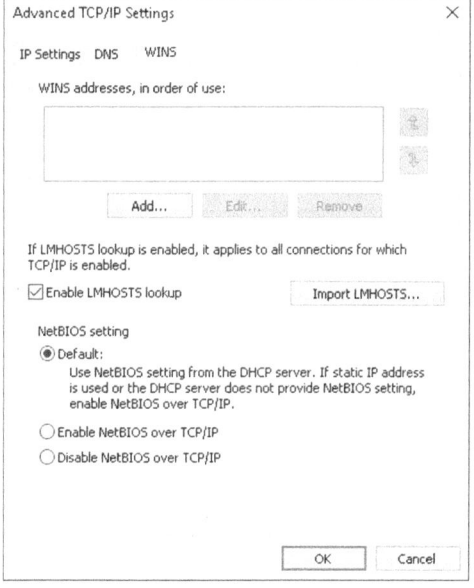

Goodheart-Willcox Publisher

Look at the **WINS addresses, in order of use** text box on your display. What address(es) has been entered? (If the network adapter has been configured to receive TCP/IP information dynamically, the WINS address section will be blank.)

_____

20. _____ Notice the **Enable LMHOSTS lookup** option in the middle of the **WINS** tab. This option refers to the lmhosts text file, which contains a list of NetBIOS names and corresponding IP addresses. This file is typically used in place of a WINS server. If enabled, the computer automatically checks the lmhosts file when attempting to resolve NetBIOS names to IP addresses. All computers in the LAN, however, must have the same contents in their lmhosts file. When a computer communicates with a different computer, it will look in the lmhosts file to find the IP address of the destination computer.

> **NOTE**
> The function of the lmhosts file has been replaced by the use of DNS servers.

21. _____ Now, look at the **NetBIOS setting** options at the bottom of the dialog box. In earlier versions of Microsoft before Windows 2000, LANs communicated by broadcasting NetBIOS name information to all devices in the LAN. Starting with Windows 2000, it became optional to conform to NetBIOS naming standards and the methods used to resolve a NetBIOS name to an IP address. The earlier operating systems required a WINS server to be running WINS services to resolve NetBIOS names to IP addresses so that network devices could communicate over the Internet, which uses IP addresses, not NetBIOS names.

The **Default** option is automatically selected when the network adapter is configured to use a DHCP service. The other two options are for enabling or disabling NetBIOS over TCP/IP. If a network consists only of Windows 2000 or later computers, you can disable NetBIOS over TCP/IP. If the network contains versions of Windows earlier than Windows 2000, enable NetBIOS over TCP/IP. Look at the NetBIOS settings on your display. What is the NetBIOS configuration for the network adapter?

_____

> **NOTE**
> WINS and DNS can coexist in a network system.

22. _____ Answer the review questions before closing any dialog boxes and shutting down your workstation.

Review Questions

1. What are the two main ways IP addresses are assigned to a network adapter?

2. What does the acronym DHCP represent?

3. What is the purpose of a DHCP server?

4. What does the acronym DNS represent?

5. What is the purpose of a DNS server?

6. What does the acronym WINS represent?

7. What is the purpose of a WINS server?

8. How can you identify an Automatic Private IP Address?

9. When is an APIPA address assigned to a network adapter?

Name _____ Date _____ Class _____

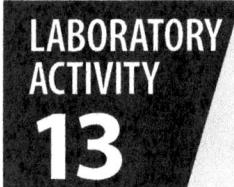

Configuring and Troubleshooting Wireless Connections

Outcomes

After completing this laboratory activity, you will be able to:
- Select a preferred wireless network from several identified networks.
- Evaluate a wireless network connection problem using the Network and Sharing Center.
- Evaluate a wireless network connection using the **Status** link of the **Network & Internet** dialog box.
- Evaluate a wireless network connection problem using the **Troubleshooting problems** of the **Network and Sharing Center** dialog box.
- Check if a wireless network is using security and what type of security is being used.

Introduction

In this laboratory activity, you will explore the features and options associated with making a new wireless network connection. The general configuration of a wireless device will automatically make a wireless connection when the preferred wireless network is in range. Mobile devices are often reconfigured to connect to another wireless network when available, for example in an airport, a coffee shop, a hotel, a school, or another location.

When performing this lab activity in a school lab environment, you may have problems caused by the computer being used by a previous student. For example, once a wireless connection is made, it is often retained even after being disconnected. You may need to delete any existing wireless connection to benefit fully from this lab activity.

A computer equipped with a wireless adapter and not connected to a wireless access point will appear in the Windows 10 task menu similar to that in the following screen capture.

Goodheart-Willcox Publisher

A list of all available wireless networks will be displayed. They will be listed in descending order with the strongest wireless signals at the top and the weakest wireless signals at the bottom. You will also see the strength of the wireless signal indicated by a green bar graph. The more green bars, the stronger the signal. **Secured** or **Open** is listed beside the name of the wireless network. An **Open** network has not configured any security, such as Wired Equivalent Privacy (WEP), Wi-Fi Protected Access (WPA2), and WPA3. Note, WEP should no longer be used. If the wireless network is labeled **Secured**, you will need to know the security passphrase or encryption key to gain access.

Navigating to **Settings>Network & Internet** will open the **Status** dialog box. If there is no established wireless connection, then the box will read **No Internet access** as shown below.

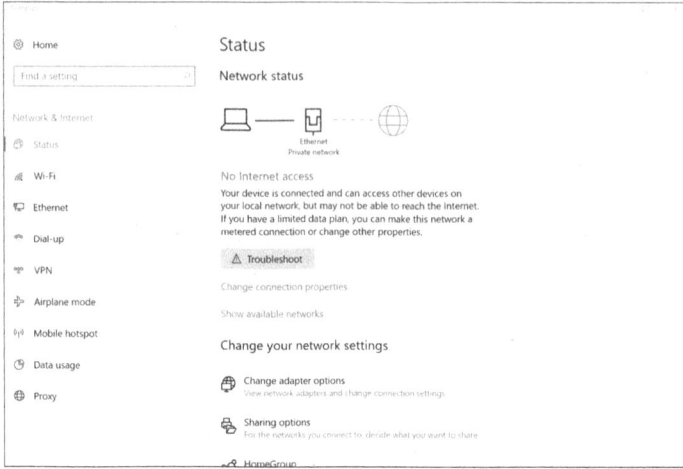

Goodheart-Willcox Publisher

Once a wireless connection is made, you will see the name of the wireless network appear in the **Status** box. The name should match the name of the network you selected from the task bar, similar to the following.

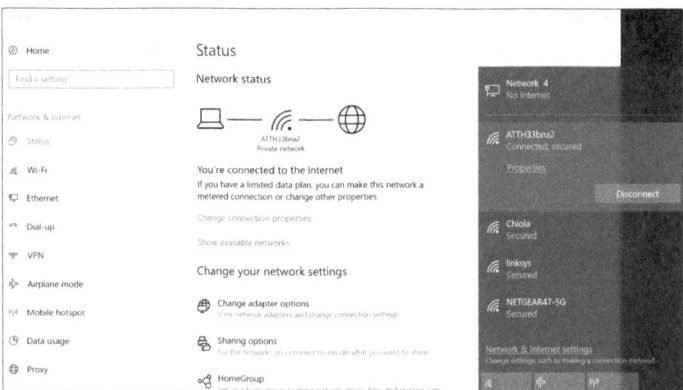

Goodheart-Willcox Publisher

Once connected to a network, you can view information about the type of security being used to protect the wireless connection by clicking on the **Property** link of the network device in the list of available networks. A dialog box similar to the one in the following screen capture will appear.

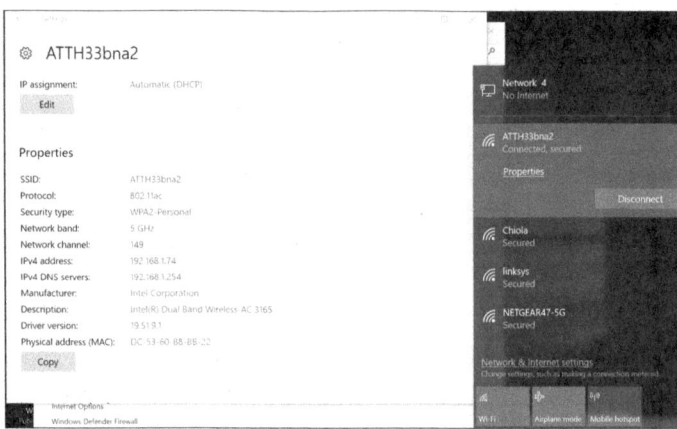

Goodheart-Willcox Publisher

Name _____

In the screen capture, you can see that the **ATTH33bna2** network is using WPA2-Personal security method. You will need the passphrase or pre-shared key to access the network.

To make a connection to a wireless network location, you select the wireless network from the list and then click the **Connect** button. Even after connecting to a wireless access point, you could still experience problems. Look at the following screen capture comparing a good wireless connection with one experiencing problems.

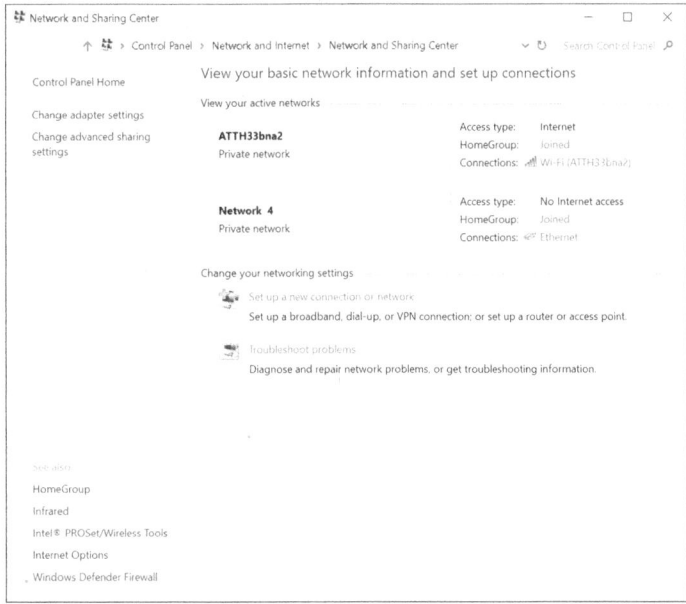

Goodheart-Willcox Publisher

The connection experiencing problems indicates a problem with the label **No Internet access**. Even though there is a problem with the wireless access point, the signal strength indicated is excellent and a connection to the wireless network connection known as **ATTH33bna2** has been indicated. This screen capture was taken from a network with a failed wireless router. The router could still broadcast a signal but could not support a connection to a computer, Internet access, or provide an IP address through its DHCP service. Look at the following screen captures comparing network status information.

Goodheart-Willcox Publisher

The good connection is recording packet activity for both "Sent" and "Received." Previously, a bad connection may show statistics for packets being sent but not for those received. In Windows 10, there is simply no network device visible if there is a bad connection or no connection. Poor signal strength will usually only support a very low data rate (1 Mbps to 5 Mbps). Excellent signal strength will support a data rate of 36 Mbps to 54 Mbps or higher, depending on the wireless standard design of the adapter, such as 802.11g or 802.11n.

Clicking the **Details** button will display the **Network Connection Details** dialog box, allowing you to view important details about the wireless adapter, similar to the following screen capture.

Goodheart-Willcox Publisher

When a connection fails, the computer is issued an APIPA IPv4 address that starts with 168.254. A good connection will have an IPv4 address other than an APIPA address. In the screen capture of the completed network connection, the IPv4 address starts with 192.168, which indicates a typical private IPv4 address, such as the type used by a home-office router or gateway. The connection could also have a different IPv4 address, but the most common default assigned IPv4 address starts with 169.254.

Wireless networks viewed in the taskbar have unique names. These names represent each network's respective SSID. This is a good reason you should change the default name of a WAP to a descriptive name other than the default name. If all wireless networks used the same wireless router with the same default SSID, it would cause connection problems. A person using a laptop who changes physical locations to such a location as a hotel in a large city could have several WAPs in range of their room. The laptop would try to connect to the strongest signal of the WAP with the same name automatically. Because the WAP could be using a security method such as WEP, the user would not be able to connect to the WAP. The user would most likely not know the reason for the failure. All the typical user would know is that they cannot establish a connection to the desired WAP and it keeps prompting them for a password or such.

Always reassign a WAP SSID. Never leave the default SSID. The main reason is security. A hacker can easily obtain the default SSID of any wireless device by brand from the Internet and usually the default password as well. A hacker then can access and reconfigure the WAP to meet their own needs. Hacking a WAP is quite common if the technician has not changed the default SSID and the default administrative password. You probably will not have more than one or two WAPs within reach of your lab computer.

The Network and Sharing Center in Windows 10 does not have a network map similar to the one seen in Windows 7. Instead, users can determine their wireless connectivity through the **Network & Internet** menu. To view available wireless networks in Windows 10, navigate to **Start>Settings>Network & Internet>Wi-Fi**, as shown in the following screen capture. Alternatively, you can access available networks by right-clicking the networking icon in the notification area.

Name _____

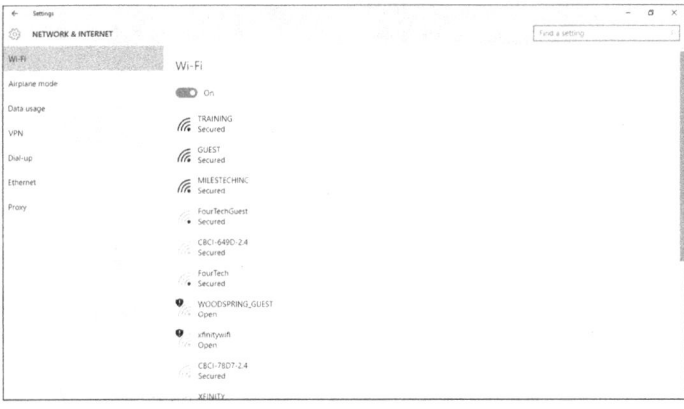

Goodheart-Willcox Publisher

Ensure your Wi-Fi is turned on and select the desired network from the list. Once you select a network, you will have the opportunity to configure the connection to connect automatically if you so choose. After you have selected a network, and clicked the **Connect** button, you will be prompted to enter the password, if the network is secured.

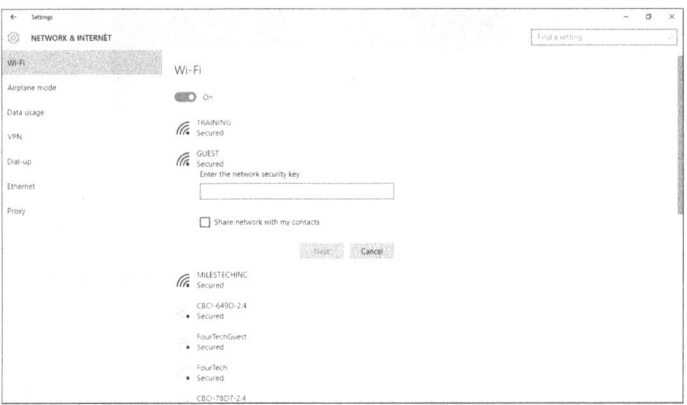

Goodheart-Willcox Publisher

Once you have successfully connected to a wireless network, you will be able to monitor your connection similarly to how you did so previously with Windows 7.

Equipment and Materials

- Windows 10 computer equipped with a wireless adapter. A laptop is preferred, but not required.
- One or more wireless access points set up in the lab area. One wireless access point should provide access to the Internet, but this is not required.
- The following information: SSID (Wireless Access Point name):

_____

Procedure

1. _____ Report to your assigned workstation.

2. _____ Boot the computer and verify it is in working order.

3. _____ Click on the Wi-Fi icon in the lower-right corner of the taskbar. If a wireless connection already exists, you will need to disconnect it. To disconnect from the WAP, simply click **Disconnect** as indicated in the following screen capture.

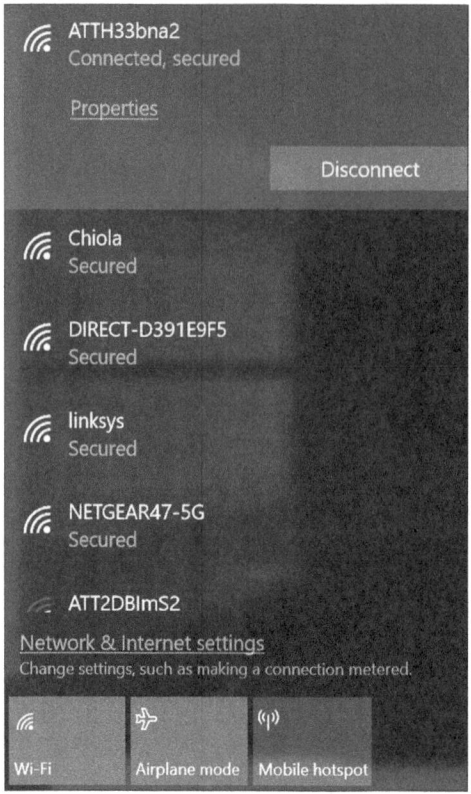

Goodheart-Willcox Publisher

4. _____ Create a new instance of a wireless connection by selecting **Connect** on the desired wireless device from the list displayed.

5. _____ Select the wireless network (SSID) that was set up for this lab activity. Some school lab environments may display many wireless networks. The wireless network inside the lab area will most likely produce the strongest signal and will be displayed at the top of the list. Select the wireless network indicated in the list of materials for this lab.

You can also connect to a network manually through the Network and Sharing Center. Once inside the Network and Sharing Center, select the **Set up a new connection or network** link. A screen similar to the following will appear.

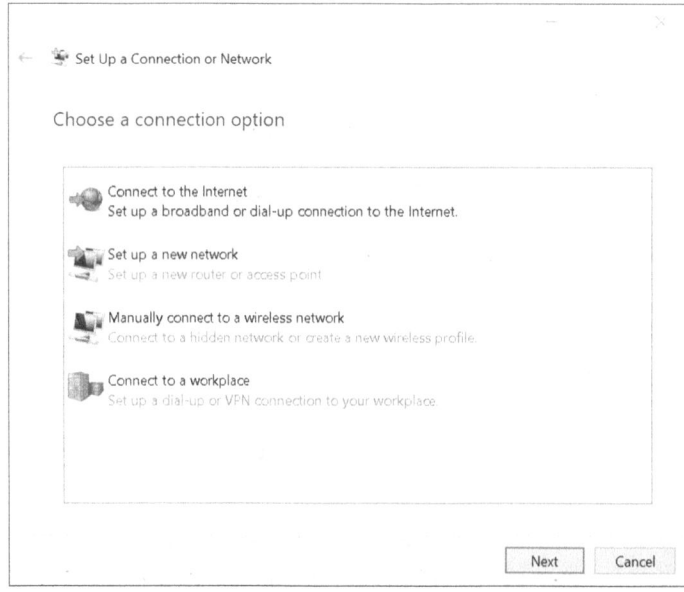

Goodheart-Willcox Publisher

Name _____

By selecting the **Manually connect to a wireless network**, you can enter the **SSID**, **Security type**, **Encryption type**, and **Security Key** for the desired network. You can also establish whether you would like the network connection to start automatically or even when the network is not broadcasting, as shown in the following screen capture.

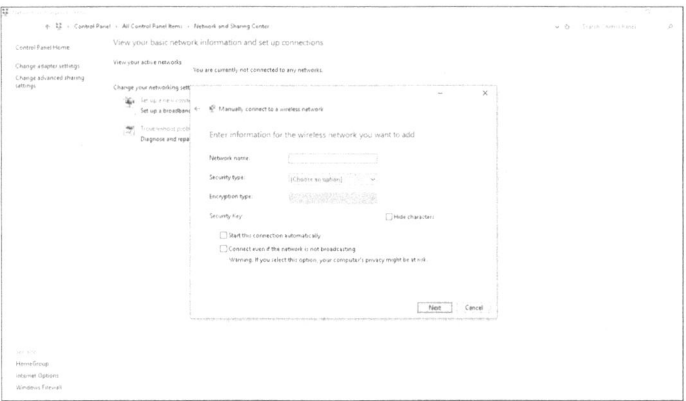

Goodheart-Willcox Publisher

If you are unable to connect to a network, you can select the **Troubleshoot problems** link from the Network and Sharing Center, which will result in a list of options similar to the following.

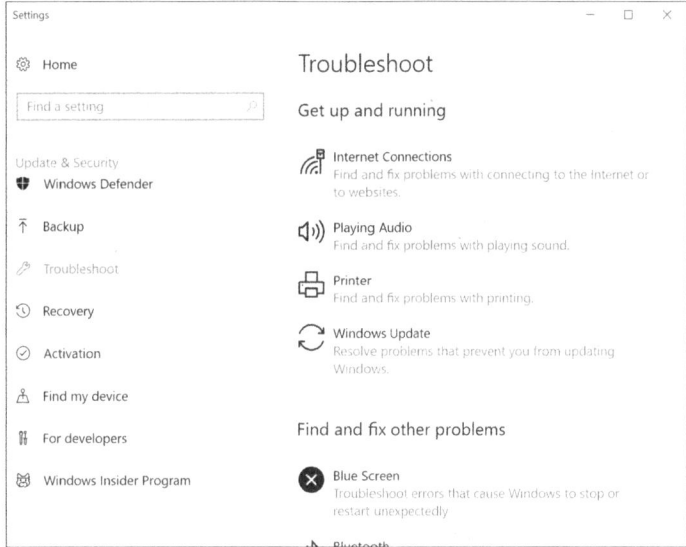

Goodheart-Willcox Publisher

Normally, the appropriate option to select would be to click **Internet Connections>Run the troubleshooter**. If this fails to fix the problem, then you should check if another computer is connected to the WAP. If another computer is connected wirelessly to the WAP, then the problem is your computer. If no one else can connect to the WAP, then the problem is most likely the WAP. You can reset the WAP and then try connecting.

6. _____ Have your instructor check your lab activity to verify a successful wireless connection.

7. _____ To gain some firsthand troubleshooting experience, disconnect the electrical power to the WAP. Open your computer's Network and Sharing Center after the power is disconnected from the WAP and view the information displayed about the wireless connection. Reconnect the power cable.

8. _____ Disconnect the cable that is used to establish the connection from the WAP to the Internet. Reconnect the power to the WAP with the Internet connection disconnected. Open the Network and Sharing Center to view the information displayed.

9. _____ Reconnect the WAP Internet connection.

10. _____ Click the list of Wi-Fi networks from the notification area of the taskbar. Click **Disconnect**.

11. _____ Disconnect the electrical power to the WAP.

12. _____ Try establishing a connection to the WAP from the computer while the electrical power is disconnected from the WAP. View the dialog boxes that are generated and try to repair the connection with the options that appear in the dialog box.

13. _____ Reconnect the electrical power to the WAP.

14. _____ Re-establish a connection to the WAP from the computer.

15. _____ Return all materials to their proper storage area and then answer the review questions.

Review Questions

1. How is a problem with a wireless connection between a computer and a WAP indicated in the Network and Sharing Center?

   _____

   _____

2. If the WAP has lost its connection to the Internet, how is it indicated in Network and Sharing Center?

   _____

   _____

3. Why should you change the default SSID of a WAP?

   _____

Name _____ Date _____ Class _____

Wireless Throughput vs. Distance

Outcomes

After completing this laboratory activity, you will be able to:
- Describe the relationship between distance and wireless network throughput.
- Describe the effect of various objects on wireless network throughput.

Introduction

In this laboratory activity, you will explore the effects of distance in relation to wireless network throughput and the effect of placing objects in the direct line of sight of wireless devices. To observe the differences in throughput, you will transfer the contents of a large file. The file should be 20 MB or larger. One way to obtain a large file is to create one with Microsoft Paint. To increase the file size, increase the color depth and picture size until the desired file size is reached. Save the file as a bitmap file. A bitmap file has a BMP file extension. A bitmap does not employ compression techniques, and thus will not reduce the size of the file when saved. Do *not* use any other file format than BMP.

Wireless LANs have become popular because of their reputation for being easy to install. Cables can be difficult to install through partitions and can be a hazard when run across or along the floor. Although wireless networks are easier to install, distance and building materials can adversely affect wireless LAN activity.

The type of material used to construct the wall affects transmission, as does the degree of the angle the signal travels through the wall. For example, if the path between the source and destination computers runs directly through the wall, the effect of the building material on transmission will be less than if the path between the source and destination computers ran at an angle through the wall. The angled path produces the same effect on the transmission as a thicker wall would. Look at the following illustration.

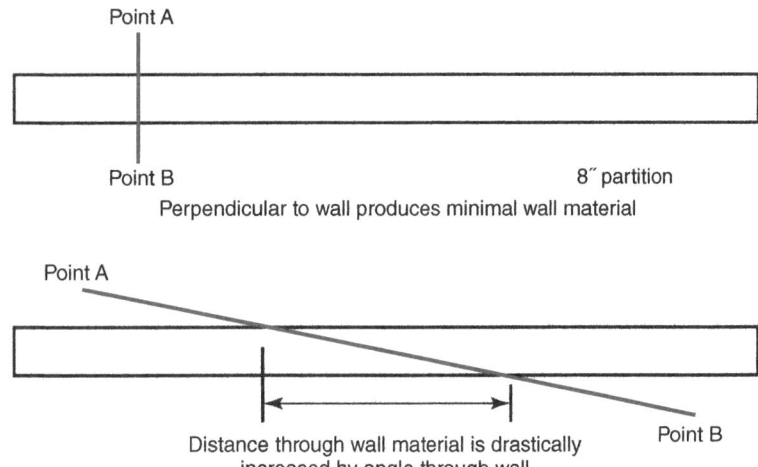

Goodheart-Willcox Publisher

As you can see, when the transmission travels directly through the wall, the distance through the material is much shorter than when the transmission travels at an angle. The angle in the example would produce three times the effect of the 8-inch wall or approximately 24 inches.

You can record throughput by measuring the amount of time it takes to transfer the file from source to destination. You can also observe the effects of throughput by looking at the signal strength indicator in the **Wireless Network Connection Status** dialog box. To access the **Wireless Network Connection Status** dialog box, open the Network and Sharing Center. Click **View Status** for the wireless network connection. Or simply type "Wi-Fi" in the search box of Windows 10. A dialog box similar to the following will display.

Goodheart-Willcox Publisher

You will see the effects of signal strength in the bar graph. You will also see a change in the speed rating. As distance is increased, the speed will drop. The throughput of the signal will also decrease as the distance increases. Increasing the distance will cause the signal to become weaker at the receiving computer and become more susceptible to radio interference. Radio interference will corrupt packets and cause the packet to be resent. The overall effect is loss in throughput.

Equipment and Materials
- Windows 10 computer configured with a wireless network adapter
- Laptop configured with a wireless network adapter
- Measuring device, such as a tape measure or yardstick, to measure distances

Procedure

1. _____ Report to your assigned computers (laptop and PC).

2. _____ Boot the computers and verify they are in working order.

3. _____ Place the laptop 3 feet from the PC.

4. _____ Create a large bitmap file on one of the computers.

5. _____ Transfer the file to the other computer and record in the following chart the amount of time it takes. Repeat this step five times.

Name _____

Transfer	File Size	Time	Throughput
1			
2			
3			
4			
5			
Average			

6. _____ Calculate the average time and average throughput.

7. _____ Increase the distance between computers to 25 feet.

8. _____ Transfer the file to the other computer and record in the following chart the amount of time it takes. Repeat this step five times.

Transfer	File Size	Time	Throughput
1			
2			
3			
4			
5			
Average			

9. _____ Calculate the average time and average throughput.

10. _____ Increase the distance between computers to 50 feet.

11. _____ Transfer the file to the other computer and record in the following chart the amount of time it takes. Repeat this step five times.

Transfer	File Size	Time	Throughput
1			
2			
3			
4			
5			
Average			

12. _____ Calculate the average time and average throughput.

13. _____ Test the effect of walls and doors on throughput. Use the **Wireless Network Connection Status** dialog box to observe the effects. First, test data transmission directly through the wall and then at an acute angle (less than 90 degrees) through the wall.

14. _____ Answer the review questions.

15. _____ Return all materials to their proper storage area.

Review Questions

1. Describe the effect on throughput in relationship to distance.

   _____

   _____

2. What is the major benefit of wireless LAN?

   _____

   _____

3. What are some concerns of wireless LAN throughput in relation to distance?

   _____

   _____

   _____

Name _____ Date _____ Class _____

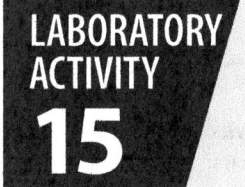

Wireshark Network Protocol Analyzer

Outcomes

After completing this lab activity, you will be able to:
- Identify common encapsulation protocols.
- Interpret protocol details.
- Use Wireshark to open previously saved captures.
- Use Wireshark to save a capture.

Introduction

In the Chapter 5 laboratory activity, you were introduced to the Wireshark network protocol analyzer. In this laboratory activity, you will take a closer look at various Wireshark options. A complete understanding of all Wireshark options and functions cannot be covered in a single laboratory activity. This laboratory activity covers only what you need to know to get you started analyzing frame and packet contents. In future laboratory activities, you will use Wireshark to observe the following:

- How a workstation announces its presence to other workstations.
- How the network browser operates.
- How a workstation properly shuts down or disconnects from a network.
- How files are exchanged (shared).
- How information is retrieved from the Internet.
- How e-mail is transferred.
- How security is implemented during network logon.

Additional options and functions are presented in these upcoming laboratory activities. For now, only the options and functions needed to run elementary laboratory activities are covered.

In this lab activity, you will see how data is encapsulated. Encapsulation involves several different protocols, one encapsulated inside another. A Wireshark capture file is used in this laboratory exercise and will be provided by your instructor. The file name is **Wireshark Sample 1**. Using this file, you will look at the way a collection of protocols is assembled into a complete packet and frame. Pay particular attention to which protocol requires addressing information for the destination and source.

> **NOTE**
> Wireshark laboratory activities are based on Wireshark 3.6.7, which is the latest version at the time of this writing. Screen capture images and exact procedure steps may not exactly match this lab activity when using a newer version of Wireshark.

Equipment and Materials

- Two or more Windows 10 or later computers connected as a peer-to-peer network
- USB storage device
- Wireshark Sample 1 file
  Wireshark Sample 1 file location: _____

Procedure

> **NOTE**
> Contents of a capture will vary according to what services are running at the time the capture was made, as well as the type of devices and operating systems running in the network. When making captures, the use of a network hub is ideal. Networking devices such as switches, routers, and firewalls may limit the captures.

1. _____ Report to your assigned workstation(s).
2. _____ Boot the computers and make sure they are in working order.
3. _____ Open Wireshark. A screen similar to the following will display.

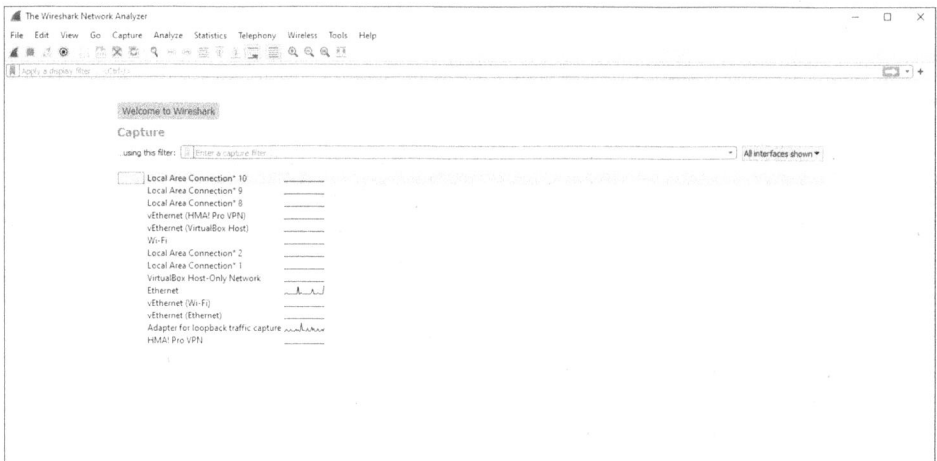

Goodheart-Willcox Publisher

4. _____ Select **Capture>Options**. The **Wireshark Capture Interfaces** dialog box will display. Select the appropriate network adapter and click the **Start** button. You may also select the appropriate network adapter located in the **Capture** section of the screen. The capture will automatically start when you select the interface.

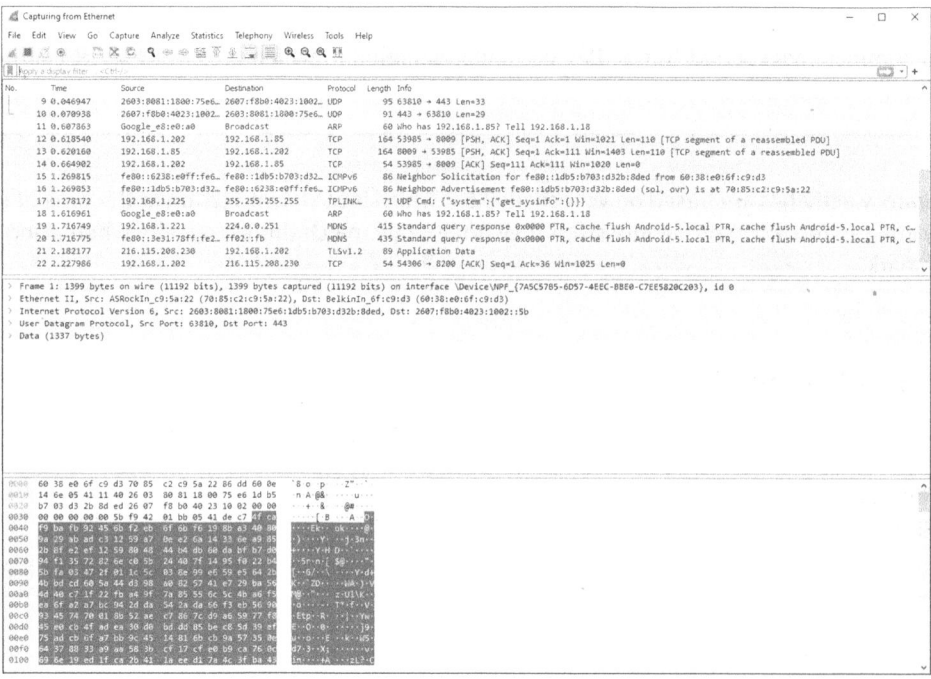

Goodheart-Willcox Publisher

Name _____

5. _____ After one or two minutes, stop the capture by selecting **Capture>Stop** or by clicking the **Stop** icon located in the menu bar.

Goodheart-Willcox Publisher

6. _____ After the capture is stopped, scroll through the captured frames and inspect the packets and protocols.

7. _____ Save the capture as a file on your computer or on a device such as a USB storage device. If you try to start a new capture, Wireshark will automatically prompt you to save the file or discard it. The dialog box that will appear will look similar to the following.

Goodheart-Willcox Publisher

You can also save a file from the main interface by selecting **File>Save** or **File>Save As**. Notice in the menu that you can also use the shortcut keys [Ctrl] [S] or [Shift] [Ctrl] [S].

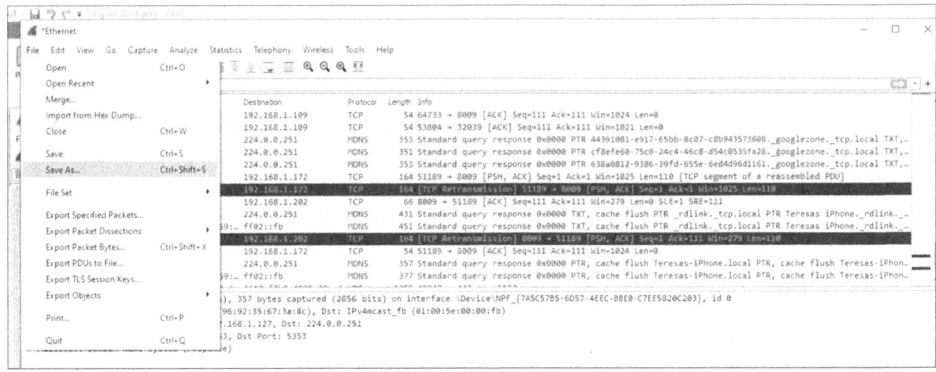

Goodheart-Willcox Publisher

To save a capture, you can also click the **Save** icon, as shown in the following screen capture.

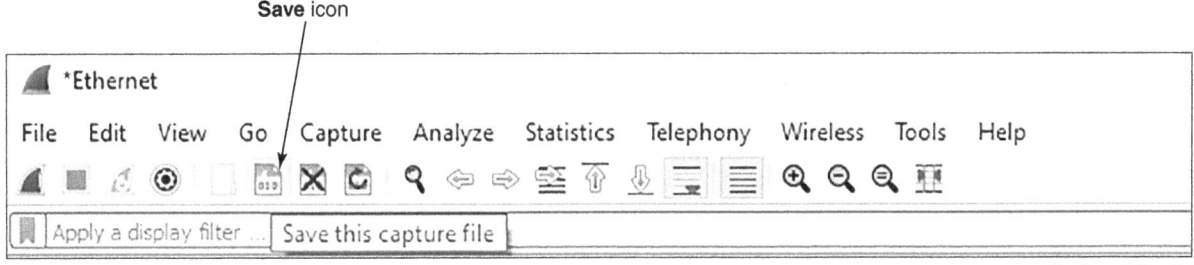

Goodheart-Willcox Publisher

Laboratory Activity 15   Wireshark Network Protocol Analyzer   73

8. _____ After selecting any of the **Save** or **Save as** options, a dialog box similar to the following will display.

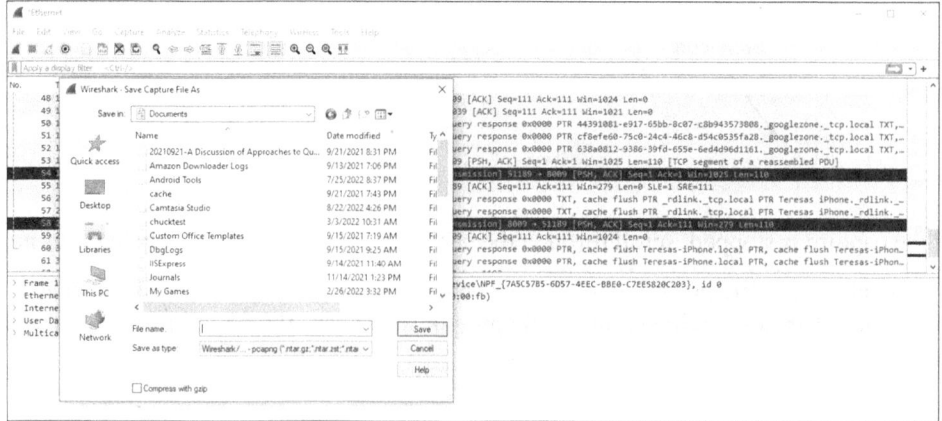

Goodheart-Willcox Publisher

Use the dialog box to locate the folder or directory to which you want to save the capture. You must name the capture to save it. You should always use a meaningful name for the capture. For example, if you are studying the ARP protocol, you may wish to name the saved capture "ARP capture" or something similar. Also, notice that in the **Packet Range** section, there are options that will allow you to save part of the capture. You can save a single frame or an entire range.

For this exercise, save the capture you just created to your USB storage device if indicated by your instructor. Call your instructor to inspect your progress after saving the capture.

> **NOTE**
> Only save captures to the location indicated by your instructor.

9. _____ Now, you will explore some of the configuration options. Open the **Wireshark Capture Options** dialog box by selecting **Capture>Options** from the menu bar. You can also press the [Ctrl] [K] combination.

10. _____ After selecting **Options**, a dialog box similar to the following will display.

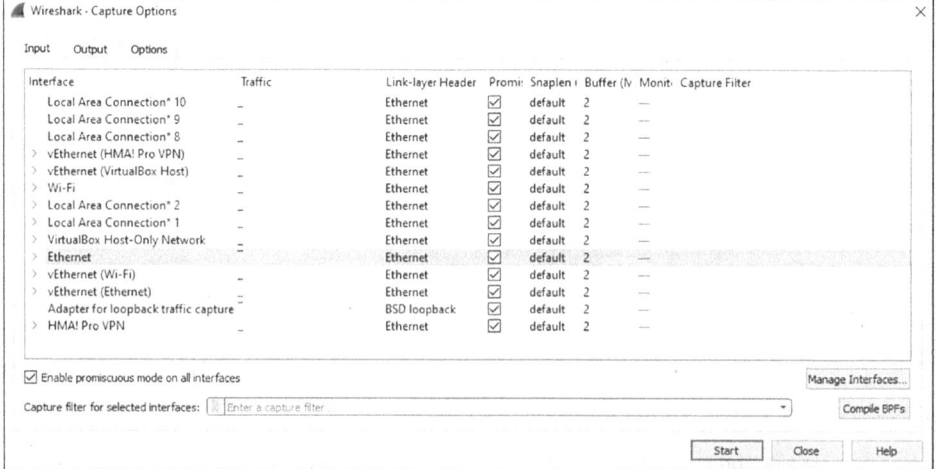

Goodheart-Willcox Publisher

Look over the **Wireshark Capture Interface** dialog box carefully. Notice that there are three tabs for configuring captures:

Input

Output

Options

Name _____

The **Input** section allows you to select a local or remote interface. **Enable promiscuous mode on all interfaces** option is selected by default. Yours may not be selected by default when the computer is shared by other students. Also, notice the **Capture Filter** text box, which will allow you to preselect specific types of captures based on protocol(s) or specific devices or locations.

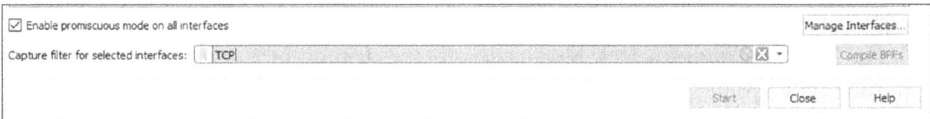

Goodheart-Willcox Publisher

The **Output** tab allows you to create a permanent capture file and select the desired output format for the file. You can also opt for Wireshark to create multiple files if a trigger condition is met. Trigger conditions can be established by selecting the **Create a new file automatically option**. After selecting the option, users can request new files be created after a given number of kilobytes, megabytes, or gigabytes have been met. Users can also set a ring buffer in this area.

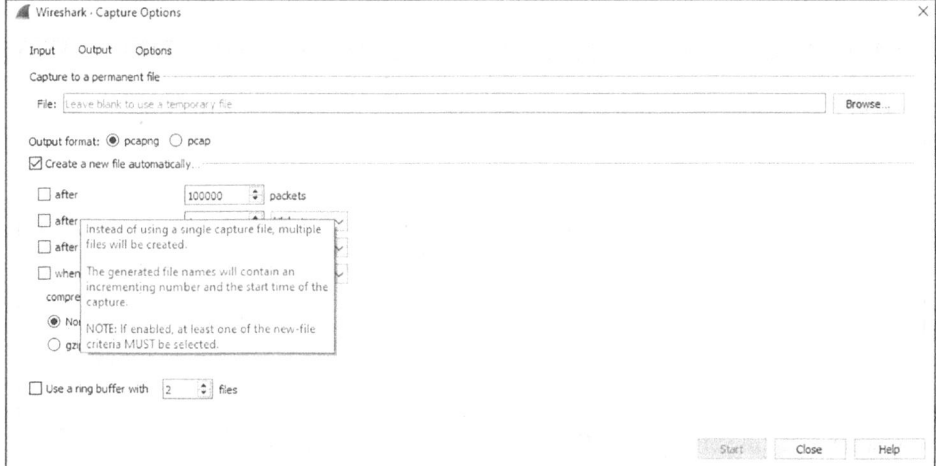

Goodheart-Willcox Publisher

The **Options** tab houses three sections of options: **Display Options**, **Name Resolution**, and **Stop capture automatically after**. The **Display Options** section allows you to specify how you want to view packets while they are being captured. The **Name Resolution** section is very handy for identifying items by name rather than by number. For example, the MAC manufacturer name can be displayed instead of the MAC address. The **Stop capture automatically after** section allows you to stop a capture series automatically after a specific lapse time, the size of the capture in megabytes, or a specific number of packets.

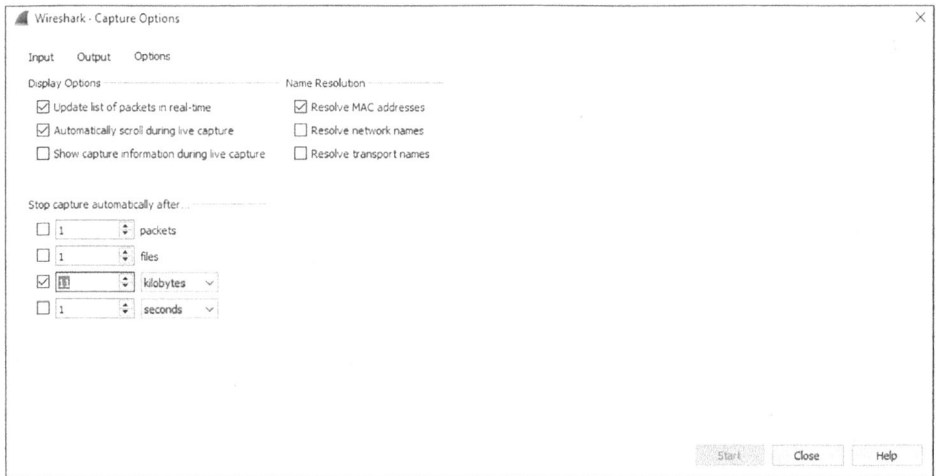

Goodheart-Willcox Publisher

11. _____ Close the **Wireshark Capture Options** dialog box and any other open Wireshark dialog boxes.

12. _____ Restart the Wireshark protocol analyzer and open the **Wireshark Sample 1** file. To open a file, select the **File>Open** or use the [Ctrl] [O] key combination. Navigate to the location of the **Wireshark Sample 1** file. Highlight the file and then click **Open**.

13. _____ Look at the protocols listed in the **Protocol** column. Notice that the protocols are displayed as acronyms. To see the full protocol name, select the packet with the desired protocol. The name of the protocol will appear in the middle pane.

14. _____ In the middle pane, notice the Ethernet II protocol. This protocol encapsulates all the other protocols. Looking at the Ethernet II section, you will see that the MAC address of the source and destination have been identified as Src: 00:0c:41:eb:89:df and Dst: 00:04:5a:4d:f1:0b. Expand the contents of the Ethernet II protocol by clicking the box with the arrow next to the protocol. You will see additional information.

15. _____ Look at the Internet Protocol section in the middle pane. The source and destination IP addresses are associated with this protocol. The source IP address is 192.168.0.3, and the destination IP address is 192.168.0.1.

16. _____ Now, look at the next major protocol for frame 1: Transmission Control Protocol (TCP). Notice that the TCP protocol lists the ports associated with the protocol. The port for the source is 139, and the port for the destination is 1091. The complete address (MAC address, IP address, and the port number) of the source and destination is contained inside the three protocols: Ethernet II, IP, and TCP. This frame is an example of a connection-oriented transmission because all information for the source and destination is contained in the frame.

17. _____ Look at the bottom pane. It contains data from the packet selected in the top pane. The left side is displayed in hexadecimal, and the right side is a mixture of ASCII and indistinguishable characters that cannot be expressed in ASCII. Most of the time, this information will be meaningless. At other times, you will be able to read specific information, especially when the contents of the packet contain plain text files.

18. _____ Select the **Statistics>Capture File Properties**. You should see a dialog box similar to the one in the following screen capture. The **Statistics>Capture File Properties** dialog box provides you with a quick summary of statistics for the capture.

Goodheart-Willcox Publisher

Name _____

19. _____ Close the **Wireshark Capture File Properties** dialog box and then select **Statistics>Protocol Hierarchy**. You should see a dialog box similar to the one in the following screen capture.

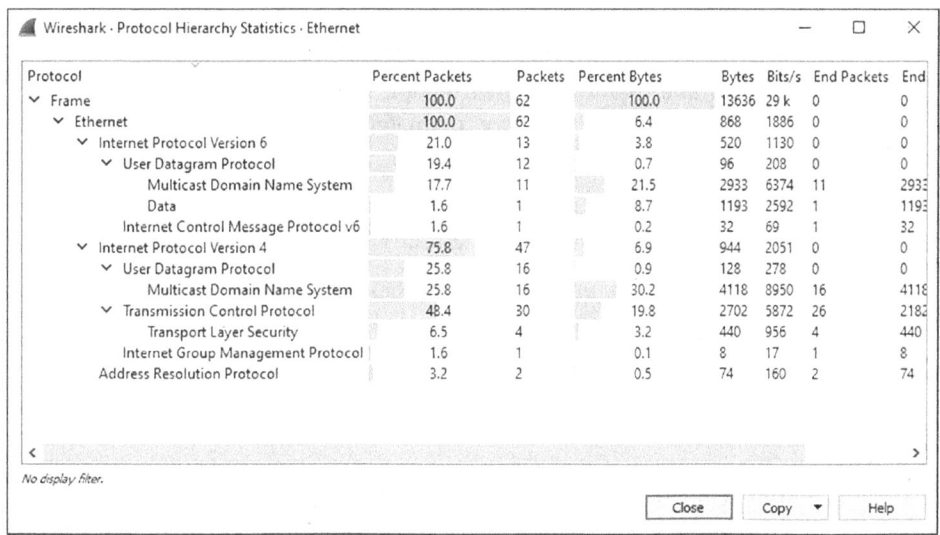

Goodheart-Willcox Publisher

The **Wireshark Protocol Hierarchy Statistics** dialog box provides you with a detailed list of statistics about each protocol captured and identified. Look over the list of protocols and notice that the gray bar in each of the **Percent Packets** column indicates the direct proportion of the protocol to the total amount of protocols captured. For example, Ethernet comprised 100 percent of the frames captured, IP comprised 75.8 percent, TCP comprised 48.4 percent, and so on.

20. _____ Close the **Wireshark Protocol Hierarchy Statistics** dialog box.

21. _____ Now you will become more familiar with using the Wireshark protocol analyzer. Answer the following questions about the Wireshark Sample 1 file capture.

What protocol(s) are used to encapsulate TCP?

_____

What protocol(s) are used to encapsulate ARP?

_____

What protocol(s) are used to encapsulate SMB?

_____

What does the acronym SMB represent?

_____

What two port numbers are associated with TCP in frame 4?

_____

How many seconds elapsed between the first and second frame captured?

_____

How many frames total were captured?

_____

How many minutes did the protocol analyzer run to capture all of the frames?

_____

22. _____ Close the Wireshark Sample 1 file by selecting **File>Close**.

23. _____ Start the protocol analyzer and capture your own sample of network activity. To generate network activity, access a shared folder on the network. After approximately one minute, stop the capture and view the contents. If you are not able to capture any contents, call your instructor for assistance.

24. _____ Save the contents of your first capture to the USB storage device. Use your name as the name of the captured file. Call your instructor to check your lab activity and look at the saved capture file.

25. _____ Select HelpContents and familiarize yourself with the help file contents. The Help file will provide you with a lot of valuable information about the operation of Wireshark.

26. _____ Answer review questions and then return all materials to their proper storage area.

Review Questions

Choose answers based on the following protocols: Ethernet, IP, TCP, SMB.

1. Which protocol provides a field for the MAC address?

_____

2. Which protocol provides a field for the IP address?

_____

3. Which protocol provides a field for the port number?

_____

4. Which protocol provided no address information or port number?

_____

5. How does SMB know where to deliver a packet of data?

_____

_____

Name _____ Date _____ Class _____

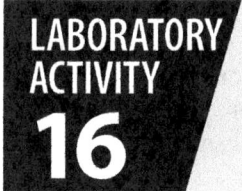

LABORATORY ACTIVITY 16
Wireshark OSI Model Exploration

Outcomes

After completing this laboratory activity, you will be able to:
- Use the Wireshark Network Protocol Analyzer to match protocols to the OSI model.
- Identify the protocols responsible for MAC address, IP address, and port numbers.
- Explain how protocols encapsulate data and other protocols.

Introduction

In this laboratory activity, you will use the Wireshark Network Protocol Analyzer to compare the relationship of specific protocols to the layers of the OSI model. You can typically determine the OSI layer a protocol aligns with by looking at its relative position in the hierarchy of protocols in the Wireshark program. Look at the following screen capture. Notice that the hierarchy of protocols is displayed in the middle pane of the Wireshark screen. Each frame that is selected displays its own hierarchy. The typical hierarchy lists the protocol related to the bottom-most OSI layer at the top of the pane.

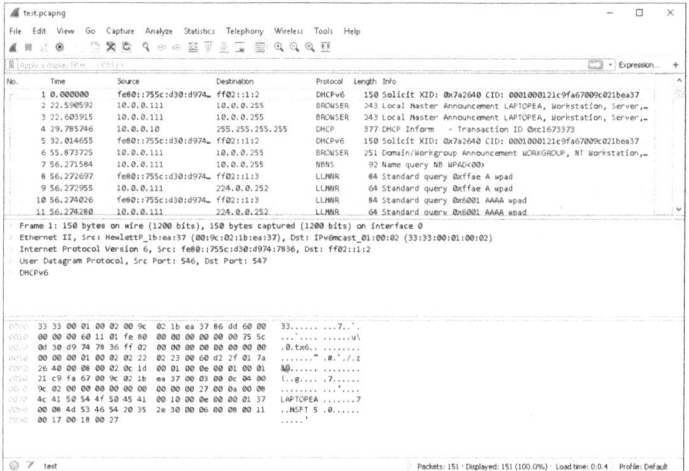

Goodheart-Willcox Publisher

Clicking the arrow at the beginning of the information line can reveal more information about each protocol listed in the hierarchy. This information may reveal items such as the source, destination, MAC, and port addresses.

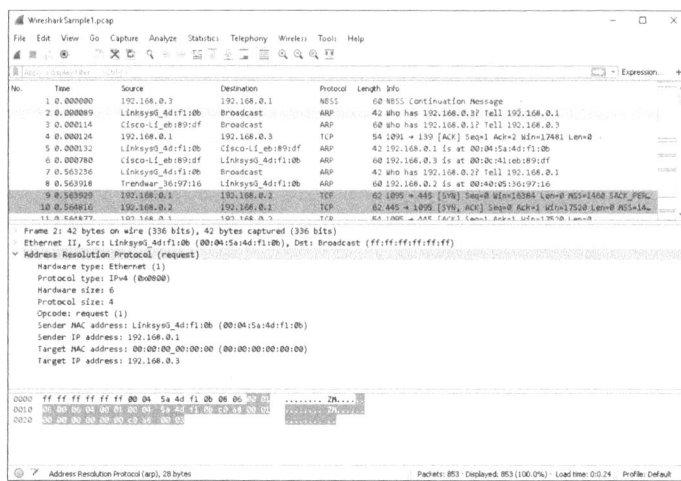

Goodheart-Willcox Publisher

According to the OSI model, the Ethernet II protocol is a Layer 2 protocol. It contains the MAC address of the destination and source. The Internet Protocol is a Layer 3 protocol. It contains the IP address of the destination and source. The User Datagram Protocol is a Layer 4 protocol. It contains the source and destination port numbers. The remaining protocols are upper-level protocols (Layers 5, 6, and 7). Unless you know the function of these upper-level protocols, it is not easy to determine their location in the OSI model. Many protocols span more than one layer because they perform more than one function.

In this laboratory activity, you will open and inspect a Wireshark capture file (provided by your instructor) and identify to which OSI layer each protocol in the capture should be assigned. Layers 5, 6, and 7 are combined for this activity. Layer 1 does not exist for this activity.

Equipment and Materials

- Windows 10 computer with Wireshark installed
- Wireshark Sample 2 file
  Wireshark Sample 2 file location:

_____

Procedure

1. _____ Report to your assigned workstation.

2. _____ Boot the computer and verify it is in working order.

3. _____ Start the Wireshark Network Protocol Analyzer utility.

4. _____ Open the Wireshark Sample 2 file.

5. _____ Place an *X* in the corresponding OSI model layer in the table and write out the protocol name for each protocol displayed in the capture.

Protocol	Layer 2	Layer 3	Layer 4	Layers 5, 6, 7	Protocol Name
Ethernet II					
ARP					
IP					
TCP					
UDP					
SMTP					
POP					
NBNS					
HTTP					
SMB2					
DNS					
LLMNR					
ICMP					
RIPv2					

6. _____ After completing the table, go on to answer the review questions.

7. _____ Return the computer to its original condition.

Name _____

Review Questions

1. Which protocol was found at Layer 2 throughout this lab activity?

   _____

2. Which protocols were found at Layer 3 throughout this lab activity?

   _____

3. Which protocols were found at Layer 4 throughout this lab activity?

   _____

4. Which protocols were not specifically identified, but are typically found at Layers 5, 6, and 7?

   _____

5. What protocols are used to encapsulate the upper-level (Layers 5, 6, and 7) protocols?

   _____

6. Which protocol uses the MAC address to identify the location of the destination and source?

   _____

7. Which protocol uses the IPv4 address to locate the source and destination?

   _____

8. Which protocols use the port number to identify the source and destination?

   _____

9. Explain how protocol encapsulation provides all the required information for data packet delivery.

   _____

   _____

Notes

Name _____ Date _____ Class _____

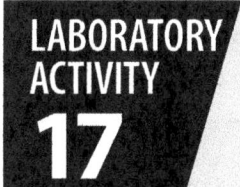

Observing ARP, LLMNR, and NBNS with Wireshark

LABORATORY ACTIVITY 17

Outcomes

After completing this laboratory activity, you will be able to:
- Explain the sequence of activities that occurs when a workstation connects to a peer-to-peer network.
- Explain the sequence of activities that occurs when a workstation disconnects from a peer-to-peer network.
- Interpret the contents of an ARP packet.
- Recall the purpose of ARP.
- Recall the purpose of NBNS.
- Interpret the contents of an NBNS packet.
- Recall the purpose of LLMNR.
- Interpret the contents of an LLMNR packet.
- Identify a broadcast packet by the destination IP address.
- Recall the purpose of multicast.
- Identify the address of IPv4 and IPv6 multicast.

Introduction

In this laboratory activity, you will use the Wireshark protocol analyzer to observe the sequence of activities that occur when a workstation connects to and disconnects from a peer-to-peer network. You will specifically examine three protocols: Address Resolution Protocol (ARP), Link-Local Multicast Name Resolution (LLMNR), and NetBIOS Name Server (NBNS).

When a workstation with a static IP address is booted, it will perform two tasks: check if the workstation's IPv4 address is duplicated on the LAN and announce to the network browser that it has joined the workgroup. The workstation uses ARP to verify that the workstation's IPv4 address is not assigned to another workstation on the LAN. This verification is known as "gratuitous ARP request" or simply "ARP." ARP uses the Ethernet MAC address ff:ff:ff:ff:ff:ff to broadcast to all workstations when performing the verification.

The workstation then announces to the network browser that it has joined the workgroup. The Microsoft network browser is a software utility that maintains a central list of information about network devices and enables users to view the network devices. The NetBIOS Name Server (NBNS) protocol is used to carry the information about the workstation name. It is also used to match IP addresses to NetBIOS names. NBNS is designed to support the Windows Internet Naming Service (WINS). When the network browser receives this information, it adds the workstation's NetBIOS name to the browser list of workstations.

When you use Wireshark to observe the connectionless process, you will see the name of the workstation listed multiple times. This occurs for two reasons. First, the protocol used to broadcast the information is connectionless; hence, it does not guarantee packet delivery. The packet is sent repeatedly to ensure that the information is delivered. Second, the workstation performs more than one role and is identified by using a NetBIOS suffix attached to the name of the workstation. For example, a workstation called Station1 may appear in the listing as Station 1 <00> and Station1 <20>. The <00> designates the workstation as a workstation. The <20> designates the workstation as a file server if it contains at least one file for sharing on the network. Some other common NetBIOS suffixes are as follows:

A. 00 = workstation
B. 01 = master browser
C. 20 = file server
D. 21 = Remote Access client
E. 1B = domain master browser

NOTE
There are over 30 possible NetBIOS suffixes.

A Class C network is identified by the first three octets: 192.168.000. The last octet is used to identify the individual device on the Class C network. For example, Workstation A is 192.168.000.00**1**, and Workstation B is 192.168.000.00**2**. When a packet is broadcast to all devices in the 192.168.000 network, 255 is used in the last octet: 192.168.000.**255**.

> **NOTE**
> While performing the lab activity, the assigned network browser may attempt to update the browser listings. This can cause the sequence of displayed generated frames to be deceiving when viewed. Look at the source IP address to check if the first set of Ethernet frames captured is from Workstation B and not from Workstation A updating the browser lists. If the first frame captured is not ARP captured from Workstation B, you should run the experiment again.

The results for this lab activity will vary greatly during a live capture if you are using an older version of Windows. Windows Vista and later use both the IPv4 and IPv6 protocol suites. As a result, there will be quite a difference in contents when a capture from an older version of Windows is compared with one from Windows Vista or later.

The Wireshark Sample 3 file and Wireshark Sample 4 file are taken from a Windows XP capture containing only IPv4 packets. They will be used to provide a much simpler capture for example purposes.

Wireshark Sample 5 file was created using two Windows 7 computers connected directly together using a crossover cable to form a small peer-to-peer network. One computer ran the Wireshark protocol analyzer while the other computer was booted. Look at the three protocols (ARP, LLMNR, NBNS) that first appear during the boot process of Windows 7.

ARP is used to match the IPv4 address to the MAC address. LLMNR is a Microsoft protocol used for name resolution for IPv6. NBNS is another Microsoft protocol and is used for name resolution for legacy operating systems using IPv4.

A live Wireshark capture from a real peer-to-peer network will produce many more protocols because there will be much more protocol activity. You will most likely see protocol activity such as DHCP, SMB, Browser, HTTP, and LANMAN. Do not be overwhelmed by the number of frames and all the mysterious protocol acronyms. You will cover many protocols throughout this course. For now, we will concentrate on the three protocols directly associated with network device identification: ARP, NBNS, and LLMNR.

Duplicate IP Addresses

You cannot have duplicate IP addresses on a network even if you create the IP address manually.

When Windows 10 detects a duplicate IPv4 address, it automatically configures the network adapter using a special IPv4 address that starts with 169.254. The 169.254.xxx.xxx address is known as an Automatic Private IP Address (APIPA) and will range from 169.254.1.0–169.254.254.255. Newer versions of Windows use IPv6 for local link communications and do not require a valid IPv4 address. IPv6 uses Neighbor Discovery protocol to detect duplicate IP on a network.

Multicast Addresses

Multicast addresses are used for topology discovery, gateway discovery, and group membership. A computer or network device uses the multicast address to notify other devices on the local link when they join a network. You will see the IPv4 multicast address of 224.0.0.252 and the IPv6 multicast prefix address of ff02::1:3. These are standard multicast addresses. When these addresses are used, the broadcast is confined to the local link and will not pass through a network router.

Equipment and Materials

- Two Windows 10 workstations connected as a peer-to-peer network. One workstation should have Wireshark installed. Workstations must be configured with a static IP address.
- Wireshark Sample 3 file
  Wireshark Sample 3 file location:

Name _____

- Wireshark Sample 4 file
  Wireshark Sample 4 file location:

_____

- Wireshark Sample 5 file
  Wireshark Sample 5 file location:

_____

Procedure

1. _____ Gather the required materials and report to your assigned workstation(s).

2. _____ Boot the computers and verify they are in working order and that Wireshark is installed on one of the workstations.

3. _____ Start the Wireshark protocol analyzer and then open the **Wireshark Sample 3** file. This is a sample of a Windows computer starting up. Windows is using only IPv4 addresses. You will see ARP and NBNS.

4. _____ Look at the Ethernet II broadcast destination address and the ARP addresses. Use the screen capture below to assist you in finding the locations.

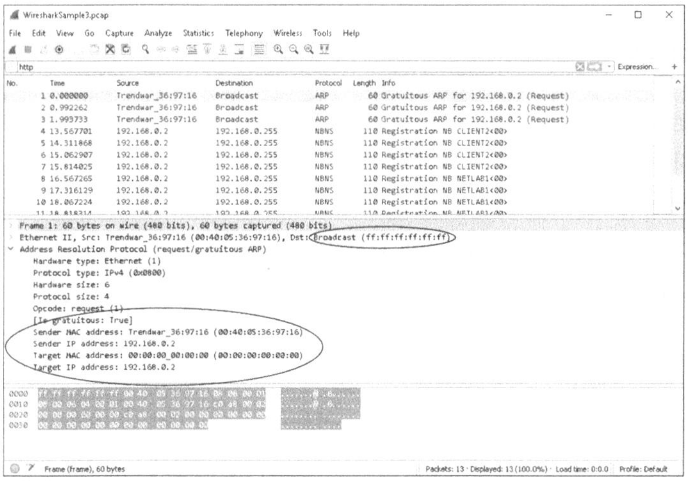

Goodheart-Willcox Publisher

What is the Ethernet II broadcast address?

_____

What is the ARP target MAC address?

_____

What is the total number of ARP requests?

_____

What protocol is used to encapsulate ARP?

_____

5. _____ Look at the third frame with the NBNS protocol. What is the destination address of NBNS frame 4?

6. _____ Select an NBNS frame with the mouse so that you can see the contents of the packet displayed in the middle section of the Wireshark screen and answer the following:

Is NBNS carried inside a TCP or UDP packet?

_____

Is NBNS considered connection-oriented or connectionless?

_____

Which protocol or protocols are used to encapsulate the NBNS protocol?

_____

7. _____ Close the Wireshark Sample 3 file.
8. _____ Open the Wireshark Sample 4 file. This file contains an example of a workstation shutting down. As you can see in the example, the browser protocol and the NBNS protocol is used to announce the shutdown of the workstation.

What is the destination IPv4 address used by both Browser and NBNS?

_____

Which protocols are used in frame 2?

_____

9. _____ Close the Wireshark Sample 4 file.
10. _____ Open the Wireshark Sample 5 file.
11. _____ Expand frame four so you can see the contents of the Link-Local Multicast Name Resolution (LLMNR) protocol and the name of the computer workstation. Notice the name of the workstation Windows7Ultimate is located in all three panes, as shown in the following screen capture.

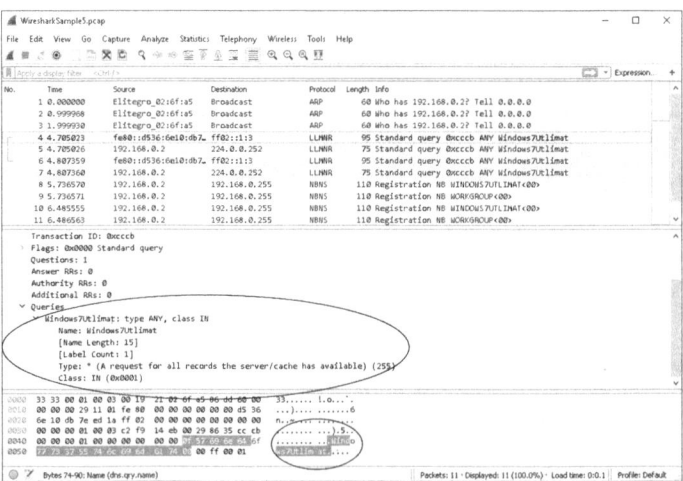

Goodheart-Willcox Publisher

The bottom pane shows the raw data that is transferred using the LLMNR protocol. The middle pane shows the converted raw data, which provides viewable information about the LLMNR packet contents.

12. _____ Select frame eight to view the contents of an NBNS packet.

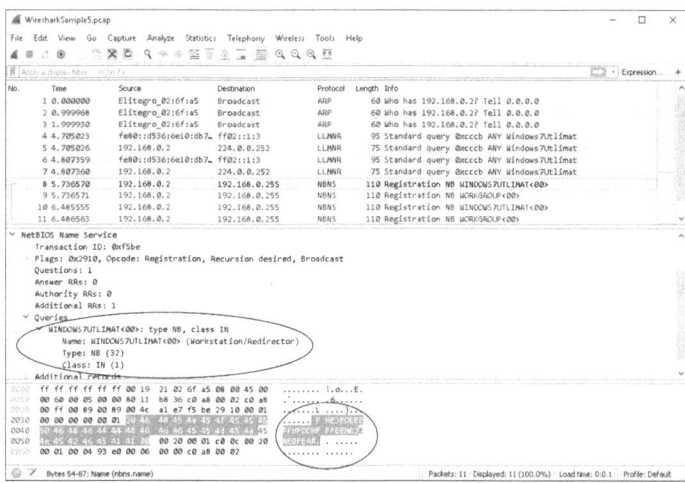

The NBNS packet identifies the name of the workstation **Windows7Ultimate**. The bottom pane with raw data is encrypted. The workstation name does not appear in plain text as it did in the LLMNR raw data content.

As you can see, when both IPv4 and IPv6 are configured for a network adapter, three different protocols are used to identify the workstation: ARP, LLMNR, and NBNS. Only NBNS encrypts the contents of the packet.

Look closely at the destination IPv6 address for the LLMNR protocol. It will always be **ff02::1:3**.

Look at the destination IPv4 address for the LLMNR protocol. It will always be **224.0.0.252**.

Now you will proceed to make your own capture and view the contents.

13. _____ Use the **ipconfig/all** command at each workstation and record the MAC address matching each workstation IP address.

Workstation A

MAC: _____

IP address: 192.168.000.1

Workstation B

MAC: _____

IP address: 192.168.000.2

14. _____ Shut down **Workstation B**.

15. _____ Start the Wireshark protocol analyzer on **Workstation A**. Be sure to select the proper interface card.

16. _____ Boot **Workstation B**. The Wireshark protocol analyzer will capture frames generated during the boot process of **Workstation B**.

17. _____ Wait approximately 1 minute and then stop the Wireshark protocol analyzer. The captured set of Ethernet frames will automatically display in the Wireshark GUI. The first frame captured must display the ARP protocol. If not, repeat the capture process.

18. _____ Answer review question 1 based on this capture.
19. _____ Unplug Workstation B from the network and then reboot the workstation.
20. _____ Attempt to change Workstation B IP address to match Workstation A creating a duplicate IP address.
21. _____ Answer the remaining review questions and then restore the computers to their original configurations. You may save the Wireshark capture for later study and review.

Review Questions

1. What are the first two tasks carried out by a peer-to-peer workstation as it completes the boot process?
   _____
   _____

2. What would be the broadcast IP address for the last octet of a Class C network address identified as 192.168.000?
   _____

3. What is the destination Ethernet MAC address of a broadcast to all devices on a local network?
   _____

4. What does the acronym NBNS represent?
   _____

5. What is the purpose of NBNS?
   _____
   _____
   _____

6. What does the NetBIOS name suffix <20> indicate?
   _____
   _____

7. What is the purpose of LLMNR?
   _____
   _____

8. What does the acronym LLMNR represent?
   _____

9. What is the multicast destination address for IPv4?
   _____

10. What is the multicast destination address IPv6?
    _____

11. What is the purpose of multicast?
    _____
    _____

Name _____ Date _____ Class _____

Observing Background Communication with Wireshark

Outcomes
After completing this laboratory activity, you will be able to:
- Identify common protocols used to support network background communication.
- Summarize what generates network background activity.

Introduction
In this laboratory activity, you will become familiar with the various activities that take place in the background of a peer-to-peer network. These background activities occur without user intervention. The general purpose of the background communication is to keep the browser information up to date by identifying users and equipment connected to the network. Other causes of background activity are:
- equipment such as routers sending out information about routes, which are constantly updated;
- mail client software automatically checking for e-mail;
- the operating system continually looking for existing and newly configured plug-and-play devices connected to the local area network;
- the workstation periodically checking for software and hardware updates; and
- servers periodically updating information about users and devices and storing the information in their database.

> **NOTE**
> The amount of activity generated by checking for updates will vary according to the hardware devices and the software programs in the computer system.

This normal background activity can be confusing when studying protocol activity. Most of the background activity can be eliminated by filtering the capture.

You will see references to computers in the Wireshark Sample 6 capture for this lab that are not turned on. For example, if a computer shares a printer with other computers, the name of the computer will show up in broadcast even when it is not connected to the network (turned off). This is because the computers connected to the network constantly check the status of other computers and devices on the network. If the computer is configured to access another computer's printer, you will see frames soliciting information about the status of the other computer and printer.

The Wireshark Sample 6 file used with this lab activity was created from a network containing a workstation with Internet access, several other workstations, and a printer. This sample capture will be very different from the sample capture you take during this lab activity.

Equipment and Materials
- Two computers running Windows 10 and configured as a peer-to-peer network with no Internet access
- Wireshark Sample 6 file
  Wireshark Sample 6 file location:
  _____

> **NOTE**
> Be sure the firewall is not enabled on either workstation.

Procedure

1. _____ Report to your assigned workstation(s).
2. _____ Boot both computers. Wait two to three minutes for network activity to settle down, and then open the Wireshark network analyzer.
3. _____ Open **Capture>Options>Options** and check that **Update list of packets in real-time** and **Automatically scroll during live capture** options are enabled. See the following screen capture.

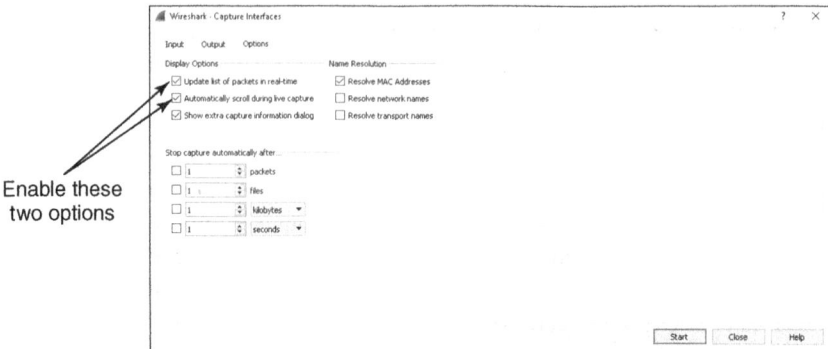

Goodheart-Willcox Publisher

The **Update list of packets in real-time** option allows you to see the packets being captured as they are used. The **Automatically scroll during live capture** option causes the display window to scroll down as it fills with frames. This way, you will always see the very last frame captured as it occurs.

4. _____ Click **Start** to start the capture.
5. _____ Observe the packets being captured and wait approximately 20 minutes before stopping the capture.
6. _____ After you have stopped the capture, open the **Wireshark Protocol Hierarchy Statistics** dialog box by selecting **Statistics>Protocol Hierarchy**. A window similar to the following will appear.

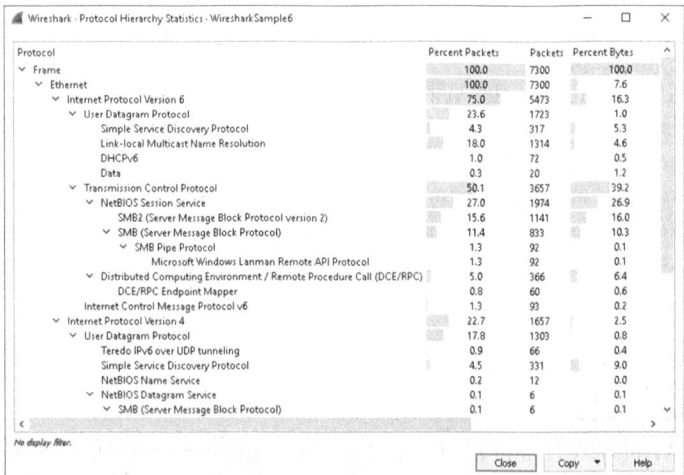

Goodheart-Willcox Publisher

Notice that the protocols are listed in their encapsulation order in the **Protocol** column. The percent of packets per protocol is indicated as a percentage and as a blue bar in the **Percentage** column.

Name _____

Use the information in the **Wireshark Protocol Hierarchy Statistics** dialog box to answer the following questions:

How many frames were captured?

_____

What were the most common three protocols identified in the protocol column?

_____

What was the purpose of most of the background activity?

_____

7. _____ Save your capture on a flash drive, naming the file FirstnameLastname_P2P_idle20min. Use your name in place of *FirstnameLastname*.

8. _____ Open the Wireshark Sample 6 file provided by your instructor. This capture should be somewhat similar to the one you just made. Use the Wireshark Sample 6 capture to answer the review questions.

9. _____ Return all materials to their proper storage area.

Review Questions

1. How many frames were captured?

_____

2. What was the purpose of most of the background activity?

_____
_____

3. What were the most common three protocols identified in the **Protocol** column?

_____

4. What is the general purpose of network background communication while a system is idle?

_____
_____
_____

5. What are some other causes of background activity?

_____
_____
_____

Notes

Name _____ Date _____ Class _____

Observing Ping with Wireshark

Outcomes

After completing this laboratory activity, you will be able to:
- Use Wireshark to identify the protocols used to transport ping packets.
- Use Wireshark to read the data contents of a ping packet.

Introduction

In this laboratory activity, you will use Wireshark to capture ping packets sent between a source computer and a destination computer. You can use two workstations connected through a hub, switch, or crossover cable. If the two workstations are connected to a network that contains other workstations running at the same time you are performing the capture, you will need to filter the capture using the workstation's IPv4 address. Filtering by using the workstation's IPv4 address will eliminate the other packet activity and make the capture contents easier to read.

The **ping** command uses the ICMP or ICMPv6 protocol to carry the echo request. The version of the ICMP protocol depends on which operating system you are using and the format of the **ping** command issued. The following summarizes what occurs when using various formats of the **ping** command on a Windows Vista or later computer:

- **Ping** with the destination computer's IPv4 address forces ICMP to be used.
- **Ping** with the destination computer name uses ICMPv6 by default.
- **Ping -4** forces ICMP to be used.
- **Ping** with the IPv6 destination address forces ICMPv6 to be used.

When the **ping** command is issued on a Windows XP or earlier computer, ICMP is used by default. This is because Windows XP and earlier operating systems use only IPv4 for local area network communication. Windows Vista and later (including Windows 11) use IPv4 or IPv6.

> **NOTE**
> ICMP is understood to represent ICMPv4 and does not usually appear with the "v4" designation.

Equipment and Materials

- Two Windows Vista or later computers connected as a peer-to-peer network using a hub, switch, or crossover cable

> **NOTE**
> If more than two workstations are connected together as a local area network, you will need to filter the Wireshark capture limiting the captures to only the two workstations identified as source and destination.

Procedure

1. _____ Report to your assigned workstation(s).
2. _____ Boot both computers and verify they are in working order.
3. _____ Designate one of the computers as the source and the other as the destination.
4. _____ Run **ipconfig** and record the IP address of the source and destination computers.

   Source IPv4 address:

   _____

Source name:

_____

Destination of IPv4 address:

_____

Destination name:

_____

5. _____ On the source computer, open Wireshark and start a capture.

6. _____ Open the command prompt on the source computer and issue the **ping** command using the destination computer's IPv4 address. Note the protocol (ICMP or ICMPv6) used to carry the ping echo request.

7. _____ Start another capture and then ping the destination workstation by name. Note the protocol (ICMP or ICMPv6) used to carry the echo request.

8. _____ Start another capture and then ping the destination computer using the destination computer's name and the **-4** switch. Note the protocol (ICMP or ICMPv6) used to carry the ping echo request.

9. _____ Repeat the observations until you are sure of the results of using the **ping** command and the destination computer's IPv4 address, the **ping** command and the destination computer's name, and the **ping -4** command and the destination computer's name.

10. _____ Answer the review questions and then return all materials to their proper storage areas.

Review Questions

1. Which protocol is used to carry a ping request using the **-4** switch?

   _____

2. What protocol is used to carry the ping request when identifying the destination by workstation name?

   _____

3. What is the total number of bytes contained in the Ethernet frame that utilizes the ICMP protocol?

   _____

4. What is the total number of bytes contained in the Ethernet frame that utilizes the ICMPv6 protocol?

   _____

5. What is the total number of bytes contained in the data field of ICMP?

   _____

6. What is the total number of bytes contained in the data field of ICMPv6?

   _____

7. Describe the contents of the ICMP data field that is readable.

   _____

8. Describe the contents of the ICMPv6 data field that is readable.

   _____

9. What other identification of the source and destination besides the IP address is present in the Ethernet frame of the ping echo request and reply for both the ICMP and ICMPv6? (Hint: Look in the Ethernet frame.)

   _____

Name _____ Date _____ Class _____

LABORATORY ACTIVITY 20
Installing Windows Server 2022

Outcomes

After completing this laboratory activity, you will be able to:
- Summarize the overall installation process for Windows Server 2022 Standard.
- Differentiate between a system upgrade and a custom (clean) installation.
- Identify the minimum hardware requirements for Windows Server 2022 Standard.
- Recall the guidelines used to create a secure server password.
- Carry out proper procedures to install Windows Server 2022.

Introduction

In this laboratory activity, you will perform a custom installation of Windows Server 2022 Standard edition. This lab activity can be used as a guide for installing other Microsoft Server editions because they have very similar installation procedures. One can download a trial version of Server 2022 or access it via Azure cloud at www.microsoft.com/en-us/evalcenter/evaluate-windows-server-2022.

If you have experience installing Windows operating systems, you will find the procedure for installing Windows Server 2022 Standard very similar. If the hardware you are using is compatible, then the installation will be very easy. Basically, all you do is follow a series of screen presentations that ask some very basic questions. The following table lists the hardware requirements for Windows Server 2022 Standard.

Hardware Component	Specifications
Processor	Minimum 1.4 GHz 64-bit processor or faster; recommended is 3.1 GHz 64-bit processor multi-core
Memory	Minimum 2GB; recommended 16 GB
Disk Space	Minimum 160GB
Display	VGA
Installation Drive	DVD drive

In earlier versions of Windows Server, the minimum requirements will differ for 32-bit and 64-bit systems. The major difference was the speed of the CPU, the amount of RAM, and the required disk space. However, Windows Server 2022 only comes in a 64-bit version. Most newly purchased computers will exceed the minimum requirements, but older systems that will be upgraded should be checked carefully to ensure they meet the minimal specifications.

Windows Server 2022 does not require activation and does not require a product key for evaluation purposes. Your instructor may request that you do not activate the copy of Windows Server 2022. You can operate Windows Server 2022 for 180 days without activation. This may be sufficient time for your course of study. It is important to note that time limits for trial versions may vary.

There are two types of server installation modes: upgrade and custom. The custom installation is also referred to as a *clean install*. When you perform a server upgrade, you replace the operating system but retain all user files such as documents and pictures. When you perform a custom installation, all user files are lost because the installation process automatically formats the partition using the default file format, NTFS.

During the installation process, one default user account, the Administrator account, is established automatically. You will be prompted to create a password for the Administrator account. The password should consist of at least seven characters and be a combination of letters (both uppercase and lowercase); special characters such as $, %, !, and #; and numbers. For example, a password such as baseball is at least seven characters, but it is not acceptable because it is a common word easily found in the dictionary. A better password based on the word baseball would be Ba$eBa11. The dollar sign is used to represent the letter *S* and the number *1* is used to represent the letter *L*. Also notice that the letter *B* is in capitalized. All these factors help create a more secure password than just a plain word. Your instructor will recommend a password for this lab activity.

At the end of the lab activity, you will see a screen used to configure the server. You will not actually configure the server in this lab activity. You will configure the server in a later lab activity.

Earlier Microsoft server systems required that you pick the server role and other specifics during the installation process. This is now done after the server operating system has been installed. During a later lab activity, you will select the server role such as a domain controller, stand-alone server, DHCP server, print server, and DNS server.

> **NOTE**
> Screen captures for this lab activity were created using a virtual copy of Windows Server 2022. Most screen captures will be a close, but not exact, match to your screen images.

Equipment and Materials

- Computer that meets the minimum hardware requirements for Windows Server 2022 Standard
- Windows Server 2022 installation DVD. (You can download the ISO file from www.microsoft.com/en-us/evalcenter/evaluate-windows-server-2022. Then you can put that on a DVD. A second option is to install Windows Server 2022 in a virtual machine. You can use any virtual machine you wish, but Oracle Virtual Box is a free download from www.virtualbox.org/wiki/Downloads.)
- The following information provided by your instructor:

Administrator password:

_____

Instructor requires product activation and product key?

_____

Create a custom sized partition for the installation?

_____

If yes, what size? _____ (160 GB Minimum)

_____

> **NOTE**
> Problems can arise in a networking lab environment that is not normally encountered in the field. Often, the hard disk drive used for the computer may have been used by a previous class and may need to be formatted or even low-level formatted to remove any existing partitions. This is especially true if the hard disk drive had a Linux partition. Linux partitions are not always detected by Microsoft operating systems. You can perform a complete clean install, and then the server fails to successfully boot. If the system meets the hardware requirements and the workstation was used by a previous class, you may need to perform a low-level format. You can also go to the hard disk drive manufacturer's website and download a diagnostic utility to inspect the hard disk drive for undetected partitions. The hard disk drive manufacturer will have all information needed to run the diagnostic software.

Procedure

> **NOTE**
> The screenshots below were taken while installing Windows Server 2022 into Oracle VirtualBox as a virtual machine.

1. _____ Report to your assigned workstation.
2. _____ Boot the server and verify it is in working order.

Name _____

3. _____ Insert the Windows Server 2022 installation DVD into the DVD drive. You must reboot the server after the installation DVD has been inserted into the drive. If the system fails to start the installation from the DVD and instead loads the contents of the hard disk drive, you will need to change the boot order in the BIOS setup.

After the workstation reboots, you will likely see a black screen with a load bar. This means that the installation media is running and files are being copied to RAM to begin the installation process.

Next, a screen will appear similar to the one in the screen capture below. You are prompted to select the appropriate language, time and currency format, and keyboard or input method.

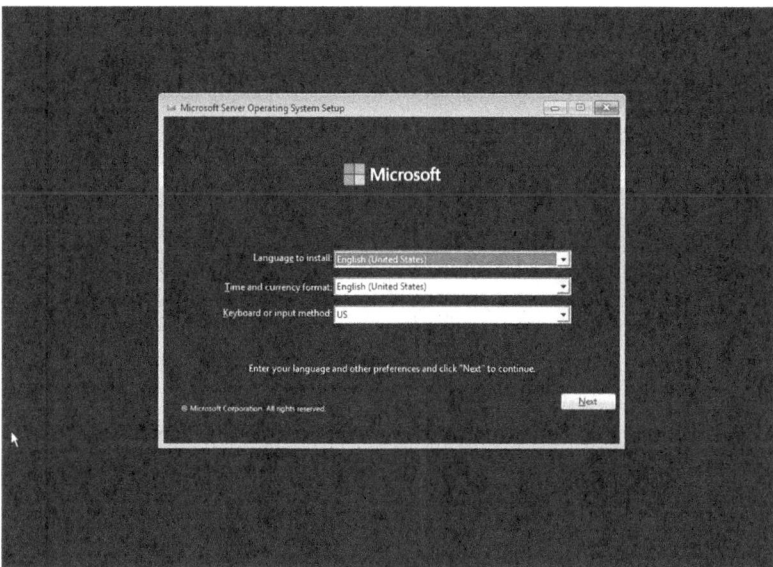

Goodheart-Willcox Publisher

4. _____ Accept the defaults and click **Next**. The next screen to appear will present you with several options: **Install now** button and **Repair your computer**.

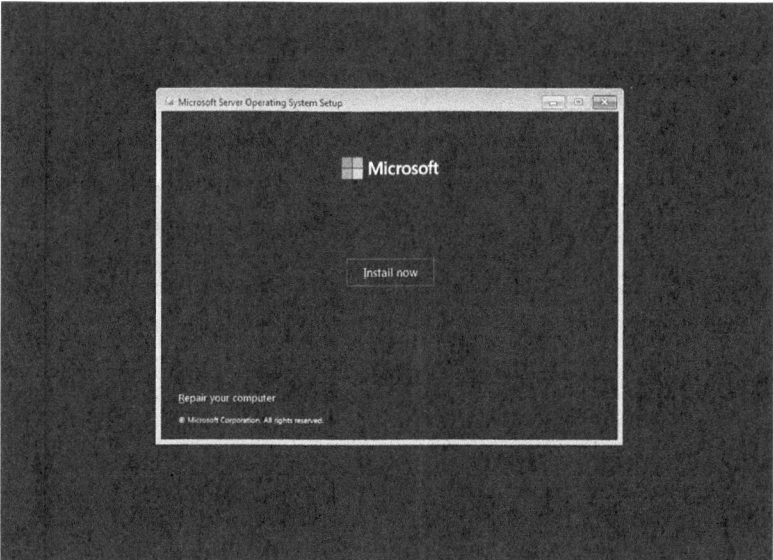

Goodheart-Willcox Publisher

5. _____ Select the **Install now** option. The next screen to appear is the product key and activation screen. Unless your instructor specifically told you to activate and enter a product key, do *not* enter the product key and be sure the **Automatically activate Windows when I'm online** option is *unchecked*. You will have 180 days if you are using the evaluation copy.

6. _____ Click **Next**. A message warning you about not entering a product key will appear on the screen. Ignore the message and click **No**. Now you will be prompted to select the server edition.

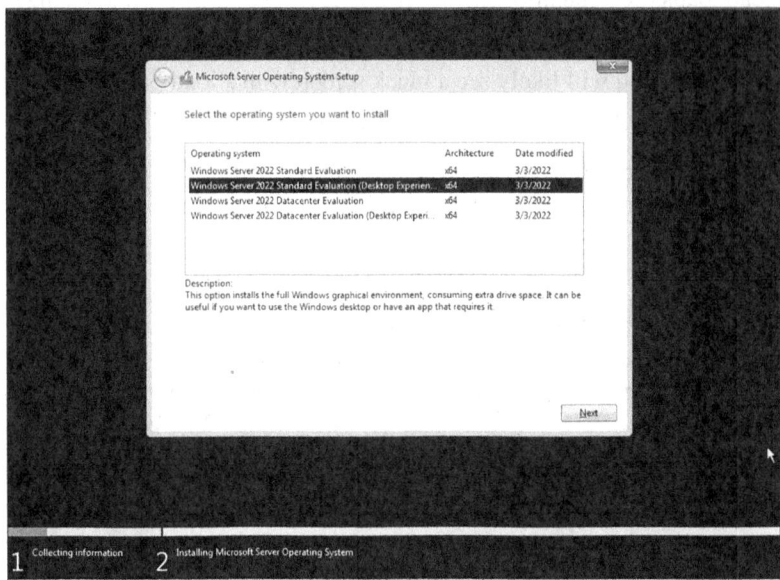

Goodheart-Willcox Publisher

7. _____ For this lab activity, select the **Windows Server 2022 Standard Evaluation (Desktop Experience)**, similar to what is shown in the previous screen capture, and then click **Next**. The license terms will appear on the screen.

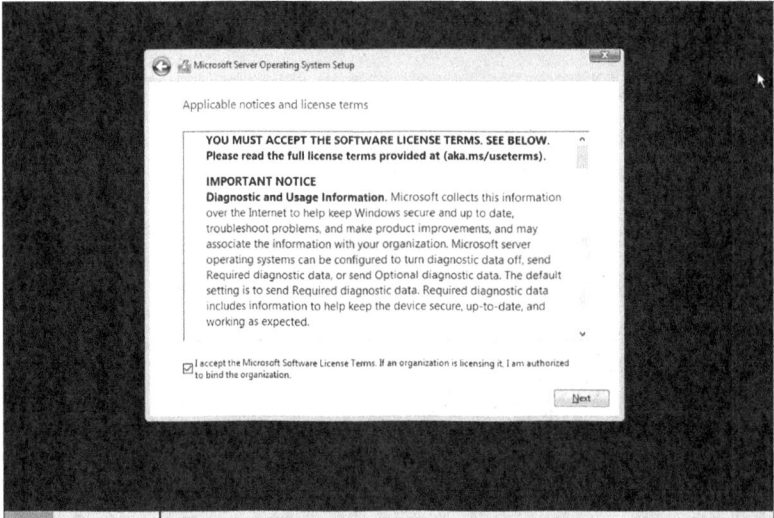

Goodheart-Willcox Publisher

Name _____

8. _____ Accept the terms to continue with the installation by selecting **I accept the license terms** and clicking **Next**. You will be presented with two choices of installation: **Upgrade: Install Windows and keep files, settings, and applications** or **Custom: Install Windows only (advanced)**.

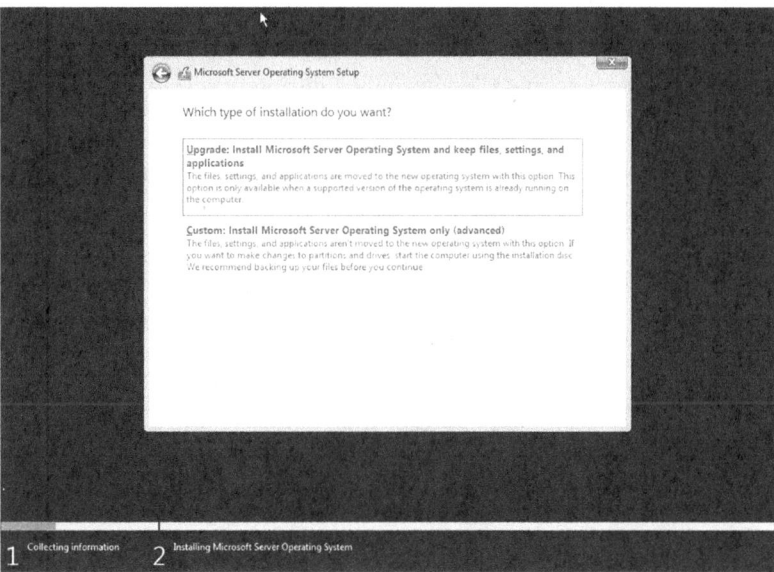

Goodheart-Willcox Publisher

The **Upgrade** option will not be available if a previous version of Windows Server was not installed on the computer. Your only option should be **Custom (advanced)**, which is also referred to as a *clean install*. When performing a custom installation, you will be presented with options to create a partition automatically or to select existing partitions. The **Custom (advanced)** option will overwrite any existing files stored in the partition on which it is installed. The **Upgrade** option will preserve any existing files that may already exist on the partition.

9. _____ Select the **Custom (advanced)** option. The installation program will perform several routine steps and identify the progress on the screen. This may take 20 minutes or more. Look at the following screen capture.

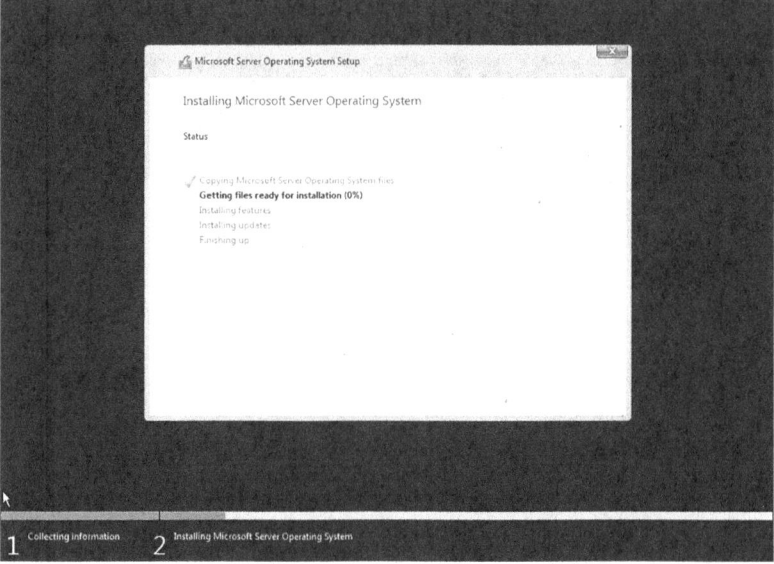

Goodheart-Willcox Publisher

The installation software will expand files and install features and updates. These steps are typically automatic with little or no user intervention. The workstation will reboot several times during this portion of the installation. The next screen image to appear is a message telling you that the password must be changed. This is a little strange since you have not tried to enter a password yet.

10. _____ Simply click **OK**. You will be prompted for the new password for the Administrator account. The Administrator is the only account installed by default during the clean installation. For this exercise, use the password as provided by your instructor.

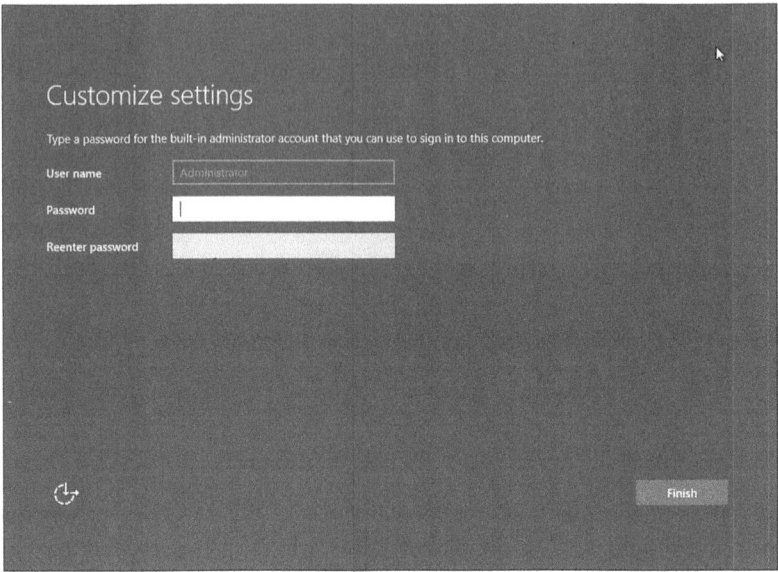

Goodheart-Willcox Publisher

Passwords should be composed of at least seven characters. The characters should contains letters, symbol(s), and number(s), for example, Pa$$word123. Review the beginning of the lab activity for the Administrator password suggested by your instructor. You will need to type the password and then retype it to confirm it. Then, you will see a notice telling you that the new password has been accepted.

The installation is now complete. You will be presented with a screen similar to this one each time the server is started.

Goodheart-Willcox Publisher

The server operating system is installed but not configured. You will configure the server in the next laboratory activity.

Name _____

11. _____ Call your instructor to inspect your project at this time. After your instructor inspects your project, you can shut down the server.

12. _____ Answer the review questions and then return all materials to their proper storage areas.

Review Questions

1. What is the minimum amount of RAM for a Windows Server 2022 Standard installation?

2. What is the recommended amount of RAM for a Windows Server 2022 Standard installation?

3. What are the two Windows Server 2022 installation options?

4. What is the difference between an upgrade and a custom installation?

5. What is another name used for *custom installation*?

6. What is the name of the default user account?

7. What are the general guidelines for creating a secure server password?

8. What file format is used by default for Windows Server 2022?

Notes

Name _____ Date _____ Class _____

LABORATORY ACTIVITY 21
Configuring Windows Server 2022 Roles

Outcomes

After completing this laboratory activity, you will be able to:
- Identify the most commonly selected roles and recall their purpose.
- Carry out proper procedures for adding the Active Directory Domain Services role.

Introduction

In this laboratory activity, you will first view the various server roles available for configuration. A Windows Server 2022 role is a specific function for the server to perform, such as DNS server, DHCP server, or file server. The following screen capture shows the initial screen for 2022.

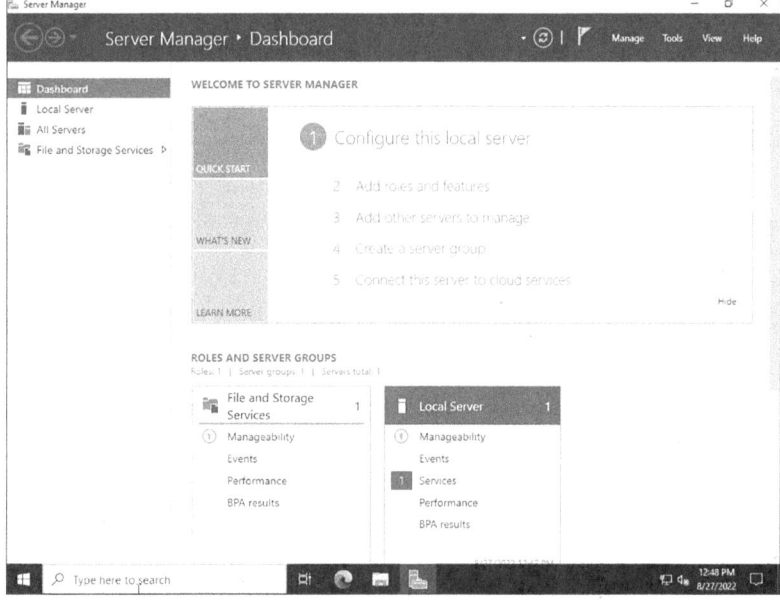

Goodheart-Willcox Publisher

From here, you can choose add roles and pick the roles you wish to add by clicking on **Add Roles**. This is shown in the following screen capture.

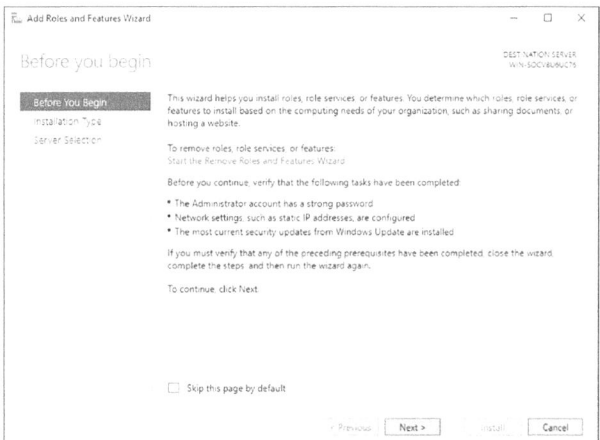

Goodheart-Willcox Publisher

Copyright Goodheart-Willcox Co., Inc.
May not be reproduced or posted to a publicly accessible website.

You will then be asked to choose either **Role-Based or feature based installation** or **Remote Desktop Service Installation**. Choose the former, as shown in the following screen capture.

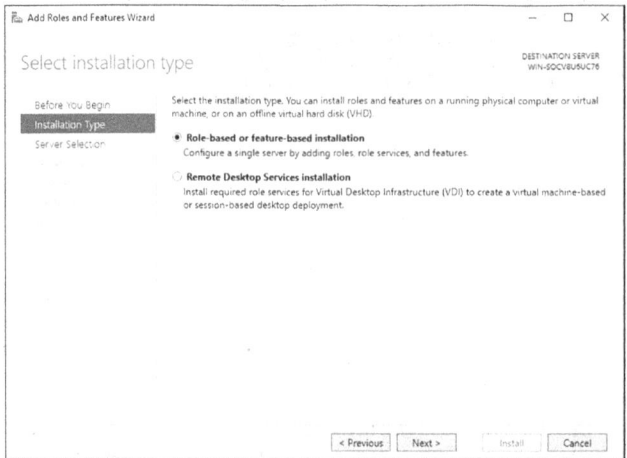

Goodheart-Willcox Publisher

Next select the specific server you wish to install on. This is designed for server pools, but in the lab situation, you will only have the single server.

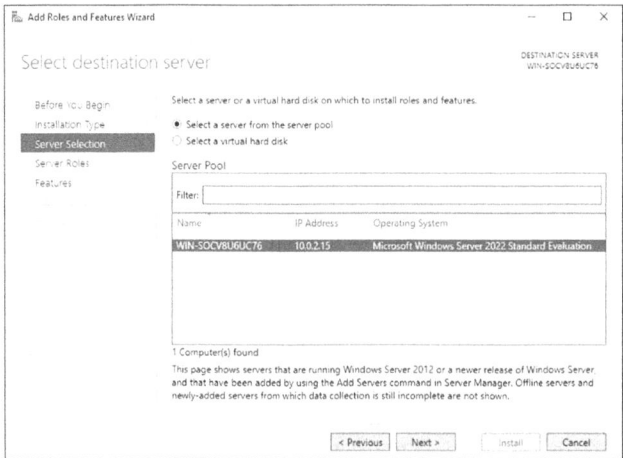

Goodheart-Willcox Publisher

After viewing the roles, you will select only Active Directory Domain Services (AD DS). You cannot add other roles such as DNS Server or File Services until after Active Directory Domain Services has been configured.

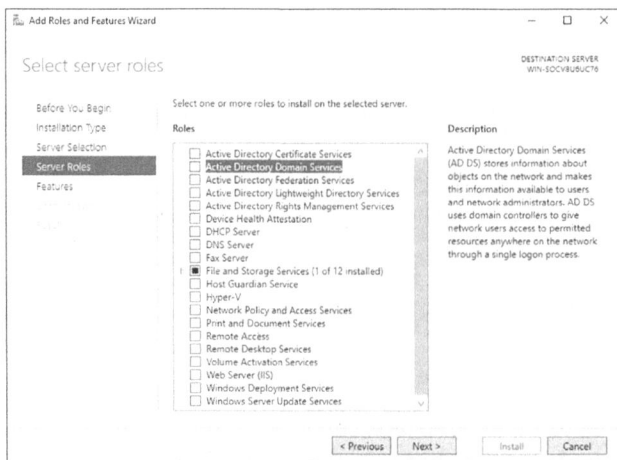

Goodheart-Willcox Publisher

104 Networking Fundamentals Lab Manual

Name _____

You can then add any features, but for our purposes leave default settings as shown in the following screen capture.

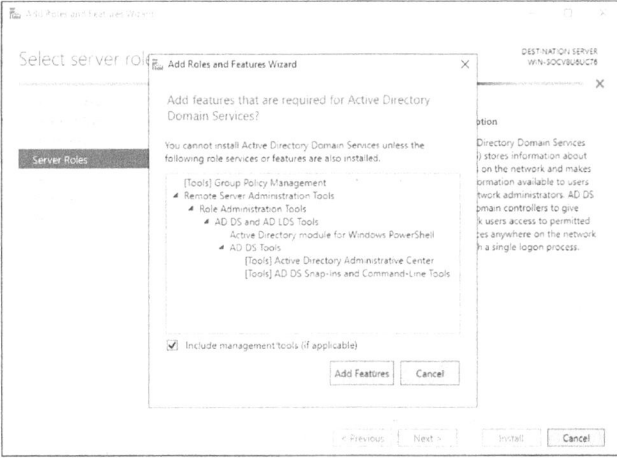

Goodheart-Willcox Publisher

It may take a few moments, during which you will see the following image.

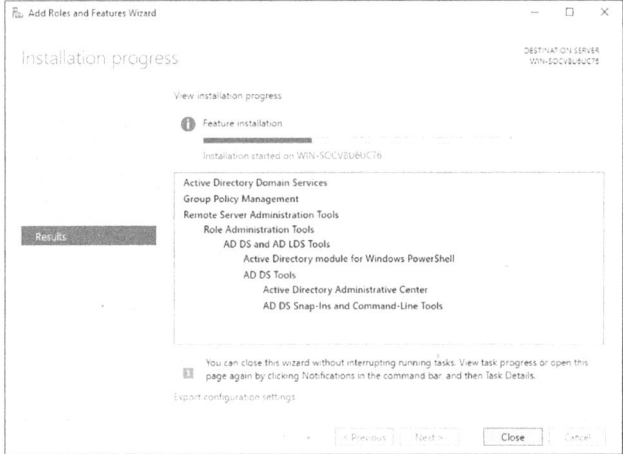

Goodheart-Willcox Publisher

In this lab, you will also assign a DNS namespace for the server. A DNS namespace is a unique name that can consist of the top-level domain name, domain name, subdomain name, and computer name each separated by a period. For example, Workstation1.corp.netclass.private consists of the computer name *Workstation1*, the domain name *corp*, the subdomain *netclass*, and the nonexistent top-level domain *private*. Some examples of real top-level domains are .com, .org, and .edu.

> **NOTE**
> Before performing this lab activity, be sure you have configured a static IPv4 address for the server.

Copyright Goodheart-Willcox Co., Inc.
May not be reproduced or posted to a publicly accessible website.

Laboratory Activity 21 Configuring Windows Server 2022 Roles 105

Equipment and Materials
- Computer with Windows Server 2022 installed
- The following information provided by your instructor:

Static IPv4 address (e.g., 192.168.001.200):

_____

Subnet mask (e.g., 255.255.255.000):

_____

FQDN (e.g., corp.netclass.private):

_____

Forest function level (e.g., Windows Server 2022):

_____

Procedure

1. _____ Report to your assigned workstation.

2. _____ Boot the server and verify it is in working order.

3. _____ Open Server Manager by selecting **Start>Server Manager**. You can also access Server Manager by opening the Start menu and typing **Server Manager** in the Search text field. The Server Manager program will appear in the list as soon as you begin typing Server Manager.

4. _____ After Server Manager opens, scroll down to **Roles and Server Groups**. There should be no role installed.

5. _____ On the Server Manager dashboard, select **Add roles and features**. Adding this role will proceed in the same manner as the role we added at the beginning of this lab. Accept the default options and click **Next**.

For this lab activity, your only real concern is that a static IP address should be configured before assigning the server roles because a static IP address is needed for DNS. Security updates and a strong password are not necessary for this lab.

6. _____ If you have already configured a static IP address, proceed to the next step. If not, abort the installation, configure a static IP address, and then proceed to the next step.

7. _____ In the **Select server roles** screen, select **Active Directory Domain Services** from the list of server roles and then click **Next**.

8. _____ The **Add Roles and Features Wizard** will appear. Click Add features to continue the installation.

9. _____ A screen will appear confirming the installation selection of roles. Notice that AD DS has been added to the list of installation steps on the left-hand side of the wizard.

10. _____ Click **Next** to continue.

11. _____ The next screen to appear is an introduction to Active Directory Domain Services and a list of "Things to Note." Read the information carefully before moving on in the lab activity. List the two "Things to Note" in the space provided.

_____

_____

12. _____ Click **Next**, then **Install** on the next screen.

The wizard will run for a few minutes to complete the installation and initialization of the chosen role. Be patient.

Name _____

13. _____ Once the server roles have finished installing, click the **Promote this server to a domain controller** link shown in the next screen.

14. _____ In the **Select the deployment operation** section of the window, choose the **Add a new forest option**. In the **Domain** text field, enter the Domain name provided by your instructor and click **Next**.

15. _____ The next screen to appear will be the **Domain Controller Options** screen. Set the Forest functional level and Domain functional level both to Windows Server 2022, and ensure that Domain Name System (DNS) server is selected. Enter and confirm the DSRM password and click **Next**.

16. _____ Accept the default options listed in the **DNS Options** screen, and click **Next**.

17. _____ The **Additional Domain Controller Options** screen will appear. Verify the domain name and make any necessary changes. Then, click **Next**.

18. _____ Confirm the locations for the Database, Log files, and SYSVOL folders, then click **Next**.

19. _____ Review and confirm your options. If everything appears to be correct, click the **Next** button.

20. _____ Verify that all prerequisite checks passed successfully, and click the **Install** button. After the installation, the server will restart.

21. _____ When the server is restarted, look at the **Start>Server Manager** dashboard and notice that there are administrative utilities related to Active Directory that were not present in the menu before configuring the Active Directory Domain Services role.

22. _____ You have now successfully completed configuring a domain controller role referred to as Active Directory Domain Services. Call your instructor to inspect your completed lab.

23. _____ Use the **Select Server Roles** screen in the **Add Roles and Features Wizard** to answer the review questions.

24. _____ Return all materials to their proper storage area.

Review Questions

1. What server role is configured by default when Windows Server 2022 is installed?
   _____

2. Which server role would you select to issue temporary IP addresses automatically to computers on the local network?
   _____

3. Which server role provides name resolution to IP addresses?
   _____

4. Which server role provides centralized printer management tasks such as sharing a printer on a network?
   _____

5. Which server role provides support for web application infrastructure?
   _____

Notes

Name _____ Date _____ Class _____

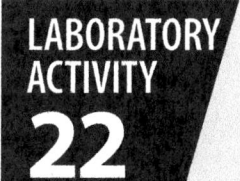

Creating a Shared Folder in Windows Server 2022

Laboratory Activity 22

Outcomes

After completing this laboratory activity, you will be able to:
- Use the File Sharing wizard to create a shared resource.
- Select the proper NTFS permissions for a share.
- Identify shared folders in Windows Explorer.
- Differentiate between share permissions and NTFS permission.

Introduction

This laboratory activity is the first of two labs that explore folder and file sharing in relation to a file server share. You will first create a folder and then configure it as a share on the local computer/server. In the next lab activity, you will add the File Server role to the server.

Creating a shared folder on a Windows 2022 server is very similar to creating a shared folder for any Windows operating system such as Windows 10. You simply create or select a folder, right-click the folder, and then select **Share with**, **Sharing**, or **Properties** from the shortcut menu to start the sharing process. After the folder is shared, you will be able to modify the share at any time.

Share and NTFS Permissions

There are two systems used to control access to files and folders: share permissions and NTFS permissions. NTFS permissions are also referred to as *security access controls*, *security access permissions*, or simply *access controls*. Share permissions are based on the FAT and FAT32 file system while NTFS permissions are based on the NTFS enhanced security of the NTFS file system. The mixture of the two systems can be very confusing because both are often referred to as *share permissions*. Technically speaking, share permissions are assigned to network shares. NTFS permissions are really security access controls used to control access to files and folders even when they are not network shares. As you work through this lab activity, many of the differences will become apparent. For example, when a device such as a CD or DVD drive is shared, only share permissions apply. When a file or folder is shared, both share permissions and NTFS permissions apply if the file system where the file or folder resides is formatted as NTFS.

Share Permissions

Share permissions are much simpler in design and have fewer options when compared to NTFS permissions. Share permissions are limited to Read, Change, and Full Control. The following table describes each share permission.

Share Permission	Description
Read	Allows user or group to view file names and subfolders, view data in files, and run programs.
Change	Allows user or group to add files and subfolders, change data in files, and delete subfolders and files.
Full Control	Allows user or group to read and change permissions and to assign permission to files and folders.

The following is a screen capture of the **Security tab** of the **Properties** dialog box for a shared folder on a Windows 2022 server. When you first share a folder, you assign **Read**, **Read/Write**, or **Remove** permissions. Notice that share permissions can be allowed or denied for a user or group.

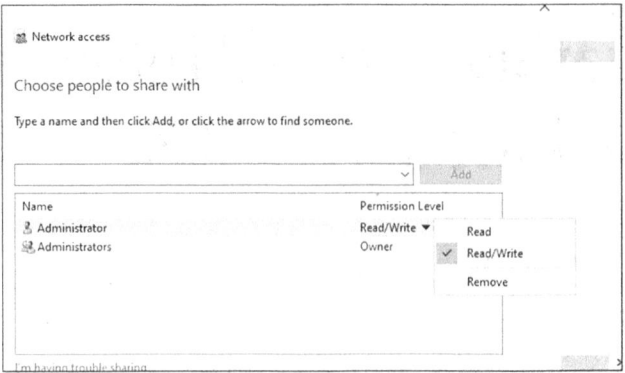

Goodheart-Willcox Publisher

Once you have shared a folder, you can use the **Properties** dialog box to assign **Full Control**, **Change**, or **Read** permissions, as shown in the following screenshot.

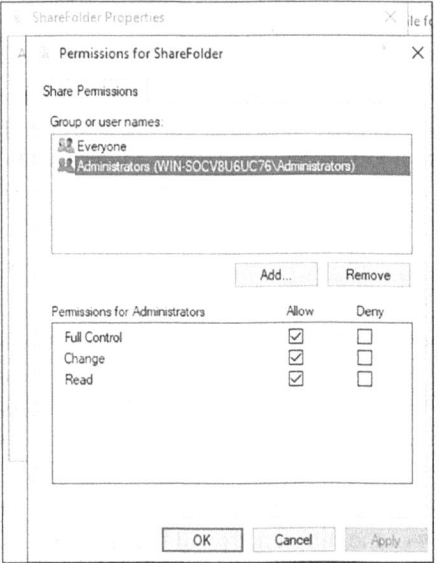

Goodheart-Willcox Publisher

NTFS Permissions

NTFS permissions are Full Control, Modify, Read & Execute, List Folder Contents, Read, Write, and Special Permissions. The following table describes each NTFS permission. Notice that there are more NTFS permissions than share permissions.

Share Permission	Description
Full Control	Allow user or group all NTFS permission except for Special Permissions to a file or folder.
Modify	Allows user or group to change file contents and delete folders. Provides the same privileges as the Read and Change share permissions.
Read and Execute	Allows user or group to read file contents and execute programs. The user or group cannot change a file's contents.
List Folder Contents	Allows user or group to view contents of a folder but does not allow the user or group to read individual files.
Read	Allows user or group to view file and folder contents.
Write	Allows user or group to change folder contents and crew new files and folders.
Special Permissions	Special Permission are additional enhanced security permission used with the NTFS file system.

Name _____

The following is a screen capture of the **Security** tab in the **Properties** dialog box for a shared folder on a Windows 2022 server. Notice that NTFS permissions can be allowed or denied for a user or group.

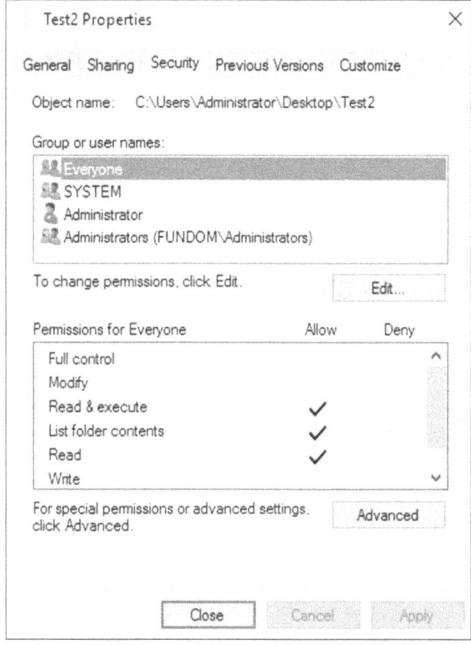

Goodheart-Willcox Publisher

Inheritance

When a folder has a set of permissions assigned, that same set of permissions is applied to all of its subfolders. The assignment of the original folder permissions to subfolders is referred to as *inheritance*. Inheritance is typically indicated in permission dialog boxes with shaded check boxes. An inherited permission can be overridden in most cases by deselecting the inherited permission (clicking the shaded check box).

Important Facts about Shares

- In Windows Server, the *Everyone* group is assigned the Read permission automatically.
- The Read permission is the most restrictive permission because users can only read the contents of the share. The only thing more restrictive is no access at all.
- The Administrator group is assigned Full Control by default.
- When sharing a device such as a DVD drive, only share permissions apply.
- Share permissions only apply when a folder is accessed across a network.
- Share permissions are lost if a folder is moved or renamed.
- NTFS permissions apply if a folder is accessed across a network or accessed locally (on the computer).
- NTFS permissions are retained when the folder is moved or renamed.
- A file or folder can have NTFS permissions without having share permissions.

You can access more information about shares and permissions using Help and Support located off the **Start** menu of Windows 10 or Windows Server.

Equipment and Materials

- Computer with Windows Server 2022 installed
- The following information provided by your instructor:

  Shared folder location (for example, C:/): _____

  Shared folder name (first initial, last name, and SharedFolder, for example, JSmithSharedFolder):

  _____

> **NOTE**
> The lab activity screen captures are based on Windows Server 2022. If you are using a different operating system, there will be some variation, but most of the instructions and screen captures will be very similar.

Procedure

> **NOTE**
> If a server is not available, you could use a Windows 7 or Windows 10 workstation.

1. _____ Report to your assigned workstation.
2. _____ Boot the server and verify it is in working order.
3. _____ Create a folder using the name and location indicated by your instructor.
4. _____ Right-click the folder and then select **Share with** from the shortcut menu. You should see a dialog box similar to following.

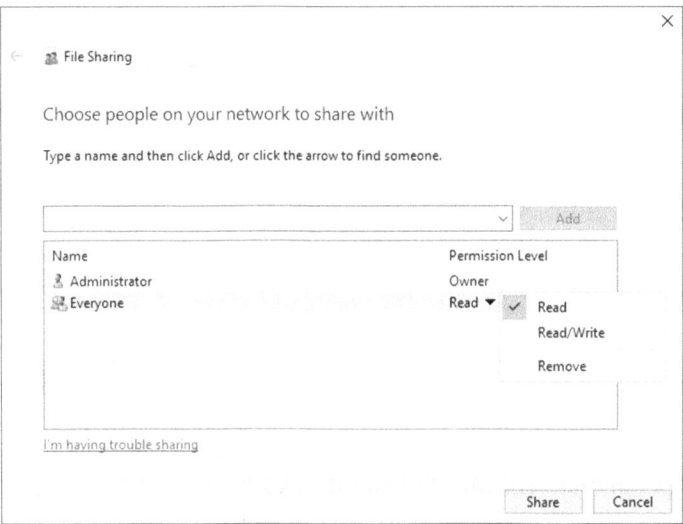

Goodheart-Willcox Publisher

By default, the folder is automatically shared with its creator. In the example below, the creator is the *Administrator*. You can select other users by using the down arrow beside the **Add** button to reveal a list of possible users or groups.

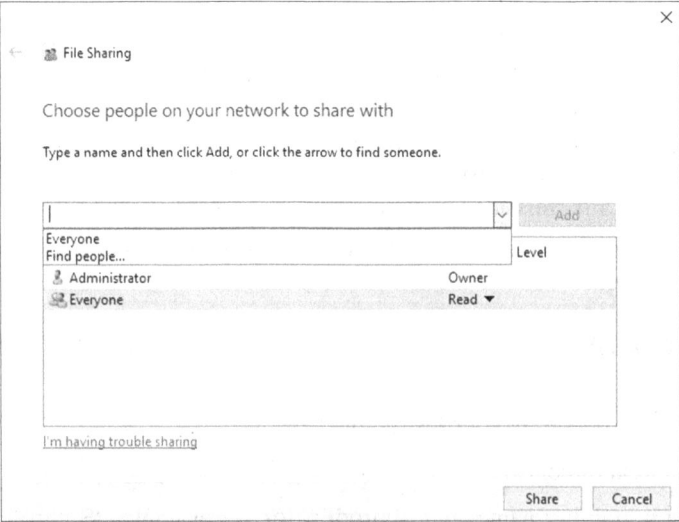

Goodheart-Willcox Publisher

In the screen capture, you see that **Everyone** is a choice. There is also an option to find or locate a possible user. If other accounts exist as local accounts on the server, their names will appear on the list.

Name _____

5. _____ Select **Everyone**. Notice that the default permission for **Everyone** is Read. This a general permission level.

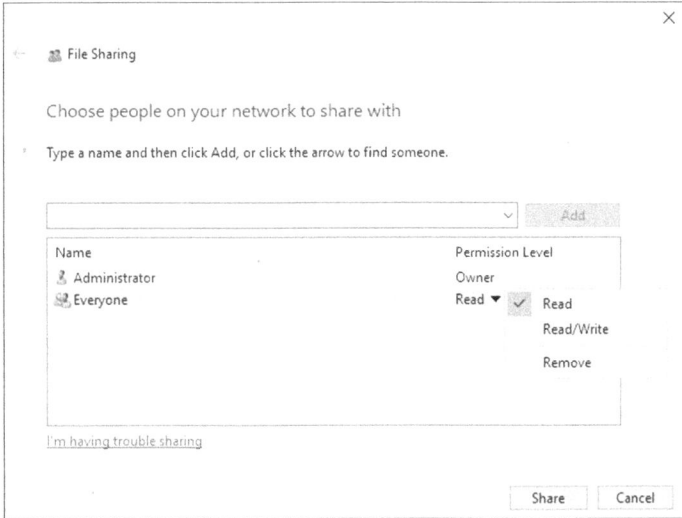

Goodheart-Willcox Publisher

6. _____ Select the down arrow next to Reader to reveal the other general permission levels associated with the folder.
- Reader has the same properties as the NTFS permission Read & Execute.
- Contributor has the same properties as NTFS permission Modify permission.
- Co-Owner has the same NTFS permission as the folder's creator, which is Full Control.

These general folder permissions are the most commonly used folder permissions. If a more restrictive or complex set of folder permissions is required, permissions can be changed later through the folder's **Properties** dialog box.

7. _____ Leave the Reader permission assigned to Everyone and click **Share**.

8. _____ The next dialog box to appear will confirm the creation of the folder share. It will appear similar to the one in the following screen capture. Notice that the shared folder has the UNC format for the share path \\WIN-S5BDSBV2M1U\Users\Administrator\Desktop\Test2.

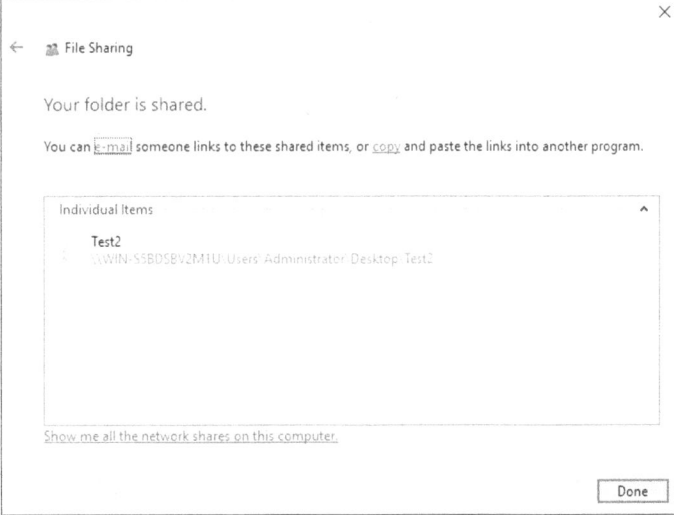

Goodheart-Willcox Publisher

Selecting the **Show me all the network shares on this computer** link will reveal all shares on the computer/server similar to the following screen capture.

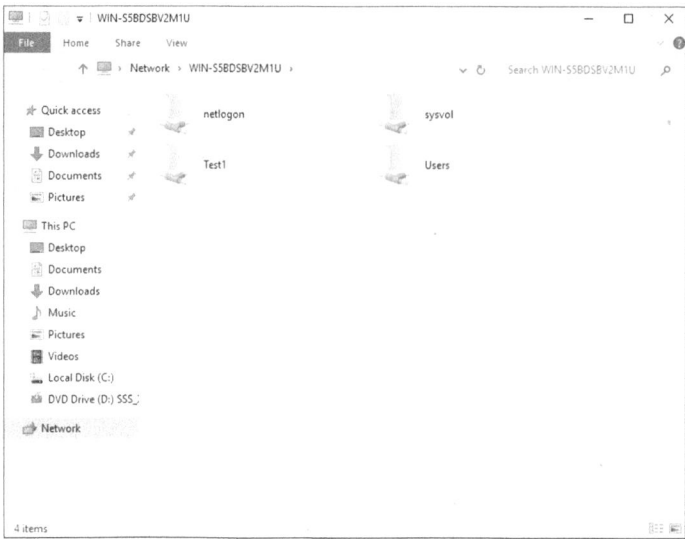

Goodheart-Willcox Publisher

Each share is displayed using the network share icon—a folder connected to a cable. Shares are identified in the navigation pane with an icon of two users side by side.

9. _____ Add files to the folder. The files will be automatically shared with all user accounts or groups you have selected.

10. _____ Locate the shared folder you just created.

11. _____ Right click the shared folder and select **Properties**. Then, select the **NTFS Sharing** tab. A dialog box similar to the following will appear.

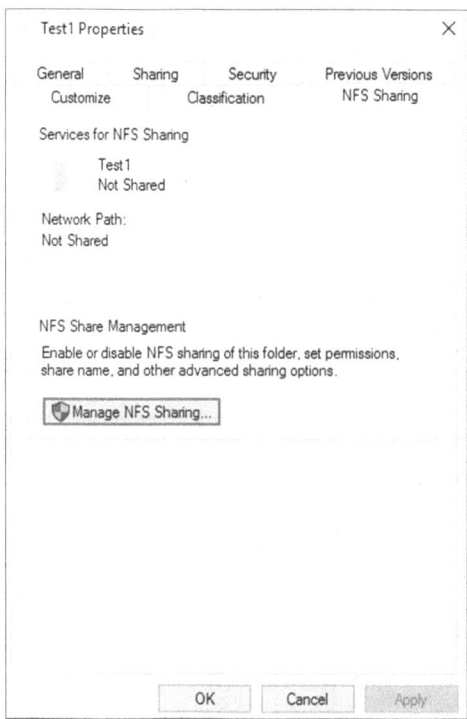

Goodheart-Willcox Publisher

Name _____

12. _____ Click the **Manage NFS Sharing** button to view share permissions and NTFS permissions. Take a minute to view the permissions settings available.

Goodheart-Willcox Publisher

13. _____ Close all open dialog boxes and then answer the review questions.
14. _____ Return all materials to their proper storage area. Leave the share you just created for the next lab activity.

Review Questions

1. What are the three permission levels associated with a locally created share?

   _____
   _____
   _____

2. What are the three available share permissions?

   _____
   _____
   _____

3. What share permissions are available for a DVD?

   _____
   _____
   _____

4. Under which folder **Properties** tab (**Share** or **Security**) are the NTFS permissions located?

   _____

5. What NTFS permission is similar to Reader?

   _____

6. Which general permission level will allow you to delete the folder share?

___

7. Which general permission level will allow a group to make changes to the share folder contents but not allow it to delete the share folder?

___

8. Which NTFS permission only allows a user or group to view the contents of a file or folder?

___

9. Which NTFS permission would you assign to a user to read, write, execute, and modify file and folder contents?

___

Name _____ Date _____ Class _____

Adding the File Server Role to Windows Server 2022

Outcomes

After completing this laboratory activity, you will be able to:
- Carry out proper procedures to add the File Server role to Windows Server 2022.
- Recall the various features provided when a server is configured as a file server.

Introduction

In this laboratory activity, you will add the File Server role to a Windows 2022 server. In Laboratory Activity 21, you configured the Active Directory Domain Controller and DNS Server roles. To add the File Server role, you will open Server Manager and select the **Add Roles and features** option. Note: When using Server 2022, there are some extra steps after Add Roles and Features. You will need to select the appropriate server from the pool every time. We covered this in a previous lab.

You can create shared folders on the server without adding the File Server role. However, the main advantage of adding the File Server role is that the wizard automatically adds special features to the file server such as DFS Namespace, DFS Replication, File Server Resource Manager, and Services for Network File System.

DFS stands for Distributed File System. It provides support for distributing files across the entire network and provides folder replication services. The File Services Resource Manager provides a suite of tools for monitoring file system resources such as disk space and generating reports. Services for Network File System supports sharing files with UNIX- and Linux-based computers.

Equipment and Materials

- Computer with Windows Server 2022 installed

Procedure

1. _____ Report to your assigned workstation.

2. _____ Boot the server and verify it is in working order.

3. _____ Open Server Manager and select the **Add Roles** option. The **Select Server Roles** screen will display.

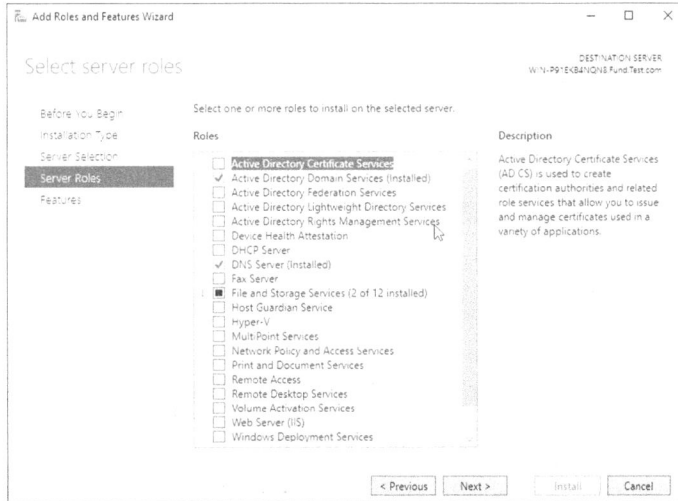

Goodheart-Willcox Publisher

4. _____ Select **File and Storage Services** from the list of server roles.

5. _____ Click the **File and Storage Services** link to read more about the file server features.

6. _____ After briefly scanning the information, close the **Files and Storage Services** help window. You will be returned to the **Add Roles and Features Wizard** screen. Click **Next** to continue.

7. _____ The next dialog box to appear will prompt you to select additional roles for the file server. Select only **Distributed File System**, **File Server Resource Manager**, and **Server for NFS**. As you select each role, information about the role will be provided on the right. Take a few minutes to read the information about each role, even the ones not selected for this exercise.

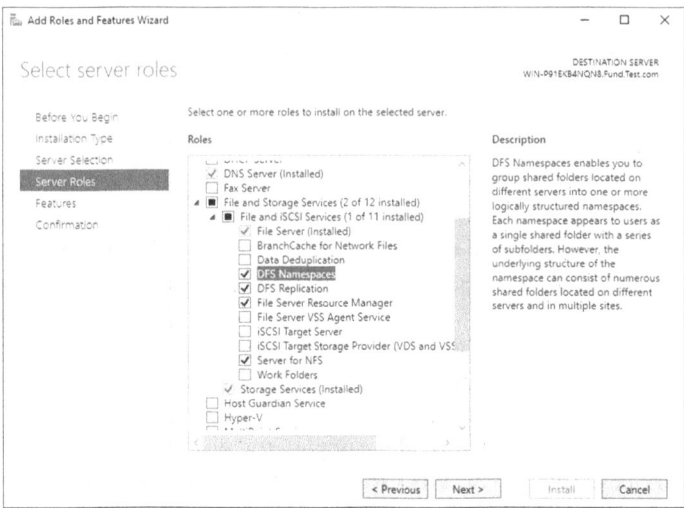

Goodheart-Willcox Publisher

> **NOTE**
> Server for NFS will be needed for a later lab activity when you install a Linux operating system computer and use it to access files on the Microsoft 2022 server.

8. _____ Click **Next**. A dialog box similar to the following will appear, prompting you to confirm installation selections. Click **Install**.

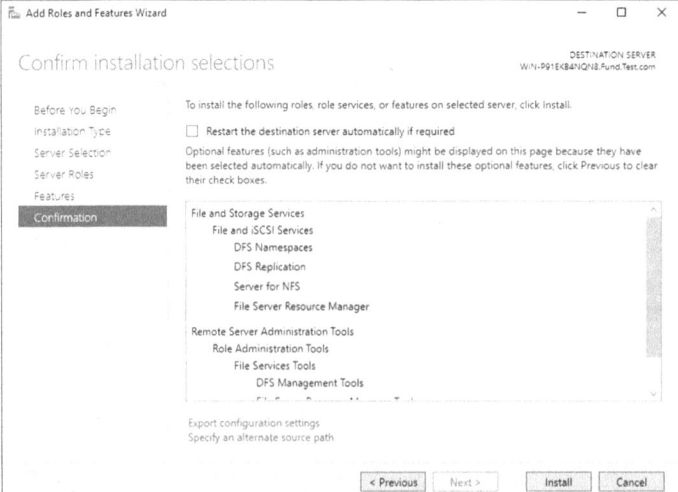

Goodheart-Willcox Publisher

> **NOTE**
> In a real network situation, a namespace would be created that reflects the purpose of the share. For example, SharedSalesFiles or SharedEngineeringProjects could be used.

Name _____

9. _____ On the Server Manager Dashboard, click on **Tools** to confirm that **DFS Management**, **File Server Resource Manager**, and **Services for Network File System (NFS)** are installed.

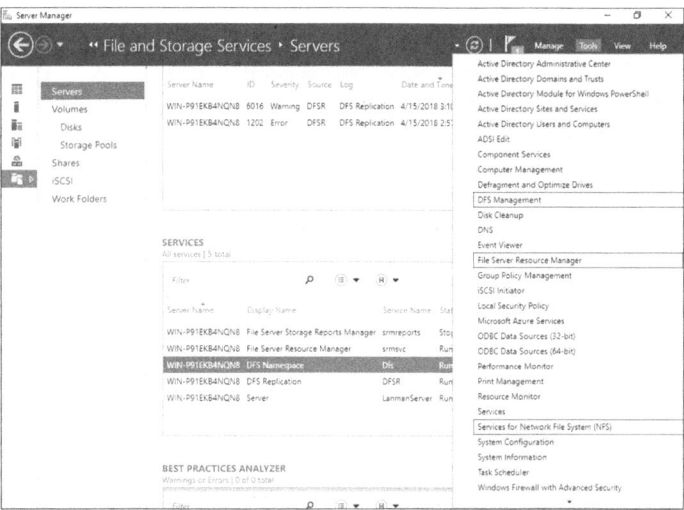

Goodheart-Willcox Publisher

10. _____ Select **Tools>DFS Management**. Click the **New Namespace** link to create a new DFS Namespace. The two types of namespace are domain-based namespace and stand-alone namespace. The *domain-based namespace* can be stored in multiple locations spread across the entire Active Directory. A *stand-alone namespace* is limited to a single server.

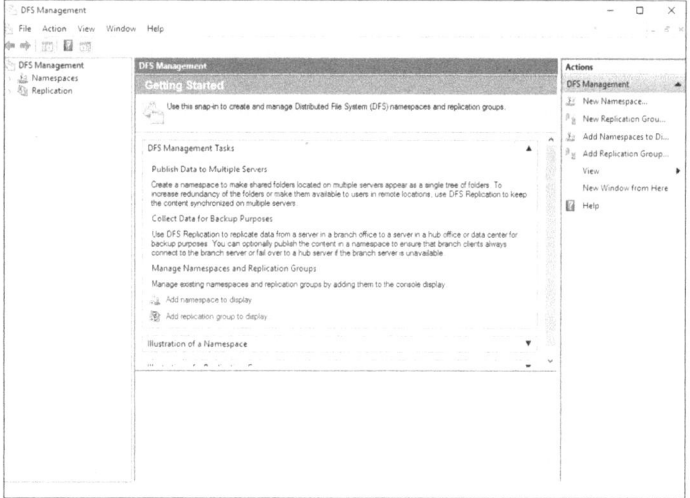

Goodheart-Willcox Publisher

11. _____ Enter the name for the namespace server and click **Next**.

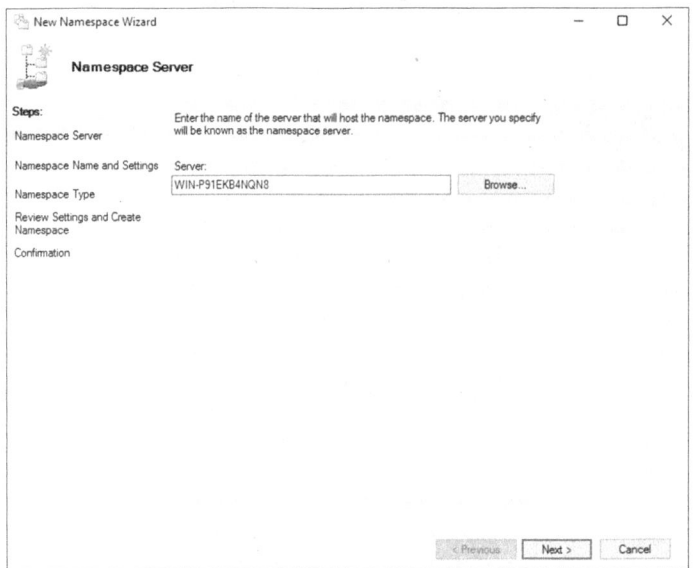

Goodheart-Willcox Publisher

12. _____ Enter the designed name for the namespace, and click the **Edit Settings** button.

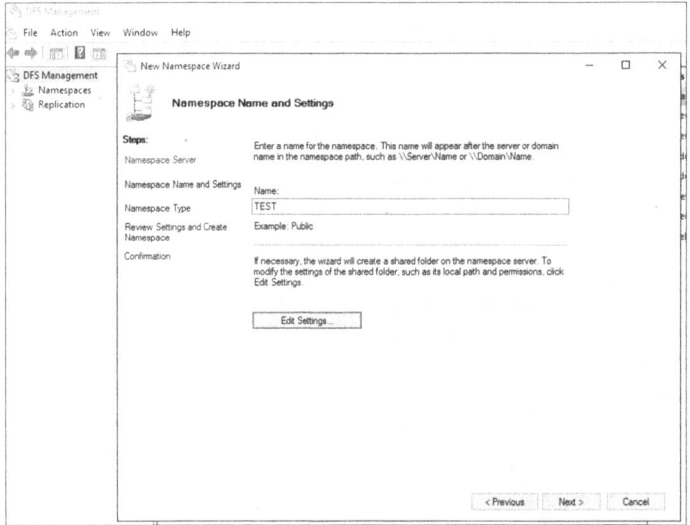

Goodheart-Willcox Publisher

Name _____

Accept the default Namespace setting and click the **OK** button to return to the New Namespace Wizard. Select **Next**.

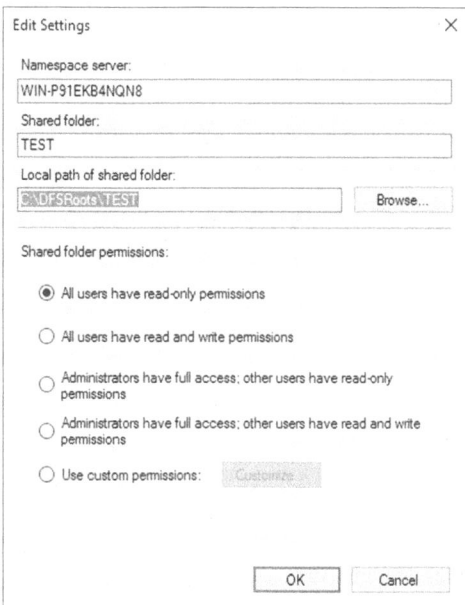

Goodheart-Willcox Publisher

13. _____ Select the type of namespace to create. A *domain-based namespace* is based on the fully qualified domain name (e.g.: \\Fund.Test.com\TEST). A *stand-alone namespace* is based on the server name (e.g., \\WIN-P91EKB4NQN8\TEST). In both examples, the names conform to the Universal Naming Convention (UNC) in which the server name follows the share name: \\Server_Name\Share_name. After you have made your selection, click **Next**.

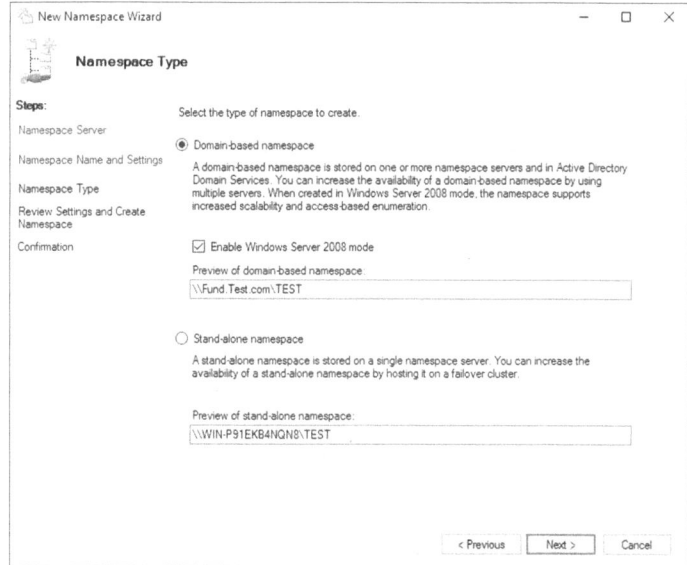

Goodheart-Willcox Publisher

14. _____ Review your settings, and click the **Create** button.

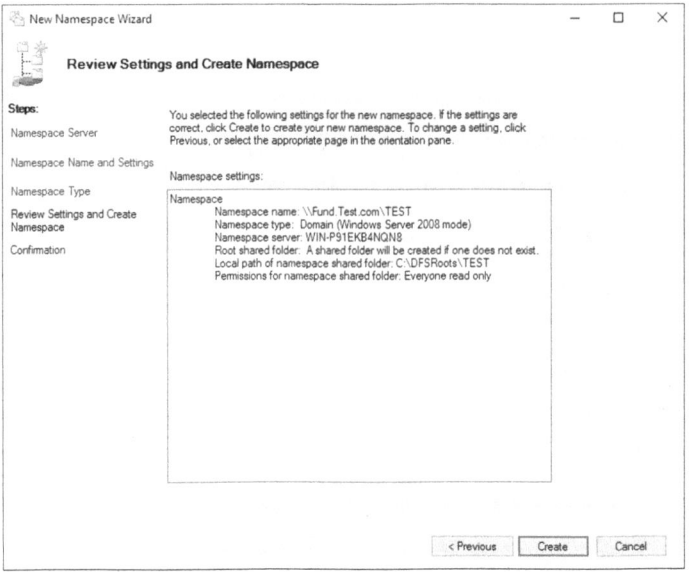

Goodheart-Willcox Publisher

The administrator can then navigate to a file location anywhere in the network or domain system and then simply select the file. It would be automatically configured as a "virtual" share in the namespace folder. When referred to as a *virtual share*, it means that the file can be located anywhere but will appear as if it is directly under the namespace folder.

15. _____ Once you confirm the namespace has been created, click the **Close** button to return to the DFS Management screen.

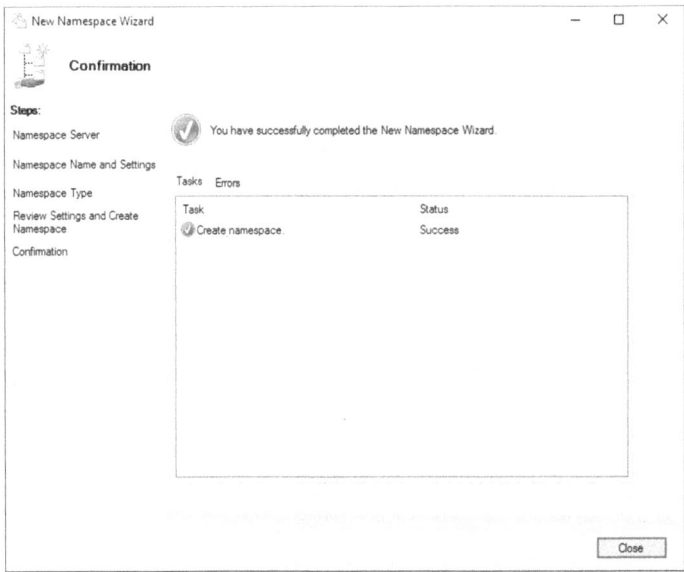

Goodheart-Willcox Publisher

Name _____

16. _____ Select the Namespaces option to view the namespace you just created. If it is not listed, seek help from your instructor.

17. _____ From the **Start** menu, right-click **Computer** and select **Manage** from the shortcut menu. You should see that the file server role (File Services) has been added to the list of server roles. When File Services is expanded, you will see Share and Storage Management and DFS Management listed. These are the same options you selected earlier in the lab activity.

18. _____ Call your instructor to check your lab.

19. _____ Answer the review questions.

Review Questions

1. Does the File Services role have to be added to enable the server to share files?

2. List four features added with the File Services role.

3. What is contained in a UNC path?

4. Write a UNC path for a share named *MyShare* located on a server called *Server1*.

5. Write a UNC for a share named *MyShare* located in a domain called *USF.edu*.

Notes

Name _____ Date _____ Class _____

Adding a Group in Windows Server 2022

Outcomes

After completing this laboratory activity, you will be able to:
- Use Active Directory Users and Computers to create a group on a Windows 2022 server.
- Summarize the administrative advantage of groups.
- Differentiate between domain local, global, and universal group scopes.
- Differentiate between distributive group types and security group types.

Introduction

In this laboratory activity, you will create a group. A *group* is a collection of user accounts that can be managed as a single unit. In a school setting, there are typically several logical groups of people, such as administrators, teachers, and students. A group can be created on the server for each of these logical groups. For example, a teachers' group can be created for all teacher user accounts. Permissions to resources, such as directory shares containing grades, financial data, school policy manuals, school forms, and software programs, can be assigned to groups instead of user accounts. Any user account added to the group automatically inherits the group's rights. This method of assigning permissions greatly reduces administrative time.

Groups can be either local or directory-based (part of the Active Directory). Local groups exist only on the individual (local) computer. Directory-based groups belong to the Active Directory and are therefore part of a domain. In this laboratory activity, you will create a directory-based group.

Directory-based groups are associated with a group scope and group type. A *group scope* defines what domains can be accessed and of how many domains the group can be a member. A *group type* refers to how the group is used—as a security group for access to shared resources or as a distribution group for e-mail distribution. You will be creating a global security–type group. The following lists group scopes and group types with a description of each.

Group Scope
- **Domain local**: Includes users from a single domain and permissions to access resources in only that domain.
- **Global**: Includes users from the domain in which it is created, but can be granted permissions to resources in other domains.
- **Universal**: Includes users from any domain and can be granted permissions to access resources in any domain.

Group Type
- **Security**: Used to assign permissions to shares.
- **Distribution**: Used only to create e-mail distribution lists.

> **NOTE**
> Do not confuse the term *local group* used in reference to a group created on a local computer with the term *domain local group* used in reference to an Active Directory group.

Equipment and Materials
- Computer with Windows Server 2022 installed
- The following information provided by your instructor:
- Group name (e.g., Group1):

Procedure

1. _____ Report to your assigned workstation.

2. _____ Boot the Windows 2022 server and verify it is in working order.

3. _____ Open **Active Directory Users and Computers** by selecting **Start> Server Manager>Tools>Active Directory Users and Computers**. A dialog box similar to the following will display.

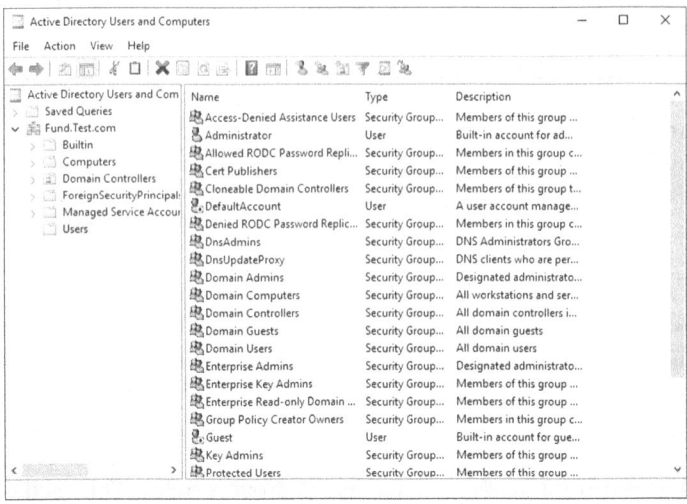

Goodheart-Willcox Publisher

4. _____ In the right pane, select the domain and the **Users** folder.

5. _____ Select **Action>New>Group**.

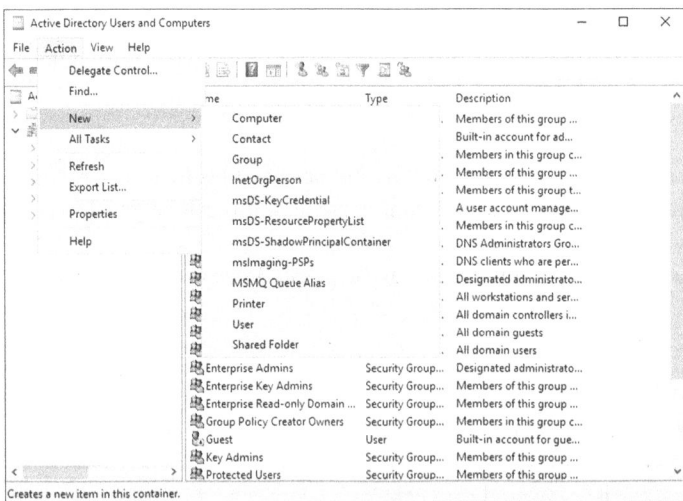

Goodheart-Willcox Publisher

Name _____

6. _____ The **New Object-Group** dialog box will display. Look at the **Group scope** and **Group type** areas and their options. The default options are **Global** and **Security**. Keep the default settings.

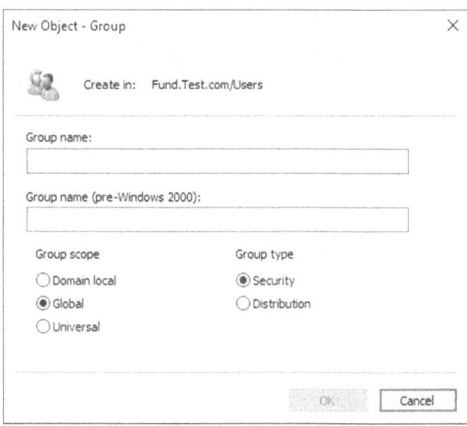

Goodheart-Willcox Publisher

7. _____ Enter the group name you listed in the **Equipment and Materials** section of this lab and then click **OK**. The new group will be created.

8. _____ Look at the **Active Directory Users and Computers** window to verify the new group has been created. If the new group was not created, call your instructor for assistance.

9. _____ Now, you will assign the user you created in the last laboratory activity to the group. To assign a user to a group, right-click the group and select **Properties** from the shortcut menu.

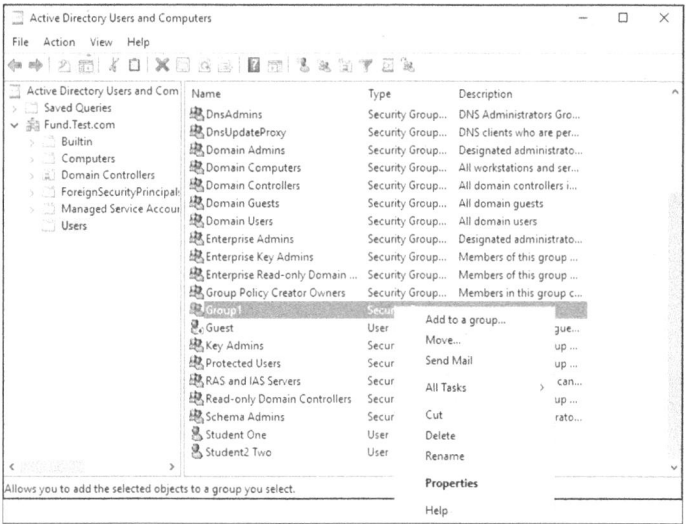

Goodheart-Willcox Publisher

Laboratory Activity 24 Adding a Group in Windows Server 2022   127

10. _____ When the group's **Properties** dialog box displays, select the **Members** tab.

Goodheart-Willcox Publisher

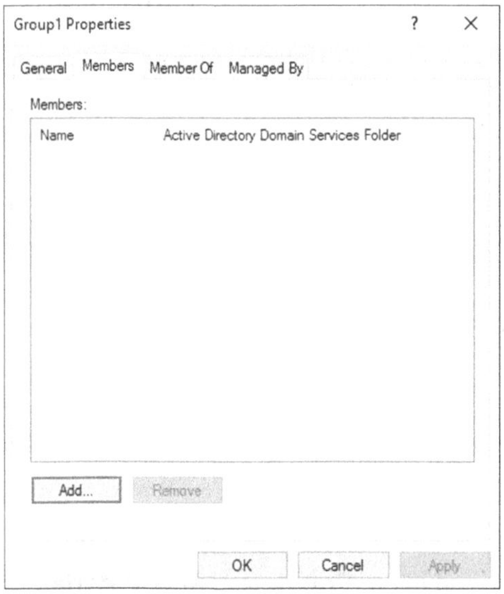

11. _____ A dialog box similar to the following will display. Notice that the new group has no members. Click **Add** to add a member to the group.

Goodheart-Willcox Publisher

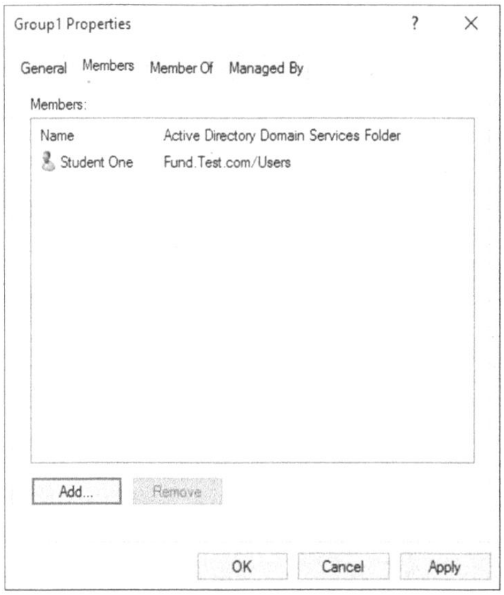

12. _____ Add members by entering the names of users in the text box or click **Advanced** to search for users.

13. _____ After you feel comfortable with creating a group and adding members to the group, answer the review questions.

Review Questions

1. What is the main purpose for creating groups?

____

2. What is the difference between a security group and a distributive group?

____

____

3. Which group scope is limited to a single domain and has access rights to that domain?

____

Name _____ Date _____ Class _____

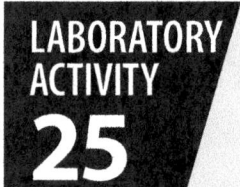

LABORATORY ACTIVITY 25

Joining a Domain

Outcomes

After completing this laboratory activity, you will be able to:
- Carry out proper procedures to join a computer to a network domain.
- Give examples of common problems associated with joining a domain.
- Summarize the Microsoft "best practice" for joining a workstation to a domain.

Introduction

In this laboratory activity, you will configure a computer to join a network domain. By default, a Windows-based computer is configured as part of a workgroup. The typical name for the workgroup is Workgroup. There is an exception for the Home version of Windows 10. This version, which cannot join a domain, uses the workgroup name MSHOME.

The following is the **System Settings** dialog box as it looks in Windows 10. If you do not see the **Join a domain** option in this dialog box, then the version of the operating system does not allow the computer to join a domain.

Goodheart-Willcox Publisher

Once the **Join a domain** option is selected, the user is prompted to enter the name of the domain they wish to join, as shown in the following screen capture.

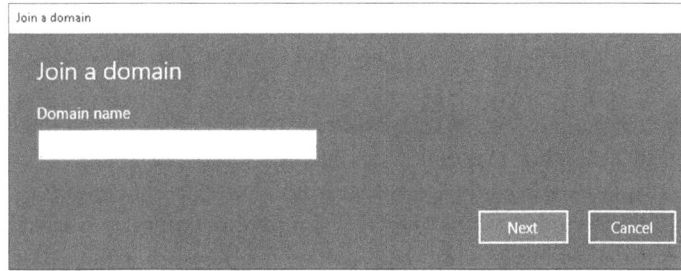

Goodheart-Willcox Publisher

Every computer that joins a domain has a security account similar to a user account. The computer must also authenticate before successfully joining the domain. Authentication is done without the user being aware that the computer is being authenticated.

Copyright Goodheart-Willcox Co., Inc.
May not be reproduced or posted to a publicly accessible website.

The following screen capture from a Windows 2022 server reveals the properties of a computer named **MYLAB1** that has become a member of the corp.chiola.com domain. Each computer in the domain must have a unique DNS name. The DNS name is a combination of the server domain name and the computer name. In the screen capture, you can see that the complete DNS name is MYLAB1.corp.chiola.com.

Goodheart-Willcox Publisher

After you join a computer to a domain, it will appear in the Active Directory Users and Computers structure. Look at the following screen capture, which shows two computers listed in the **Computers** folder under the corp.chiola.com domain tree.

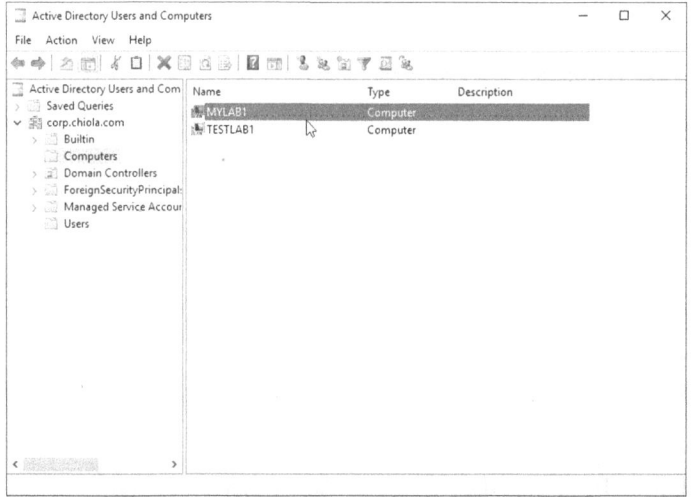

Goodheart-Willcox Publisher

The computers were added automatically when the properties of the computers were changed from a member of a workgroup called **Workgroup** to a member of a domain called **corp**. It is not always necessary to enter the complete DNS name when joining a network domain. If the DNS server is not working correctly or is unavailable, then you will need to supply the Fully Qualified Domain Name (FQDN). Joining a computer to a network in this manner is very common in a small local area network, but it is not the recommended best practice according to Microsoft. The best practice is to add the computer object to the directory structure prior to joining the computer to the domain. Adding an object to the Active Directory structure before the object is actually joined to the active directory domain is referred to as *pre-stage*.

One common reason that you may not be able to join the domain is the network adapter properties may need to be reconfigured by changing the preferred DNS to the IP address of the domain controller. Another reason is making a simple typo when entering the desired domain name. Also, each workstation must have a unique name; otherwise, it will not be able to join the domain.

Name _____

Equipment and Materials

- Computer with Windows Server 2022 installed and configured as a domain controller
- Computer running Windows 10 connected to a network containing the domain controller
- A user account on the domain controller
- The following information provided by your instructor:

User account name:

_____

User account password:

_____

Domain name:

_____

> **NOTE**
> This lab activity can be completed without a network, but you will not be able to connect to a network or verify the connection to a domain controller.

Procedure

1. _____ Report to your assigned workstation.

2. _____ Boot the computer and verify it is in working order.

3. _____ Open the **System Properties** dialog box by right-clicking **Computer** and selecting **Properties** from the shortcut menu. Select **Advanced System Settings** and then the **Computer Name** tab. Click the **Change settings** button.

4. _____ Enter the domain name.

> **NOTE**
> You will be prompted to supply an account name and password to make changes to the domain logon.

5. _____ The computer typically requires a reboot before joining a domain. You will also see a [Ctrl] [Alt] [Del] prompt to produce the typical logon screen.

6. _____ After logging on, call your instructor to inspect your lab.

7. _____ Answer the review questions and then log off of the computer.

Review Questions

1. What is typically required before joining a domain?

_____

2. To which folder of Active Directory Users and Computers is the computer name added?

_____

3. What is the Microsoft best practice method for joining a computer to a domain?
   _____
   _____

4. Is pre-staging the computer object essential to join a domain?
   _____
   _____

5. What network adapter configuration IP address might need to be changed if you encounter difficulty successfully joining a domain?
   _____
   _____

Name _____ Date _____ Class _____

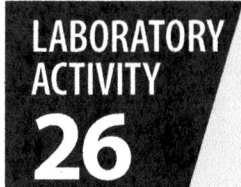

Adding the Print Services Role in Windows Server 2022

Outcomes

After completing this laboratory activity, you will be able to:
- Use the Add Roles Wizard to install the Print Services role.
- Recall the printer configuration tasks available in Print Management.

Introduction

In this laboratory activity, you will run the Add Roles Wizard to install the Print Services role. If an actual printer is available, you may go on to install a printer to the print server. At the end of this lab activity, you will start to see how easy it is to configure the most common server roles.

Equipment and Materials

- Computer with Windows Server 2022 installed

> **NOTE**
> Although it is desired, no printer is necessary for this lab activity. You can still run the lab activity and complete the review questions.

Procedure

1. _____ Report to your assigned workstation.

2. _____ Boot the server and verify it is in working order.

3. _____ Open Server Manager by selecting **Start>Server Manager>Tools**.

4. _____ After Server Manager opens, click **Manage>Add Roles and Features**. Note: When using Server 2022, there are some extra steps after Add Roles and Features. You will need to select the appropriate server from the pool every time. We covered this in a previous lab.

5. _____ Select **Print and Document Services** from the list of roles.

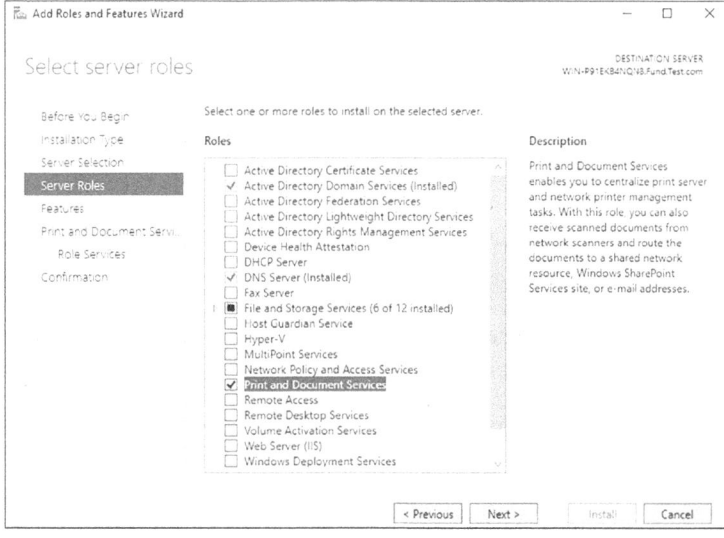

Goodheart-Willcox Publisher

You can find out more about Print Services by clicking the **Print Services** link located on the right of the screen under **Description**. Do this now and scan the information before continuing with the lab.

6. _____ Close the Print Services information window and then click **Next**. A dialog box similar to the following will appear providing important information concerning this role.

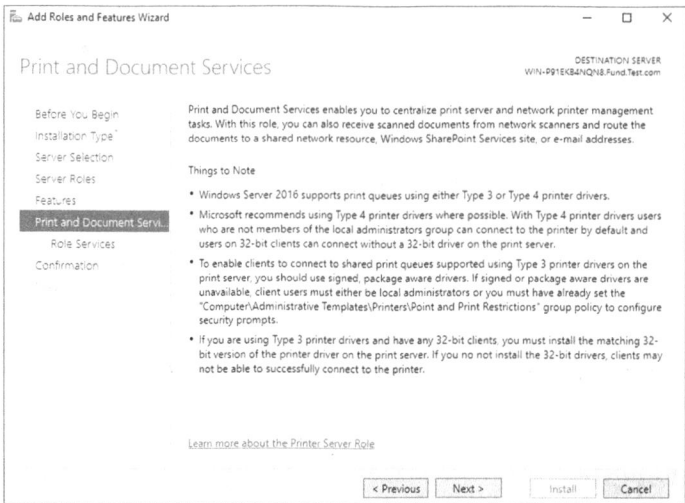

Goodheart-Willcox Publisher

A failover cluster configuration is recommended to ensure printer availability. Additional information is also available through a list of links displayed in the dialog box. You may review any of the items before continuing.

7. _____ Click **Next**. A dialog box appears presenting three Print Services roles: **Print Server**, **LPD Service**, and **Internet Printing**.

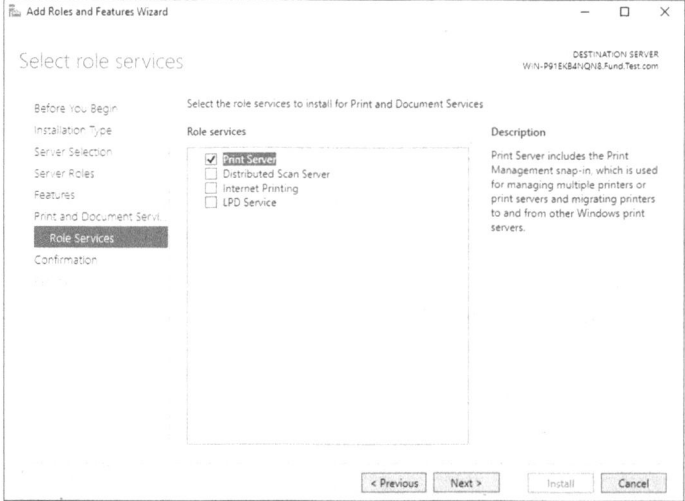

Goodheart-Willcox Publisher

To view information about any of these services, highlight the service. Information will appear on the right under **Description**.

Look at the description for LPD Service and Internet Printing. The review questions are based on the information listed here. Answer the review questions before proceeding.

8. _____ Select only the **Print Server** option. Do not select the other two options at this time.

Name _____

9. _____ Click **Next**. A dialog box confirming your choice of printer role(s) will appear.

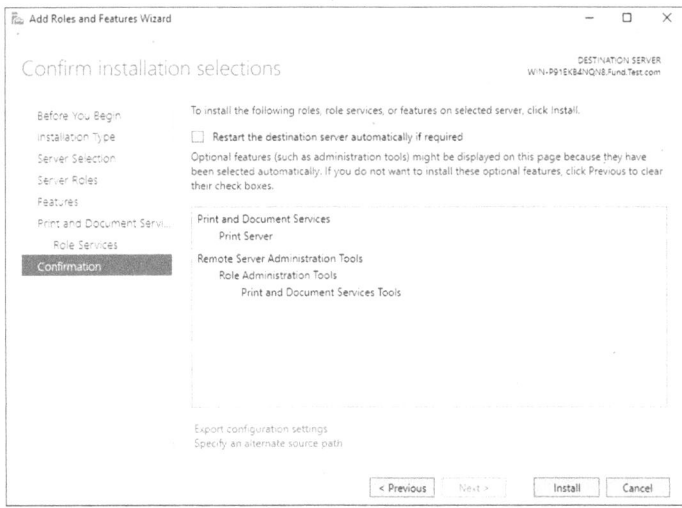

Goodheart-Willcox Publisher

10. _____ Click **Install**. After a few minutes, you will see a dialog box confirming the successful installation of the Printer Services role.

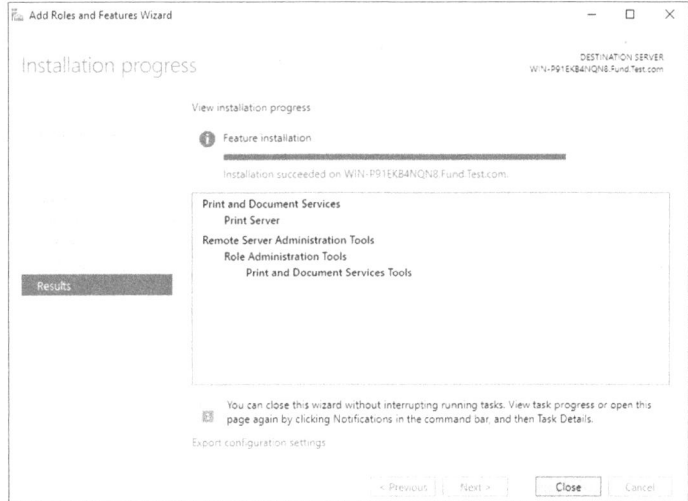

Goodheart-Willcox Publisher

11. _____ Click **Close**. If you have a printer available to connect directly to the server, do so now. The printer will be automatically detected and configured for the server.

12. _____ Open Print Management by selecting **Start>Server Manager>Tools>Print Management**. The Print Management utility becomes available when the Print Services role is installed. Print Management provides a centralized location to manage all aspects of the printer configuration, such as installing drivers and checking the status of print jobs.

Goodheart-Willcox Publisher

13. _____ Open the **Help** menu item and take a minute to look at the information provided concerning the Print Management utility.

14. _____ Close Print Management and return all materials to their proper storage areas.

Review Questions

1. What does the acronym LPD represent?

2. What does the LPD service enable?

3. What does Internet Printing create?

4. What does the acronym IPP represent?

Name _____ Date _____ Class _____

Observing Share Transactions with Wireshark

Outcomes

After completing this laboratory activity, you will be able to:
- Use Wireshark to capture a share transaction between two nodes on a network.
- Compare SMB, SMB2, SMB3, and other related protocols to the OSI model.
- Summarize why actual bandwidth exceeds the calculated bandwidth for transferring a file based on file contents.
- Summarize why segmentation is necessary.

Introduction

In this laboratory activity, you will share a file and then transfer the file while running Wireshark. You will also open and view the contents of sample capture files to learn the general concepts of what happens during a file transfer.

There are three versions of Server Message Protocol (SMB): SMB, SMB2.x, and SMB3.0. You will not necessarily see the original version identified as SMB 1.0 because when expressed as SMB it is implied that it is version one. SMB2 was first released with Windows Vista and then later incorporated into Windows 7 and Windows Server 2008. SMB3.0 was introduced with Windows 8 and Windows Server 2012. You may see all versions during the capture because Microsoft still maintains backward compatibility with earlier operating systems. Using Windows 10, 11, and Server 2022, you are more likely to see SMB 3.0.

You probably think that a simple file transfer would not be very complex. In reality, a lot of information is transferred before and after the exchange of one simple file. In the first SMB capture, **Wireshark Sample 7**, there are 252 frames. Over 200 frames are encountered before the actual file contained in the share is transferred to the client. Only one frame contains the actual contents of the small file being accessed and transferred.

Later, you will perform a file transfer based on SMB2. You will see a significant reduction in the number of frames required for a file transfer. SMB2, and now SMB3, combined many of the commands and now relies on newer security features incorporated into the operating system. This results in fewer required frames. On a local area network, SMB2 and SMB3 use the IPv6 protocol for encapsulating packets.

Microsoft uses SMB to support file- and print-sharing activities. SMB is an upper-level protocol that handles the OSI model application- and presentation-level responsibilities. SMB relies on other protocols to establish a session and to transport commands and data over the network. NetBIOS is used to set up the session and is found at the session level of the OSI model. SMB also relies on the TCP, UDP, IP, and Ethernet protocols to carry it. Look at the following table to see the relationship of the protocols.

Application Presentation	SMB, SMB2, SMB3
Session	NetBIOS
Transport	TCP & UDP
Network	IPv4 & IPv6
Data Link	Ethernet
Physical	

Notice how SMB/SMB2/SMB3 is identified at the application and presentation layers. The encapsulation process of SMB/SMB2/SMB3 also uses NetBIOS, TCP, UDP, IPv4, IPv6, and Ethernet.

You may see all versions of SMB appear in a capture series. The SMB protocol will appear when there are Windows XP or older operating systems in the network. Windows Vista and Windows 7 will typically only contain SMB2 packets. Windows 8 and later will likely only contain SMB3 packets.

Your Wireshark capture will not match the example exactly. Reasons for this include but are not limited to the following:
- Which updates or service pack(s) have been installed.
- How you access the file.
- Background activity such as time synchronization of the network by the Network Time Protocol (NTP).
- Browser update activity.
- Other workstations connected to the network.
- Antivirus software activity.
- Other software programs that use network capabilities.

Equipment and Materials
- Windows 10 workstation with Wireshark installed
- Windows Server 2022 with a folder ready to share
- Wireshark Sample 7 file

    Wireshark Sample 7 file location:

    _____

- Wireshark Sample 8 file

    Wireshark Sample 8 file location:

    _____

- Wireshark Sample 9 file

    Wireshark Sample 9 file location:

    _____

Procedure

1. _____ Gather required materials and report to your assigned workstation.

2. _____ Boot the server and the workstation and verify they are in working order.

3. _____ On the workstation, open the Wireshark program and the **Wireshark Sample 7** file.

4. _____ Look at frame 7. Notice that in the middle pane under NetBIOS Session Service the terms called and calling are used to identify the two nodes.

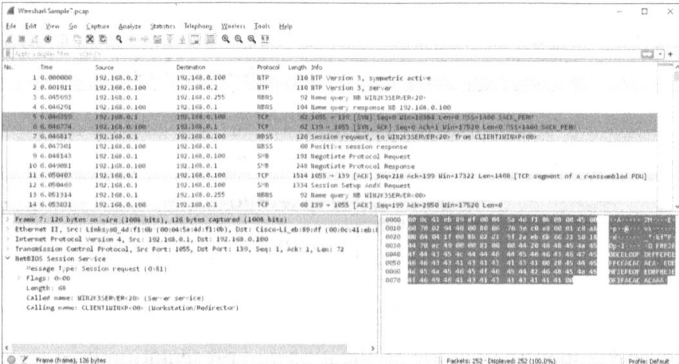

Goodheart-Willcox Publisher

In the example, the server is identified as the "called name" and the workstation is identified as the "calling name." The called and calling names are NetBIOS names.

Name _____

5. _____ Highlight frame 9. Notice in the middle pane under SMB (Server Message Block Protocol) that the particular "dialect" of SMB is negotiated.

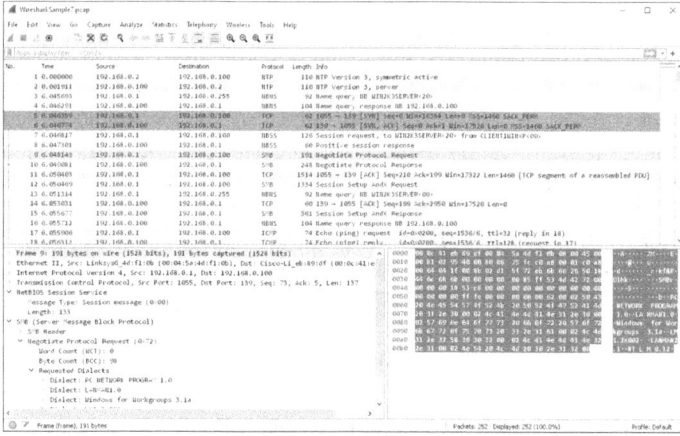

Goodheart-Willcox Publisher

SMB has been developed over many years and several "dialects" exist. A specific dialect must be agreed on to ensure the most compatible communications. An early version may not contain all the various enhancements and thus could generate errors while attempting to transfer data or while attempting to access a share.

6. _____ Highlight frame 19. Notice that the client is requesting a connection to the shares located on the server.

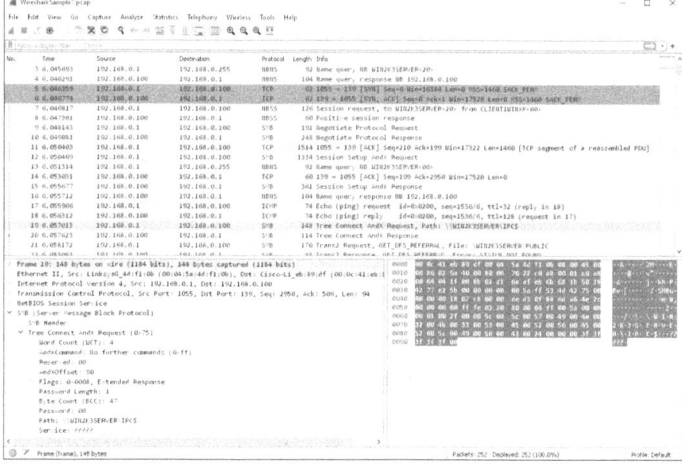

Goodheart-Willcox Publisher

Take note of the IPC$ share designation. This is a general share rather than a specific share. It is used to initiate a temporary connection between a client and server. In the following frames, more messages are exchanged concerning mostly security issues. Each step in the path to the network share is negotiated, such as the hard disk drive access, the share directory structure, and the file. On reaching frame 238, the contents of the file are finally accessed.

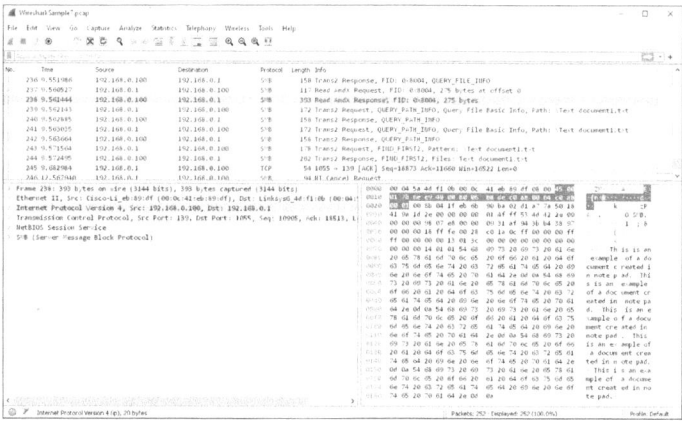

Goodheart-Willcox Publisher

You can see the actual file contents at the bottom of the screen. The words "This is an example of a document created in note pad" are displayed several times as they are in the actual contents of the file. You will create a similar file for viewing later in this lab activity. Take note of the Read AndX Response located on frame 238 of the Info column. This is an abbreviation for the SMB command used to display the contents of the file. This can only be issued after all the other command steps have been responded to correctly.

As you can see, there is a lot of network activity that takes place whenever you access a share on a client/server network. The amount of frames is significantly reduced on a peer-to-peer network system, but accessing a share still requires approximately 50 frames. This overhead should be taken into account when calculating bandwidth requirements for a network file transfer. In the Wireshark Sample 7 file containing a few lines of text, the ratio of overhead to actual file transfer bandwidth is very high. As the size of the file contents increases, the ratio is reduced.

NOTE
Calculated bandwidth, or how long it takes to download a file, is typically based on file size divided by device bandwidth. As you can see in the screen capture, many frames are required to negotiate the connection to the file before it is downloaded or transferred. This is why calculations are not accurate at all.

7. _____ Open the **Wireshark Sample 8** file. Examine frames 168 to 189.

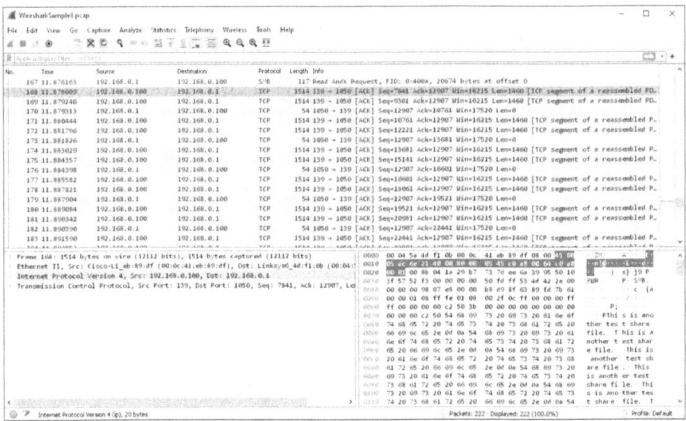

Goodheart-Willcox Publisher

Notice the series of frames using the TCP protocol. The TCP protocol is used to transfer the remaining segments of the file contents after the first segment was transferred using SMB. When a file is too large to fit inside one frame, the file must be divided into smaller sections or packets. Dividing the large collection of data into smaller packages is called *segmenting the data* or *segmentation*. The entire Ethernet frame and payload is a maximum of 1514 bytes.

8. _____ Open the **Wireshark Sample 9** file. This sample capture was created using Windows 7 and Windows Server 2008. Notice that the entire SMB2 transaction takes less than 100 frames. That's significantly a lesser amount of frames when compared to SMB.

9. _____ Highlight and examine frame 71. You will be able to view the contents of the shared file.

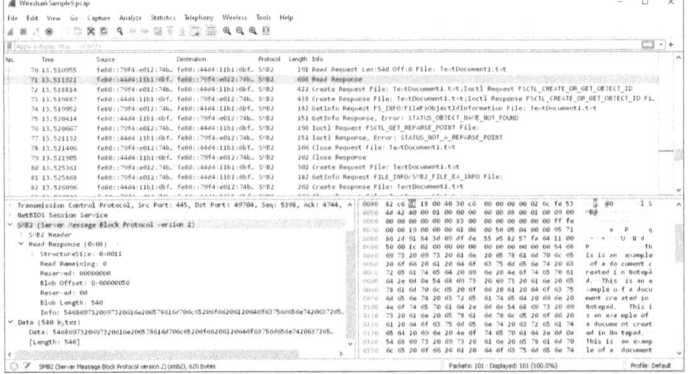

Goodheart-Willcox Publisher

Name _____

10. _____ Highlight and examine frame 66. Notice that the share permission settings for the **TextDocument1.txt** file are shown. The permissions are read and write, but not delete.

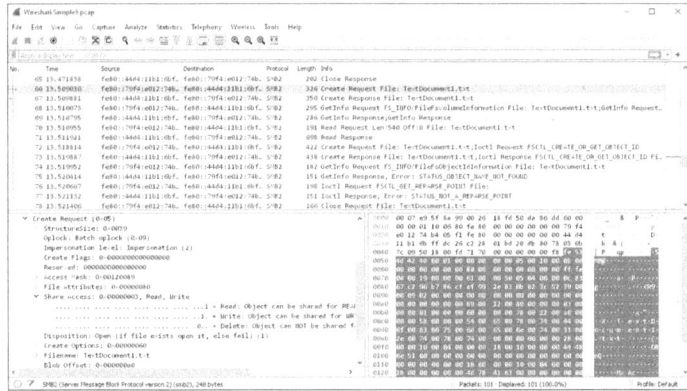

Goodheart-Willcox Publisher

11. _____ Open any frame that contains the SMB2 and the NetBIOS protocol and expand the NetBIOS Session Service entry in the middle pane. You will see that it is practically void of any critical information. SMB2 does not rely on NetBIOS name resolution when using IPv6. As you can see, all the frames identified as SMB2 use IPv6 to support packet exchanges. SMB relies solely on IPv4.

12. _____ Now you will create a document for viewing on the server. At the server, access the Notepad program. Create a document containing the sentence, "This is an example of a document created in Notepad" without the quotation marks. Copy and paste the line nine more times. You will have a total of ten lines. Save the file using the name **TextDocument1**. Create a shared folder on the server and place the document in the shared folder.

13. _____ At the workstation, start a Wireshark capture.

14. _____ From the workstation, access the text document you just created.

15. _____ After you have successfully accessed the shared document, stop the protocol analyzer capture and view its contents. Look for the captured frame that contains the contents of the document. Look for "Read Response" in the **Info** column to help locate the frame. You should be able to read the contents of the document.

16. _____ Create a document of much greater length. Copy the contents of the Notepad document to a new file called **TextDocument2**. Copy and paste the 10 lines approximately 20 to 30 more times to create a much larger document. Place the new file in the shared folder, and then access the new document from the client while Wireshark is capturing frames.

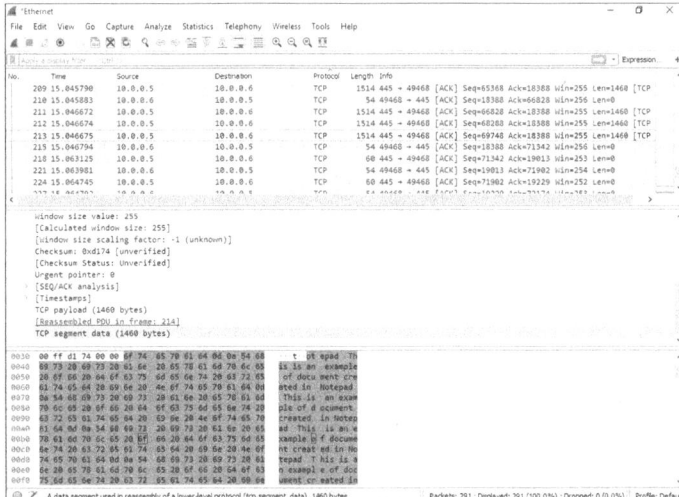

Goodheart-Willcox Publisher

17. _____ Stop the capture and then view the contents of the capture to see if you can locate the series of TCP segments used to carry the contents of the larger document.

The series of TCP protocol packets contains sections of the entire file. The last section delivered will be an SMB2 Read Response. Look for the series of segmentations in your capture. If you cannot locate this series, call your instructor for assistance.

> **NOTE**
> Large files must be segmented because TCP/IP limits the maximum size of a frame. In general, the maximum TCP segment size is 1514 bytes.

Return the server and the workstation to their original condition, and answer the review questions.

Review Questions

1. At what OSI layer(s) does the SMB/SMB2/SMB3 protocol align?

2. What other protocols does SMB/SMB2/SMB3 require to communicate with another node?

3. What is the purpose of the IPC$ share?

4. Why are there so many frames for a file transfer?

5. What is the maximum size of the Ethernet frame?

6. What is segmentation?

7. After the file contents transfer begins, which high-level protocol is used to continue transferring data to support segmentation?

8. Which protocol version, IPv4 or IPv6, is used for SMB2?

9. Why would the original SMB protocol show up in a capture series?

10. Why is calculated bandwidth much lower than actual bandwidth?

Name _____ Date _____ Class _____

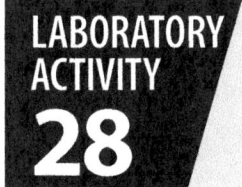

LABORATORY ACTIVITY 28: Installing Ubuntu Linux

Outcomes

After completing this laboratory activity, you will be able to:
- Carry out a default installation of Ubuntu Linux.
- Recall the three default partitions created during the Ubuntu installation process.
- Summarize the purpose of various installation options.

Introduction

In this laboratory activity, you will install the Ubuntu Linux operating system. You can download a copy from the Ubuntu organization located at https://ubuntu.com/download/desktop. If this web address is no longer valid, conduct an Internet search using the key words Ubuntu Linux download.

The two main problems typically encountered during a Linux installation are hardware compatibility and understanding terminology unique to UNIX/Linux operating systems. While hardware compatibility issues have become less of a problem, the terminology problem still exists. However, there is no need to understand Linux terminology fully to complete a successful installation process. This does not mean you do not need to understand the terminology for operating purposes; you just do not need to understand the terminology to *install* Linux.

You can also install Ubuntu Linux in a virtual machine. You may use any virtual machine software you wish, but Oracle Virtual Box is a free download from https://www.oracle.com/virtualization/solutions/try-oracle-vm-virtualbox. The install in these lab instructions was done by installing Ubuntu into Oracle Virtual Box.

GNU Grub is the default installation program for Ubuntu. You can start the installation process in similar fashion to performing a Windows operating system installation. Place the Ubuntu installation DVD into the DVD drive. The disk will be detected automatically, and the installation program will be started. You can also place the installation DVD into the drive and then reboot the computer. If the installation does not start from the DVD after the reboot, you may need to configure the boot device sequence so that the DVD drive is listed as the first boot device. You will need to configure the boot options in the BIOS setup.

During the Ubuntu installation, the hard drive will be automatically divided into three partitions and formatted. The three partitions are /swap, /home, and / (root). The /swap partition is used in similar fashion to the Windows swap partition. The /swap partition supplements the available RAM. The /home partition is used for user home directories. The Linux operating system is installed in the root partition symbolized by the backslash (/) symbol. This partition is also called the *system partition* and is where all the required operating system files are installed. It is not used for user storage.

During the installation process, you will create a password. The password should consist of a combination of uppercase and lowercase letters as well as numbers and special keyboard symbols. You can even use spaces in a password. If the password does not meet the complexity recommendations, you will generate a warning message. The complexity of the password is not mandatory, just strongly recommended.

To find out more information about Ubuntu Linux, go to the Ubuntu tutorials page at https://ubuntu.com/tutorials To learn more about other Linux versions, look at the Linux organization website located at http://www.linux.org.

> **NOTE**
> When performing this lab, do *not* make changes to the recommended default configuration unless told to do so by your instructor.

Equipment and Materials

- Ubuntu set of DVD discs or ISO file with a Virtual Machine
- Computer meeting the following requirements:
- 512 MB RAM
- 5 GB or more available hard disk space
- CPU: Intel Pentium 1 to 4 or Xeon; AMD Duron, Athlon, Athlon XP, Athlon MP, Athlon 64, or Sempron
- The following information, provided by your instructor:

Root password:

_____

Username:

_____

User password:

_____

Additional usernames:

_____

Procedure

1. _____ Gather all required materials and report to your assigned workstation.

2. _____ Boot the computer and then place the first installation DVD in the DVD boot device.

> **NOTE**
> You may need to access the BIOS setup program to reconfigure the computer to boot from the DVD device first rather than from the hard disk drive.

3. _____ With the Ubuntu installation DVD in the DVD drive, reboot the system to start the installation. Alternatively, load the .iso file into a virtual machine. In a few seconds, you will be presented with several options similar to those in the following screen capture.

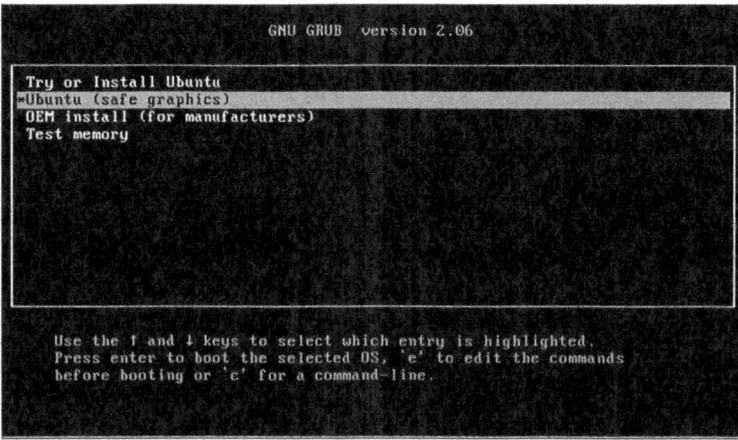

Goodheart-Willcox Publisher

Name _____

4. _____ Select **Ubuntu (safe graphics)**. There will be a few seconds delay, then you will see the following screen.

Goodheart-Willcox Publisher

There will be a small spinning circle in the lower right hand corner. As long as this is spinning, things are moving along just fine. You will then be presented with a graphical user interface wizard that will guide you through the steps.

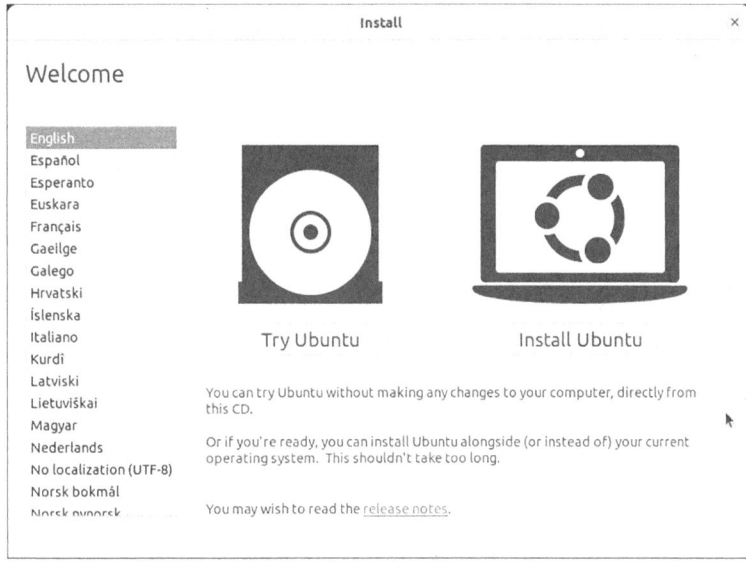

Goodheart-Willcox Publisher

5. _____ For the purposes of this example, we will install with English; however, feel free to use any language you choose. The next screenshot shows the selection of keyboard layout and language choice.

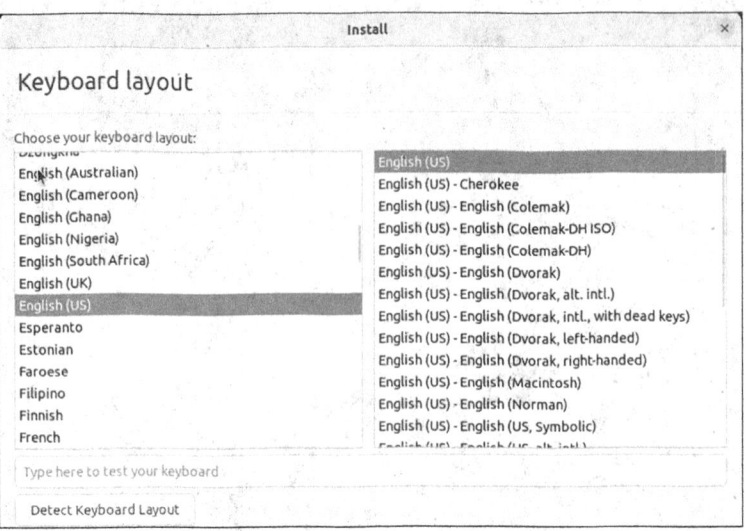

Goodheart-Willcox Publisher

6. _____ Click **Next**. The next screen involves installation and updates. On this screen and the next, please use default settings.

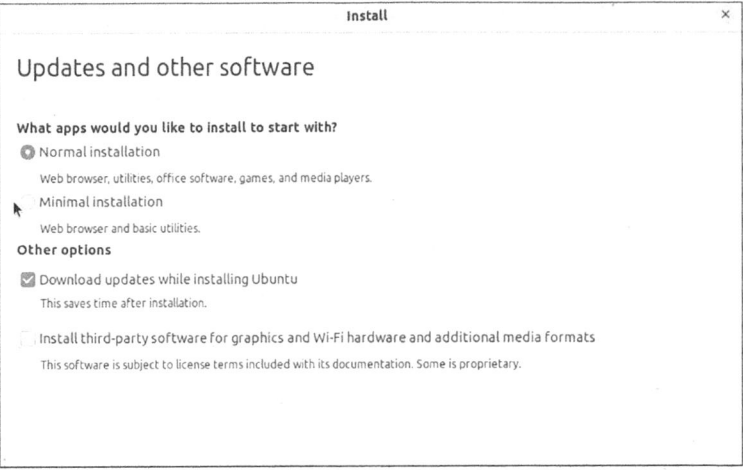

Goodheart-Willcox Publisher

7. _____ Click **Next** to continue. The installation program will probe the system to identify hardware and determine if any partitions are already created and if an operating system is already installed. This will take a few minutes. You will then be asked how to install. For the purposes of this example, we will choose the default **Erase disk and install Ubuntu** as shown in the following screenshot.

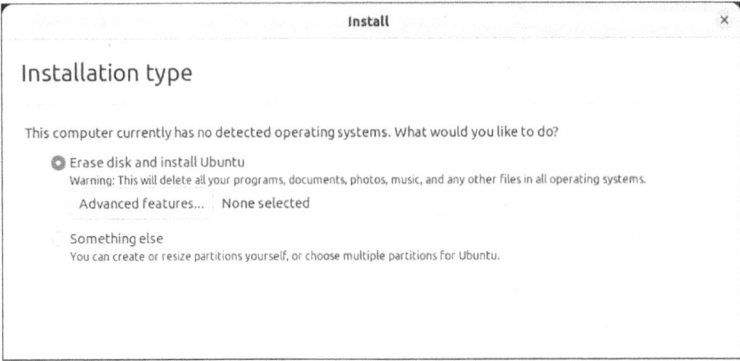

Goodheart-Willcox Publisher

Name _____

8. _____ You will be prompted to accept the changes you have made, then you will be asked to set the clock and select the time zone. You can adjust the time by selecting the desired location from the **Region** and **Time Zone** drop-down menus, or you can select **Next** to accept the default settings.

Goodheart-Willcox Publisher

9. _____ Next you will enter your name, computer name, username, and password.

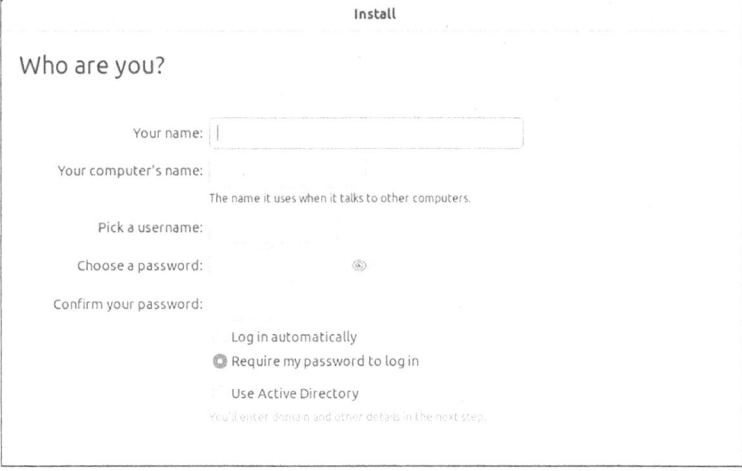

Goodheart-Willcox Publisher

Then you will see a series of screens with information as the files are being copied to the device. These will look like what you see in the following screenshot. This part of the install takes several minutes.

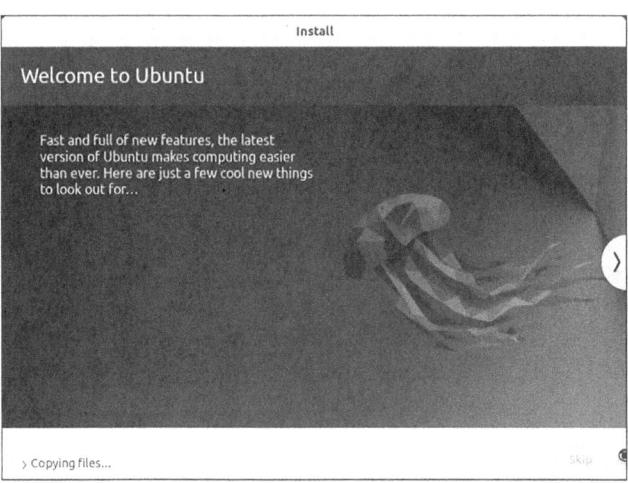

Goodheart-Willcox Publisher

10. _____ You will now be notified that installation is complete and restart your computer.

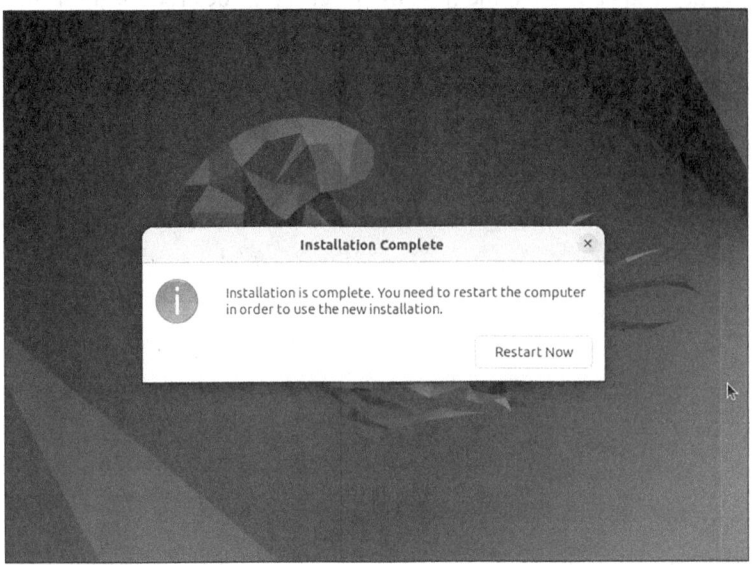

Goodheart-Willcox Publisher

11. _____ Call your instructor to inspect your lab activity.

12. _____ Go on to answer the review questions. Return all materials to their proper storage areas.

Review Questions

1. What is the default installation program for Ubuntu?

   _____

2. What are the three partitions in the Ubuntu installation?

   _____

3. What is another name for the root partition?

   _____

4. What elements should be incorporated into a secure Linux password?

   _____
   _____

5. Can spaces be used in the password?

   _____

Name _____ Date _____ Class _____

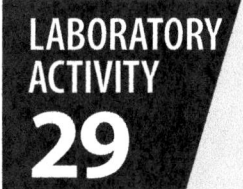

Adding a New User in Ubuntu

Outcomes
After completing this laboratory activity, you will be able to:
- Create a new user account on an Ubuntu Linux system.

Introduction
In this laboratory activity, you will create and edit a new user account on an Ubuntu Linux system. There are two general types of user accounts: local user and domain user. In this lab activity, you will create a local user account, which is a user account on the Linux computer. A domain user account is associated with a client/server network.

Equipment and Materials
- Computer with Ubuntu installed
- The following information provided by your instructor:

Root password:

_____

LDAP server password (if required):

_____

First new user account name (for example, Student1):

_____

Second new user account name (for example, Student2):

_____

First new user password (for example, Pa$$wOrd):

_____

Second new user password (for example, Pa$$wOrd):

_____

NOTE
The user account password can be the same for both user accounts.

Procedure
1. _____ Report to your assigned workstation.
2. _____ Boot the computer and log on to the KDE system using your assigned user account or as root.

3. _____ Click on **Apps**, then search for users. Find the settings for users.

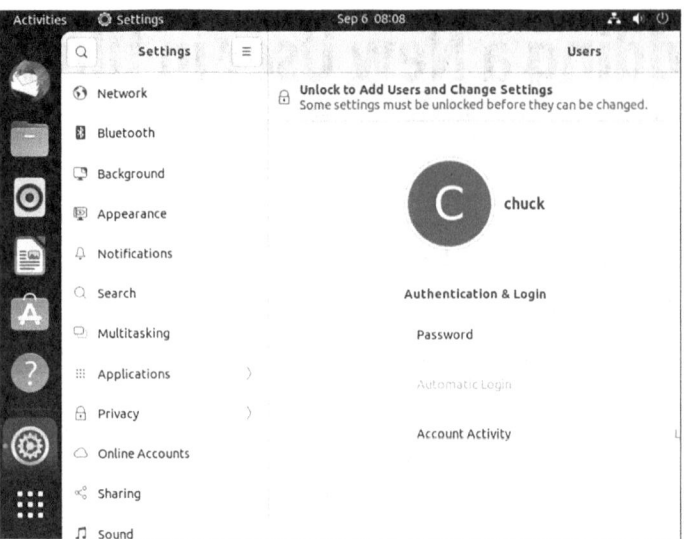

Goodheart-Willcox Publisher

4. _____ Add a user by clicking the **Add User** button.

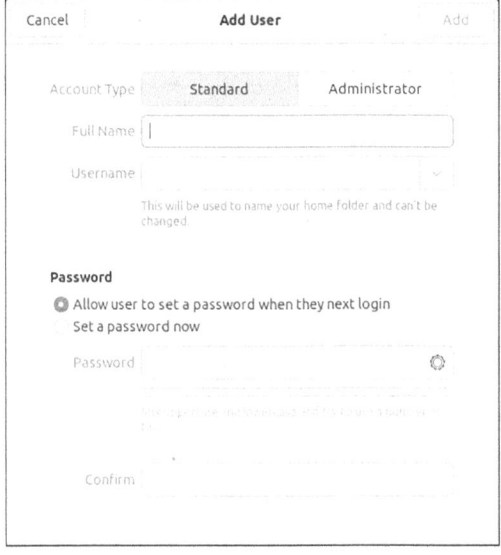

Goodheart-Willcox Publisher

Only the root user has permission to create a new user account. If you are already logged on to the system and are not the root, you will be prompted for the root password when attempting to change the system configuration.

Name _____

5. _____ When you are prompted for the root user password, you are automatically granted permission to make system changes such as creating a new account. Adding a user is quite simple, as shown below. Set the password provided by your instructor.

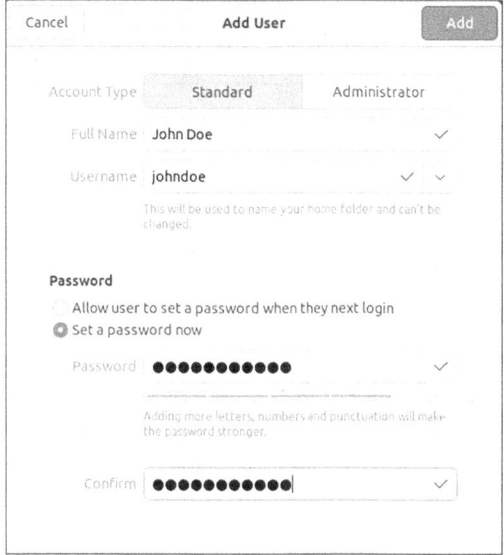

Goodheart-Willcox Publisher

6. _____ After adding a user, close Ubuntu and answer the review questions.

Review Questions

1. What are the two general types of user accounts?

    _____

2. Who is authorized to create a new user account?

    _____

3. If you create a new user account and are not the root, what will happen?

    _____

4. What kind of user account is used with a Linux computer?

    _____

5. What kind of user account is used with a client/server network?

    _____

Notes

Name _____ Date _____ Class _____

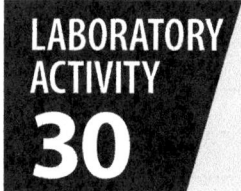

Introduction to KDE Terminal Konsole

Outcomes

After completing this laboratory activity, you will be able to:
- Use the KDE Terminal Konsole to enter basic commands.
- Use the commands **ls**, **ls -al**, **dir**, **mkdir**, and **whoami**.
- Recall the functions of the commands **ls**, **ls -al**, **dir**, **mkdir**, and **whoami**.
- Identify three common troubleshooting commands.

Introduction

This laboratory activity introduces you to one of the many command-line interfaces available in UNIX/Linux operating systems and to a few of the most basic commands. The command-line interface you will be using for this lab activity is the console called *Konsole*. It is also referred to as a *terminal*.

> **NOTE**
> In the KDE system, many features are written with the capital letter *K* in place of the first letter to reflect the fact it was modified for the KDE system.

The original UNIX system did not use a graphical user interface (GUI) but rather was a command-line interface (CLI) similar to the command prompt in Windows operating systems. The CLI is referred to as a *shell*. Even today, the CLI is used to issue commands on a Linux server to minimize system resources. For example, there is no need to start the GUI on the server to add a new user to an existing system. Starting the GUI reduces system performance because the GUI requires RAM to run. A GUI affects the overall performance of the server when it is supporting many users (clients). Using the command line interface will have minimal effect on server performance.

Another reason for learning to use the CLI is when the GUI fails to load. When the GUI fails to load, the CLI may be the only way to repair the server.

There are many different command line interfaces used in UNIX/Linux. Two very well-known CLI shells are Bourne Again Shell (bash) and Korn Shell (ksh). When the shell is incorporated into a desktop system, it is referred to as a *shell console* or *terminal emulator*.

An important difference between commands issued in UNIX/Linux is that they are case-sensitive. This means that commands designed to be issued in lowercase letters will not be recognized if issued in uppercase letters. Microsoft Windows systems recognize commands in uppercase or lowercase.

In UNIX/Linux, certain commands are restricted to use by the superuser or root and cannot be issued by ordinary users. For example, the **fdisk** command will not be recognized by the Linux system except when issued by the superuser. The following table contains a list of the most common UNIX/Linux commands. Notice that many of them are similar to those found in Microsoft Windows.

Command	Description
cd	Change the current directory
clear	Clear the display area
dir	Display the current directory
finger	Display information about the current user
halt	Shut down the system
ifconfig	Show IP configuration information; similar to Microsoft **ipconfig**
l	List files in the current directory
ls	List files in the current directory
ls –a	List both hidden and system files
ls –l	List files in long fashion
man	Access the manual pages
mkdir	Make or create a new directory
ping	Similar to Microsoft **ping** command
pwd	Print or display the current working directory path
reboot	Reboot the system
rm	Remove or delete a file
rmdir	Remove or delete a directory
su	Switch from the current user
touch	Create a file
traceroute	Similar to Microsoft **tracert**
who	Display all users currently logged on
whoami	Display who the current user is

To leave or close the KDE Konsole issue the **quit** command at the prompt. Alternatively, you can select **Session>Close session** or **Session>Quit** on the Konsole screen.

> **NOTE**
> Previous versions of KDE Konsole used the **Quit** menu item to end a session.

Equipment and Materials
- Computer with openSUSE 42.3 or later installed

> **NOTE**
> You can perform this lab activity on most versions of SUSE Linux as well as some other Linux operating systems.

Procedure

1. _____ Report to your assigned workstation.
2. _____ Boot the computer and log on using your assigned user account, not as root.

Name _____

3. _____ Open the KDE Konsole (**Application Launcher>System>Konsole**).

Goodheart-Willcox Publisher

4. _____ Issue the **ls** command and note what appears on the screen. The **ls** command consists of lowercase letters *L* and *S*. You should see a display of directories and files similar to the ones in the following screen capture.

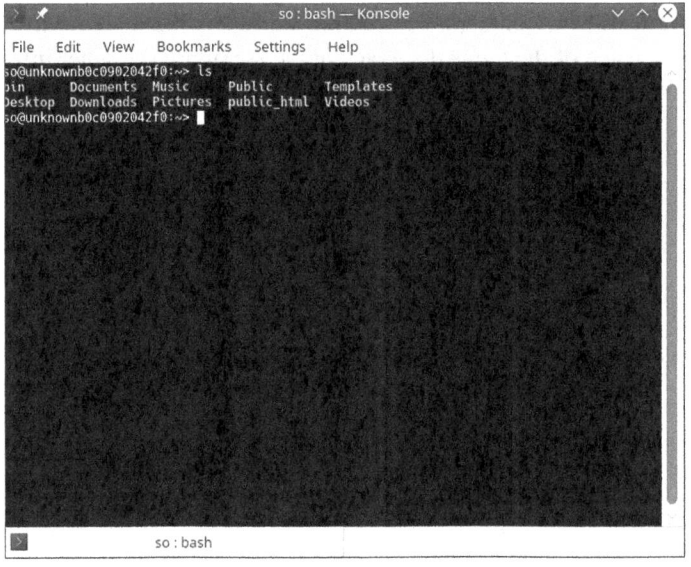

Goodheart-Willcox Publisher

5. _____ Issue the **ls** command using uppercase letters instead of lowercase letters. What is the result?

_____

6. _____ The **ls** command has switches that will modify the command. Two switches often used are **-a** and **-l**. The **-a** switch modifies the **ls** command to list all files. This means it will show hidden and system files also. The **-l** switch modifies the **ls** command to list the files in long list fashion. Issue the command **ls -al** and observe the results. You should see a screen display similar to the following.

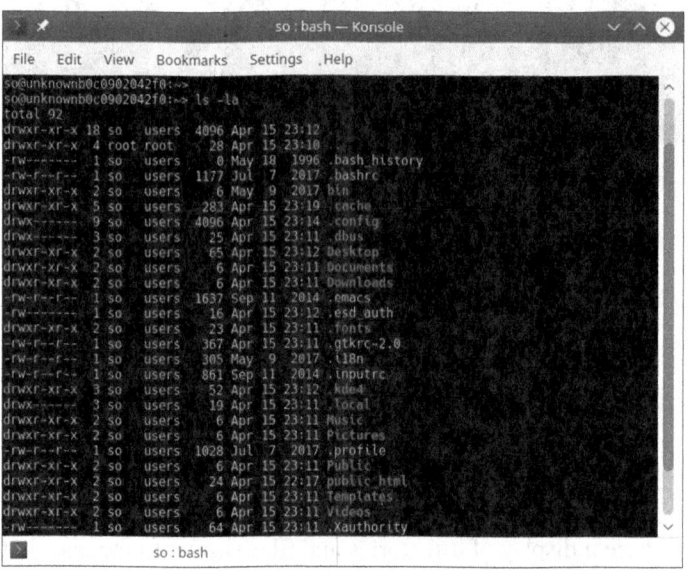

Goodheart-Willcox Publisher

All the information about the files and directories is displayed across the screen. Information about the file is read from left to right. The name of the file is displayed at the far right. The other information about the file will be explained in detail in a later lab activity. For now, you are just becoming familiar with how to use Konsole.

7. _____ Enter the **l** (lowercase L) command and observe the results.

8. _____ Now issue the **dir** command. The directories should be listed.

9. _____ Create an empty file by using the **touch** command. Issue the command touch **zfile** and then view the current directory contents using the **l** or **ls** command to verify the creation of the new file called zfile. The file should appear at the bottom of the list.

10. _____ Now create another file called zzfile and verify its creation using the **l** or **ls** command.

11. _____ Create a directory called zdir using the **mkdir** command, for example, mkdir zdir. Verify the creation of the zdir directory using the **l** or **ls** command.

12. _____ You can remove or delete the directory by using the **rmdir** command. Files can be removed or deleted using the **rm** command. To remove the directory, simply issue the command **rmdir** followed by the name of the directory, for example, **rmdir zdir**. To remove a file, simply issue the **rm** command followed by the file name, for example, **rm zfile**. Remove the zdir directory and the zfile and zzfile files using the appropriate commands. Verify they have all been removed using the **l** or **ls** command.

13. _____ Issue the **whoami** command to display the current user. The current user account name should be displayed.

14. _____ Issue the **who** command to display current information about the user.

15. _____ Another useful command that will allow you to view current information about the user is **finger**. Issue the command **finger** and view the results.

16. _____ Log on as a different user using the **Switch user** option (**Application Launcher>Leave>Switch user**). A message dialog box will ask if you would like to create a new session using desktop 2. You will also see an option asking if you would like to lock the current screen or desktop. Do not select the option to lock the screen.

Name _____

17. _____ After the new user session loads, open Konsole and issue the **whoami**, **who**, and **finger** commands. Observe the results of each command and write a brief summary of the observation.

whoami:

_____

who:

_____

finger:

_____

18. _____ Log off the current user and return to your own logon session.

> **NOTE**
> Do *not* shut down the system. Select the **Logoff** option.

19. _____ Some commands require the root password or you must be logged on as the root. You need not log off and back on as the root. A quick way to change to the root is to issue the **su** command. You will be prompted for the root password. After providing the root password, you will be issuing commands as the root user. You will remain the root user until you exit the CLI or switch to another user.

20. _____ Enter **exit** and then the **su root** command followed by the root password.

21. _____ You can shut down or reboot the Linux computer from the Konsole using the commands **halt** and **reboot**. The **halt** command will shut down the computer, and the **reboot** command will reboot the computer. Try each command now. Notice that a message will be broadcast to all users that the system will halt or reboot as applicable. You must be the root to perform these commands.

22. _____ Standard in all versions of UNIX/Linux is the user manual referred to as the man pages or manual pages. The manual pages are written in text-only format. To access the manual pages, enter the **man** command at the prompt followed by the command you want information about. For example, **man finger** will display information in the man pages about the **finger** command, including options and arguments. Issue the **man finger** command now and observe the results. You can use the [Enter] key or [Spacebar] to view additional lines of text. The [Spacebar] key displays an additional page and the [Enter] key displays one additional line of text. After you finish viewing the information, you can use the lowercase [q] key to quit or close the man pages. You can also use the mouse to close the manual pages.

23. _____ Close the manual pages.

24. _____ Display information about the **ls** command using the man pages by entering **man ls**.

25. _____ Display information about the **su**, **finger**, and **who** commands.

26. _____ Another handy command is **pwd**. The **pwd** command displays the current working directory (the directory structure you are presently in when you issue the command). For example, when the user "richard" issues the **pwd** command, that user's exact location in the directory structure will be displayed as related to their home directory. The results will be similar to /home/username. Issue the **pwd** command now and observe the results.

27. _____ Three very important troubleshooting commands are **ping**, **traceroute**, and **ifconfig**. The **ping** command is issued in a similar fashion as **ping** when using the Windows command prompt. The one big difference is that when you issue the **ping** command in Linux, it will continually repeat until you use the keyboard combination [Ctrl][C]. Enter ping 127.0.0.1. Wait for the results and then use the [Ctrl][C] key combination to stop the ping.

28. _____ Issue the **ping** command again, but this time use the ping 127.0.0.1 -c command followed by a number. The **-c** represents count, which is the number of times to issue the **ping** command. For example, ping 127.0.0.1 -c4 will result in only four pings being issued. Try the command now: ping 127.0.0.1 -c4.

29. _____ The Linux **traceroute** command is similar to Microsoft's **tracert** command and produces similar results. If your Linux workstation is connected to the Internet, try issuing the **traceroute** command now to a known Internet location such as www.g-w.com, for example, **traceroute** www.g-w.com or some other known URL. Observe the results.

> **NOTE**
> Any user can issue a **ping** command but only the root can issue the **traceroute** command.

30. _____ The **ifconfig** command is similar to the **ipconfig** command used in Windows. Issue the **ifconfig** command at the command prompt and observe the results. You should see the assigned IP address for the network adapter.

31. _____ Access the man pages to learn more about the **ping**, **traceroute**, and **ifconfig** commands.

32. _____ Review the commands used in this lab activity.

33. _____ Answer the review questions.

Review Questions

1. What is the name of the KDE terminal emulator?

2. What does the acronym CLI represent?

3. Why would a system administrator use the command-line interface rather than a graphical user interface?

4. What command ends the Konsole session?

5. What command can be used to list all the files in a directory including the hidden files?

6. What command is used to display the current logged on user?

7. What command is used to display all currently logged on to the system?

8. What command can be used to display more detailed information about the user other than **whoami**?

9. What command is used to create an empty file?

10. What command is used to stop or shut down the system?

11. What command is used to remove or delete a file?

Name _____

12. What command is used to delete or remove a directory?
   _____

13. Who can use the **halt** command?
   _____

14. What are the results of the following command ping 127.0.0.1 -c8?
   _____
   _____

15. What keyboard combination is used to stop the **ping** command?
   _____

16. What command would you use to find more information about the **finger** command?
   _____

17. List the two most common reasons for a student to issue a command incorrectly from the Konsole command prompt.
   _____
   _____
   _____

Notes

Name _____ Date _____ Class _____

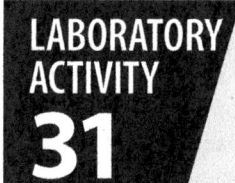

LABORATORY ACTIVITY 31
Exploring the Linux File System

Outcomes
After completing this laboratory activity, you will be able to:
- Differentiate between the Linux and Microsoft directory and file structure.
- Recall UNIX/Linux file and directory permissions.
- Use the GUI to modify file and directory permissions.
- Identify the services used to share directories and files between UNIX/Linux and Microsoft operating system users.

Introduction
In this laboratory activity, you will explore the Linux directory structure. You will explore and modify directory and file permissions using the graphical user interface (GUI). The Linux directory structure is mostly similar across all the various Linux distributions. You may have some slight differences based on what Linux distribution you are using (Ubuntu, Open SUSE, Kali, etc.) and what version of that distribution you are using. The Linux directory structure is hierarchical. The top of the directory is the root directory represented by the forward slash (/) symbol. The Linux system does not use letters in the directory structure to represent the top of the directory structure or partitions as in NTFS and FAT systems. There is no C drive in the directory structure, only /.

> **NOTE**
> Do *not* confuse the / directory with the /root directory. The /root directory is the root user's home directory.

When a new user account is created, a home directory is automatically created for the new user account. Look at the /root directory contents in the following screen capture. The Linux application used in the screen capture is Dolphin. Dolphin is a KDE file manager application. It is similar to Windows Explorer. If you are using a different Linux distribution, you might have a different file manager. However, all file managers look and operate in similar fashion. Look at the following screen capture to become familiar with the Dolphin interface.

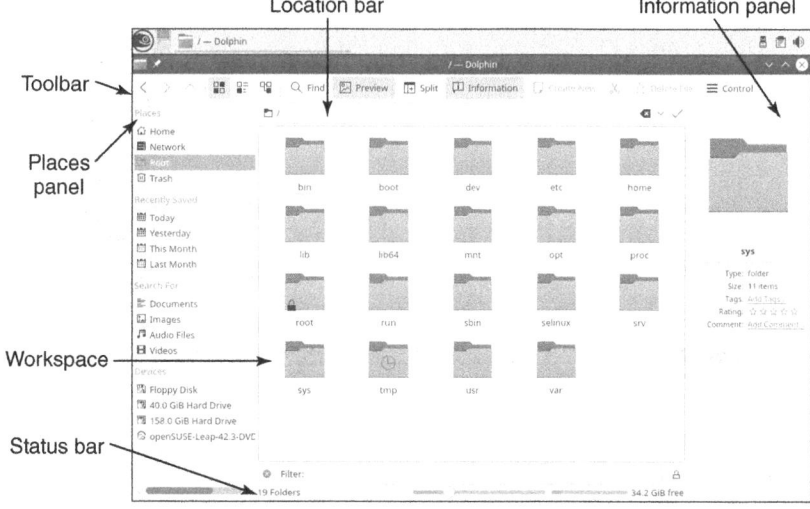

Goodheart-Willcox Publisher

The location bar, at the top, allows you to enter a path to a folder such as /home/student1/documents. This will result in opening the documents folder belonging to the student1 account. When **Network** is selected from the Places Panel, various network locations are revealed. When **Root** is selected, the top-level directories in / are displayed as they are in the previous screen capture. Notice that the forward slash (/) symbol is in the location bar. This indicates the root of the directory structure. Notice that the default directory names shown in the workspace are in lowercase letters. Also notice that one of the folders shown is called **home**. The following screen capture shows the contents of the /home directory.

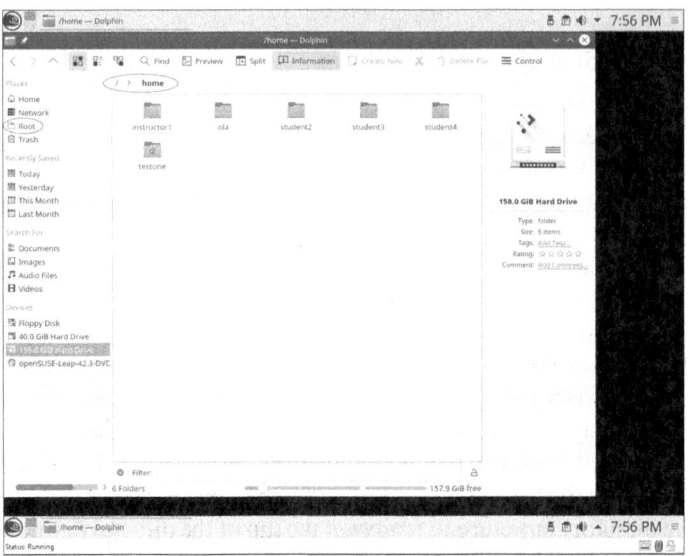

Goodheart-Willcox Publisher

You can see that there are many different user accounts in the /home directory such as ola, testone, student2, instructor1, and more. When a user account is created, a corresponding directory with the username is created. The directory with the user account name is where that particular user will store their files and applications by default. The next capture shows the contents of the user directory for user account ola.

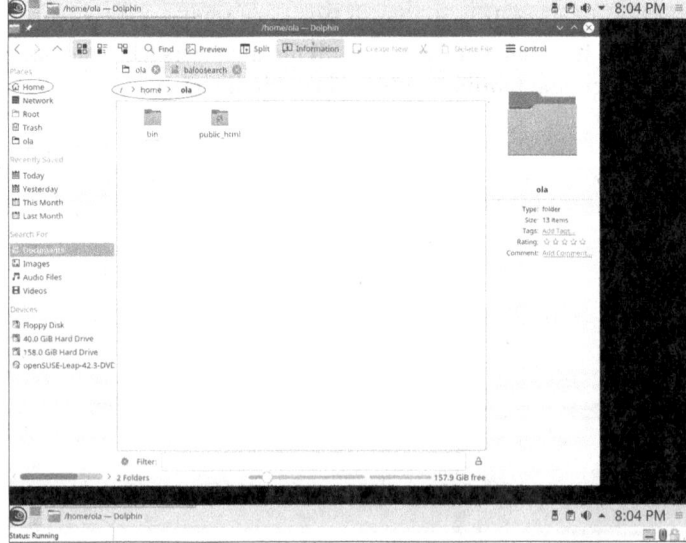

Goodheart-Willcox Publisher

In the screen capture, Home has been selected from the Places Panel, which has automatically redirected the view to the default user's home directory. In this case, the default user is ola, as indicated in the location bar as />home>ola.

There are three large arrows in the Dolphin menu bar: the **Up** arrow, the **Back** arrow, and the **Forward** arrow. The **Up** arrow automatically takes you up one level in the directory structure. The **Back** arrow takes you back to the last displayed view of the directory. The **Forward** arrow returns you to the previously viewed menu after you have used the **Back** arrow.

Name _____

There are three main differences between Microsoft NTFS and FAT directory structures and the UNIX/Linux directory structure. File and directory names are case-sensitive in UNIX/Linux operating systems; they are not case-sensitive in Microsoft Windows operating systems. Microsoft Windows uses the backslash (\) character in the directory structure. UNIX/Linux operating systems use the forward slash (/). Look at the following screen capture that compares a Linux file path with a Windows file path.

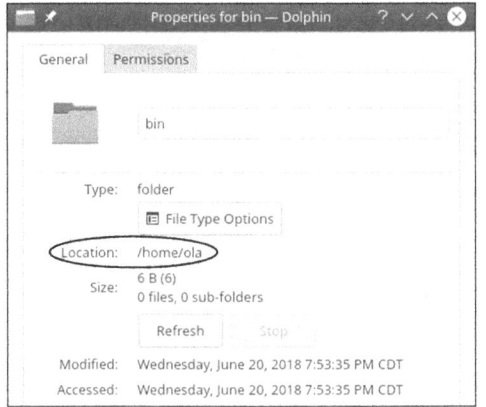

Linux User Path

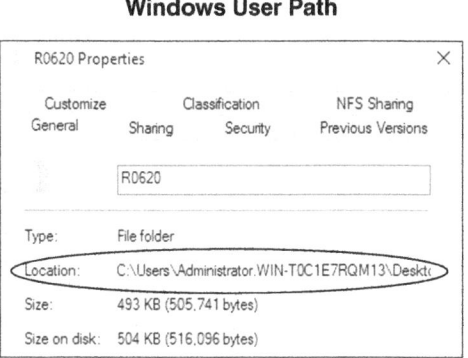

Windows User Path

Goodheart-Willcox Publisher

Windows operating systems use letters such as C, D, and E to identify partitions and storage devices. UNIX/Linux uses mount points identified by the forward slash (no letter) followed by the partition or directory name. Devices such as DVD drives and USB drives are located in the directory structure typically under the /media directory in Linux and the /mnt directory in many other Linux systems such as Red Hat.

There are two different applications for file management in KDE: Dolphin and Konqueror. Dolphin is the default KDE file manager. Konqueror functions as both a web browser and a file manager. In fact, all web browsers can also be used to navigate files and directories.

Equipment and Materials

- Computer with Linux installed
- The following information:

User account name:

_____

User account password:

_____

Root password:

_____

Procedure

1. _____ Report to your assigned workstation.

2. _____ Boot the computer and log on using your assigned user account, *not* as root. Later, you may need the root password to access certain configuration options.

3. _____ After you log on, open Dolphin by selecting the icon in the KDE Panel that resembles a file cabinet.

Goodheart-Willcox Publisher

4. _____ You should now see the Dolphin file manager similar to the one presented in the lab introduction.

5. _____ Select **Home** located from the Places Panel to reveal the home directory contents associated with your user account.

6. _____ Right-click one of the folders to reveal a shortcut menu with various options similar to that in the following screen capture. These same options are available in the menu bar, but the right-click method is more convenient.

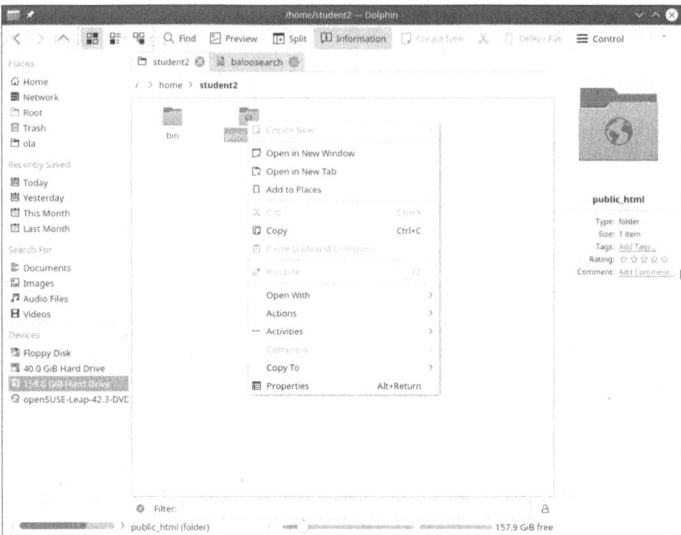

Goodheart-Willcox Publisher

7. _____ Select **Properties** from the shortcut menu. The **General** tab should be displayed by default and will appear similar to that in the following screen capture. The **General** tab provides information such as the folder's location.

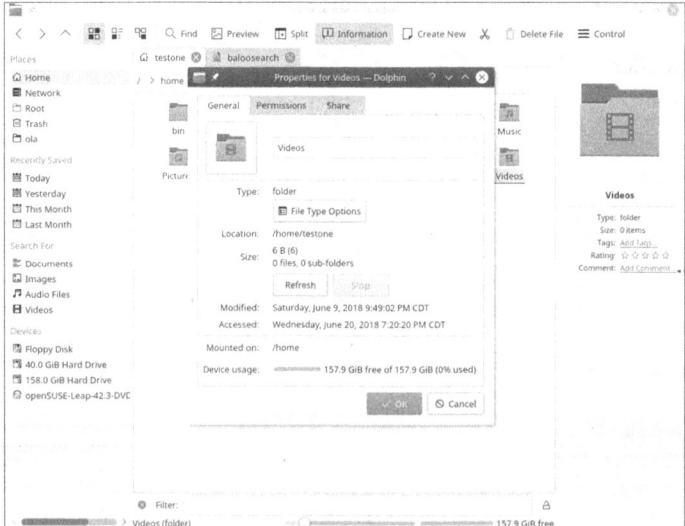

Goodheart-Willcox Publisher

Name _____

8. _____ Now select the **Permissions** tab.

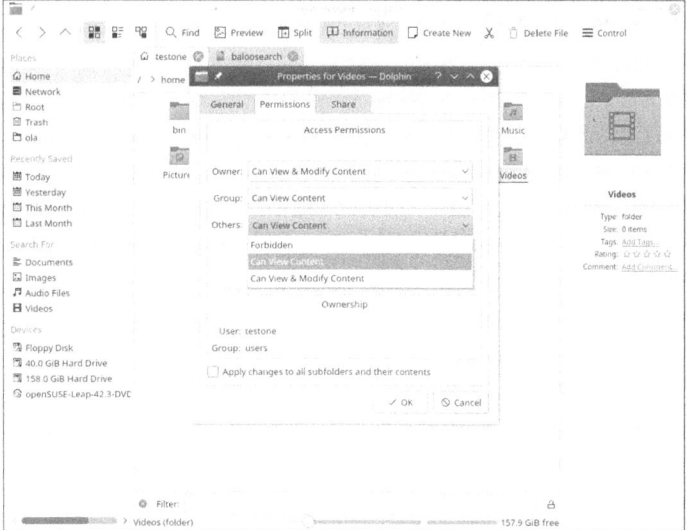

Goodheart-Willcox Publisher

9. _____ The three general access permissions are the following:
- Forbidden
- Can View Content
- Can View & Modify Content

10. _____ The **Advanced** button will allow you to configure the typical Linux set of permissions.

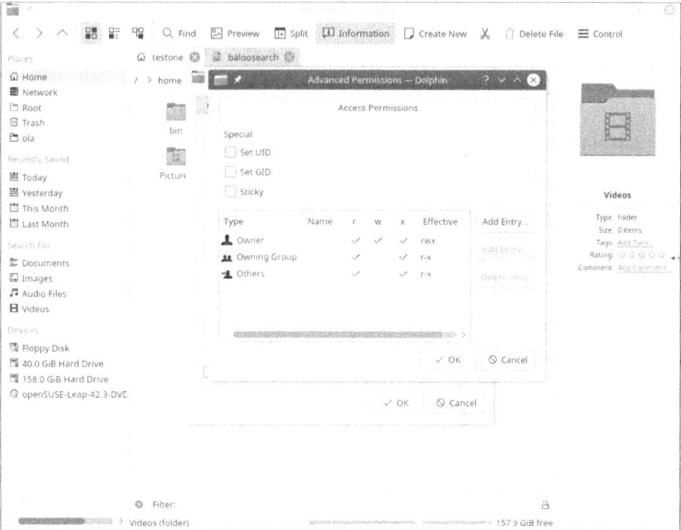

Goodheart-Willcox Publisher

11. _____ The advanced permissions are the following:
- Read (r)
- Write (w)
- Execute (x)

12. _____ The Dolphin file manager refers to these as "advanced permissions," but read, write, and execute are the standard UNIX/Linux set of permissions.

13. _____ Close the **Advanced Permissions** dialog box and select the **Share** tab. The **Share** tab allows you to configure the folder for sharing. The **Share with Samba (Microsoft Windows)** checkbox will allow you to configure the selected folder or file for sharing.

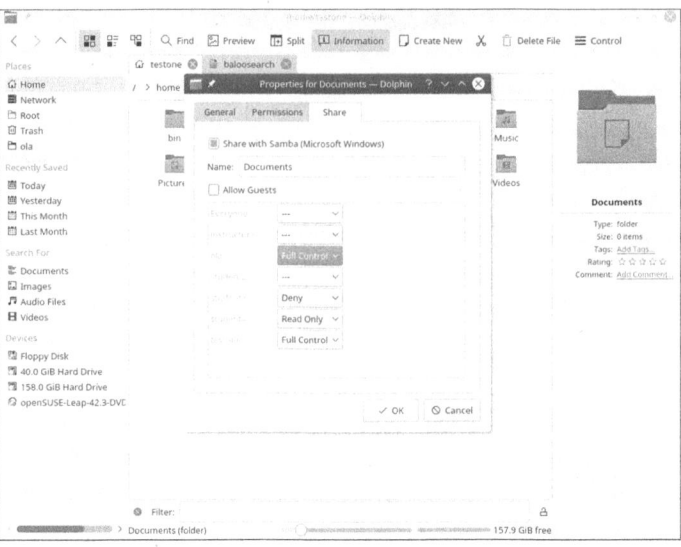

Goodheart-Willcox Publisher

14. _____ Check the **Share with Samba (Microsoft Windows)** checkbox.

15. _____ Take a few minutes to explore the various directory and folder options. Also, practice accessing and navigating Dolphin.

16. _____ Answer the review questions.

Review Questions

1. What are the three general Linux file and directory permissions?

   _____
   _____
   _____

2. What are the three major differences between the Microsoft file and directory structure and the Linux file and directory structure?

   _____
   _____
   _____
   _____
   _____

3. What does UNIX/Linux use in place of a partition identified by the colon and letter symbol?

   _____
   _____

4. What general file permission would you apply to allow users to modify the contents of a memo?

   _____

Name _____

5. What file permission would you apply to allow a user to only view the contents of a memo?
   _____

6. Which service is used to allow Windows operating system users to access files on a UNIX/Linux computer over a network connection?
   _____

7. Which service is used to allow UNIX/Linux operating system users to access files on a Windows computer over a network connection?
   _____

Notes

Name _____ Date _____ Class _____

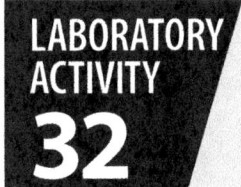

LABORATORY ACTIVITY 32
Introduction to Samba

Outcomes
After completing this laboratory activity, you will be able to:
- Carry out proper procedures to install and configure the Samba service.
- Use the Dolphin file manager to browse the local area network.
- Identify Samba shares on the network.
- Differentiate between Samba shares and NTFS shares.
- Use the **net view** command to view all available computers on the local network.

Introduction
In this laboratory activity, you will explore how to configure the Samba service on a Linux computer. Samba allows Microsoft computers to access files on a UNIX/Linux system. NFS is used to support sharing between UNIX/Linux computers and to allow UNIX/Linux computers to access Windows shares. Windows Server 2022 can be configured for NFS so that UNIX/Linux operating system users can access shares on the Windows Server.

> **NOTE**
> When viewed with a protocol analyzer at a Windows computer, you will see SMB, SMB2, SMB3, or CIFS identified as the application level protocol used to support share transfers for both Samba and NFS.

Samba is generally referred to as a *service* and includes a software package that allows a computer to serve as a Samba server or as a Samba client. Samba is generally not configured automatically in UNIX/Linux. It generally needs to be configured and started as a service on the host computer. Today, many versions of Linux operating systems automatically configure Samba and NFS when a directory or file is configured for sharing.

When a peer-to-peer network is configured to share files and printers, all computers must be members of the same workgroup. This means all computers in the same peer-to-peer should have the same workgroup name.

All computers including the Samba server should have an identical user account configured with identical passwords. For example, a user account with a username such as **student1** and password **Pa$$word123** must be created on each computer. The identical accounts may already exist from previous labs.

Computers in the local area network will have the same IPv4 subnet mask and the same network address. For example, all computers should have 255.255.255.0 for a subnet mask and 192.168.0.xxx for an IPv4 address. The 192.168.0 indicates the network address and the xxx indicates the computer or host address. The host address is unique for each computer on the network. Be aware that each computer typically generates a random IPv6 address. All local network traffic uses an IPv6 address to exchange frames and packets.

Before you install the Samba service, you should exchange pings between a Windows computer and the Linux computers. This will verify that TCP/IP is configured on each computer and is working correctly.

A handy tool is the **net view** command. When issued from the command prompt of a Windows computer, all locally connected computers are identified, even Linux computers.

When run, the **net view** command will show the names of all networked Linux computers as well as their Samba versions and their Linux operating system versions. Be aware that a firewall can prevent seeing other computers in the peer-to-peer network. You should disable the firewall on each computer for this lab activity. Be aware that you typically must enable sharing on each computer before it can be viewed by other members of the peer-to-peer network.

When using Samba, packet exchanges are somewhat slow, and you may experience slight delays before changes to the configuration take effect. Some versions of Linux require a reboot before the new configuration takes effect. Typically, there will be a message to inform you if a reboot is necessary. Be sure to read all messages as they appear on the screen when performing the configuration.

Equipment and Materials

- Two computers Linux or later installed
- Computer with Windows 10 or Windows 11 installed
- The following information provided by your instructor:

Linux root password:

_____

Matching user account name and password:

_____

Workgroup name:

_____

Domain name:

_____

Procedure

1. _____ Report to your assigned workstation.

2. _____ Boot and log on to the Linux computers and the Windows computer and verify they are in working order.

3. _____ Write down the computer name and IPv4 address assigned to each computer. Use the **ipconfig/all** command on the Windows computer and use the **ifconfig** command on the Linux computers to view the assigned addresses.

> **NOTE**
> At the Linux computer, you need to be the root to use the **ifconfig** command. The command prompt will provide the name of the Linux workstation.

Linux computer 1 name: _____

Linux computer 1 IPv4 address: _____

Linux computer 2 name: _____

Linux computer 2 IPv4 address: _____

Windows computer name: _____

Windows computer 1 IPv4 address: _____

4. _____ Exchange pings between the computers to ensure they are in the same network and that the TCP/IP stack is configured correctly. You can use one computer, such as the Windows computer, to ping the others. This will generally confirm the TCP/IP connections. Do this before progressing in the lab activity. If you cannot exchange pings, call your instructor for assistance.

Name _____

On one of the Linux computers, open YaST and then select **Network Services>Windows Domain Membership** as indicated in the following screen capture.

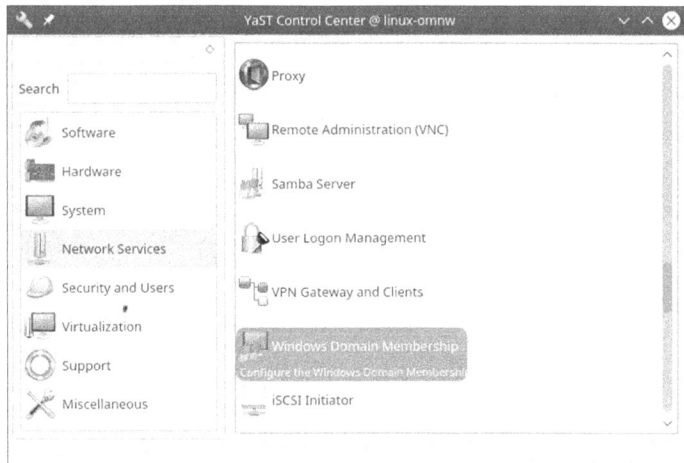

Goodheart-Willcox Publisher

This is a feature in Linux that allows for a much easier configuration as a member of a Windows domain or workgroup.

5. _____ In the **Windows Domain Membership** dialog box, type in the name of the Windows workgroup the Linux computers will be joining. For example, enter Workgroup, which is the default Windows 10 workgroup name. Your instructor may be using a different workgroup name for this project. Also, select the **Allow Users to Share Their Directories** option. Click **OK** when finished to close the dialog box and return to the YaST Control Center.

Goodheart-Willcox Publisher

6. ____ From the YaST Control Center, access **Network Services>Samba Server**. This option is used to configure a Samba server.

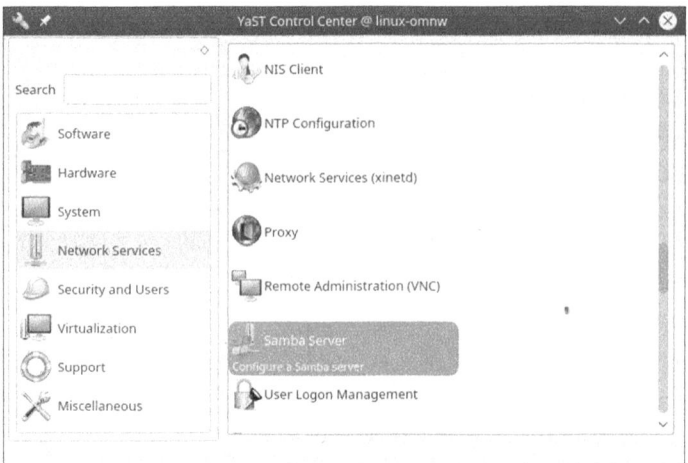

Goodheart-Willcox Publisher

The **Samba Configuration** dialog box should open to the **Shares** tab. If not, select the **Shares** tab now. All available shares should be listed. If the desired share is not listed, add it by clicking the **Add** button and entering the share name, share description, and share path. Click **OK**.

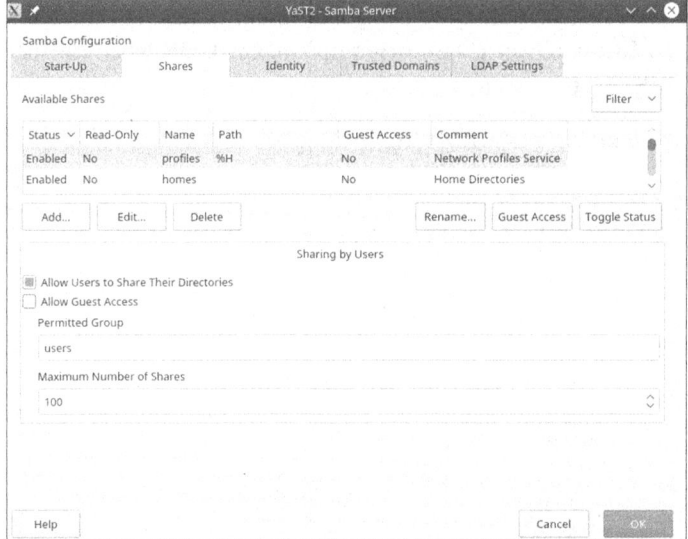

Goodheart-Willcox Publisher

Name _____

7. _____ Select the **Start-Up** tab and then select the **During Boot** option. This will allow the Samba service to start automatically each time the Linux computer is started. If not selected, the service must be manually started after the computer is booted. Click **OK**. The computer should be configured as a Samba server allowing Windows computers to access its shares.

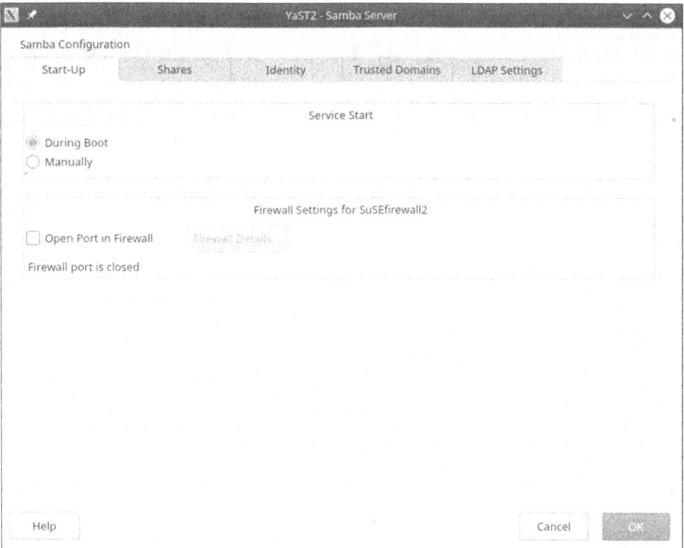

Goodheart-Willcox Publisher

8. _____ Repeat steps 5 through 8 on the other Linux computer.

9. _____ At the Windows computer, type Network in the **Search** box and then click **Network** from the **Programs** list. Network will open and look similar to that in the following screen capture.

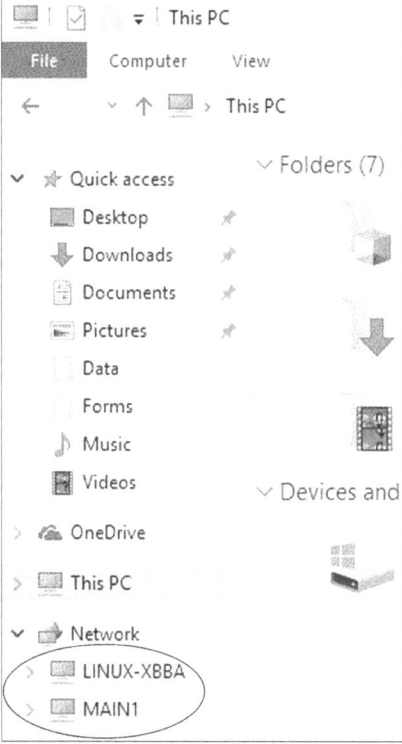

Goodheart-Willcox Publisher

In the screen capture, you will see that the Linux computers have identical icons as the Windows computers. Only the assigned names are different. If the Linux computers are not viewable on your Windows computer, restart the Linux computers.

10. _____ At the Windows computer, open the command prompt and issue the **net view** command. You should see all local computers listed, including the Linux computers. If not, call your instructor for assistance.

11. _____ At either Linux computer, open Dolphin.

12. _____ Select the **Network** option from the **Places Panel**. You should see results similar to that in the following screen capture such as the **Network**, **Network Services**, **Samba Shares**, and **Add Network Folder** icons. Your view may be different, especially if your workstation is shared by other students.

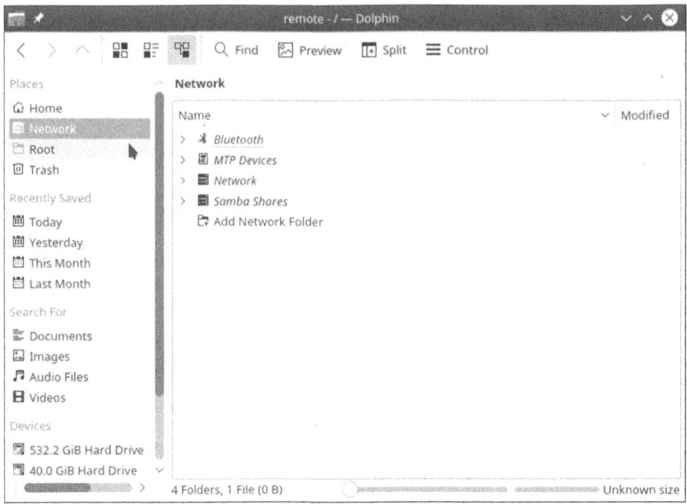

Goodheart-Willcox Publisher

13. _____ Click **Samba Shares**. A list featuring the workgroup name you selected will display.

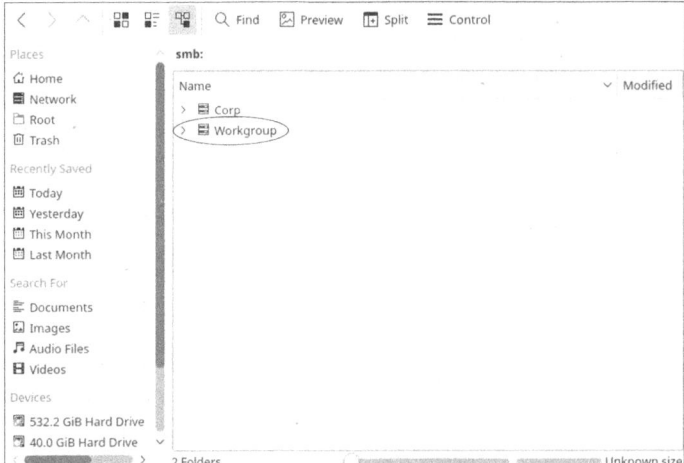

Goodheart-Willcox Publisher

Name _____

14. _____ Click **Workgroup**. You should see the computers that are members of the workgroup similar to that in the following screen capture.

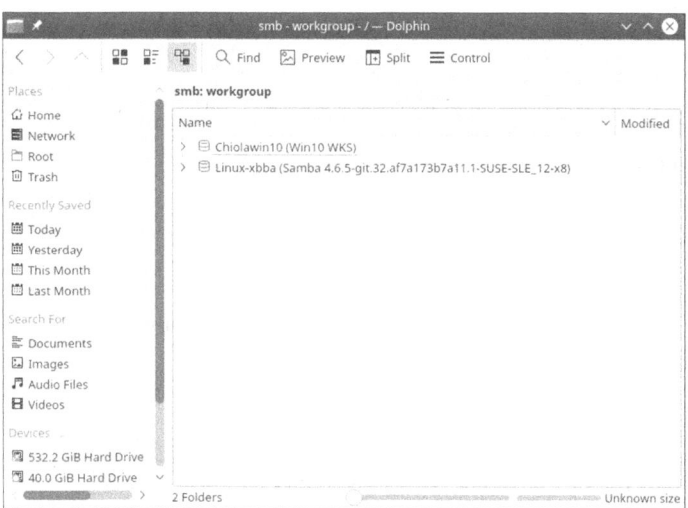

Goodheart-Willcox Publisher

If you do not see any computers, try pressing [Alt] [F2], which will produce a dialog box. Enter smb:/// in the text box and then press [Enter]. This is not performed from the terminal or command prompt. The key combination is performed while Dolphin is opened. Be sure to include the three slashes. This is not a typo. This is a Linux text command that should produce the workgroup. If not, call your instructor for assistance.

15. _____ Click one of the Linux computer icons. Wait a few seconds and you should see the available shares similar to that in the following screen capture.

Goodheart-Willcox Publisher

16. _____ Use the **Back** arrow to go back or simply select the **Network** from the **Places Panel**.

17. _____ Navigate back into the workgroup. This time, access a Windows share.

18. _____ Return all computers to the configuration specified by your instructor.

19. _____ Answer the review questions.

Review Questions

1. What is the purpose of Samba?

2. What is the purpose of NFS?

3. What does a successful ping exchange between a Microsoft computer and a Linux computer indicate?

4. What service is available in Linux that supports access to a Windows Domain?

5. What command can be entered from a Windows command prompt that will display all local area network computers?

6. What will be listed under the Net View **Remark** column, which will help identify Linux computers?

Name _____ Date _____ Class _____

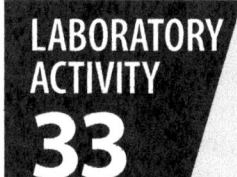

Inspecting and Defragmenting Partitions

Outcomes

After completing this laboratory activity, you will be able to:
- Use the Disk Management utility to inspect hard disk drive partitions.
- Use the Optimize Drives utility to defragment hard disk drive partitions.

Introduction

In this laboratory activity, you will inspect and defragment the hard disk drives on a Windows 2019 or Windows 2022 server using the Disk Management and Optimize Drive utilities.

The Disk Management utility allows you to inspect the condition of the server's hard disk drives. The Disk Management utility can be accessed through **Start>Administrative Tools**. It can also be accessed through **Server Manager>Tools>Computer Management**.

Information such as the drive's storage capacity, unused disk space, file system type (FAT, NTFS), and disk type (basic, dynamic) will display. Look at the following figure. Notice that the bottom pane reveals a graphical view of the server's hard disk drive configuration. It also displays details about the drive and its partitions. The first physical drive is named Disk 0. One partition of Disk 0 is labeled C:. The first drive also contains an unallocated area and other partitions that have not been assigned drive letters. The unallocated area contains no partitions and is unformatted at this time. The term *unallocated* indicates an unformatted and unpartitioned area on a primary partition. Both Disk 0 and Disk 1 are basic disks. Disk 1 contains NTFS as well as FAT- partitions. If a partition is marked *free space*, it means that the area is an extended partition that can be used to create logical drives.

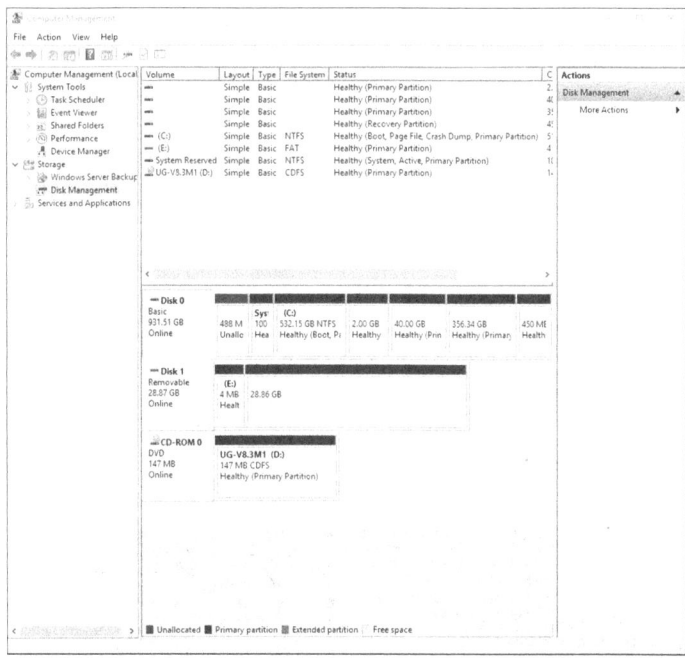

Goodheart-Willcox Publisher

Right-clicking the disk identification area in the bottom pane reveals a shortcut menu with the option to convert the drive to dynamic disk. A different shortcut menu displays when you right-click the partition. This shortcut menu allows you to change the volume label and to view the partition's properties.

Information about the system's drives is also revealed in the top pane. Notice the information presented about partition C, which states it is a simple (layout), basic (type), NTFS (file system) partition that is healthy (status). It also indicates that it is a system and boot partition as well as an active partition with a page file and other attributes.

The Optimize Drive utility is used to enhance disk access performance by organizing files into contiguous sectors. Files are stored in small areas on the disk drive called *sectors*. The smallest sector size is 512 bytes. If a file is larger than the sector size, it is stored in two or more sectors. As files are added, deleted, and modified on the hard disk drive, files become fragmented. Fragmented means that a file is no longer stored in contiguous sectors.

> **NOTE**
> The size of a sector depends on the storage capacity of the hard disk drive and the type of file system used, such as FAT32 and NTFS.

The Optimize Drives utility, called Disk Defragmenter in earlier versions of Windows, can be accessed from **Properties>Tools**, as shown in the following screen capture.

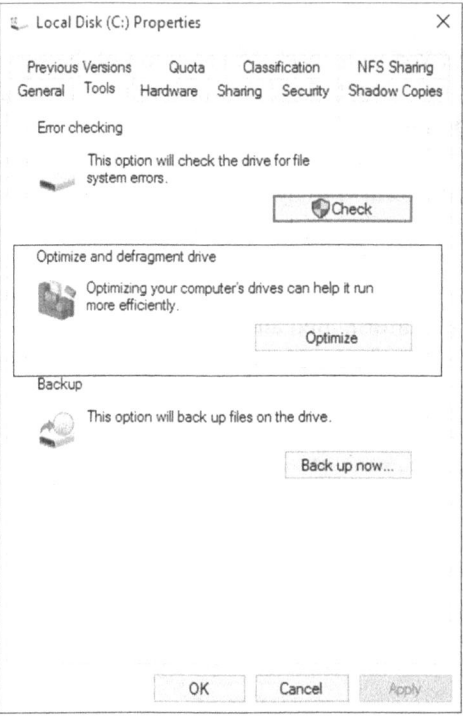

Goodheart-Willcox Publisher

The Optimize Drives utility can also be run from the command prompt using the **defrag** command. For example, you would enter defrag e: -a to analyze drive E. A window similar to the following will display information about the size of the drive, amount of free space, and how much of the drive is fragmented. If the disk is severely fragmented, a message will appear telling you to defragment the drive.

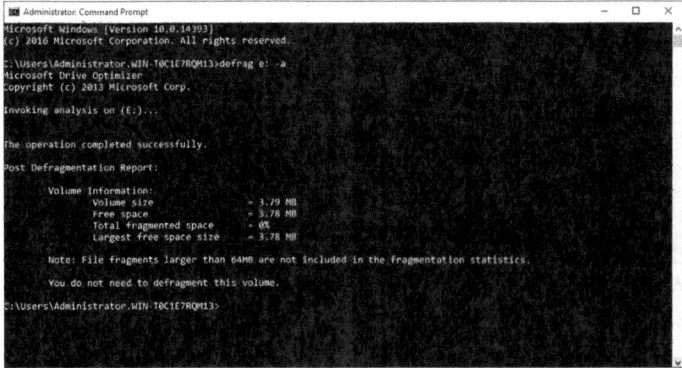

Goodheart-Willcox Publisher

Name _____

The Optimize Drives utility is similar in most versions of Windows operating systems. The following is a screen capture of the **defrag help** command results. This command reveals a list of command switches, also known as *parameters*, and several examples of the command.

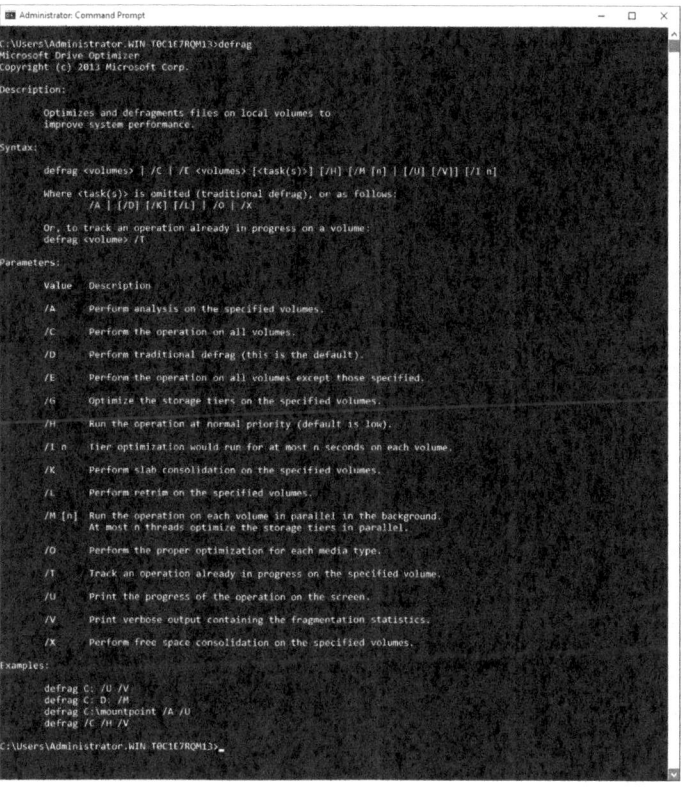

Goodheart-Willcox Publisher

Equipment and Materials

- Computer with Windows Server 2019 or Windows 2022, Windows 10 or Windows 11 installed

> **NOTE**
> The Optimize Drives utility is so similar in the various Microsoft operating systems you can use any of them to perform this lab activity. The procedure and screen captures for this lab activity were created on a Windows 10 computer.

Procedure

1. _____ Report to your assigned workstation.

2. _____ Boot the computer and verify that it is in working order.

3. _____ After logging on to the computer, open Server Manager (Windows Server 2019 or 2022) or Computer Management (Windows 10 or 11) by right-clicking **Computer** and selecting **Manage** from the shortcut menu.

4. _____ Select **Disk Management** from the right-hand pane as shown in the following screen capture. Information similar to the following about the disk drives and partitions should display.

Goodheart-Willcox Publisher

5. _____ Answer the following questions about the hard disk drive you are inspecting.

Physical size:

_____

First partition size:

_____

First partition file type:

_____

Type of partition (basic disk or dynamic):

_____

Name _____

6. _____ Right-click the C partition and select **Properties** from the shortcut menu. The **Properties** dialog box for the drive will display.

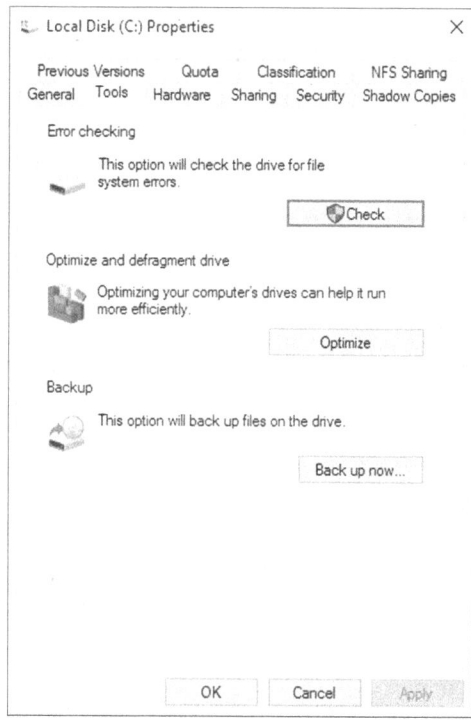

Goodheart-Willcox Publisher

7. _____ Click **Optimize**. A dialog box similar to the following will display.

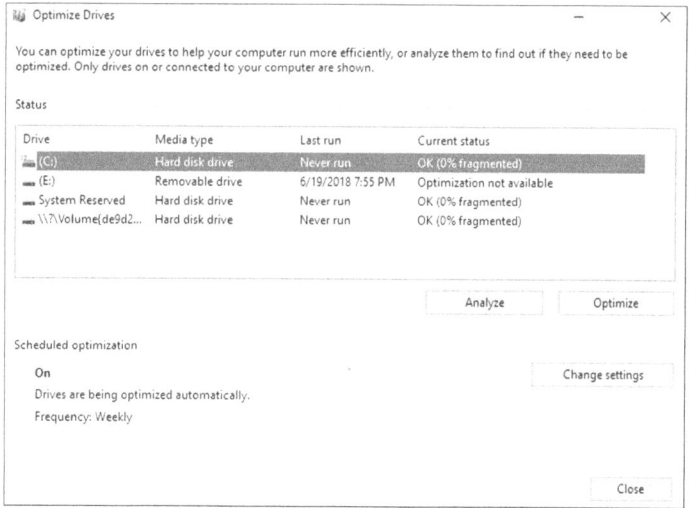

Goodheart-Willcox Publisher

The dialog box will vary somewhat according to the operating system you are using for this laboratory activity.

> **NOTE**
> You may be informed that the disk does not need to be defragmented.

Look at the **Change settings** button. The option allows you to choose a day of the week and the hour to perform a routine defragmentation of the disk drive, if necessary. Also, notice that the time of the last defragmentation appears in the **Current status** text box.

8. _____ Close Optimize Drives, the disk **Properties** dialog box, and Server Manager or Computer Management.

9. _____ Access the command prompt and enter the following command: **defrag c: -a**. The Disk Defragmenter utility should automatically start analyzing the disk. The results should display after a few minutes. Write down the analysis results in the space provided.

_____
_____
_____
_____

10. _____ Answer the review questions and then return all materials to their proper storage areas.

Review Questions

1. What information is revealed by the Disk Management utility?

_____
_____
_____

2. What is the purpose of defragmenting a hard disk drive?

_____
_____
_____

3. What command is issued at the command prompt to defragment drive C?

_____

4. In general, what is the smallest sector size?

_____

Name _____ Date _____ Class _____

Using the Disk Management Utility

Outcomes

After completing this laboratory activity, you will be able to:
- Differentiate between a partition and volume.
- Use the Disk Management utility to create, format, and remove a partition or volume.
- Use the Disk Management utility to extend or shrink a volume.

Introduction

In this laboratory activity, you will create and format a volume. You will then remove the newly created volume. A volume is a section of one or more hard disk drives treated as a single disk space. It is identified with either a drive letter or a mount point. A mount point is a location inside an existing empty folder formatted as NTFS. A mounted drive functions the same as any other volume, but it is identified by a name rather than a drive letter.

A partition is a section of one hard disk drive treated as a single disk space. Partitions and volumes identified by drive letters have a maximum of 26 possible letters. A mount point uses a name rather than a letter, which means there is no limit to the number of volumes that can be created on one or more hard disk drives.

> **NOTE**
>
> The terms *partition* and *volume* are used interchangeably today. Originally, the term *partition* was used to describe a section of a physical disk. The term *volume* was introduced with the concept of dynamic disk and the NTFS file system. A volume is a section of a physical disk, but it can also span across two or more physical disks.

In the following screen capture, the shortcut menu is shown as it appears for the unallocated portion of the hard disk drive.

Goodheart-Willcox Publisher

The only options available are **New Simple Volume**, **Properties**, and **Help**. The other options, **New Spanned Volume**, **New Striped Volume**, **New Mirrored Volume**, and **New RAID-5 Volume**, are not available because they require a second physical disk drive, which is not installed on this particular computer. Right-clicking drive C will reveal several options that are different from the unallocated drive portion as shown in the following screen capture. The available options are **Open**, **Explore**, **Change Drive Letter and Paths**, **Shrink Volume**, **Properties**, and **Help**. Note that the options **Mark Partition as Active**, **Format**, **Extend Volume**, and **Delete Volume** are unavailable on this particular computer.

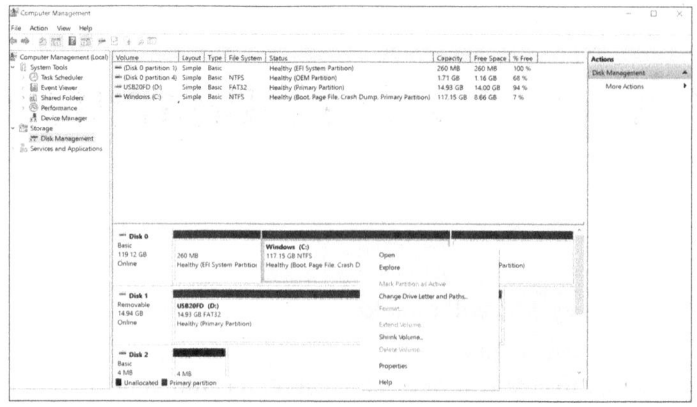

Goodheart-Willcox Publisher

Notice in the previous screen capture the System Reserved partition, which is also known as the *Microsoft Reserved Partition*. The existence of the System Reserved partition will depend on the computer firmware. There are two types of firmware: Basic Input Output System (BIOS) and Extensible Firmware Interface (EFI). The EFI is an enhanced version of the BIOS found on modern computers.

In addition, the type of partition table used, master boot record (MBR) or globally unique identifier (GUID), will depend on the firmware. MBR is the original and most common partition table used. It is supported by all current Microsoft operating systems. The globally unique identifier partition table (GPT) is an updated version of the MBR partition table. There are many advantages to the GPT, but the two most important advantages are the capability of larger partitions than MBR and exceeding the MBR limitation of four primary partitions. GPT can support disks larger than 2 TB; MBR cannot. MBR partition table supports only four partitions or three partitions and one extended partition. GPT can support up to 128 partitions.

> **NOTE**
>
> All disks with a GPT also contain an MBR partition table. The reason is to protect the GPT from older software utilities that may think that the MBR partition table is missing and try to repair or recreate it, thus damaging the GPT.

NTFS has two classifications of disks: dynamic and basic. Basic disk refers to the original Microsoft Disk Operating system (MS-DOS) style of partitioning and formatting a disk. Dynamic disk was first introduced with the Windows 2000 operating system and has continued on to Windows 11. Basic disk is created by default. It can then be converted to dynamic disk. Dynamic disk overcomes many limitations of basic disk.

Basic Disk	Dynamic Disk
Can be accessed by MS-DOS programs, such as Fdisk.	Cannot be viewed or modified by Fdisk. Uses the DiskPart utility instead to view and modify volumes/partitions.
Does not support RAID configurations.	Required for RAID configurations on Microsoft computers.
Cannot span multiple physical disks.	Can span multiple physical disks.
Cannot use mount points.	Uses mount points.

Name _____

Equipment and Materials

- Windows 10 or Windows 11 computer. The hard disk drive should have unallocated space available. (A server is not required for this laboratory activity.)
- Simple volume size (5 GB recommended): _____

> **NOTE**
> Because of limited class time, you may wish to create and format a small partition. The amount of time for the lab will be directly related to the size of the partition you format.

> **NOTE**
> Do *not* alter the partitions on the computer without explicit permission of your instructor.

Procedure

1. _____ Report to your assigned workstation.

2. _____ Boot the computer and verify that it is in working order.

3. _____ Open Computer Management and then select **Disk Management**.

4. _____ Right-click the unallocated disk space area and then select **New Simple Volume** from the shortcut menu. The **New Simple Volume Wizard** dialog box will automatically appear similar to the one in the following screen capture.

Goodheart-Willcox Publisher

> **NOTE**
> The exact appearance of the New Simple Volume Wizard will vary somewhat according to the operating system you are using.

5. ____ Click **Next** to continue. A dialog box similar to the following will display prompting you for the simple volume size in megabytes.

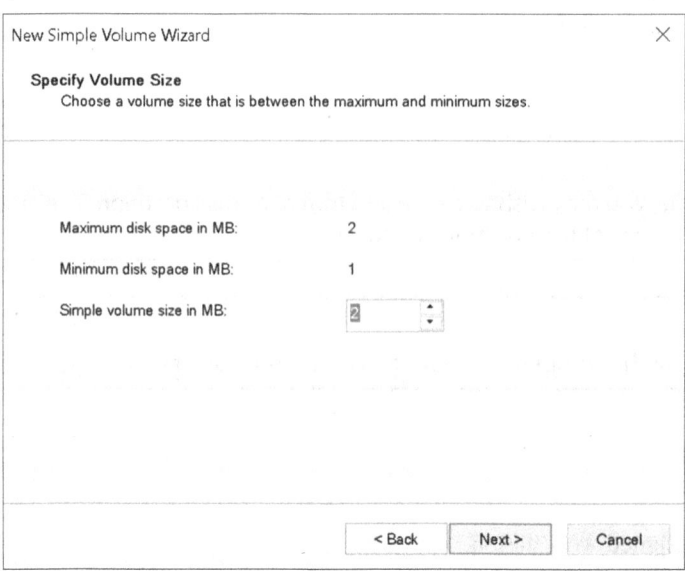

Goodheart-Willcox Publisher

For this laboratory activity, enter the value of the new simple volume as indicated by your instructor at the beginning of this lab activity. The recommended value is 5 GB.

6. ____ Click **Next**. A dialog box similar to the following will prompt you to assign a drive letter for the partition. Notice that you also have the option to mount the volume in an empty NTFS folder. This allows you to use a folder rather than a drive letter.

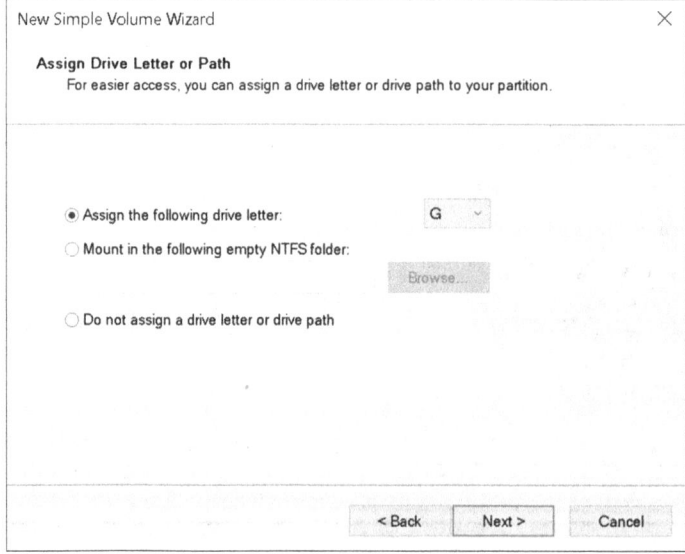

Goodheart-Willcox Publisher

186 Networking Fundamentals Lab Manual

Name _____

7. _____ Click **Next**. You will be prompted for the file system type and allocation unit size. The default file system is NTFS, but you may also choose FAT32. The default allocation unit size is automatically selected by the New Simple Volume Wizard, but the minimum size is 512 bytes.

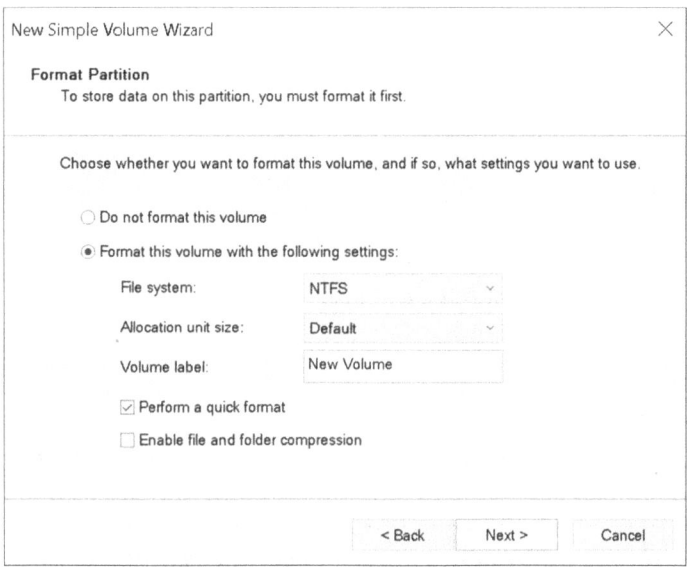

Goodheart-Willcox Publisher

There may also be an option for a volume label, which is a name for the partition. The default name is New Volume, but you could name it anything you like. The volume label cannot exceed 32 characters for NTFS and 11 characters for FAT. Similar to file naming restrictions, it cannot contain spaces or any of the following characters: *? | . , ; + = [ ] < >

8. _____ Click **Next**. A summary of the settings you selected will be displayed for your review. You can accept the settings, go back and make appropriate changes, or cancel the operation.

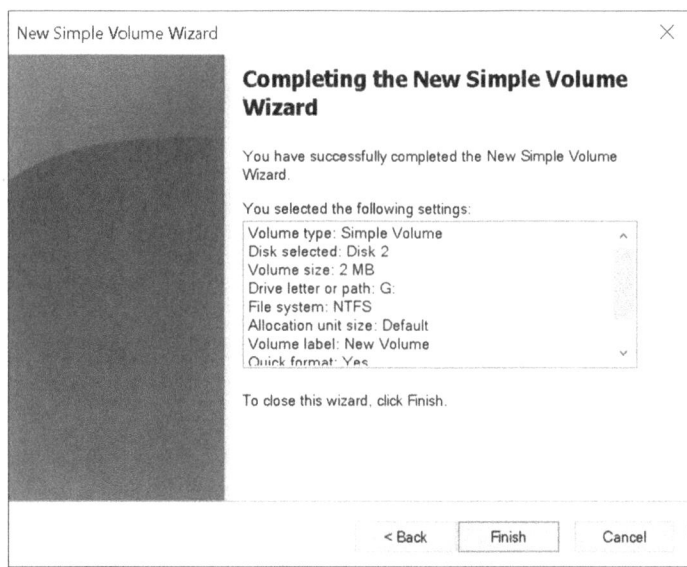

Goodheart-Willcox Publisher

9. _____ Click **Finish**. The new partition will be created and formatted as specified. The format operation should take a few minutes. The larger the partition, the longer it will take.

10. _____ After the partition has been formatted, have your instructor inspect your new partition.

11. _____ Remove the new partition by right-clicking of the partition and then selecting the **Delete Volume** from the shortcut menu.

12. _____ Answer the review questions and then return all materials to their proper storage areas.

Review Questions

1. _____ How is the first physical drive identified?
   A. Disk 0
   B. Disk 1
   C. Disk A:
   D. Drive 1

2. What is the difference between a partition and a volume?

   _____

   _____

3. What is the maximum number of primary partitions that can be created using MBR?

   _____

4. What is the maximum number of partitions that can be created using GPT?

   _____

Name _____ Date _____ Class _____

Installing a RAID System

Outcomes

After completing this laboratory activity, you will be able to:
- Use the Disk Management utility to install a RAID 1 system.
- Summarize how fault tolerance is achieved using a RAID 1 and RAID 5 system.

Introduction

In this laboratory activity, you will install and configure a RAID 1 system, also known as a *mirror* or *duplex* configuration. RAID 1 uses two disk drives. Each hard disk drive contains a volume that is a duplicate of the other. RAID 1 is one way of providing fault tolerance. RAID 5 is another. It requires three hard disk drives. The data is striped across all three drives. If one of the three drives fails, it can be replaced by a new hard disk drive. After the failed drive is replaced, the stripe of data is automatically rebuilt based on data and information stored on the other two drives.

Microsoft operating systems require that dynamic disk be used for RAID configurations. Therefore, when creating a RAID configuration on a basic disk, a dialog box will appear with a warning stating that if you convert a basic disk to a dynamic disk, any operating systems contained on the volume, aside from the boot volume, will not start. If your workstation contains a multiboot operating system, you may not be able to boot any operating system other than the default.

The following screen capture shows how a mirror configuration will appear in the Disk Management utility. Notice that both physical disks have been converted to dynamic disk and that both physical disks share a mirrored partition (F). Also, notice that the mirrored partitions are the same size. Every time data is saved to partition F, the data is saved to both partitions labeled as F:. The mirror ensures redundancy and prevents data loss caused by a failed drive. The only disadvantage is that it takes longer to save data because the data is written twice, once to each drive.

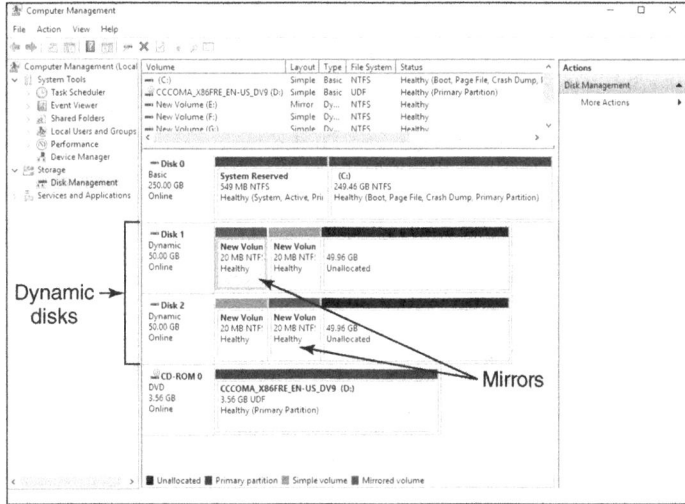

Goodheart-Willcox Publisher

> **NOTE**
> This lab can also be performed using software to create a RAID system.

Equipment and Materials

- Computer with Windows Server 2016, 2019, or 2022 installed (Note, this lab activity can also be performed on a Windows 10 or Windows 11 computer.)
- ATA or SATA hard disk drive to match existing hard disk drive if using hardware RAID
- A set of tweezers if using an ATA drive (You will need this to remove jumpers when configuring the drives as slave and master.)
- Antistatic wrist strap
- Flat-tip or Phillips screwdriver

> **NOTE**
> This lab activity is based in part on knowledge acquired in the previous lab activity.

> **NOTE**
> The instructor may wish you to remove the mirror configuration and the newly added hard disk drive so that the computer can be used by other students. Check with your instructor to verify if the computer should be returned to its original condition.

Procedure

1. ____ Gather all required materials and report to your assigned workstation.

2. ____ Boot the computer and verify it is in working order.

3. ____ If using hardware RAID, check if there is unallocated disk space on the first hard disk drive (Disk 0) that can serve as part of the mirrored disk set.

4. ____ Shut down the computer and unplug the power cord before installing the second hard disk drive (Disk 1). Be sure to follow the manufacturer's installation recommendations and procedures. Remember to use an antistatic wrist strap during this procedure.

5. ____ After the second drive (Disk 1) has been installed, reboot the computer. The second hard disk drive should be automatically detected and initialized. If the drive is not automatically detected, access the Disk Management utility and select **Action>Rescan Disks** from the menu. If the drive is still not detected, call your instructor for assistance.

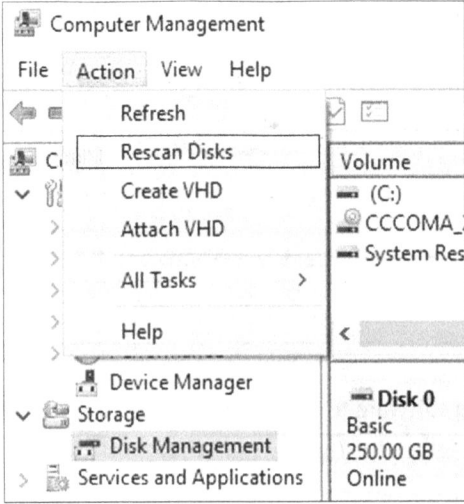

Goodheart-Willcox Publisher

Name _____

> **NOTE**
> Because you are in a school laboratory environment, the exact procedure could vary because the disk could have been mirrored in a previous class. If it has, check with your instructor before proceeding.

6. _____ Create a small partition (approximately 20 GB) on Disk 0. Format the partition as NTFS.

7. _____ To start the RAID configuration, right-click the 20-GB partition on Disk 0 then select the **Add Mirror** option from the shortcut menu. You will be prompted to select the location of the mirror drive. It will be Disk 1.

8. _____ Disk Management will automatically mirror the drives. When finished, you should be able to view two identical partitions on Disk 0 and Disk 1. They should have the same drive letter and be the same size.

9. _____ Call your instructor to verify your lab. After inspecting your lab activity, your instructor may want you to restore the computer to its original state by removing the mirror, newly created partition, and additional drive. Check with your instructor before continuing this lab activity. If your instructor wants you to return the computer to its original state, go on to step 10. If not, answer the review questions.

10. _____ To remove the mirror, right-click the Disk 1 mirror and select **Remove Mirror** from the shortcut menu. The mirror will be automatically removed, leaving only the 20-GB partition on Disk 0. You can remove the 20-GB partition from Disk 0 by right-clicking the partition and selecting **Delete Volume** from the shortcut menu. When you are finished, call your instructor to view the Disk Management configuration.

11. _____ Power off the computer and remove the second hard disk drive (Disk 1).

12. _____ Power on the computer to verify it is in working order.

13. _____ Return all materials to their proper storage area and then answer the review.

Review Questions

1. Which RAID configuration (RAID 0, RAID 1, or RAID 5) requires at least three physical drives?

   _____

2. Which RAID configuration provides no fault tolerance?

   _____

3. Which type of disk is required for Windows Server RAID systems: basic or dynamic?

   _____

4. Which RAID type provides the fastest data access?

   _____

5. You have just configured Disk 0, partition F as RAID 1 with the mirror located on Disk 1. What letter is used to identify the mirrored partition on Disk 1?

   _____

Notes

Name _____ Date _____ Class _____

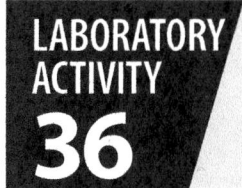

Configuring a DHCP Server

Outcomes
After completing this laboratory activity, you will be able to:
- Summarize how IP addresses are assigned from an address pool.
- Recall the purpose of reserved addresses.
- Recall the purpose of a lease period.
- Use the Add Roles Wizard to configure a scope on a DHCP server.

Introduction
In this laboratory activity, you will configure the DHCP Server role on a Windows 2016 or 2019 server. A DHCP server is responsible for automatically issuing IP addresses to DHCP clients. The DHCP server draws IP addresses from a pool of addresses indicated in the scope. The *scope* is an administrative grouping of DHCP clients. A Windows workstation is configured by default to receive an IP address, called a *dynamic address*, from a DHCP server. A workstation that is configured to receive a dynamic address is called a *DHCP client*.

An IP address dynamically assigned to a DHCP client has a maximum lease period. The default lease period for Windows Server 2016/2019 is eight days. After the lease period expires, the IP address is released and is made available to the IP address pool. Before the lease expires, the client will attempt to contact the DHCP server and renew the lease. The lease period prevents a DHCP client from using an IP address from the pool when it is no longer needed. Some network administrators set the lease period quite short, such as to an hour or less. This is especially true when there are an insufficient number of IP addresses for the number of DHCP clients on the network.

Not all network devices receive dynamic addresses. Certain devices, such as servers and printers, must use static addresses so clients requiring their services can locate them. When included in a DHCP scope, these types of static addresses are considered reserved addresses. Reserved addresses are matched to the MAC address of the network device requiring a constant IP address.

You will use the Add Role Wizard to configure and add the DHCP Server role. The major stages (**Add Role Wizard** screens) of the DHCP Server role configuration are as follows:

1. Network Connection Bindings
2. IPv4 DNS Settings
3. IPv4 WINS Settings
4. DHCP Scopes
5. DHCPv6 Stateless Mode
6. IPv6 DNS Settings
7. DHCP Server Authorization
8. Confirmation

At each of these stages, you will either enter information required to configure the DHCP server or accept the default settings.

NOTE
Be aware that the new DHCP role you create will automatically send a new IPv4 address to other workstations that connect to the same local area network. This may cause a problem for other student workstations, and may prevent them from accessing the Internet.

Equipment and Materials
- Windows 2016 or 2019 server
- Windows 10 or Windows 11 computer for verifying the DHCP operation (optional)
- The following information provided by your instructor:

Parent domain name (server domain name):

_____

Preferred DNS address (can be the same as DHCP server):

_____

Scope name:

_____

DHCP address pool: _____ to _____

Reserved address block: _____ to _____

MAC addresses of reserved address devices:

_____

_____

Lease duration:

_____ days

_____ hours

_____ minutes

> **NOTE**
> The DHCP server must be configured with a static IP address. Use static IPv4 address 10.0.0.100 and subnet mask 255.0.0.0 for the DHCP server.

Procedure

1. _____ Report to your assigned workstation.

2. _____ Boot the server and verify it is in working order.

Name _____

3. _____ Open Server Manager (**Start>Administrative Tools>Server Manager**). You should see a screen similar to the following.

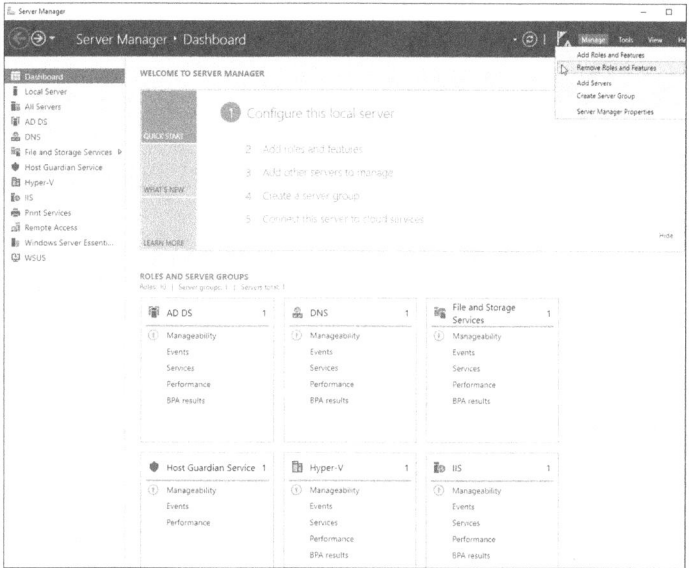

Goodheart-Willcox Publisher

4. _____ Select **Manage>Add Roles and Features**, which is located on the right side of the screen. Click **Next** until you see a dialog box similar to that in the following screen capture.

NOTE
The server may already be configured for the DHCP Server role. If it is, call your instructor for assistance. You will need to remove the DHCP Server role before proceeding in the lab activity.

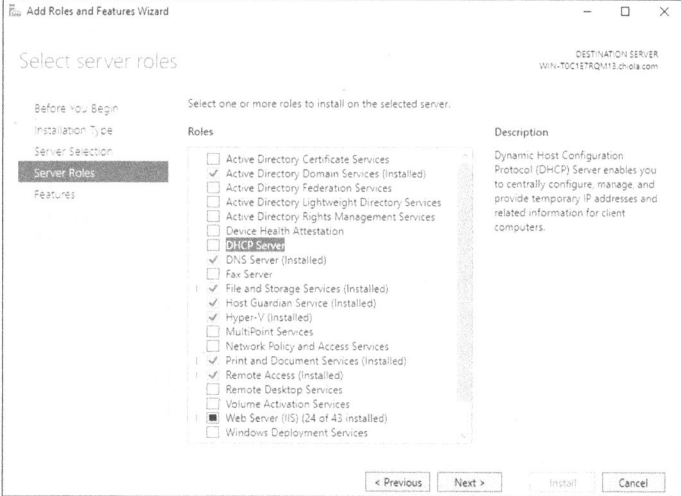

Goodheart-Willcox Publisher

5. _____ Select the **DHCP Server** role. Then, look at the description on the right as related to Dynamic Host Configuration Protocol (DHCP) Server before moving on to the next step.

6. ____ Click **Next**. A dialog box similar to the following will appear.

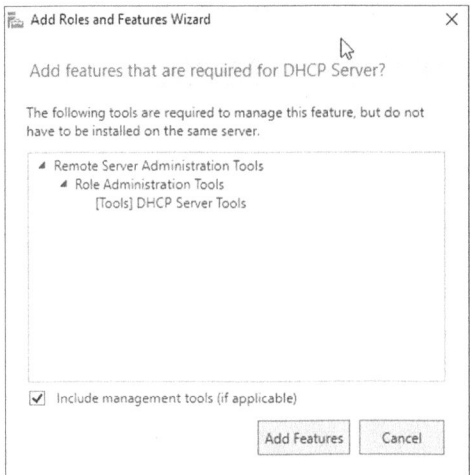

Goodheart-Willcox Publisher

Click **Add Features**.

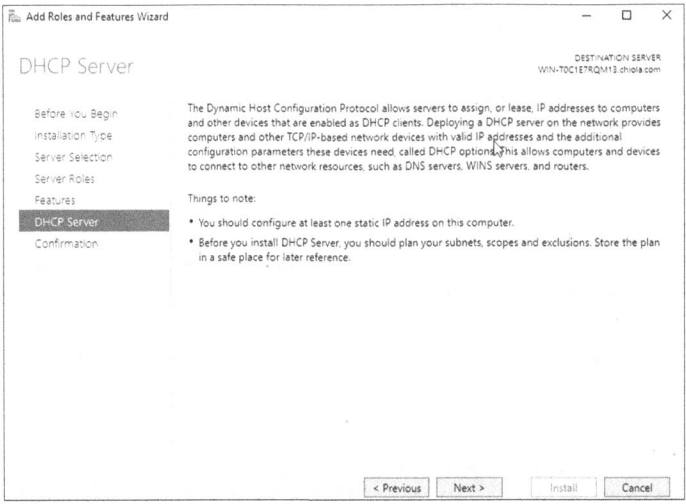

Goodheart-Willcox Publisher

Take a few minutes to read the information presented in the dialog box as it relates to DHCP. Notice in the section titled *Things to note* that the computer acting as the DHCP server should be configured with a static IP address. Also notice that it is recommended to make a plan for the subnets, scopes, and exclusions before configuring the DHCP server. It is also suggested that you make a record of the DHCP configuration and store it in a safe place. This will not be necessary for this lab activity as you have already received this information from your instructor.

Name _____

7. _____ When you are finished reading the information, click **Next** twice. You should see a confirmation screen, similar to the following screen capture.

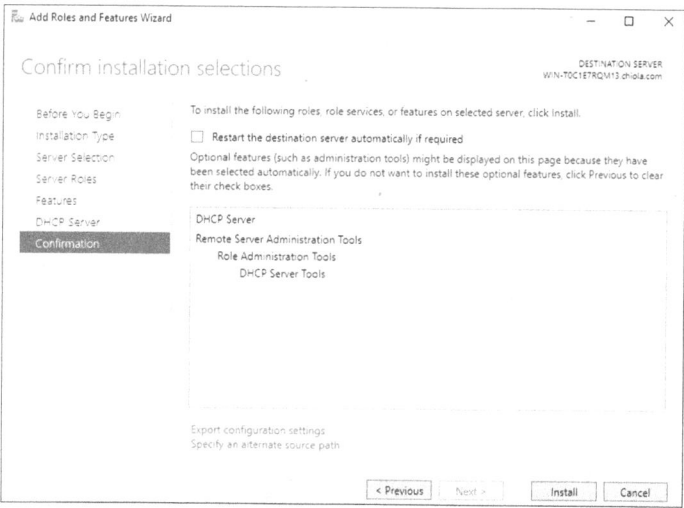

Goodheart-Willcox Publisher

Click **Install**. Close the dialog box after installation.

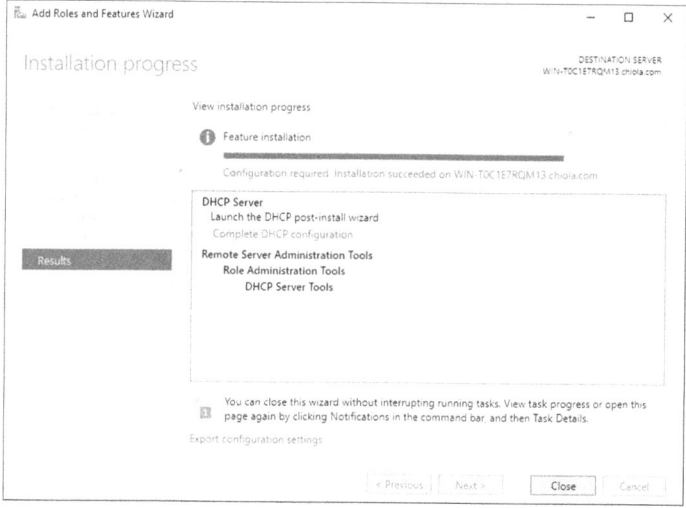

Goodheart-Willcox Publisher

8. _____ On the Server Manger dashboard, select **DHCP** from the left-side panel. Click **More...** to reveal a dialog box similar to the following.

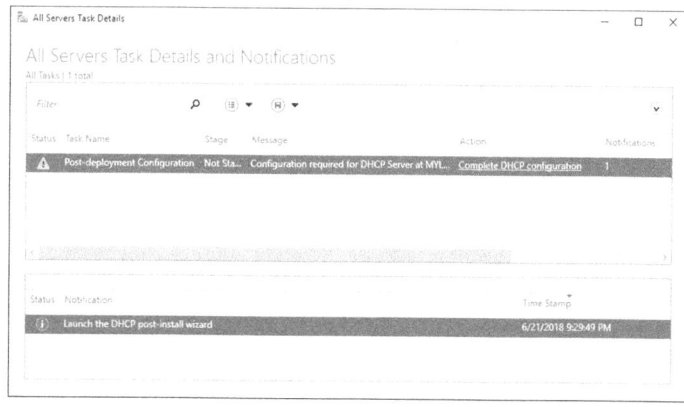

Goodheart-Willcox Publisher

Copyright Goodheart-Willcox Co., Inc.
May not be reproduced or posted to a publicly accessible website.

Laboratory Activity 36   Configuring a DHCP Server   197

9. _____ Click the **Complete DHCP configuration** link to complete the DHCP installation. Click **Next**. Accept the default for **Use the following user's credentials** and click the **Commit** button.

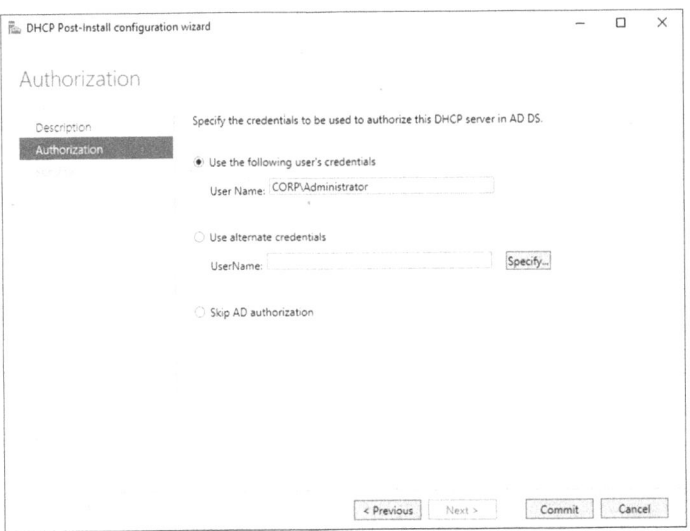
Goodheart-Willcox Publisher

Close the summary dialog box.

10. _____ Select **Server Manager>Tools>DHCP**. Click on the server's IP address and make sure that the IPv4 and IPv6 icons have green check marks, as shown in the following screen capture.

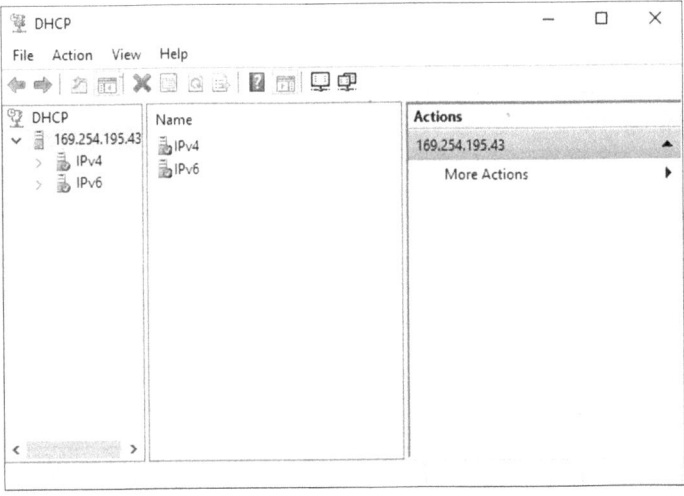
Goodheart-Willcox Publisher

11. _____ Right-click the IPv4 icon and select **New Scope**.

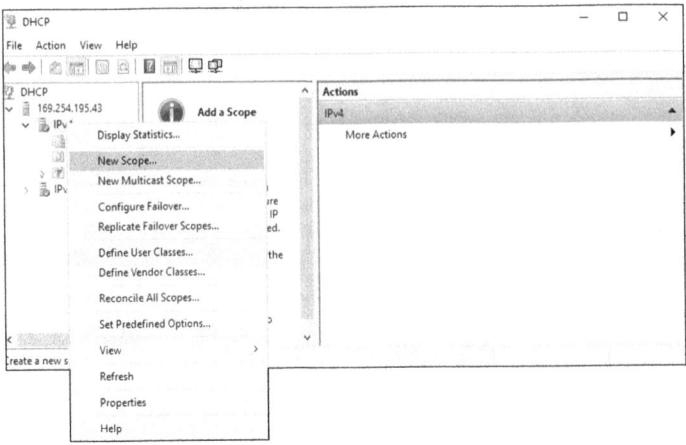
Goodheart-Willcox Publisher

198   Networking Fundamentals Lab Manual

Name _____

Click **Next** and complete the **Name** and **Description** fields.

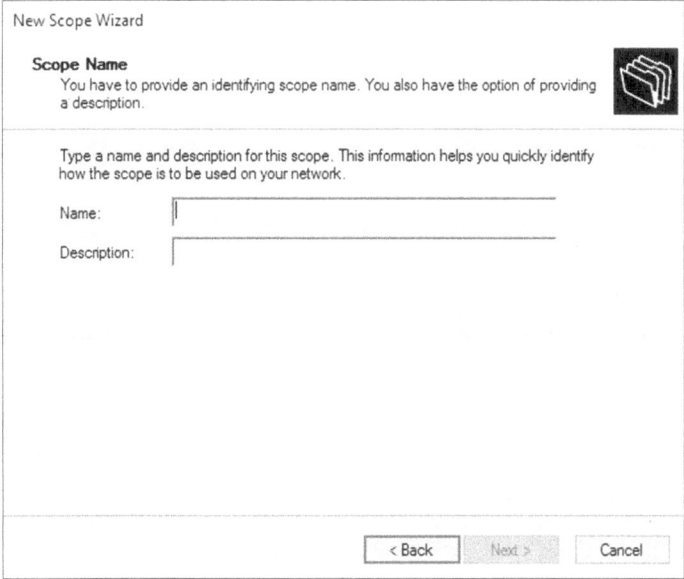

Goodheart-Willcox Publisher

Enter Network1 for both the scope name and description. Select **Next** when finished.

12. _____ You will be prompted to enter an IP address range. Use the IP address range and subnet mask reference in the Equipment and Materials portion of this lab to complete this screen.

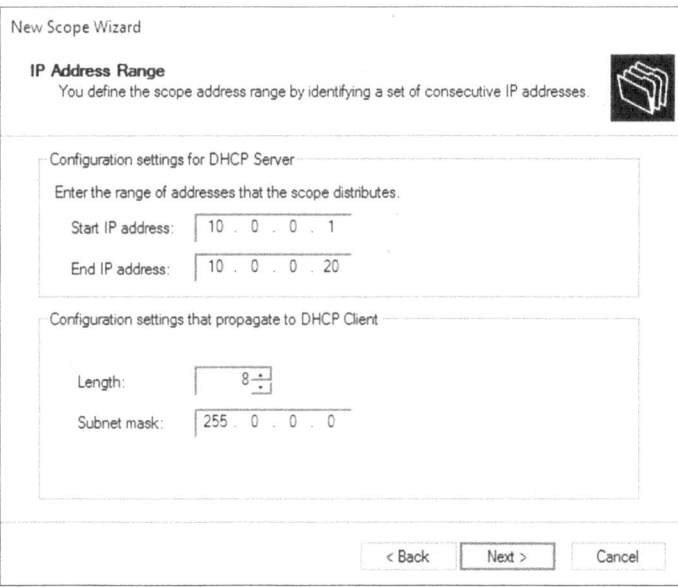

Goodheart-Willcox Publisher

When finished, click **Next**.

Laboratory Activity 36   Configuring a DHCP Server   199

13. ____ Click **Next** on the **Add Exclusions and Delay** dialog box to reach the **Lease Duration** menu.

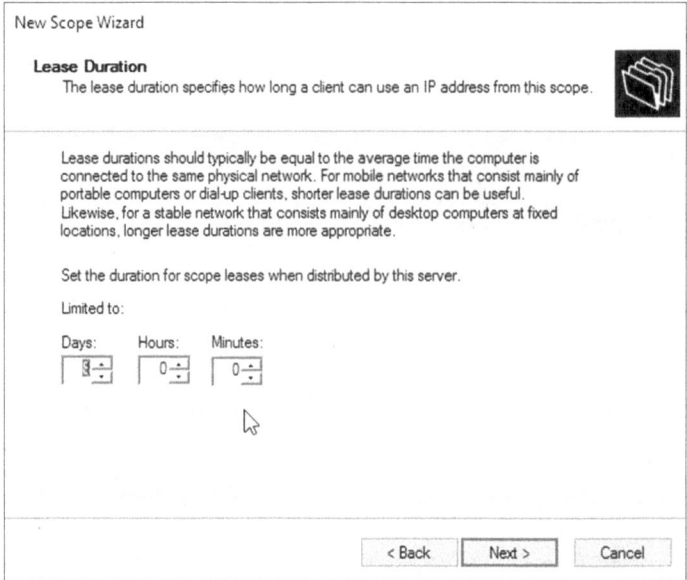

Goodheart-Willcox Publisher

Accept the default lease duration of 8 days, and click **Next**. You should a screen similar to the following.

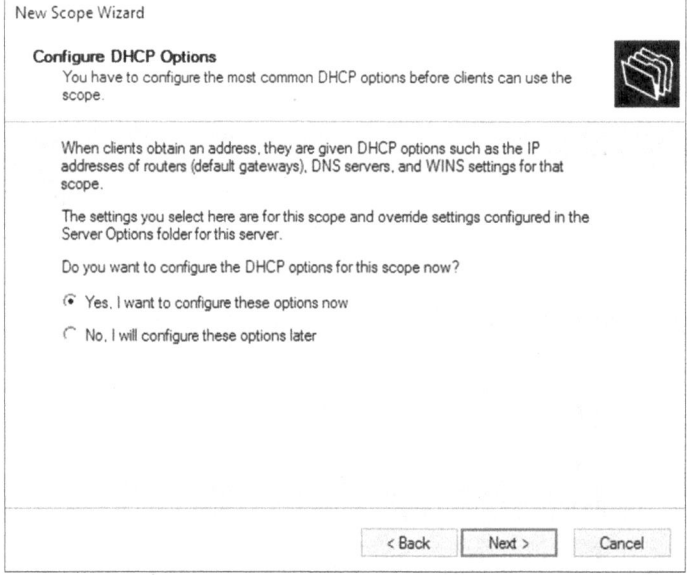

Goodheart-Willcox Publisher

14. ____ Select the **Yes, I want to configure these options now** option on the **Configure DHCP Options** dialog box and click **Next**.

15. ____ Accept the default on the **WINS Servers** dialog box. This dialog box prompts you for WINS server setting. These settings ensure backward compatibility with older Windows operating systems. A WINS server is not required for networks that only contain Windows 2000 and later operating systems. Click **Next**.

Name _____

16. _____ The next dialog box to appear should be the **Router (Default Gateway)** menu.

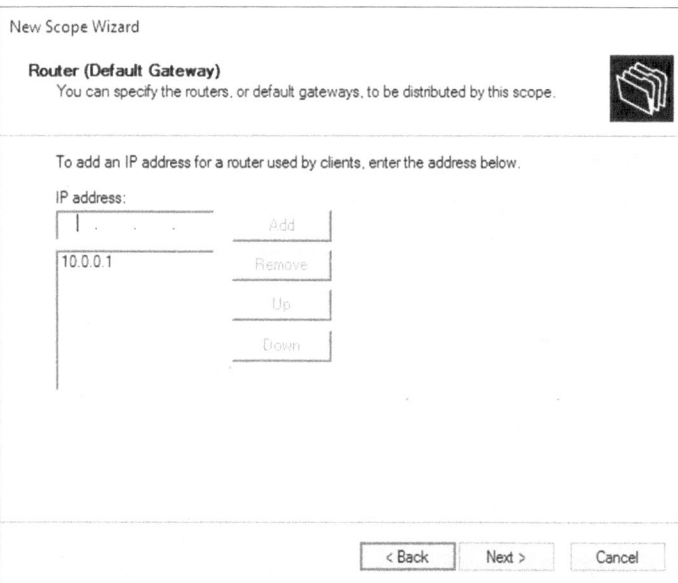

Goodheart-Willcox Publisher

Enter the default gateway and click the **Add** button. The default gateway is optional because the operating system will automatically identify the default gateway. Click **Next**.

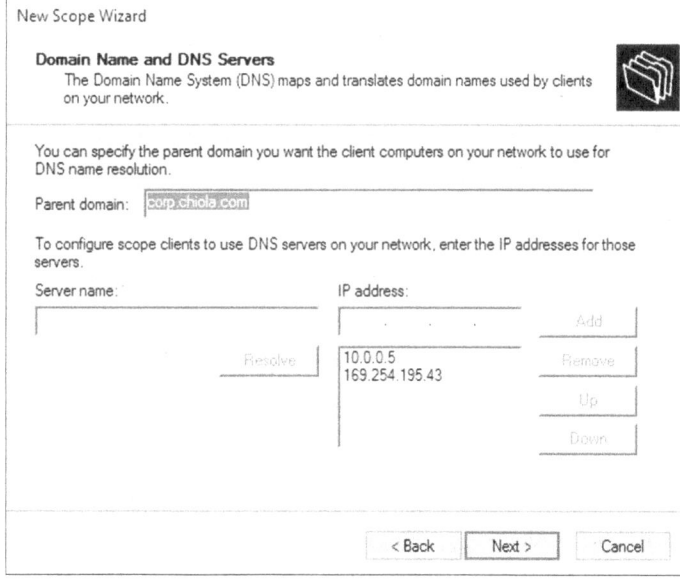

Goodheart-Willcox Publisher

17. _____ The above dialog box prompts you for DNS **Parent domain**, **Server name**, and **IP address**. Enter the information as listed in the Equipment and Materials section of this lab and click **Next**.

18. _____ The next screen you see should be the **Activate Scope** menu.

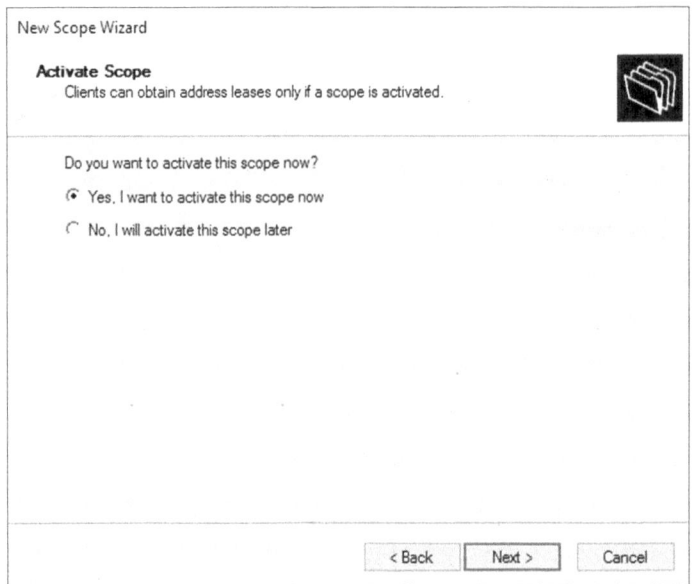

Goodheart-Willcox Publisher

Select **Yes, I want to activate this scope now** and click **Next**.

19. _____ Click **Finish** to complete the DHCP scope activation.

20. _____ On the DHCP window, expend the **IPv4** icon to verify the scope.

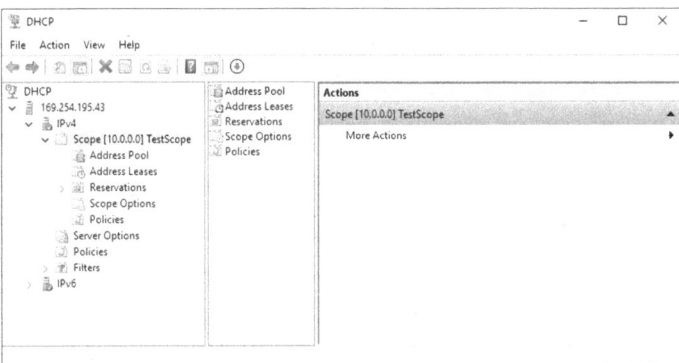

Goodheart-Willcox Publisher

21. _____ Boot the Windows 10 (or Windows 11) computer, which should be connected to the same network as the DHCP server. Use the **ipconfig** command to view the IPv4 address issued.

Name _____

22. _____ At the Windows 2016 (or 2019) server, open Server Manager and then view the address lease assigned to Windows 10 (or 11) computer. You will be able to see the computer name and domain location and the assigned IPv4 address.

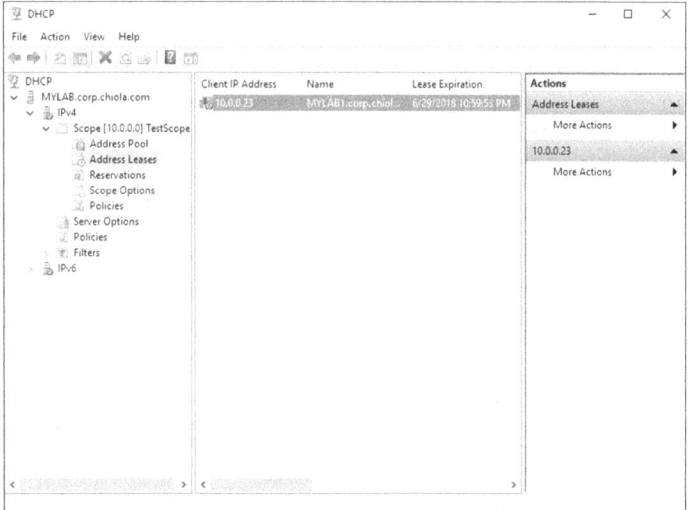

Goodheart-Willcox Publisher

23. _____ Call your instructor to inspect your laboratory activity at this time. With your instructor's permission, you may practice configuring additional DHCP server scopes.

24. _____ After completing the DHCP configuration, you can remove the DHCP Server role by selecting **Start>All Programs>Administrative Tools>Server Manager**. In Server Manager, select **Roles Summary>Remove Roles**. The **Remove Roles Wizard** will display. Deselect the DHCP Server role as shown in the following screen capture. You must restart the server to complete the removal of the DHCP Server role.

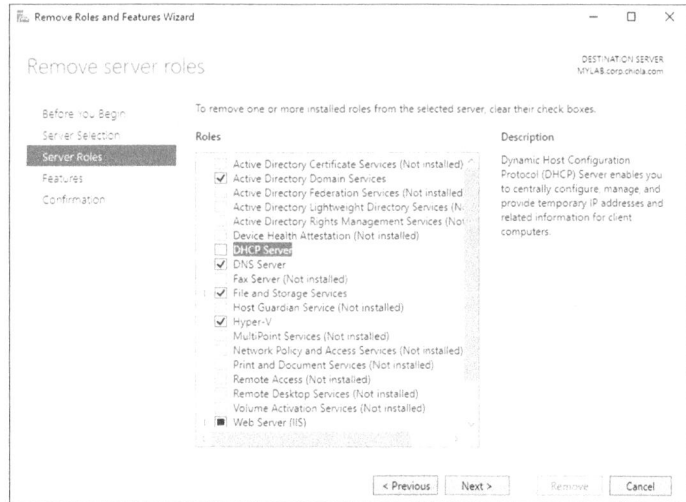

Goodheart-Willcox Publisher

25. _____ Call your instructor to verify the DHCP Server role has been removed.

26. _____ Answer the review questions.

Review Questions

1. What does the acronym DHCP represent?

2. What is the default IP configuration (static or dynamic) of a Windows workstation?

3. What is the purpose of a reserved address?

4. What is a lease period?

5. In what order does a DHCP server assign IP addresses?

6. What happens when the DHCP server is configured for IPv6 stateless mode?

Name _____ Date _____ Class _____

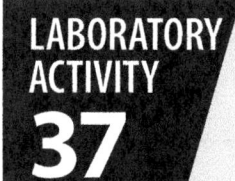

Observing APIPA

Outcomes
After completing this laboratory activity, you will be able to:
- Recall the purpose of Automatic Private IP Addressing (APIPA).
- Identify the APIPA address range.

Introduction
In this laboratory activity, you will observe the Automatic Private IP Addressing (APIPA) feature. APIPA was first introduced in Windows 98 second edition and continues through to Windows 11. The purpose of APIPA is to assign an IP address automatically to a workstation to allow it and the other workstations to communicate in the local area network when the DHCP server cannot be contacted. APIPA generates a Class B IP address when a workstation is configured to obtain a dynamic IP address. This means that a local area peer-to-peer network is automatically created to support communication between workstations. All the workstations will have an APIPA-generated IP address within the range of 169.254.0.1 to 169.254.255.254 and a subnet mask of 255.255.0.0.

You can check if the computer is using an APIPA address by issuing the **ipconfig** command from the command prompt. A response of an IP address within the APIPA range means that the workstation is running the APIPA service. An APIPA assigned IP address is a good way to identify a problem between the workstation and a DHCP server when troubleshooting a network problem. The following table describes the **ipconfig** command used with various switches.

Command	Description
ipconfig	Reveals the IP address configured for the network adapter(s).
ipconfig/all	Reveals detailed information about the network adapter(s).
ipconfig/renew	Renews the IP address of the network adapter(s).
ipconfig/release	Releases the IP address resulting in 0.0.0.0 as the IP address of the network adapter(s), unless a DHCP server is connected to the local network.

Equipment and Materials
- Microsoft Windows 10 or later computer connected to a network with a DHCP server

Procedure

1. _____ Report to your assigned workstation.

2. _____ Boot the computer and verify it is in working order.

3. _____ Run **ipconfig** from the command prompt to identify the assigned IP address. Write the IP address in the space provided.

4. _____ Disconnect the network cable at the hub that is connected to the DHCP server. This will simulate a DHCP server failure.

5. _____ At the computer, open the command prompt and issue the command **ipconfig/release** to release the assigned IP address.

6. _____ Issue the command **ipconfig** and observe the new IP address assignment. Write this IP address in the space provided.

Copyright Goodheart-Willcox Co., Inc.
May not be reproduced or posted to a publicly accessible website.

7. _____ Issue the **ipconfig/renew** command. Be patient. The command will appear to lock up the workstation. It will take a short period of time to activate the APIPA address as a result of the failure to locate the DHCP server. Write the error that appears on the screen in the space provided.

_____

_____

8. _____ Issue the **ipconfig** command and observe the APIPA address that is assigned to the computer. Write the APIPA address in the space provided.

_____

9. _____ Reconnect the DHCP server and then use the **ipconfig/renew** command to generate a new IP address from the DHCP server.

10. _____ Use the **ipconfig** command to observe the new IP address assigned by the DHCP server. Write this address in the space provided.

_____

11. _____ Repeat the procedure until you understand the concept of APIPA and the **ipconfig/renew** and **ipconfig/release** commands and their effect on the IP address assignment of the workstation.

12. _____ Answer the review questions.

Review Questions

1. What does the acronym APIPA represent?

_____

2. What subnet mask is used for APIPA?

_____

3. What class (Class A, Class B, or Class C) of network is APIPA?

_____

4. What are the first two octets of an APIPA IP address?

_____

5. What is the purpose of APIPA?

_____

_____

6. What would an APIPA address assigned to a workstation indicate while troubleshooting an Internet connection problem?

_____

_____

Name _____ Date _____ Class _____

Configuring an Alternate IPv4 Address

Outcomes

After completing this laboratory activity, you will be able to:
- Use the **Internet Protocol Version 4 (TCP/IPv4) Properties** dialog box to configure an alternative IPv4 address.
- Give examples of when an alternate IPv4 address might be required.

Introduction

In this laboratory activity, you will configure a workstation for an alternate IPv4 address. Laptop computers often require more than one IPv4 address when they are used at home and at work. The laptop may be configured with a dynamic address to connect to a network at home and require a static IPv4 address to connect to the network at work.

Alternate IPv4 configuration options are only available when a workstation has been configured for DHCP. If a static address is assigned to the workstation, you will not be able to configure an alternate address. A workstation configured with an alternate IPv4 address will automatically attempt to connect to the network when a DHCP server cannot be located.

Windows operating systems are automatically configured for DHCP by default when first installed. The Automatic Private IP Address (APIPA) feature is also enabled by default. If a workstation cannot establish a connection with a DHCP server, it will automatically assign an IPv4 address to itself in the range from 169.254.0.1 to 169.254.255.254 with a subnet mask of 255.255.0.0. The APIPA feature allows a workstation to communicate with other workstations on a network in the event of a DHCP server failure.

The APIPA feature is disabled when a computer is configured with an alternate IPv4 address. Starting as far back as Windows Vista, Windows computers use IPv6 to communicate in the local area network. With IPv6 enabled, APIPA is not needed to communicate on the local area network should the DHCP server fail; however, the computer will not be able to access remote locations on the Internet that require an IPv4 address.

Equipment and Materials

- Windows 10 or later computer connected to a network
- The following information provided by your instructor:
  Static IPv4 assignment:

  _____

Procedure

1. _____ Report to your assigned workstation.

2. _____ Boot the computer and verify it is in working order.

3. _____ Use the **ipconfig/all** command to verify the network adapter settings. Record the information in spaces provided.

   IPv4 address:

   _____

   Subnet mask:

   _____

Default gateway:

_____

DNS server:

_____

4. _____ If the computer is configured to obtain an IPv4 address automatically, proceed to step 5. If the computer is not configured to obtain an IPv4 address automatically, configure it now by opening the **Local Area Connection Status** dialog box. Click the **Properties** button.

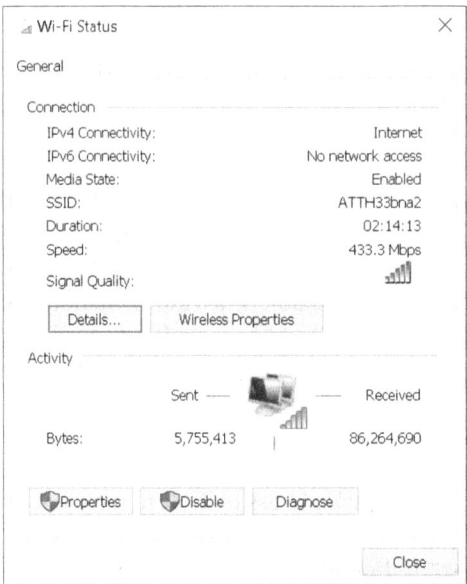

Goodheart-Willcox Publisher

The **Local Area Connection Properties** dialog box will display. Highlight **Internet Protocol Version 4 (TCP/IPv4)**, and then click **Properties**. A dialog box similar to the following will appear. Select the **Obtain an IP address automatically** option and then click **OK**. Then, click **Close** to close the dialog boxes.

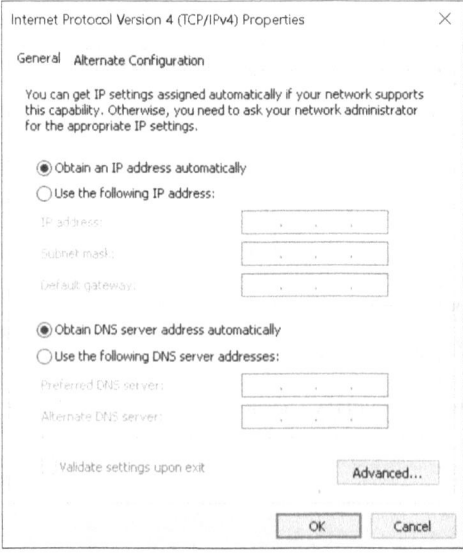

Goodheart-Willcox Publisher

Name _____

5. _____ Open the **Local Area Connection Properties** dialog box.

6. _____ Select the **Alternate Configuration** tab. A dialog box similar to the following will appear.

Goodheart-Willcox Publisher

NOTE
The **Alternate Configuration** tab is only available when the workstation is configured to obtain an IP address automatically. If the computer is configured for a static IPv4 address, the **Alternate Configuration** tab will not be available.

7. _____ Select the **User configured** option, which allows you to configure a static IPv4 address for the network adapter. Pay particular attention to the **Preferred DNS server** and the **Preferred WINS server** options. These two options do not need to be configured, but when they are, connections are established quicker on the network. Also, notice that **Automatic private IP address** and the **User configured** options use radio buttons. The use of radio buttons means you can only use one option or the other, not both. Therefore, when selecting the **User configured** option, APIPA is disabled.

8. _____ Click **OK**. The computer has now successfully been configured for an alternate IPv4 address. Call your instructor to inspect your lab activity.

9. _____ Restore the workstation to its original TCP/IP settings, and then answer the review questions.

Review Questions

1. When might a person use an alternate IPv4 address?

2. You attempt to configure an alternate IPv4 address for your computer and you find the feature is not available. What might be the cause for the feature not to be available?

3. When configuring an alternate IPv4 address, what other two optional addresses may be configured that will provide a faster network connection?

4. How is the APIPA feature affected by a static IPv4 address configuration?

Name _____ Date _____ Class _____

Configuring ICS

LABORATORY ACTIVITY 39

Outcomes

After completing this laboratory activity, you will be able to:

- Recall the purpose of NAT.
- Identify the three groups of private IP addresses associated with NAT.
- Differentiate between a public and a private IP address.
- Use the **Local Area Connection Properties** dialog box to configure a workstation as an ICS host.
- Use the **Local Area Network (LAN) Settings** dialog box to configure a workstation as an ICS client.

Introduction

In this laboratory activity, you will configure Microsoft's Internet Connection Sharing (ICS) feature, which allows multiple workstations to share a single Internet connection. ICS is Microsoft's implementation of Network Address Translation (NAT). NAT is a standard developed by the Internet Engineering Task Force (IETF), which allows one public IPv4 address to translate into multiple private IPv4 addresses. The following private IPv4 addresses are associated with NAT:

- 10.0.0.0–10.255.255.255
- 172.16.0.0–172.32.255.255
- 192.168.0.0–192.168.255.255

> **NOTE**
> ICS is only designed to support private IPv4 addresses in the range of 192.168.0.0 to 192.168.255.255.

Private IPv4 addresses are also referred to as *non-routable IPv4 addresses*. This is because they are blocked by default by a router and cannot be used to communicate directly across the Internet.

A workstation or server configured to share an Internet connection using Microsoft ICS is called an *ICS host*. A workstation configured to access the Internet through an ICS host is called an *ICS client*. The ICS host must be running for the ICS host to be able to connect to the Internet. The ICS host not only provides a connection to the Internet, but also acts as a DHCP server, automatically issuing a private IPv4 address to each ICS client.

An additional network adapter card may need to be installed in the ICS host if the Internet connection is being provided directly through a DSL or cable modem. An additional network adapter installed in the ICS host is not required if the ICS host connects to the Internet directly by a dial-up telephone modem, router, or gateway device.

Look at the following figure. Notice that two network interface cards are located in the ICS host. One network interface card is configured with the public address and connects directly to the ISP provider. The other network interface card is configured with a private IPv4 address and is used to share the connection with one or more other clients.

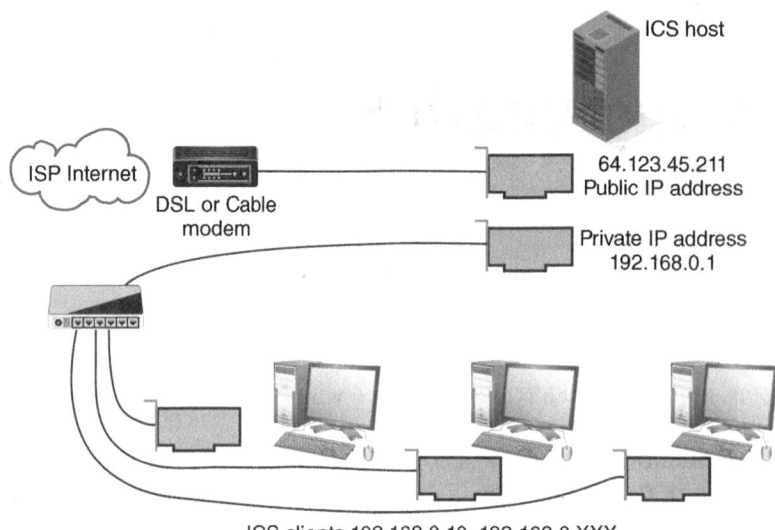

Goodheart-Willcox Publisher; (modem and hub icons) Vadim Ermak/Shutterstock.com; (server icon) aShatilov/Shutterstock.com; (workstation icons) romvo/Shutterstock.com

The ICS configuration can be set up during the initial network configuration or later manually. ICS is very easy to configure. At the workstation designated as the ICS host, you must first configure two network interface cards. The Internet connection is configured with the public IPv4 address provided through the ISP. The LAN connection is assigned the IPv4 private address of 192.168.0.1 and subnet mask 255.255.255.0. The ICS clients in the LAN should be configured for DHCP. IPv4 addresses in the range of 129.168.0.1 to 192.168.0.255 are automatically assigned to ICS clients using the DHCP feature of the ICS host.

Keep in mind that a router or gateway device can provide NAT and share Internet access with all clients in the LAN. A router typically supports a full range of private IPv4 addresses. The router connects directly to the Internet provider via a DSL or Cable modem connection. The network cable from the client workstations can be plugged into the router's RJ-45 ports. Typical ICS devices also provide wireless connection service to wireless devices such as laptops. If more wired connections are needed than the number provided by the ICS device, a hub or switch can be connected to the ICS device.

Equipment and Materials

- Two Windows 10 or later computers (One must have either two LAN connections built into the motherboard or an additional network adapter, such as a wireless adapter.)
- DSL, cable modem, or a dial-up telephone modem (Required to access the Internet.)
- A hub or a switch (Needed to share the connection to the ICS client. You can use a crossover cable instead to connect the ICS host to the ICS client.)
- The following information provided by your instructor:

Static IPv4 address:

_____

Subnet mask:

_____

Name _____

DNS server 1:
_____

DNS server 2:
_____

Internet access username:
_____

Internet access password:
_____

Procedure

1. _____ Gather the required materials and then report to your assigned workstation.

2. _____ Boot the Windows computers and verify they are in working order.

3. _____ If necessary, shut down the computer designated to be the ICS host and install the additional network adapter. If the additional adapter is installed, proceed to step 4.

4. _____ On the ICS host, the default name of the installed network adapter is Local Area Connection. Each additional network adapter will have the same name followed by a sequential number, for example, Local Area Connection 2. For this lab activity, you will need to rename the Local Area Connection name that connects the ISP to the ISP connection. To do this, open the Network and Sharing Center and then select **Change adapter settings**.

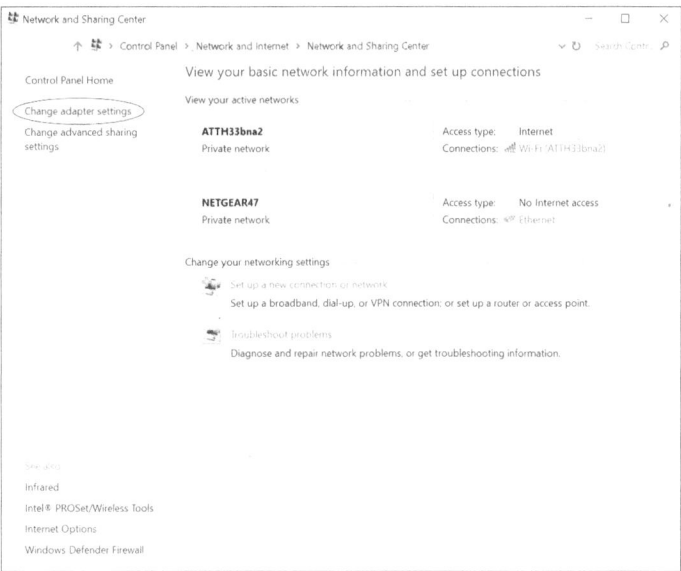

Goodheart-Willcox Publisher

5. _____ Right-click the Network adapter icon connecting to DSL or cable modem and select **Rename** from the shortcut menu. Rename it to WAN (Wide Area Network). Select the Network adapter icon connecting your router and select **Rename** from the shortcut menu. Rename it to LAN (Local Area Network).

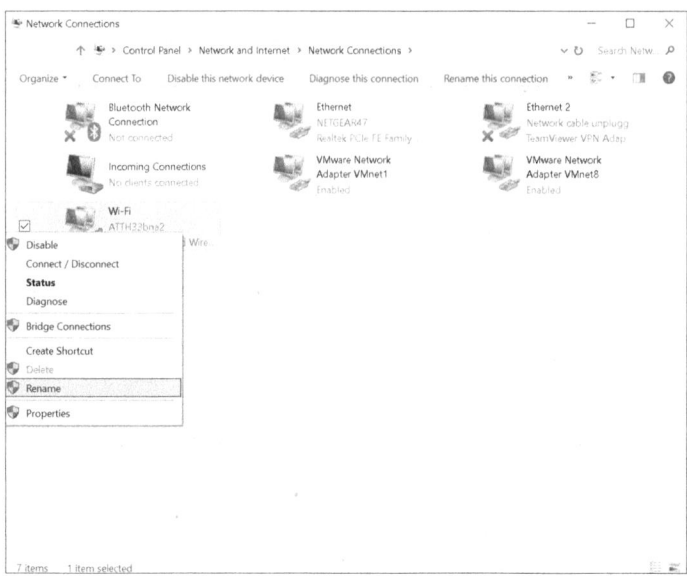

Goodheart-Willcox Publisher

6. _____ Right-click the WAN icon again and then select **Properties** from the shortcut menu.

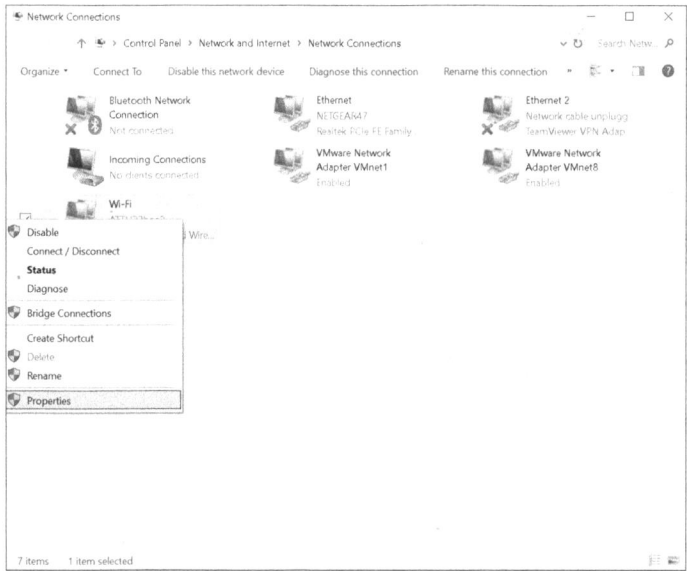

Goodheart-Willcox Publisher

Name _____

7. _____ When the **WAN Properties** dialog box appears, select the **Sharing** tab. Notice there are two options that allow the network adapter to be configured for ICS. Select both options.

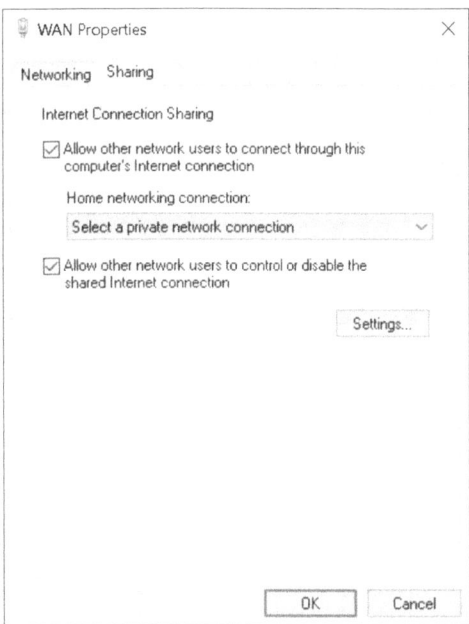

Goodheart-Willcox Publisher

8. _____ From the **Home networking connection:** drop-down menu, select the adapter connected to your router.

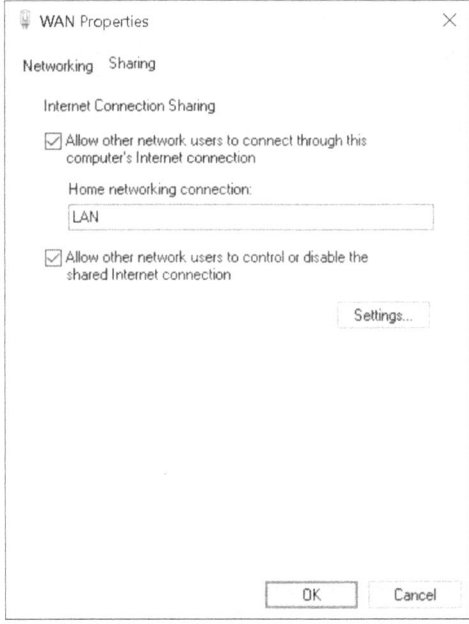

Goodheart-Willcox Publisher

Take a few minutes to review Internet Connection Sharing by conducting an online search with the keywords Using ICS.

9. _____ When you are finished reviewing the information, close your bowser window by clicking the X in the top right-hand corner. Click **OK** to close the **WAN Properties** dialog box.

10. _____ At the ICS client, open the **Internet Properties** dialog box (**Start>Control Panel>Network and Internet>Internet Options**). Select the **Connections** tab and then click the **LAN settings** button.

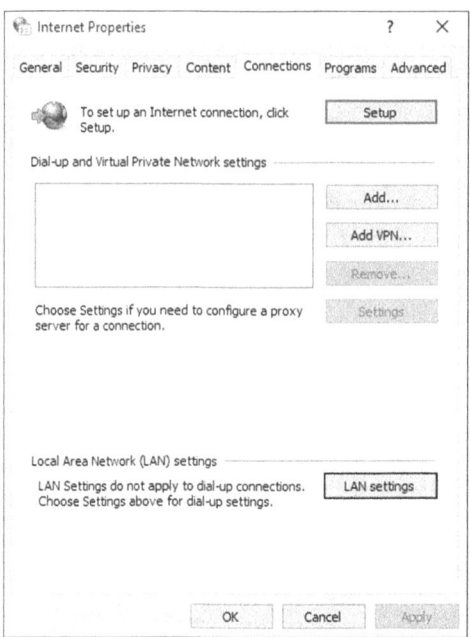

Goodheart-Willcox Publisher

11. _____ When the **Local Area Network (LAN) Settings** dialog box appears, select the **Automatically detect settings** option. Leave the other options unselected. The ICS client network adapter will now accept the private IPv4 address from the ICS host.

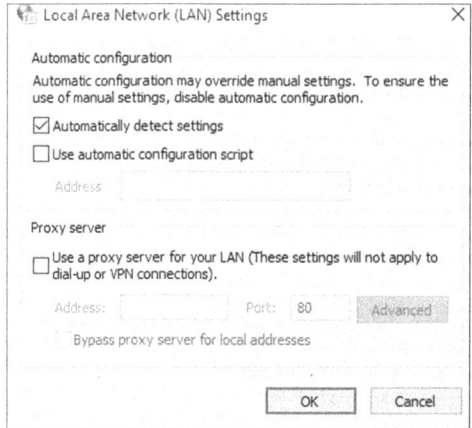

Goodheart-Willcox Publisher

12. _____ Close all open dialog boxes, and then test the Internet connection from the ICS client. Remember that the ICS host must be running in order for the ICS client to connect to the Internet through the ICS host.

13. _____ Use the **ipconfig** command to verify the assigned IPv4 address of the ICS host and ICS client.

14. _____ Have your instructor inspect your laboratory activity.

15. _____ Return the computers to their original configuration. You can use System Restore to return the computers to their original configurations quickly and easily.

16. _____ Return all materials to their proper storage areas and then complete the review questions.

Name _____

Review Questions

1. What does the acronym ICS represent?

   _____

2. What does the acronym NAT represent?

   _____

3. What is the purpose of NAT?

   _____

   _____

   _____

4. What are the three private IPv4 address ranges?

   _____

   _____

   _____

5. What is the difference between a public and a private IPv4 address?

   _____

   _____

   _____

   _____

Notes

Name _____ Date _____ Class _____

LABORATORY ACTIVITY 40
Observing DHCP Commands with Wireshark

Outcomes

After completing this laboratory activity, you will be able to:
- Recall the purpose of the Bootstrap Protocol.
- Explain what happens when the **ipconfig/release** command is issued.
- Explain what happens when the **ipconfig/renew** command is issued.
- Use the **Local Area Connection Properties** dialog box to disable and enable the IPv6 protocol.

Introduction

In this laboratory activity, you will use Wireshark to observe the protocol actions that occur when the **ipconfig/release** and **ipconfig/renew** commands are issued. The **ipconfig/release** command causes the assigned IPv4 address to be released from the network adapter configuration. When the IPv4 address is released, the workstation has no assigned IPv4 address. The **ipconfig/renew** command causes the workstation network adapter to request a new IPv4 address from the DHCP server.

For this lab activity, you will need two computers connected to a network with a DHCP server: one configured for DHCP and the other with Wireshark installed. If Wireshark is installed on the workstation using the **ipconfig/release** command, Wireshark may quit working. Wireshark must maintain a connection to the network to work properly. This may not be possible when the IPv4 address is released.

The two IPv4 addresses used for communication between the DHCP client and server are 0.0.0.0 and 255.255.255.255. The IPv4 address 0.0.0.0 is reserved for use by the client when requesting an IPv4 assigned address from the DHCP server. The 255.255.255.255 IPv4 address is also reserved and is known as the *IPv4 broadcast address*. The workstation requesting the IPv4 address does not yet know the assigned IPv4 address of the DHCP server, so it sends out the DHCP request to destination location 255.255.255.255. The DHCP server accepts all broadcasts to 255.255.255.255. The DHCP server then selects the next available IPv4 address from the pool of IPv4 addresses and sends it to the requesting workstation with the 0.0.0.0 IPv4 address. After the requesting workstation accepts the new IPv4 address, it will no longer use the 0.0.0.0 address. As you can see, the automatic assignment of the IPv4 address is quite simple.

You will see the Bootstrap Protocol (BOOTP) identified by Wireshark at the start of the IPv4 address request. BOOTP facilitates IP request when the network adapter is configured for DHCP. If you look closely at the BOOTP packet contents, you will see it contains the same last IPv4 address used by the workstation. This is normal. The just-released IPv4 address will be the first new IPv4 to be issued from the pool of IPv4 addresses.

To identify in the Wireshark capture the workstation making the DHCP request, record the workstations' MAC address before performing the capture. The MAC address can be used to identify the workstation originating the DHCP request. Looking at all of the frame captures can be quite confusing. The MAC address will help you to identify the proper frame more easily.

Equipment and Materials

- Two Windows 10 or later computers connected to a network with a DHCP server (one computer should be configured for DHCP; the other should have Wireshark installed)
- Wireshark Sample 10 file

Wireshark Sample 10 file location: _____

Procedure

1. _____ Report to your assigned workstation(s).

2. _____ Boot the Windows workstations and verify they are in working order.

3. _____ On the workstation configured for DHCP, check the current IPv4 configuration by issuing the **ipconfig/all** command from the command prompt. Record the information in the spaces provided.

   IPv4 address:

   _____

   Subnet mask:

   _____

   Default gateway:

   _____

   Preferred DNS server:

   _____

   DHCP enabled (yes or no):

   _____

   MAC address:

   _____

4. _____ On the workstation with Wireshark installed, open the **Wireshark Sample 10** file and look at frames 105 through 111. Notice that in frame 105, the IPv4 address is released. In the next frame, the workstation is requesting an IPv4 address from the DHCP server. The source IPv4 address of the requesting workstation is 0.0.0.0. It uses the broadcast IPv4 address 255.255.255.255 to contact the DHCP server. The protocol used to send the request for a DHCP IPv4 address is BOOTP.

   In the next few frames, the IPv4 address 192.168.1.104 is issued to the workstation. The workstation then sends out an ARP request to verify no other device has been assigned the 192.168.1.104 IPv4 address. This precaution ensures that each IPv4 address in the local network is unique.

   You cannot duplicate IP addresses in the same local area network. When a duplicate address is found, the workstation sending the ARP request will disable its own network adapter. This might occur when one of the IPv4 addresses found in the DHCP pool of addresses has been manually assigned as a static IPv4 address to some device such as a printer. Static IPv4 addresses used on the local area network with a DHCP server should be reserved by registering them with the DHCP server.

5. _____ Open frame 110 and closely look at the contents of BOOTP. If you expand the contents, you will see that the workstation is requesting its original IPv4 address of 192.168.1.104 from the DHCP server. Do not automatically think that a brand new IPv4 address is assigned. The old IPv4 address is typically available and will be assigned to workstation. This is the reason that you see workstations with a consistent IPv4 address even when configured for DHCP.

6. _____ Close the **Wireshark Sample 10** file.

Name _____

7. _____ Before starting your own capture, you may wish to disable the IPv6 protocol to make it easier to observe the IPv4 DHCP function. To disable the IPv6 protocol, open the **Local Area Connection Properties** dialog box. Deselect **Internet Protocol Version 6 (TCP/IPv6)** and then click **OK**.

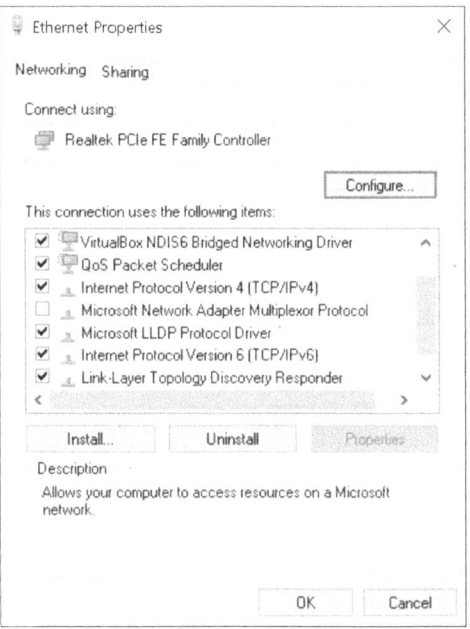

Goodheart-Willcox Publisher

8. _____ Start a Wireshark capture.

9. _____ On the workstation configured for DHCP, open a command prompt and issue the **ipconfig/release** command followed by the **ipconfig/renew** command.

10. _____ Stop the Wireshark capture and then inspect the contents of the frames. You can quickly locate the start of the DHCP renewal process by looking for the frame containing the first 0.0.0.0 source IPv4 address.

11. _____ Using the captured contents as a reference, answer the review questions.

12. _____ After completing the review questions, return the workstations to their original configuration. Do not forget to enable the IPv6 protocol on the Wireshark computer.

13. _____ Return the workstation to its original configuration.

Review Questions

1. What protocol is used to issue the DHCP request?

_____

2. DHCP requests are carried by which type of packet: TCP or UDP?

_____

3. Which two IPv4 addresses are used to communicate between a workstation and a DHCP server?

_____

4. What IPv4 address is used by a workstation when requesting an IPv4 address from the DHCP server?

_____

5. To what IPv4 address does the workstation send the DHCP request?

_____

6. List the protocols used to encapsulate BOOTP.

_____

7. What is the purpose of BOOTP?

_____

_____

8. What port numbers are associated with BOOTP?

_____

9. What command issued from the command prompt will generate a new IPv4 address from the DHCP server?

_____

10. What command issued from the command prompt will release the assigned IPv4 from the network adapter?

_____

Name _____ Date _____ Class _____

Laboratory Activity 41: Observing ICS Activity with Wireshark

Outcomes

After completing this laboratory activity, you will be able to:
- Explain the boot process of an ICS client.

Introduction

In this laboratory activity, you will set up a simple experiment and then observe the results. You will use the results to answer the review questions.

In the following image, there are two arrangements that can be used when observing ICS activity with Wireshark. In the first arrangement, Wireshark is run from the ICS host. In the second arrangement, Wireshark is run from a workstation that is not part of the ICS configuration. The experiment will not produce the desired results if you run Wireshark from the ICS client. Also, Wireshark must be running before you turn on the ICS host.

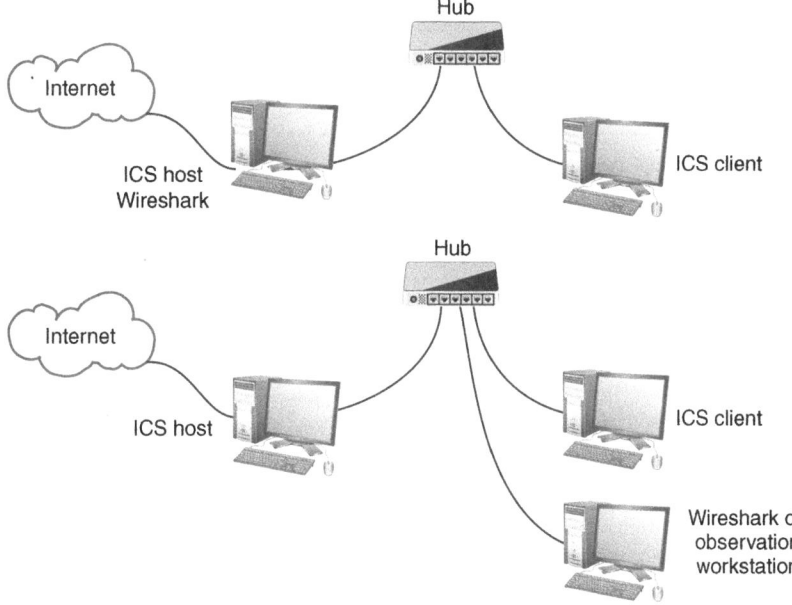

Goodheart-Willcox Publisher; (hub icon) Vadim Ermak/Shutterstock.com; (workstation icons) romvo/Shutterstock.com

In either of the two network arrangements, Wireshark will capture all of the network traffic between the workstations. After performing a Wireshark capture, you will view the contents and then answer the review questions.

Equipment and Materials

- Two Windows 10 or later computers (if using the first configuration), one with Wireshark installed on the ICS host
- Three Windows 10 or later computers (if using the second configuration), one with Wireshark installed on the computer that will not be part of the ICS configuration

Procedure

1. _____ Report to your assigned workstation(s).

2. _____ Boot the Windows computers and verify they are in working order.

3. _____ Shut down the ICS client.

4. _____ Verify the ICS host has an Internet connection.

5. _____ Start a Wireshark capture.

6. _____ Boot the ICS client and then connect to the Internet from this workstation.

7. _____ After successfully connecting to the Internet, stop the Wireshark capture.

8. _____ Examine the captured series of frames/packets.

9. _____ Answer the review questions.

Review Questions

1. From where did the ICS client receive its IPv4 address?

   _____

2. What IPv4 address did the ICS client use when making the request?

   _____

3. What IPv4 address is used by the ICS host for the local area network?

   _____

4. What IPv4 address is used by the ICS host for the Internet connection?

   _____

5. Which computer acted like a DHCP server?

   _____

Name _____ Date _____ Class _____

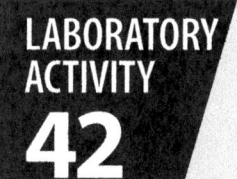

Using Microsoft Calculator for Binary Conversion

Outcomes

After completing this laboratory activity, you will be able to:
- Use the Microsoft Calculator menu to change the view from standard to scientific.
- Use the Microsoft Calculator to convert binary numbers to decimal.
- Use the Microsoft Calculator to convert decimal numbers to binary.

Introduction

Calculator is a program that comes with most Microsoft Windows operating systems. Knowing how to use the Calculator program for binary conversion will prove valuable when studying subnet masks.

The Calculator program is located at **Start>All Apps>Calculator**. In Windows 10 and 11, many views are available, as shown in the following screen capture. To switch views, select the view type from the **Menu** button.

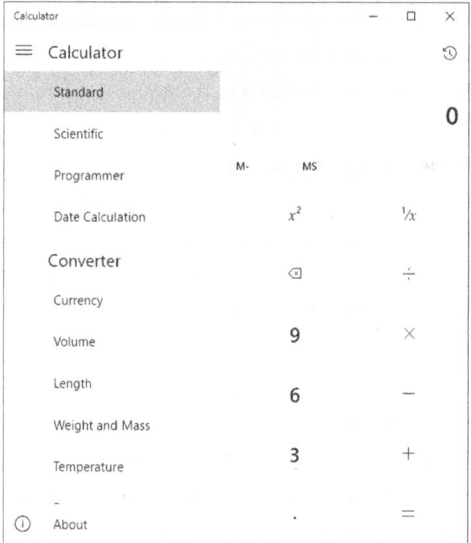

Goodheart-Willcox Publisher

For this lab activity, you will select the **Programmer** view. This view was not available in versions of Windows prior to Windows 7; the closest view type was **Scientific**. The Programmer view is handy for converting binary numbers to decimal and decimal numbers to binary. When Calculator is in Programmer view, the options **HEX**, **DEC**, **OCT**, and **BIN** are listed. Selecting one of these options configures the calculator to accept numeric values of the type chosen or changes the value in the display window to that type. For example, if you want to enter a binary value, you would first select the **BIN** option before entering the binary value. To convert the binary value to a decimal value, you would select the **DEC** option. The binary value will automatically convert to decimal.

The following screen capture shows the Windows 10 Calculator in **Programmer** view. Notice that the options **HEX**, **DEC**, **OCT**, and **BIN** are listed in a box on the left side of the calculator.

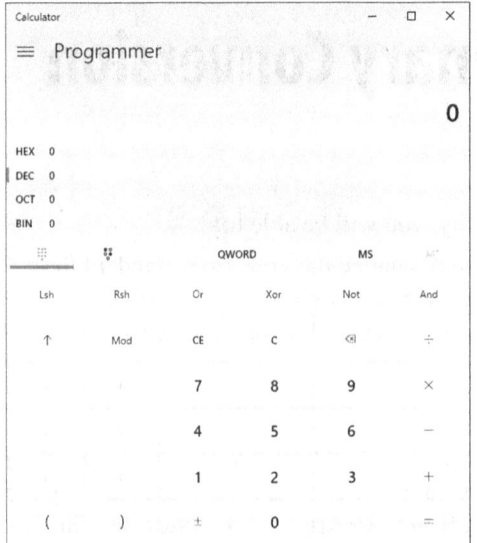

Goodheart-Willcox Publisher

Equipment and Materials

- Windows 10 or later computer

Procedure

1. _____ Report to your assigned workstation.

2. _____ Boot the computer and verify it is in working order.

3. _____ Open the Calculator program.

4. _____ Select the **Programmer** option from the **Menu** button.

5. _____ Convert the following binary numbers to decimal. Before entering the binary number, be sure to set the calculator to binary by selecting the **BIN** option. After you have entered the binary number, select the **DEC** option to convert it to decimal. Record the decimal number in the space provided. To clear a value from the display window, click the C button. Do not forget to select the **BIN** option before entering the next binary number.

    1101 =
    _____

    1111 =
    _____

    0001 =
    _____

    0010 =
    _____

Name _____

6. _____ Convert the following decimal numbers to binary. Before entering the decimal number, be sure to select the **DEC** option. After you have entered the decimal number, select the **BIN** option to convert it to binary. Record the binary number in the spaces provided.

25 =

_____

30 =

_____

124 =

_____

8 =

_____

16 =

_____

Review Questions

1. Use Calculator to convert the following binary numbers to decimal.

    A. 0011 =

    _____

    B. 0100 =

    _____

    C. 0101 =

    _____

    D. 11 =

    _____

    E. 111 =

    _____

    F. 1111 =

    _____

    G. 11111 =

    _____

    H. 111111 =

    _____

    I. 1111111 =

    _____

    J. 11111111 =

    _____

    K. 10000000 =

    _____

L. 11000000 =

M. 11100000 =

N. 11110000 =

O. 11111000 =

2. Use the Calculator program to convert the following decimal numbers to binary.
   A. 32 =

   B. 64 =

   C. 128 =

   D. 256 =

   E. 512 =

   F. 1024 =

   G. 2048 =

   H. 4096 =

   I. 111 =

   J. 15 =

Name _____ Date _____ Class _____

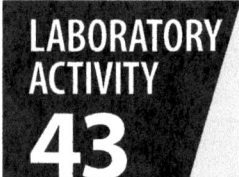

Observing the Effects of an IPv4 Subnet Mask

Outcomes

After completing this laboratory activity, you will be able to:
- Explain the effects subnetting has on viewing computers in a physical network.
- Identify the network address associated with an IPv4 subnet mask.
- Identify the broadcast address associated with an IPv4 subnet mask.

Introduction

In this laboratory activity, you will experiment with a subnetwork configuration. Two or more logical networks can be created from a single physical network by assigning an IPv4 subnet mask such as 255.255.255.192. The following table lists four subnets that have been created by using the subnet mask 255.255.255.192.

Subnet	Subnet ID	Subnet Range	Broadcast
0	192.168.0.0	192.168.0.1–192.168.0.62	192.168.0.63
1	192.168.0.64	192.168.0.65–192.168.9.126	192.168.0.127
2	192.168.0.128	192.168.0.129–192.168.0.190	192.168.0.191
3	192.168.0.192	192.168.0.193–192.168.0.254	192.168.0.255

The four subnets are identified as subnets 0 through 3. The subnet ID is the IPv4 address. For example, subnet 0 uses 192.168.0.0 as the network address. The range of IPv4 addresses available for subnet 0 are 192.168.0.1 through 192.168.0.62. The IPv4 address 192.168.0.63 is reserved as the broadcast address. The broadcast address is used to send a broadcast packet to only members of subnet 0.

Subnets are typically created for security reasons. Workstations in different networks cannot see each other in the **Network** folder, though they can still communicate. Keeping a department's workstations out of sight from users in other departments can add to security. Users will be less likely to seek out and browse a workstation that is not in their assigned department. For example, you may want all of a company's financial workstations on a separate network so that users in other departments will be less likely to explore them.

During the laboratory activity, you will use the **Network** folder to view the computers in the local area network and how they are affected by changing the assigned subnet.

The **Network** folder relies on Network Discovery protocols. To provide backward compatibility with previous versions of Windows operating systems, the **Network** folder relies on protocols such as NetBIOS Name Server (NBNS), Link-Local Multicast Name Resolution (LLMNR), LANMAN, and SMB. Whether a workstation appears depends on the operating system and the method used to view the other computers in the local area network.

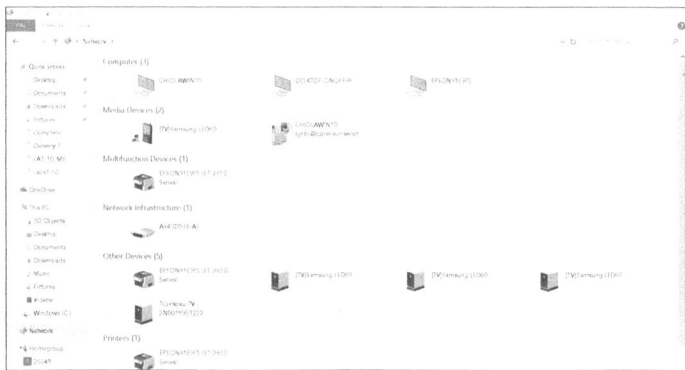

Goodheart-Willcox Publisher

Copyright Goodheart-Willcox Co., Inc.
May not be reproduced or posted to a publicly accessible website.

Each time the Network Discovery protocols send packets out to explore the local area network, the results are cached and will display the cache contents for a period of time depending on the operating system and structure of the network. Be patient.

> **NOTE**
> For this lab activity, you should disable the IPv6 protocol in the **Local Area Network Properties** dialog box. This will ensure that the results you view are based on the IPv4 protocol, not the IPv6 protocol.

Equipment and Materials

- Two Windows 10 computers configured as a peer-to-peer network

Procedure

1. _____ Report to your assigned workstation(s).

2. _____ Boot the computers and verify they are in working order.

3. _____ Configure the computers to be in the same subnet by assigning IP address 192.168.0.5 to one and 192.168.0.6 to the other. Both should have the same subnet mask of 255.255.255.192.

4. _____ Test the connection between the two computers using the **ping** command. Was the ping successful (yes or no)?

   _____

5. _____ Open the **Network** folder. Can you see both computers (yes or no)?

   _____

6. _____ Change the assigned IP address of 192.168.0.6 to 192.168.0.70. The two workstations are now in different subnets.

7. _____ Test the connection between the two computers using the **ping** command. Was the ping successful (yes or no)?

   _____

8. _____ Open the **Network** folder. Can you see both computers (yes or no)?

   _____

9. _____ Call your instructor to inspect your lab activity.

10. _____ Assign a new IPv4 address to both computers based on the same subnet mask. Run both previous tests and observe the results.

11. _____ Now, assign the IP address 192.168.0.63 to one of the computers. Make sure to check the **Validate settings upon exit** checkbox. The 192.168.0.63 is the broadcast address that corresponds with subnet 0. If Windows 10 detects a problem, the Windows Network Diagnostic utility will run automatically to troubleshoot and attempt to fix the problem. The Windows Network Diagnostic dialog box will present two options. Click on the **Skip this step** link. Record the error message displayed in the Windows Network Diagnostic window in the space provided below.

    _____

12. _____ Try assigning the subnet ID 192.168.0.64. Make sure to check the **Validate settings upon exit** checkbox. The network address is used to identify the network and should not be assigned. Again, a Windows Network Diagnostic dialog box will appear and present two options. Click on the **Skip this step** link. Record the error message displayed in the Windows Network Diagnostic window in the space provided below.

    _____

Name _____

13. _____ Experiment by assigning other similar subnet mask IP addresses.

14. _____ Return all materials to their proper storage area and return both computers to their original configurations. Be sure to enable the IPv6 protocol on each computer.

15. _____ Answer the review questions.

Review Questions

1. Can you successfully see workstations on a different subnet mask that are in the same physical local area network?

   _____

2. Can you successfully ping workstations assigned to different subnets on the same physical local area network?

   _____

3. Can you successfully ping workstations on the same subnet?

   _____

4. Why can't the IPv4 address 192.168.0.64 be assigned to a workstation in this lab activity?

   _____

5. Why can't the IPv4 address 192.168.0.191 be assigned to a workstation?

   _____

6. Convert the last octet (host) of the subnet 0 broadcast IP address to binary. You may use the Windows Calculator.
   192.168.0.63 =

   _____

7. What binary pattern represents a broadcast?

   _____

8. What binary pattern would represent a network?

   _____

Notes

Name _____ Date _____ Class _____

Route Print Command

Outcomes

After completing this laboratory activity, you will be able to:
- Interpret a routing table.
- Recall the role of a default gateway.
- Use the **route print** command to view a routing table.

Introduction

In this laboratory activity, you will inspect the routing table of a typical computer and identify the default gateway router. Gateways are important for establishing TCP/IP connections between different network segments. A gateway is usually a router.

Network adapters are associated with a routing table. A routing table provides information about network connections to and from the network adapter based on IP addresses and subnet masks. The information contained in the routing table can be viewed by issuing the **route print** command from the command prompt.

To better understand the information in a routing table, first look at the results from the **ipconfig/all** command shown in the following screen capture. Notice that the network adapter is assigned the IP address of 192.168.1.74 with a subnet mask of 255.255.255.0. The default gateway for the workstation's network adapter is 192.168.1.254.

Goodheart-Willcox Publisher

In this case, the default gateway is a gateway router used to connect several workstations to the Internet through a cable modem. Now, look at the following screen capture of a routing table generated by issuing the **route print** command. You will see both the IPv4 and the IPv6 routing information displayed. The routing table is divided into three major sections: Interface List, IPv4 Route Table, and IPv6 Route Table.

```
C:\Users\25348>route print
===========================================================================
Interface List
 20...80 3f 5d c0 71 a2 ......DisplayLink Network Adapter NCM
  7...dc 53 60 b8 bb 23 ......Microsoft Wi-Fi Direct Virtual Adapter #5
  3...de 53 60 b8 bb 22 ......Microsoft Wi-Fi Direct Virtual Adapter #6
 19...dc 4a 3e a6 7b 4e ......Realtek PCIe FE Family Controller
 16...00 50 56 c0 00 01 ......VMware Virtual Ethernet Adapter for VMnet1
 21...00 50 56 c0 00 08 ......VMware Virtual Ethernet Adapter for VMnet8
 22...dc 53 60 b8 bb 22 ......Intel(R) Dual Band Wireless-AC 3165
  4...00 ff 0f 45 43 e6 ......TeamViewer VPN Adapter
  9...dc 53 60 b8 bb 26 ......Bluetooth Device (Personal Area Network)
  1...........................Software Loopback Interface 1
===========================================================================

IPv4 Route Table
===========================================================================
Active Routes:
Network Destination        Netmask          Gateway       Interface  Metric
          0.0.0.0          0.0.0.0    192.168.1.254    192.168.1.74     40
          0.0.0.0          0.0.0.0         10.0.0.1        10.0.0.2     35
         10.0.0.0    255.255.255.0         On-link         10.0.0.2    291
         10.0.0.2  255.255.255.255         On-link         10.0.0.2    291
       10.0.0.255  255.255.255.255         On-link         10.0.0.2    291
        127.0.0.0        255.0.0.0         On-link        127.0.0.1    331
        127.0.0.1  255.255.255.255         On-link        127.0.0.1    331
  127.255.255.255  255.255.255.255         On-link        127.0.0.1    331
      192.168.1.0    255.255.255.0         On-link     192.168.1.74    296
     192.168.1.74  255.255.255.255         On-link     192.168.1.74    296
    192.168.1.255  255.255.255.255         On-link     192.168.1.74    296
     192.168.22.0    255.255.255.0         On-link     192.168.22.1    291
     192.168.22.1  255.255.255.255         On-link     192.168.22.1    291
   192.168.22.255  255.255.255.255         On-link     192.168.22.1    291
     192.168.36.0    255.255.255.0         On-link     192.168.36.1    291
     192.168.36.1  255.255.255.255         On-link     192.168.36.1    291
   192.168.36.255  255.255.255.255         On-link     192.168.36.1    291
        224.0.0.0        240.0.0.0         On-link        127.0.0.1    331
        224.0.0.0        240.0.0.0         On-link     192.168.22.1    291
        224.0.0.0        240.0.0.0         On-link     192.168.36.1    291
        224.0.0.0        240.0.0.0         On-link         10.0.0.2    291
        224.0.0.0        240.0.0.0         On-link     192.168.1.74    296
  255.255.255.255  255.255.255.255         On-link        127.0.0.1    331
  255.255.255.255  255.255.255.255         On-link     192.168.22.1    291
  255.255.255.255  255.255.255.255         On-link     192.168.36.1    291
  255.255.255.255  255.255.255.255         On-link         10.0.0.2    291
  255.255.255.255  255.255.255.255         On-link     192.168.1.74    296
===========================================================================
Persistent Routes:
  None

IPv6 Route Table
===========================================================================
Active Routes:
 If Metric Network Destination      Gateway
  1    331 ::1/128                  On-link
 19    291 fe08::/64                On-link
 19    291 fe08::1234/128           On-link
 16    291 fe80::/64                On-link
 21    291 fe80::/64                On-link
 19    291 fe80::/64                On-link
 22    296 fe80::/64                On-link
 21    291 fe80::4985:d3e8:25ad:c0db/128
                                    On-link
 16    291 fe80::adb0:1291:6b47:22ec/128
                                    On-link
 22    296 fe80::b8cc:2929:92fb:16f9/128
                                    On-link
 19    291 fe80::c838:5922:c888:4652/128
                                    On-link
  1    331 ff00::/8                 On-link
 16    291 ff00::/8                 On-link
 21    291 ff00::/8                 On-link
 19    291 ff00::/8                 On-link
 22    296 ff00::/8                 On-link
===========================================================================
Persistent Routes:
  None

C:\Users\25348>route print_
```

Goodheart-Willcox Publisher

The Interface List contains information related to the network adapters installed in the local computer. The table displays the network adapter MAC address for the network adapter "dc 4a 3e a6 7b 4e Realtek PCIe GBE Family Controller." The routing table only shows the routes for the network-connected adapter.

On your system, you might also see that there are several interfaces with "00 00 00 00 00 00" as the assigned MAC address. These represent virtual network adapters used for IPv6 transition technologies such as Teredo and ISATAP. Both technologies are designed to tunnel IPv6 packets through IPv4 networks.

Name _____

Now, look at the IPv4 Route Table section. This section displays a list of active routes associated with the network adapter. Most of this information was provided when the network adapter was configured. Notice that the table has five headings: Network Destination, Netmask, Gateway, Interface, and Metric.

- *Network destination* refers to a destination network address, not to a specific network adapter. For example, when the interface address 192.168.1.74 is assigned with a subnet mask of 255.255.255.0, the network destination address is 192.168.1.0.
- *Netmask* is similar to the subnet mask with the exception that all 0s are used to indicate the default gateway netmask, and all 255s are used to indicate the default broadcast netmask. Relatively new is the 240.0.0.0 multicast netmask.
- *Gateway* is the gateway.
- *Interface* is the local network adapter card.
- *Metric* is an assigned value for a particular route. The metric values are used to compare the various routes to take when more than one route exists. Typically, the lowest numeric metric is chosen first.

The first line in the IPv4 Route Table displays the destination of the route as 0.0.0.0. When the Network Destination column is filled with 0.0.0.0, it indicates the default route or default gateway. In the example, the row for this entry indicates that the default gateway is 192.168.1.254 and the local network adapter IP address is 192.168.1.74. You can use the following table as an aid for interpreting the table information concerning IPv4 network destinations.

Type	Network
Default route	0.0.0.0
Loopback	255.0.0.0
Multicast	224.0.0.0
Broadcast	255.255.255.255

The IPv6 Route Table has four headings: If (interface), Metric, Network Destination, and Gateway. In the IPv4 Route Table, the default route or default gateway is indicated by 0.0.0.0. In the IPv6 routing table, the default route or default gateway is indicated by ::/0.

Some computer motherboards are equipped with two network adapters. For example, a computer configured as an Internet Connection Server (ICS) has one network adapter to connect to the Internet and another network adapter to connect to network. When a computer is equipped with more than one network adapter, it is referred to as a *multi-homed computer*.

Failure to connect to the proper default gateway can result in network communication failure and or unusual communication results. The default gateway in a typical network setting is usually a router. A router can maintain a table of routes that are either automatically updated or manually entered. When values are manually entered into the routing table, they are referred to as static values or static addresses. When routers update their table values automatically, they use protocols designed specifically for that purpose. The protocols communicate with joining routers and exchange information about other network locations. These routing tables are used to make decisions as to what is the best route to take when delivering a packet across a WAN.

Equipment and Materials

- Windows 10 computer with Internet access

Procedure

1. _____ Report to your assigned workstation.
2. _____ Boot the computer and verify it is in working order.
3. _____ Open the command prompt and enter ipconfig/all. Then press **Enter** to run the command.

4. _____ Record the following information:

Host name:

_____

IPv4 address:

_____

IPv4 subnet mask:

_____

Default gateway:

_____

IPv6 address:

_____

IPv6 default gateway:

_____

5. _____ At the command prompt enter route print. Then press **Enter** to run the command.
6. _____ Identify the IPv4 default gateway. Look for 0.0.0.0. in the **Network Destination** column.
7. _____ Does the default gateway in the IPv4 Route Table match the default gateway identified by **ipconfig/all** command?

_____

8. _____ How is the IPv6 default gateway address identified?

_____

9. _____ At the command prompt type and run route/? to see more information about the **route** command.
10. _____ Return all materials to their proper storage area and then answer the review questions.

Review Questions

1. What is the role of the default gateway?

_____

_____

2. What command is used to display the routing table?

_____

3. What information is contained in the first line of an IPv4 Route Table?

_____

_____

4. What does the netmask of 0.0.0.0 indicate?

_____

Name _____

5. What other information is contained in the IPv4 Route Table besides the default gateway IP address and the local network adapter IP address?

   _____
   _____
   _____

6. What would be the result of using the wrong gateway IP address when configuring a network adapter?

   _____
   _____

7. What is a *metric*?

   _____
   _____
   _____

8. How is the default IPv6 gateway indicated?

   _____

9. What is the IPv4 multicast netmask?

   _____

10. What is the IPv4 broadcast netmask?

    _____

Notes

Name _____ Date _____ Class _____

Performing a System Backup and Restore

Outcomes
After completing this laboratory activity, you will be able to:
- Use Windows Backup and Restore to backup files.
- Use Windows Backup and Restore to restore files.

Introduction
In this laboratory activity, you will use the Windows Backup and Restore utility in Windows 10. Windows Server 2016 uses the Windows Server Backup utility, which is customized to meet the server role. However, backup terminology for all Microsoft operating systems is similar, though it may change somewhat for each generation of operating system to match the latest technology better.

Backing up system and user files is a critical part of maintaining a network system. In this laboratory activity, you will create a folder on the hard disk drive to use as the location for the files you back up. In a real scenario, you would most likely use an internal drive, external drive, CD/DVD disc, USB flash drive, or network storage location. Backing up to a location on the default hard disk drive is not recommended because if the hard disk drive fails, you will lose the backup. Although, you could have two separate hard disk drives installed and use the second hard disk drive as a backup location. The most common backup location for networked computers is a network attached storage (NAS) device.

> **NOTE**
> The automatic backup function requires internal disk storage, external disk storage, or a network storage location to be used. Automatic backups will not be successfully performed for media such as CD/DVD discs or USB flash drives because they must be present at the time of the automatic backup, which is unlikely. If the CD/DVD disc or USB flash drive is not present, the automatic backup will not occur.

RAID 2 and RAID 5 systems perform a similar function as a backup. The difference is that RAID systems are continuous backup systems, which means they always have the very latest copy of system and data files. Traditional backup systems are not continuous and can result in lost data.

There are several types of backups identified by Windows Backup and Restore: Full reset, Recovery, File restore. A *Full reset* is an exact copy of a hard drive, including all system settings, programs, and files. It can be used to recover the entire operating system as well as all user files. In Windows 10, you can reset the computer to a clean configuration. All personal files will be whipped.

A *Recovery* contains all of the required files to repair the operating system but does not back up user files such as documents. In case of hardware failure, system corruption, or virus infection, you can initiate a recovery process to reinstall Windows from a backup image.

A *File restore* is performed in the event of an accidental deletion of folder or file. Windows 10 has a built-in tool that can be used to restore the deleted folder or file. This tool is called *File History*. The primary function of this tool is to save copies of local files so it can easily be restored when needed. File History was introduced in Windows 8.

Windows 10 also includes the Windows 7 Backup and Restore tool. Restoring files in Windows 10 is much faster and easier than previous versions of Windows. You can access the backup solution by opening **Setting>Update & Security>Backup** as shown in the following capture.

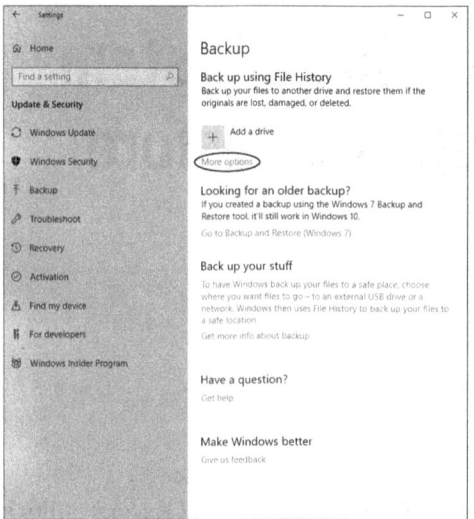

Goodheart-Willcox Publisher

You can add a drive to back up your files. The **More options** link provides the opportunity to fine-tune the backup options.

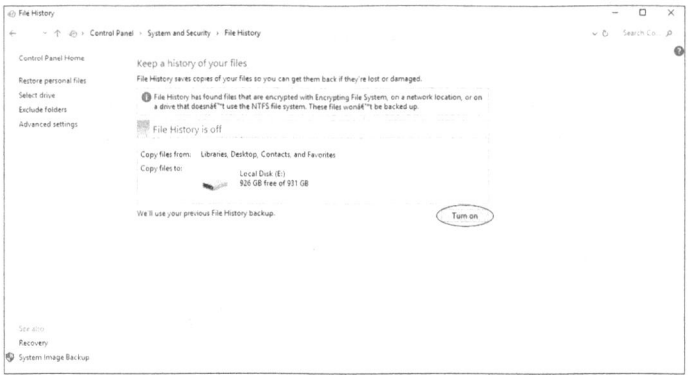

Goodheart-Willcox Publisher

Click the **Turn on** button to activate the drive to which you want to back up files.

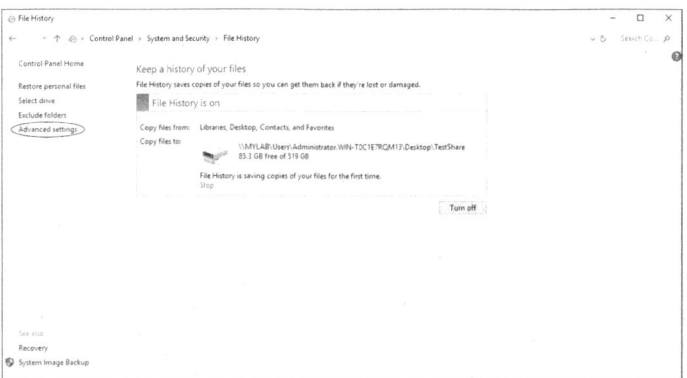

Goodheart-Willcox Publisher

Click **Advanced Settings** to choose how long you want to keep the versions of your backup and the frequency of taking backups.

Name _____

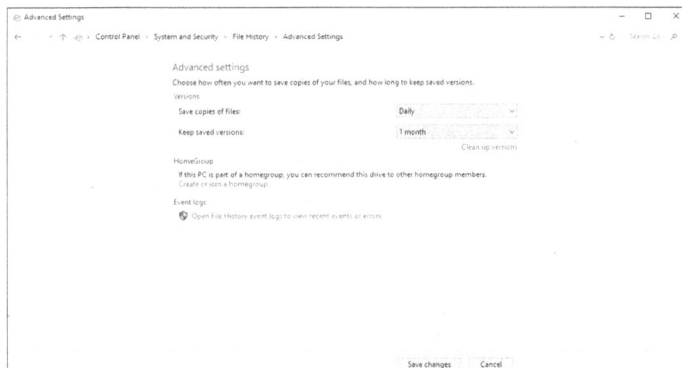

Goodheart-Willcox Publisher

If you decided to use another drive, you must stop using the currently configured backup drive. You can also add folders or remove folders that you want to back up in the Backup options menu, as shown in the following screen capture.

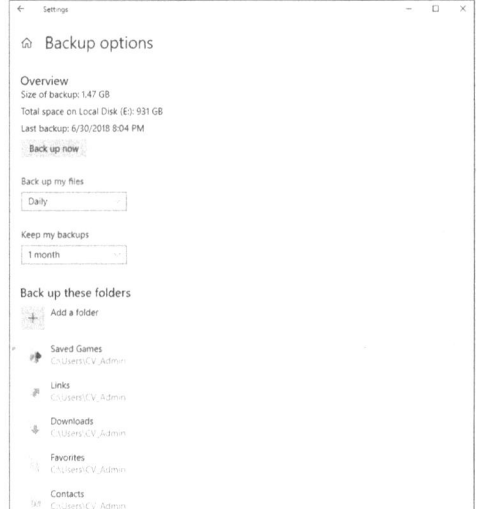

Goodheart-Willcox Publisher

Equipment and Materials
- Windows 10 computer
- The following information provided by your instructor:

   Backup location:

   _____

   Save or delete the backup after completing the laboratory activity?

   _____

> **NOTE**
> The backup location will indicate if you need additional materials to perform this laboratory activity. For example, the backup location can be a USB-connected external hard disk drive.

Procedure

1. _____ Gather the required materials and then report to your assigned workstation.

2. _____ Boot the computer and verify it is in working order.

3. _____ Create a network folder on the Instructor's system called **Practice Backup Folder**. If your instructor has provided you with a different backup location or media, create the Practice Backup Folder at that location. The folder will serve as the destination for the files you back up.

4. _____ To access Backup and Restore, select **Start>Control Panel>System and Security>File History**.

Goodheart-Willcox Publisher

5. _____ Click on the **Select drive** link to add the network drive from your instructor.

6. _____ Select the **Advanced settings** option and then follow the screen prompts. Select the desired values for how long saved copies of the files and how long saved versions will be stored. Click the **Save changes** button to set these parameters and close the screen. A backup copy of your files will be taken for the first time.

Goodheart-Willcox Publisher

7. _____ After completing the backup, call your instructor to inspect your laboratory activity.

8. _____ Now, open Windows File Explorer to inspect the location of the backup files. The backup files are located in the folder specified by your instructor.

9. _____ Perform a restore operation by clicking the **Restore personal files** link in the Backup and Restore utility. Depending on the size of the backup, restoring the files can take quite a while.

10. _____ After you have finished the laboratory activity, return all materials to their proper storage areas. Delete or save the backup folder you created as indicated by your instructor.

11. _____ Answer the review questions.

Name _____

Review Questions

1. What is the default for File History to check designated drives and folder for changes?

   _____

2. What is the default backup period for a History File?

   _____

3. Can File History back up files to the C: drive?

   _____

Notes

Name _____ Date _____ Class _____

Creating a Web Page Using HTML

Outcomes

After completing this laboratory activity, you will be able to:
- Identify the four fundamental markup tags used for designing a simple web page.
- Recall the function of a web browser.
- Create a web page.
- Use a web browser to view an HTML-coded page.

Introduction

In this laboratory activity, you will create a web page using hypertext markup language (HTML). In the next laboratory activity, you will post the page on your local area network for viewing by other workstations. This will simulate an office intranet.

Web browsers interpret and then display web-page content written in code such as HTML. HTML code allows web-page contents to be displayed identically regardless of the computer's hardware type or operating system. The four fundamental markup tags used for designing a simple web page are listed in the following table. These tags are used to identify certain elements of a web page, such as its code type and title.

Markup Tag	Description
<html>	Informs the Internet browser of the code type used.
<head>	Identifies the first part of the web page, which contains the title.
<title>	This title is not to be confused with a title that will be displayed on the page itself. Search engines use the title to identify the web page. This title is not displayed on the page, but it will typically appear in the title bar.
<body>	Contains the content of the web page.

NOTE
HTML code is not case-sensitive.

HTML tags must precede the content they are to identify or format. End tags are used at the end of the contents to indicate to the web browser where the identification or format should end. An end tag is similar to an HTML tag, but begins with a slash. For example, the end tag for the <B> HTML tag is </B>.

When writing HTML code, you should use a text editor such as Notepad. Do *not* use a full word-processing program such as Microsoft Word. Using a full word-processing program can cause a web page to display incorrectly. The code interpreted by the web browser must be written in a simple ASCII code. Most word-processing programs use many different fonts and formatting code that cannot be interpreted correctly by a web browser.

A web page can be saved with the .htm or .html file extension. For this laboratory activity, you will save the web page with the .htm file extension. Other HTML tags are used to format the web page's contents. These tags are listed in the following table.

HTML Tag	Description
<P>	Format the contents as a paragraph
<P ALIGN =CENTER>	Format as a center-aligned paragraph
<P ALIGN=LEFT>	Format as a left-aligned paragraph
<P ALIGN=RIGHT>	Format as a right-aligned paragraph
<B>	Format as bold
<I>	Format as italic
<U>	Format as underlined
<FONT COLOR="blue">	Format font color as blue
 	Insert a line break (two breaks equal the effect of one <P>)
<H1> to <H6>	Indicates the heading size (H1 is the largest; H6 is the smallest)

Microsoft Office Word is a word-processing application used to create document-type files and is capable of also creating web page files. For this lab activity, do *not* use Microsoft Office Word to create the web page. Use the Microsoft Notepad application instead. You may experiment with the Microsoft Word application after completing this lab activity, but only with your instructor's permission.

Equipment and Materials

- Windows 10 or later computer

Procedure

1. _____ Report to your assigned workstation.
2. _____ Boot the computer and verify it is in working order.
3. _____ Create a directory on drive C using your name as the folder title. This is where you will store your web page.
4. _____ Open a text editor such as Notepad.
5. _____ Type the following:

   <html>

   <head>

   <title>This is the title.</title>

   </head>

   <body>

   This is my first web page written in HTML code.

   </body>

   </html>

6. _____ Save the web page as a text file (with the **.txt** extension) in the directory you created. Then, save the web page as an HTML file (with the **.htm** extension). A file saved as a text file is interpreted as a plain ASCII file. A file saved as an HTML file is interpreted as a web page.

Name _____

7. _____ To view the web page, navigate to the **.htm** file and then right-click the file. From the shortcut menu, select **Open with>Windows Edge**.

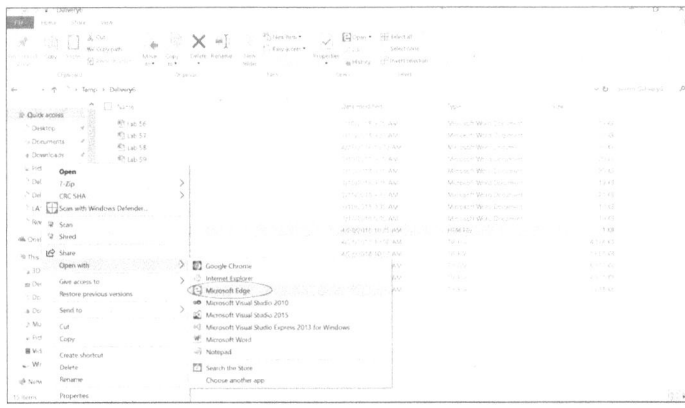

Goodheart-Willcox Publisher

8. _____ You can also simply click the file and it should open in Microsoft Edge unless it is not the default viewer for HTML type documents. Notice that the HTML version of the file has the Microsoft Edge letter *e* icon that is used to represent files that are in browser format.

9. _____ When the browser opens the page, it should appear exactly as it would if viewed through an Internet connection. You should not see any tags, only the contents. If the web page fails to display or if you receive an error message, ask your instructor for assistance. The most common problems are generally generated by errors when coding the page. Be sure to check your web page code for errors.

10. _____ After successfully displaying your first web page, modify the page so that it looks like the following:

    <html>

    <head>

    <title>This is the title and cannot be seen in the displayed page.</title>

    </head>

    <body>

    <H1>This is an H1 heading.</H1>

    <H6>This is an H6 heading.</H6>

    <H1>This is my first Web page written in HTML code.</H1>

    </body>

    </html>

11. _____ Save the file using first a text file and then as an HTML file.

12. _____ Open the web page using Microsoft Edge to view the page changes.

13. _____ You can view the code used to create an HTML web page being displayed by Internet Explorer. Simply right-click the web page while it is viewed in Microsoft Edge and then select **View Source** from the shortcut menu. The HTML code will be revealed if the page was written using standard HTML code. You may have to select the **DOM Explorer** tab to view the HTML code.

14. _____ Modify your code by using other HTML tags. For example, use <B> and <FONT COLOR> to create a headline in your web page. Experiment with other tags and attributes. Retain your work from this laboratory activity for the next laboratory activity.

15. _____ If you have Internet access, you can perform a Google search to find much more information about HTML coding and web-page creation. One excellent source of information is W3schools located at www.w3schools.com. It even has an HTML coding simulator so that you can practice code online and instantly see the results. Information about many more web-page coding languages is also available. You might want to try inserting an image into your web page.

16. _____ Answer the review questions and then return all materials to their proper storage area.

Review Questions

1. What are the four fundamental markup language tags used for creating a simple HTML web page?

2. What file extensions are used to identify an HTML file?

3. What does the acronym HTML represent?

4. What is the function of a web browser?

5. True or False: HTML tags are case-sensitive.

6. What is the most common problem for an HTML coded page to fail to display properly?

7. What tag is used to indicate the end of a paragraph?

8. What tag is used to create the largest heading font?

Name _____ Date _____ Class _____

Creating an Intranet Web Page

Outcomes

After completing this laboratory activity, you will be able to:
- Identify the default directory location for a web page.
- Identify the common file names for the default web page.
- Carry out simple diagnostics if a web page fails to display.
- Construct a simple intranet.

Introduction

In the last laboratory activity, you created a simple web page using HTML coding. In this laboratory activity, you will configure your web page as the home page for a simple intranet, similar to one that could be found in a small office.

When a web browser is directed to a website, it looks for a default web page on that site. A default web page can be named **default.htm**, **default.html**, **index.htm**, **index.html**, or **index.asp**. For this laboratory activity, you will save your web page as **default.htm**. After the web page is saved, you will place it in the C:\inetpub\wwwroot directory, as shown in the following screen capture. The C:\inetpub\wwwroot directory is created when Microsoft's Internet Information Service (IIS) is installed.

Goodheart-Willcox Publisher

Notice that the complete path is C:\inetpub\wwwroot. By default, when a web page is placed in this directory, it will automatically be given file permissions that permit access to anonymous users. If the web page were not given these permissions, anonymous users would receive a message saying that they do not have permission to access or to view the web page.

To access the intranet website, enter http://<computer_name> or the IPv4 address of the workstation into the Microsoft Edge address bar. You may also add the port number to the IP address. For example, you can enter 192.168.0.5:80, where 192.168.0.5 is the IP address of the computer hosting the web page and :80 is the port number for the web-page service. If you have problems accessing the web page across the network, try the following:

- Ping the localhost from the computer hosting the web page to verify that the TCP/IP protocol is configured.
- Ping the host from a different computer on the network to verify that there is a complete cable connection.
- Check if Windows Firewall is turned off or is configured to allow access to HTTP port 80.

There is extensive information about IIS available at the Microsoft IIS website located at www.iis.net. If you visit the website during this lab activity, please be brief. The information is quite extensive, and you could use too much lab time reviewing the information and not be able to complete the lab activity.

The key steps for posting a web page and viewing from another computer on the same local area network are as follows.

1. Enable IIS on the web server.
2. Create a document and save it as an HTML file.
3. Rename the file to "default" and then place a copy on the web server in the C:\inetpub\wwwroot directory.
4. Access the default web page from any computer on the local area network using the web server IPv4 address, for example, http://192.168.0.5.

The web page will not be viewable from a distant Internet location because you are using a private IPv4 type address. When a page is hosted by a web-hosting service, a public IPv4 address is assigned to the default web-page location.

Equipment and Materials

- Two Windows 10 or later computers connected as a peer-to-peer network

Procedure

1. _____ Report to your assigned workstation(s).

2. _____ Boot the computers and verify they are in working order.

3. _____ Check if IIS has been installed on one of the computers. You can check if it is installed by accessing **Start>Control Panel>Programs and Features>Turn Windows** features on and off. Check if Internet Information Services and Internet Information Services Hostable Web Core have been enabled. If not, simply select the appropriate check box to enable the features.

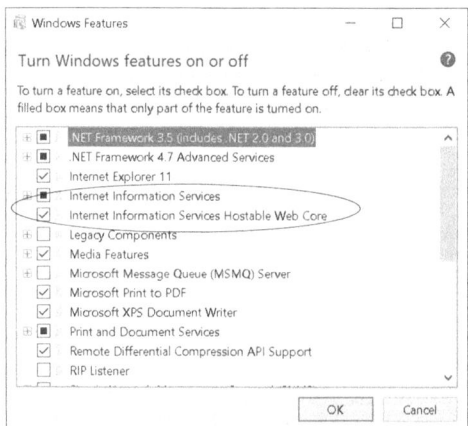

Goodheart-Willcox Publisher

4. _____ After enabling the IIS service, you can check if the service is running by entering "localhost" into the address bar.

Goodheart-Willcox Publisher

Name _____

You will replace the function of the default IIS page with your own web page. The two web pages can coexist in the same directory. Your web page will be renamed default.htm, making it the default web page for the computer.

5. _____ Copy the web page you created in the last laboratory activity to the C:\inetpub\wwwroot directory. You must include the file extension .htm. You can leave the iisstart.htm page in the directory. The iisstart.htm page will not interfere with the results of this lab activity. Look at the following screen capture to see an example of a default page added to the wwwroot folder.

Goodheart-Willcox Publisher

Notice the default.htm file is placed inside the wwwroot directory folder, which resides inside the inetpub directory folder.

6. _____ Access the default page from the other workstation, not the host. Use the following methods: IP address (http://192.168.0.5), IP address and the port number (http://192.168.0.5:80), and the name of the web-hosting computer (http://Station1). You should be able to view the default home page using any one of the three methods. Call your instructor to check your work.

7. _____ Now, you will view some of the IIS properties associated with the web page you created. Open Computer Management. The IIS Manager is located under **Services and Applications** folder located in the left-hand pane.

Goodheart-Willcox Publisher

8. _____ Take a few minutes to explore the many configuration options available through the IIS Manager console. Do *not* make any changes at this time.

9. _____ Return the computers to their original configuration and then answer the review questions.

Review Questions

1. Where is the default directory location for the web page?

   _____

2. What file names are used to identify the default web page?

   _____

3. What will happen when you type localhost into the Microsoft Edge address bar?

   _____

   _____

4. List three simple diagnostic steps to perform if a web page does not display.

   _____

   _____

   _____

5. Why is the default web page not viewable across the Internet?

   _____

Name _____ Date _____ Class _____

LABORATORY ACTIVITY 48
Observing E-Mail Activity with Wireshark

Outcomes

After completing this laboratory activity, you will be able to:
- Explain the operation of SMTP, IMAP, and POP3 servers.
- Identify port numbers assigned to IMAP, POP3, and SMTP.
- Identify which protocols are used to encapsulate SMTP.

Introduction

In this laboratory activity, you will use Wireshark to capture e-mail packets as they travel to and from your computer. You will examine the capture and identify the port numbers assigned to IMAP, POP3, and SMTP. You will also identify the protocols used to encapsulate SMTP.

Sending and receiving e-mail is a simple operation. When you send e-mail, the e-mail is uploaded to a Simple Mail Transport Protocol (SMTP) server. E-mail is received from or downloaded from an Internet Message Access Protocol (IMAP) server, a Post Office Protocol (POP3) server, or an HTTP server, commonly referred to as a *web e-mail server*. IMAP and POP3 are true e-mail protocols written expressly for e-mail communications. HTTP is not an e-mail protocol but rather a means to access your e-mail using a web browser.

The following screen capture represents a portion of a typical Windows e-mail configuration dialog box. Notice the choices for setting up an e-mail account. Users can enter the domain address of an incoming and outgoing e-mail server. Previously, Windows allowed you to customize the type of incoming server. The outgoing mail server uses SMTP to upload or send out e-mail. Port number 25 is associated with SMTP. Also, when you enter the name of the SMTP server, SMTP is typically incorporated into the name of the server such as **smtp.ameritech.yahoo.com**.

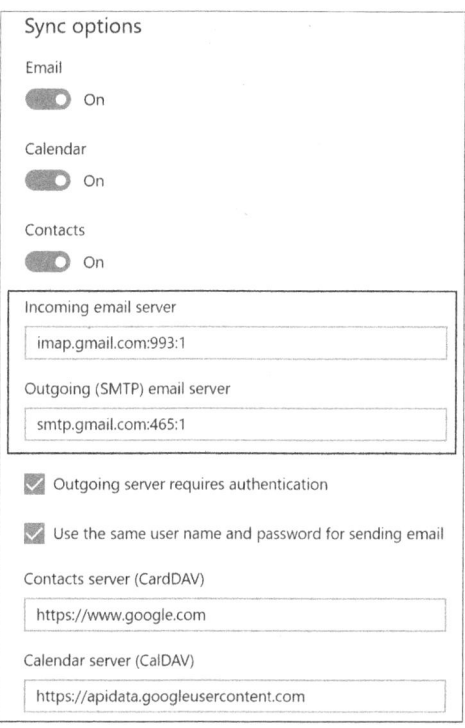

Goodheart-Willcox Publisher

One server may be used for both uploading and downloading e-mail, or two separate servers can be used. Each server may use the same name or have two different names. For example, Comcast uses mail.comcast.net for its incoming mail server and smtp.comcast.net for its outgoing mail server.

In the following screen capture, you can see a typical POP e-mail connection sequence as it appears in Wireshark. The user is establishing a connection to the ISP e-mail account. Notice that there are 11 POP e-mail messages being downloaded. POP is used to download e-mail messages.

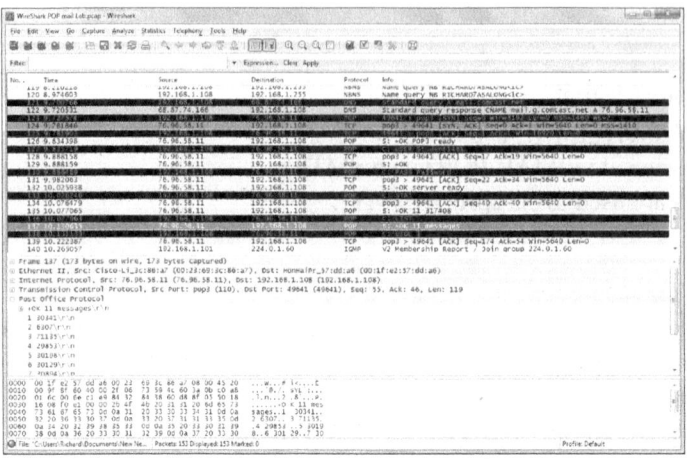

Goodheart-Willcox Publisher

In the next screen capture, the SMTP protocol is used to upload an e-mail being sent to Student1@rmroberts.com. The exact series of packets will vary depending on the type of e-mail client being used as well as which e-mail service provider is accessed. When performing the lab activity, your series of e-mail packets in the capture will not match the packets presented in the screen captures.

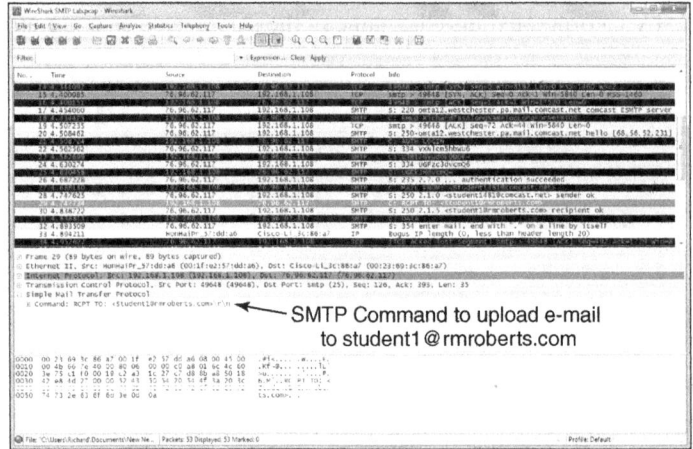

Goodheart-Willcox Publisher

Equipment and Materials

- Windows 10 or later computer with an Internet connection and Wireshark installed
- E-mail account

NOTE
You must have an e-mail account to perform this laboratory activity.

Name _____

Procedure

1. _____ Report to your assigned workstation.
2. _____ Boot the computer and verify it is in working order.
3. _____ Establish a connection to the Internet.
4. _____ Open Wireshark. To limit the amount of background activity being captured, start the Wireshark capture just before sending the e-mail message in the next step.
5. _____ Create an e-mail message and send it to yourself.
6. _____ After the e-mail has been successfully sent, stop the Wireshark capture and review its contents. Answer the following questions. Record your answers in the spaces provided.

    Which protocol was used to access and download the e-mail: POP, IMAP, or HTTP?

    _____

    Can you view the contents of the e-mail message (yes or no)?

    _____

7. _____ Start another capture and then send a short e-mail message to yourself or to any other e-mail address.
8. _____ After the e-mail has been successfully sent, stop the capture.
9. _____ Scan the capture for the protocols and packets used to send the e-mail. Answer the following question, writing your answer in the spaces provided.

    Which e-mail protocol was used to send the e-mail?

    _____

10. _____ You may run the laboratory activity again or until you feel comfortable with the results.
11. _____ Answer the review questions.

Review Questions

1. What are the three major e-mail protocols, not including HTTP?

    _____

2. Which e-mail protocol is designed to support e-mail uploads to the mail server?

    _____

3. Which e-mail protocols are designed to support downloading e-mail from the mail server?

    _____

4. Which protocol was designed to allow you to access e-mail using a web browser and is not an exclusive e-mail protocol?

    _____

5. What port number is associated with IMAP?

    _____

6. Which port number is associated with POP3?

    _____

7. Which port number is associated with SMTP?

___

8. Which major protocols are used to encapsulate SMTP?

___

Name _____ Date _____ Class _____

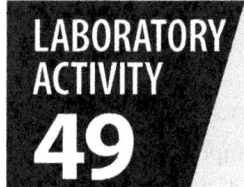

Configuring FTP

Outcomes

After completing this laboratory activity, you will be able to:
- Identify the URL heading for accessing an FTP site.
- Differentiate between FTP site properties displayed in Windows Explorer and Computer Management.
- Use Computer Management to install and configure the File Transfer Protocol (FTP) service.

Introduction

In this laboratory activity, you will install and configure the File Transfer Protocol (FTP) service for a peer-to-peer network. You will also create a document for the FTP server using a text editor, such as Notepad. Once the document is created, you will copy it to the FTP directory, **C:\inetpub\ftproot**. The latest version of IIS FTP service associated with Server 2016/2019 and Windows 10 is quite different from previous versions. The security features have been enhanced and the FTP service is disabled by default.

Although the FTP service requires that Internet Information Service (IIS) be installed, the FTP service is not installed by default when you install IIS. You will most likely need to install the FTP service in a similar fashion to the way you installed the web service in the previous laboratory activity.

There are two ways to view FTP site properties just as there are two ways to view website properties. You can access the properties of the FTP site by using Windows Explorer or Computer Management. The results of these methods are different. When the FTP site or website is accessed through Windows Explorer, properties concerning the file system are displayed. When you view the properties of the FTP site or website through Computer Management, the properties of the service configuration and associated file properties are displayed. The main purpose of Computer Management is to view and configure a service. This will become more apparent after performing this laboratory activity.

The FTP service is a great way to provide access to documents in an office Intranet. Employees can easily access informational documents, such as policy books and office forms. To access the FTP site, you would use Microsoft Edge and enter the IP address or name of the FTP server. You must replace the HTTP protocol in the URL with FTP. Look at the example in the following screen capture.

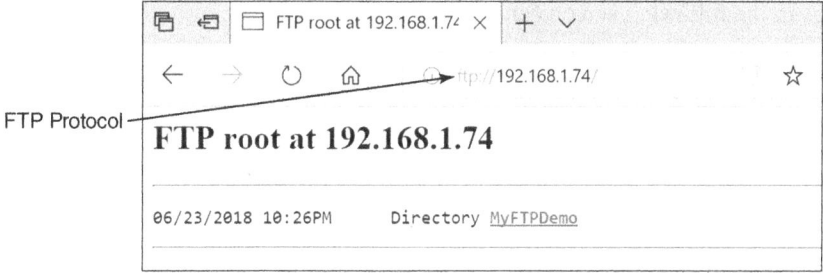

Goodheart-Willcox Publisher

As you see, the first part of the URL address is used to identify the protocol used for the communication. You may also use the port number as part of the address when accessing the site. The FTP port number is 21. For example, a complete address using the IP address of the FTP server and the FTP port number would be ftp://192.168.0.10:21.

There are known issues with the correct intended outcome of this lab activity. The FTP program and services were not intended to be used in a school environment. When multiple students share the same computer and complete the same FTP lab activity, unexpected results can occur. Fragments of the original lab activity configuration can remain and cause unexpected results in additional student labs. This lab is performed best on a computer that has never configured this lab before. Other known issues are as follows:
- You will need a local user account on the host to log on to the FTP site you create.
- You may need to set up share permissions for any folders and directories you add to the FTP site to allow access to users.

- The Windows Firewall blocks FTP access by default. You will need to reconfigure Windows Firewall to allow FTP incoming connections on the host.
- FTP and Anonymous are reserved words and cannot be used as an account name.
- FTP content, especially executable programs, are often blocked by web browsers and antivirus programs.

If you continue to have problems accessing the FTP site, set up a typical share on the host computer and see if you can access it from a remote computer. If you can access the share, then most likely you have not configured the FTP site properly. If you cannot access the share, then most likely Windows Firewall or the share user permissions are preventing access to the computer remotely.

Equipment and Materials
- Two Windows 10 or later computers configured as a peer-to-peer network

Procedure

1. _____ Report to your assigned workstation.

2. _____ Boot the computers and verify they are in working order.

3. _____ Check if the File Transfer Protocol (FTP) Service is installed on one of the computers. If the FTP service is installed, you should see the C:\inetpub\ftproot directory listed in Windows Explorer as shown in the following screen capture.

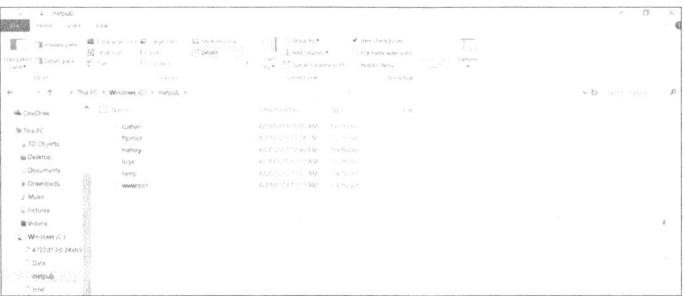

Goodheart-Willcox Publisher

Also, Computer Management will display FTP sites that have been created. Note the **Default Web Site** and **MyFTPsite** entries in the following screen capture.

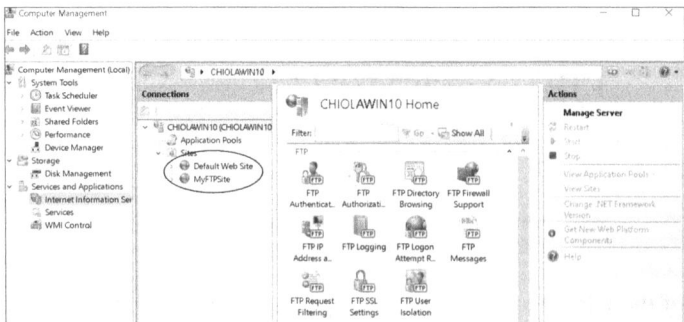

Goodheart-Willcox Publisher

If FTP has not been installed, proceed to step 4. If it has been installed, proceed to step 5.

Name _____

4. _____ To install FTP services on the workstation, open the **Windows Features** dialog box. Expand **Internet Information Services**. A list of the IIS services will display. Select the **FTP Server** option as well as **FTP Extensibility** and **FTP Service**. Click **OK**. The FTP service will be automatically installed.

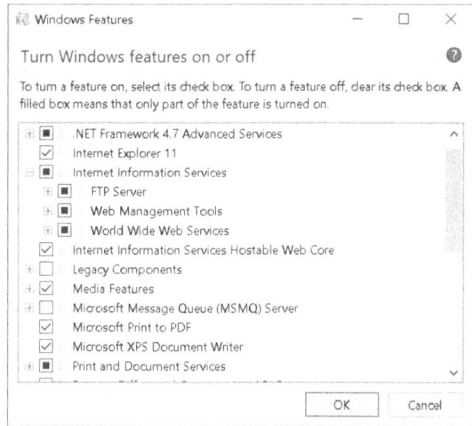

Goodheart-Willcox Publisher

5. _____ Open a text editor such as Notepad and create a document to install in the \Inetpub\ftproot directory. For the contents of your document, enter: This is a sample file for FTP demonstration. Save the file as FTP_DemoFileDocument.txt. Also, create a folder under \Inetpub\ftproot called MyFTPsite. When you are finished, you will have a document under the \Inetpub\ftproot and a folder.

6. _____ Set the permissions on the folder and document to allow everyone the right to read both.

7. _____ Open Computer Management to begin configuring the FTP site. It should look similar to that in the following screen capture.

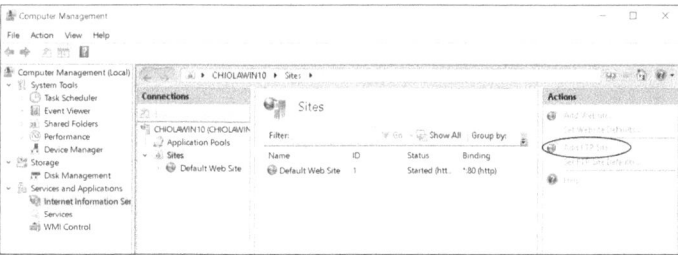

Goodheart-Willcox Publisher

Laboratory Activity 49   Configuring FTP   259

8. ____ Select the **Add FTP Site** to start the Add FTP Site wizard. This option is located in the right-most pane. The following dialog box will display prompting you for an FTP site name and for the physical path to the FTP content directory.

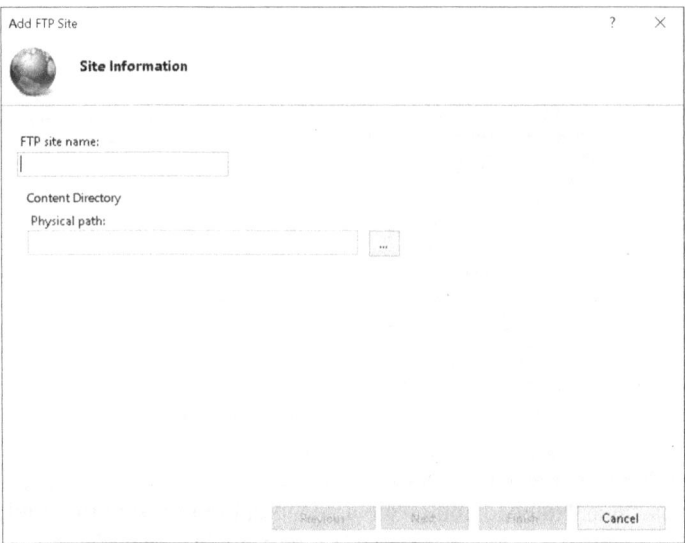

Goodheart-Willcox Publisher

9. ____ Enter MyFTPsite in the **FTP site name** text box. In the **Physical path** text box, enter the location of the ftproot directory. You can use the browse button on the right side of the text box to locate **ftproot**. The complete path should be similar to **C:\inetpub\ftproot** when located. Click **Next**. A dialog box similar to the following will display, prompting you for the FTP site IP address and security settings.

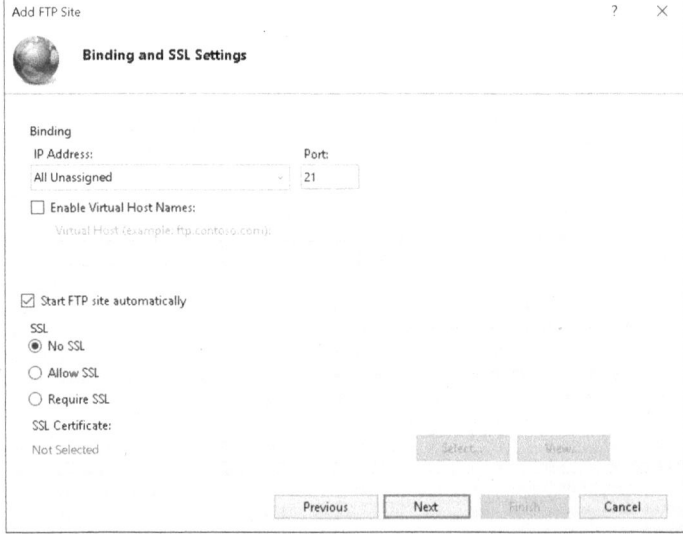

Goodheart-Willcox Publisher

260 Networking Fundamentals Lab Manual

Name _____

10. _____ The default setting in the **IP Address** text box is **All Unassigned**. Use the drop-down arrow to reveal the IPv4 address of the host. The IPv4 address should be the same as the host address. Leave the **Start FTP site automatically** option enabled. This will start the FTP service automatically every time the host is booted. Change the default **SSL** option to **Allow SSL**. Click **Next**. A dialog box similar to the following will display.

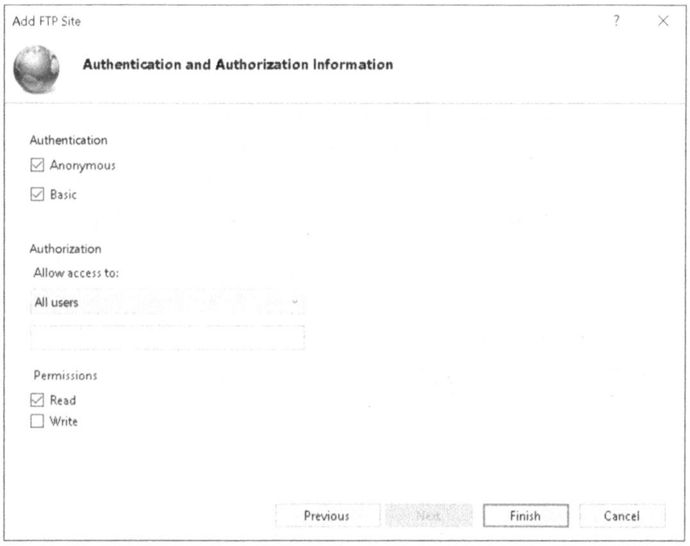

Goodheart-Willcox Publisher

11. _____ Select the **Anonymous** and **Basic** options. In the **Permissions** section, select the **Read** option. Then, click **Finish** to create the new FTP site.

> **NOTE**
> A typical FTP site allows for anonymous connections, which means that when accessing an FTP site, you do not need to supply a username or password.

12. _____ Test the new site by entering ftp:// followed by the IPv4 host address, for example, ftp://192.168.1.74. The result should be similar to that in the following screen capture.

Goodheart-Willcox Publisher

All contents, both the directories and individual files, of the FTP site will display. You may be prompted to enter a local user account name and password to access the directories and folder.

13. _____ Try accessing the new FTP site from the other computer. To do so, simply enter ftp:// and the IPv4 address of the FTP host computer into the address bar. You may be prompted for a user account name and password. If you encounter problems, call your instructor for assistance.

14. _____ Answer the review questions and return all materials to their proper storage areas. The instructor may want you to leave the new FTP site on the computer rather than remove it. Check with your instructor.

Review Questions

1. _____ Which of the following is the correct example of a complete FTP URL address?
   A. http://192.168.0.1:80
   B. http://192.168.0.1:21
   C. ftp://192.168.0.1:80
   D. ftp://192.168.0.1:21

2. What two Windows utilities allow you to view FTP site properties?
   _____

3. What is displayed when you view the properties of the FTP site through Computer Management?
   _____
   _____

4. What is displayed when the FTP site is accessed through Windows Explorer?
   _____
   _____

5. Which option in Computer Management will start the Add FTP Site wizard?
   _____

Name _____ Date _____ Class _____

Observing FTP Activity with Wireshark

Outcomes

After completing this laboratory activity, you will be able to:
- Identify protocols associated with FTP.
- Recall the purpose of the protocols associated with FTP.

Introduction

In this laboratory activity, you will use Wireshark to capture network activity associated with the File Transfer Protocol (FTP). You will first view the sample capture in the Wireshark Sample 11 file and inspect specific frame contents. Then, you will set up your own Wireshark capture.

Most FTP sites are configured for anonymous access. For this configuration, no username or password is required. In the Wireshark captures, you will see that the user's e-mail address is used as a password for the FTP site.

Near the end of the laboratory activity are several FTP sites that you can view if you have Internet access. Internet access is optional for this laboratory activity. You can still visit the sites using any computer that has Internet access, such as your home computer.

An interesting fact about connections made with FTP sites is that they are automatically included in the Windows Explorer directory structure listed under the Network folder after they are downloaded. Look at the following screen capture. Notice the FTP sites listed in the following screen capture.

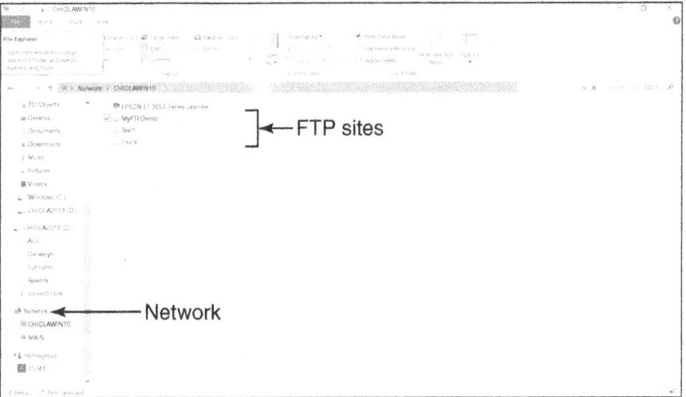

Goodheart-Willcox Publisher

FTP is used for downloading content from the Internet, such as game software applications and user manuals. When you visit the Microsoft and Novell FTP sites in the lab activity, you will see some typical files available for download.

Equipment and Materials

- Two Windows computers connected as a peer-to-peer network (one computer must be running the FTP service with at least one file available for an FTP download; the other computer must have Wireshark installed)
- Internet access (optional)
- Wireshark Sample 11 file

Wireshark Sample 11 file location: _____

_____

Copyright Goodheart-Willcox Co., Inc.
May not be reproduced or posted to a publicly accessible website.

Procedure

1. _____ Report to your assigned workstation(s).

2. _____ Boot the Windows computers and verify they are in working order.

3. _____ Start Wireshark and then open the Wireshark Sample 11 file.

4. _____ Look at frame 5. Notice that the FTP process starts with a TCP request to the destination. The destination is using IP address 192.168.0.10 and port 21. By default, port 21 is associated with an FTP site.

5. _____ Now look at frame 9. Notice that the request has been made by "USER anonymous." In frame 10, the FTP server requests the anonymous user's e-mail address. Some sites request a user's e-mail address. Typically, the e-mail address for anonymous access is IEUser@ for no e-mail address or IEUser@<your email provider> when you do have an e-mail provider and a valid e-mail address. If you do not have a valid e-mail address, the e-mail address will be simply IEUser@. The e-mail address is also used as a password for accessing the FTP site.

6. _____ Inspect any of the FTP frames. Notice that the protocol used to transfer FTP is TCP. FTP carries commands and information between a destination and source. It relies on TCP, IP, and the Ethernet protocol to deliver the contents. TCP contains the source and destination port numbers, IP contains the source and destination IP addresses, and the Ethernet protocol contains the destination and source MAC addresses.

7. _____ Close the Wireshark Sample 11 file and then start a Wireshark capture.

8. _____ Access the FTP site created in your last lab activity while running Wireshark and download the file you created for this site.

9. _____ After downloading and viewing the file, stop the Wireshark capture and inspect the frame contents. See if you can locate the beginning and end of the file transfer process.

10. _____ If you have an Internet connection available, see how a real FTP site reacts when a request is made. In your web browser, enter ftp://ftp.microsoft.com to access the Microsoft FTP site. You will see many different files available from Microsoft. You can also enter ftp://ftp.suse.com for the SUSE FTP site. Some browsers and security programs block downloads from FTP sites by default. Watch the screen closely for warning messages.

11. _____ Return the computers to their original configuration.

12. _____ Answer the review questions.

Review Questions

1. What protocol contains the destination and source IP addresses?

   _____

2. What protocol contains the destination and source MAC address?

   _____

3. What protocol contains the FTP transfer commands?

   _____

4. What is the purpose of FTP?

   _____

5. On what protocols does FTP rely to deliver its contents?

   _____

Name _____ Date _____ Class _____

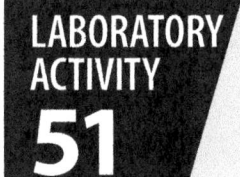

Observing HTTP Activity with Wireshark

Outcomes

After completing this laboratory activity, you will be able to:
- Recall the purpose of the HTTP protocol.
- Recall the purpose of the DNS protocol.
- Identify the protocols that support HTTP.

Introduction

In this laboratory activity, you will become familiar with the HTTP and DNS protocols and how they are used to locate and display web-server content. The DNS protocol provides a mechanism for converting domain names to assigned IP addresses. The DNS service is needed because packets are sent across the network using IP addresses, not domain names. There is no place in the address of a packet header for a domain name, only IP addresses.

After DNS resolves the host name to an IP address, HTTP is used to transmit the contents and HTML code from the website to the requesting computer. TCP, IP, and the Ethernet protocol encapsulate HTTP and provide the proper addressing to transfer information between the source and destination.

Equipment and Materials

- Two Windows 10 or later computers connected as a peer-to-peer network (One computer should have Wireshark installed.)
- Wireshark Sample 12 file

    Wireshark Sample 12 file location:

    _____

- Wireshark Sample 13 file.

    Wireshark Sample 13 file location:

    _____

Procedure

1. _____ Report to your assigned workstation(s).

2. _____ Boot the computers and verify they are in working order.

3. _____ Start Wireshark and then open the **Wireshark Sample 12** file.

4. _____ Look at frames 4 through 7. Notice that the web browser attempted to make a connection to www.microsoft.com when the browser was started. A web browser is configured to connect to a default website on startup. The computer on which this capture was taken is configured to connect to www.microsoft.com automatically when the web browser is opened. Since the computer used for the capture is not connected to the Internet, you see only the attempt to connect to the www.microsoft.com site, and not the actual transfer of web page content.

5. _____ Now, look at frame 8. Notice the attempt to connect to a web page that is located on another computer. Frames 8, 9, and 10 are a series of TCP packets used to establish a connection between the destination and source. After the connection has been established, HTTP supports the web-page transfer.

6. _____ Examine frame 12. This frame carries the contents and HTML coding of the web page. The middle pane of the Wireshark capture displays the source code of the web page. The bottom pane displays the source code of the web page in ASCII code.

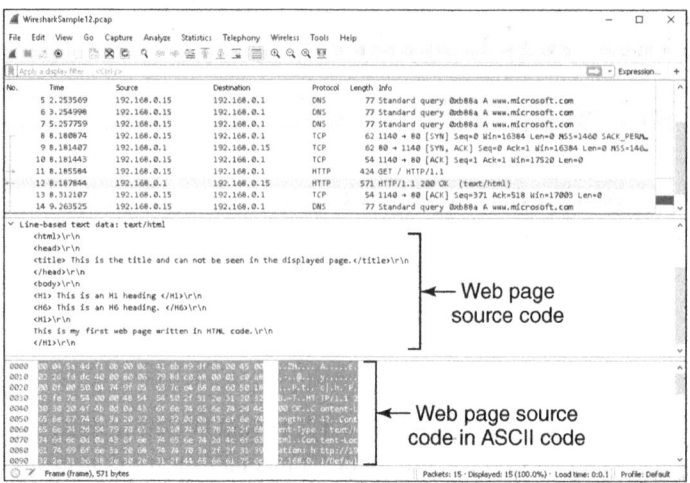

Goodheart-Willcox Publisher

7. _____ In frame 12, look in the TCP packet and locate the port information. It will indicate port 80 for the source and port 1140 for the destination. The default port for a web server is port 80. The computer requesting the web page can use most any available port to establish a connection with the web server.

8. _____ Close the **Wireshark Sample 12** file and then open the **Wireshark Sample 13** file.

9. _____ Look at frames 1 and 2. You will see a DNS query asking for the address of **www.google.com**. Frame 2 responds to the DNS query with three IP addresses that can be used to access the Google website search engine.

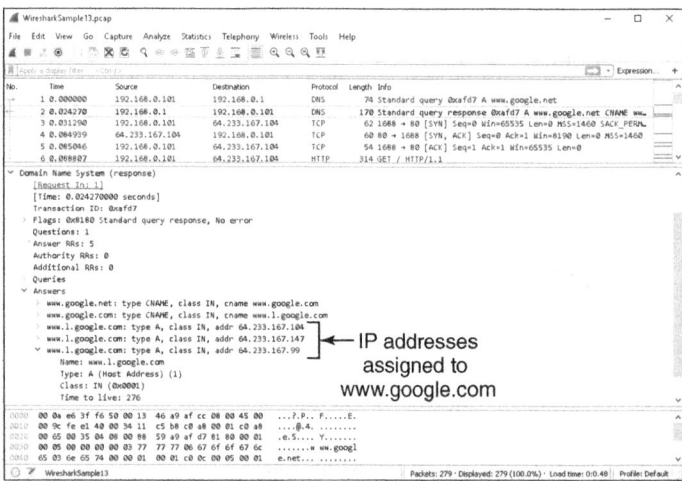

Goodheart-Willcox Publisher

10. _____ Now, look at frame 31 and 32 and see if you can determine what website is being queried and what IP address is assigned to the website. Record this information in the space provided.

11. _____ Close the **Wireshark Sample 13** file.

12. _____ If you have an Internet connection, start a Wireshark capture and then visit the **www.g-w.com** website. Stop the Wireshark capture and then inspect the contents of the frames. See if you can locate the DNS query and the IP address of the **www.g-w.com** website.

13. _____ Repeat step 12, this time accessing a different website. Verify the port address used by the website. Also, study which protocols are used to support the HTTP protocol.

14. _____ Answer the review questions.

Name _____

Review Questions

1. What is used to transmit web-page contents and HTML code from the website to the requesting computer?
   _____

2. What protocol is used to match domain names to IPv4 addresses?
   _____

3. What protocols encapsulate HTTP and provide the proper addressing to transfer information between the source and destination?
   _____

Notes

Name _____ Date _____ Class _____

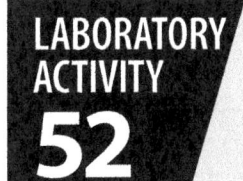

Creating a Virtual Private Network Connection

Outcomes

After completing this laboratory activity, you will be able to:
- Recall the characteristics of the Point-to-Point Tunneling Protocol.
- Recall the characteristics of the Layer 2 Tunneling Protocol.
- Use the Network and Sharing Center options to configure a VPN host and client.
- Use the **Network Connections** dialog box to verify a VPN connection.

Introduction

In this laboratory activity, you will install a virtual private network (VPN) connection between two computers on a LAN. VPN connections are made to increase security or privacy when two computers are exchanging data. The two original tunneling protocols associated with VPN connections are Point-to-Point Tunneling Protocol (PPTP) and Layer 2 Tunneling Protocol (L2TP). Today, two additional security protocols are available for VPN connection support: Secure Socket Tunneling Protocol (SSTP) and IKEv2.

PPTP is part of the TCP/IP protocol suite. It allows TCP/IP, IPX/SPX, or NetBEUI packets to be encapsulated inside PPP using the Generic Route Encapsulation (GRE) protocol. PPTP incorporates authentication, encryption, and compression. Authentication ensures that only authorized persons can open the contents of the frames. Encryption ensures that if content is captured, the information inside will remain secure. Compression allows for large collections of data to be compressed and transported in a more efficient manner.

L2TP is a proprietary protocol and has been jointly developed by Cisco Systems and Microsoft. Its characteristics are similar to those of PPTP, but there are a few differences. The main difference is that L2TP supports data transmission across Frame Relay, ATM, X.25, and TCP/IP systems.

SSTP was first introduced in Windows Vista and has continued through Windows 11. It provides a mechanism to support PPP to be transported through Secure Sockets Layer (SSL), which is associated with HTTP SSL-type connections.

IKEv2 was first introduced in Windows 7 and Windows Server 2008 and still is found in Windows 11 and Windows Server 2019. It allows for a continuous wireless network connection while moving between different Wireless Access Points. Before IKEv2, VPN connections would disconnect and need to be reestablished each time the connection was broken. With the introduction of IKEv2, this is no longer a problem.

Windows 10 has an option that allows the user to configure authentication if a user selects a built-in VPN type, for example, IKEv2, L2TP, PPTP, or Automatic.

When creating a VPN connection, you must first configure a VPN host and then a VPN client. On completion, the client will connect to the host. The host allows a remote connection to the VPN client.

After completing the VPN connection, all activities that take place between the two computers are encrypted. In other words, if you open a share on the host from the client, the transaction is encrypted.

Configuring of a VPN is accomplished using a wizard. You simply respond to a series of dialog boxes and the configuration will be automatically created. You may also manually change configuration settings after the VPN has been created. The following list contains some common causes of VPN connection problems:

- A user account on the VPN host and VPN client has not been created.
- The username and password have been incorrectly entered. (Check if the [Caps Lock] key has been accidentally enabled.)
- The network cable is unplugged.
- A firewall is blocking the connection. This is normally not a problem because the firewall in Windows 10 automatically configures itself for a VPN-type connection.
- Third-party security or antivirus software is preventing the connection.
- The Internet Connection Share (ICS) on the local network is causing the VPN connection to fail.
- A network switch, gateway, or router is blocking the VPN connection.

For additional troubleshooting help, Microsoft has a web page for VPN error codes: https://learn.microsoft.com/en-us/troubleshoot/windows-client/networking/error-codes-for-dial-up-vpn-connection.

Equipment and Materials

- Two Windows 10 or later computers configured as a peer-to-peer network

NOTE
A user account name and password must be established on both computers before starting the laboratory activity. A VPN connection relies on user authentication to complete the connection between the two computers.

Procedure

1. ____ Report to your assigned workstation(s).

2. ____ Boot the computers and verify they are in working order.

3. ____ Assign each computer a role, one as VPN host and the other as VPN client. Then, record the following information:

- VPN host name:

- VPN host IPv4 address:

- VPN host IPv6 address:

- VPN client name:

- VPN client IPv4 address:

- VPN client IPv6 address:

4. ____ At the VPN host, open the **Network and Sharing Center**, and then select the **Change adapter settings** option.

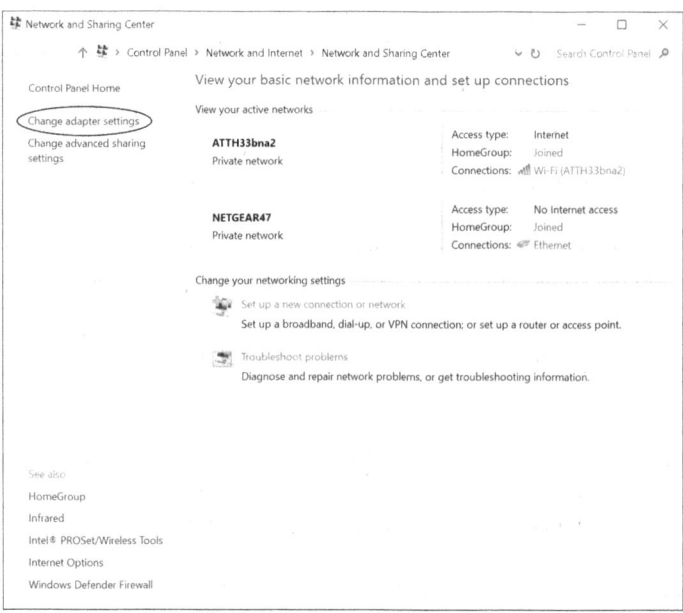

Goodheart-Willcox Publisher

Name _____

5. _____ Press the [Alt] key to reveal the menu bar. The menu bar is typically hidden from view. Select **File>New Incoming Connection**.

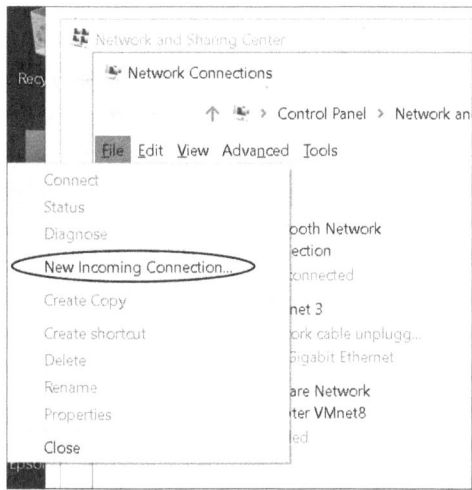

Goodheart-Willcox Publisher

6. _____ A short series of dialog boxes will appear to assist in configuring the VPN host.

7. _____ The next dialog box will allow you to either select existing user accounts or to create new user accounts for the incoming connection.

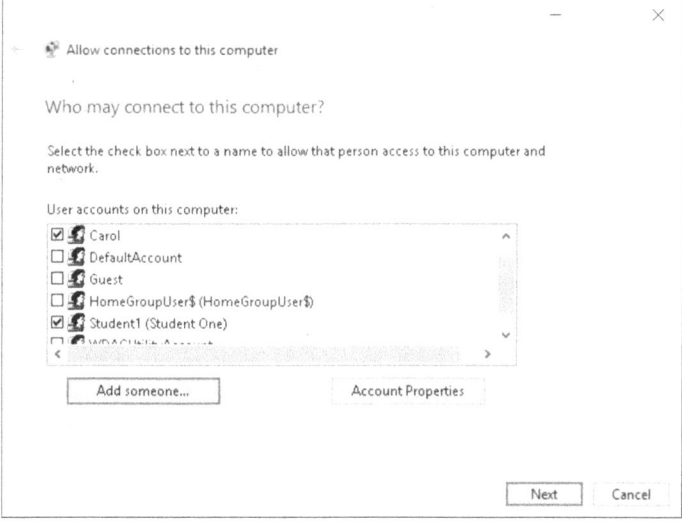

Goodheart-Willcox Publisher

Only users in the list can be authenticated and allowed to connect to this computer. Notice the **Add someone** button, which can be used to create a username and password. The **Account Properties** button allows you to change user account properties such as a forgotten password. One very important aspect about resetting a user account password is a user will no longer be able to access any files they have created on the computer. An administrator will need to intervene on behalf of the user to transfer any existing files to the user after the password is reset. Select users as directed by your instructor and click **Next**.

8. _____ The next dialog box to appear prompts you to select the VPN connection method. The options are **Through the Internet** and **Through a dial-up modem**. For this lab activity, select **Through the Internet**.

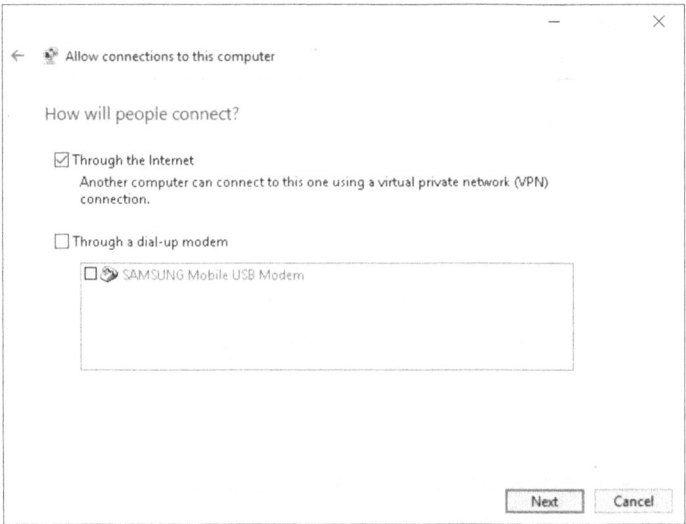

Goodheart-Willcox Publisher

9. _____ The next dialog box will prompt you to select the appropriate network software to use to support the VPN connection. By default, Internet Protocol Version 6 (IPv6) is not enabled because IPv6 is not the default Internet protocol at this time. Accept the defaults and click **Allow access**.

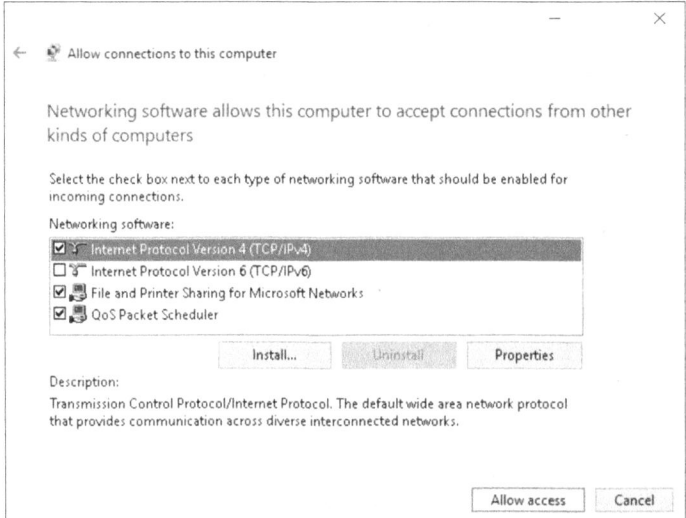

Goodheart-Willcox Publisher

Name _____

10. _____ The last dialog box to appear contains the name of the host computer. The name of the host computer is typically used to establish a connection from the client. You may also use IP address in some cases.

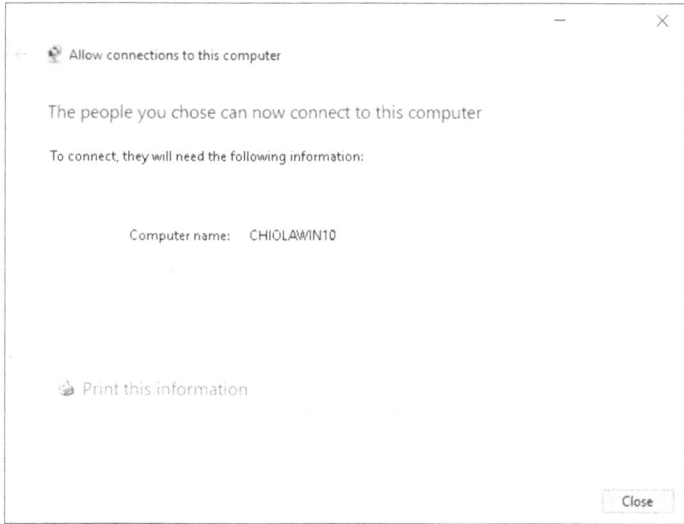

Goodheart-Willcox Publisher

There is no need to print the information because you already recorded the name at the beginning of the lab activity. Click **Close**.

11. _____ To verify that the VPN host has been successfully completed, open the **Network Connections** dialog box. You should see the new VPN connection called **Incoming Connections**, in addition to Local Area Connection. If the Incoming VPN Connection is not viewable through the **Network Connections** dialog box, call your instructor for assistance.

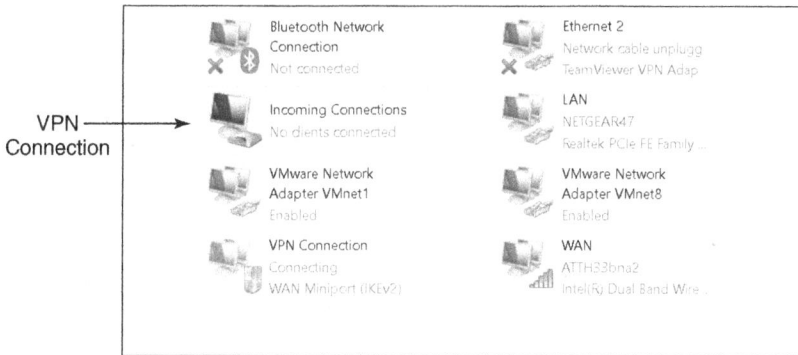

Goodheart-Willcox Publisher

12. _____ At the VPN client, start the VPN client configuration by opening the Network and Sharing Center and then selecting the **Set up a new connection or network** option.

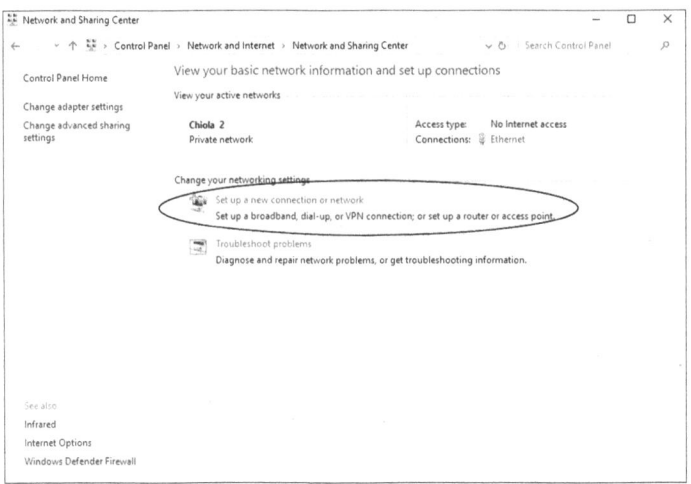

Goodheart-Willcox Publisher

13. _____ In the next dialog box, select the **Connect to a workplace** option and click **Next**.

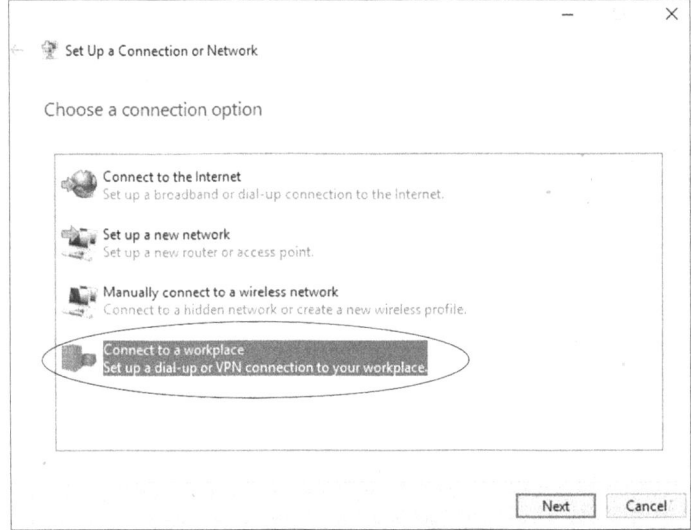

Goodheart-Willcox Publisher

Name _____

14. _____ Select the **Use my Internet connection (VPN)** option.

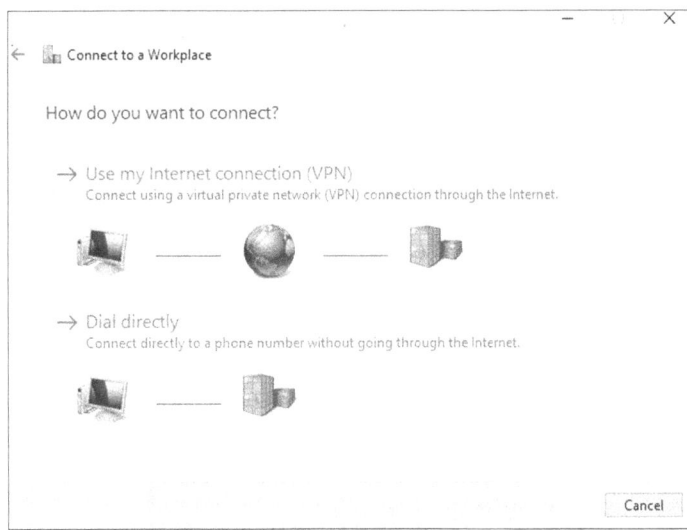

Goodheart-Willcox Publisher

15. _____ The next dialog box to appear prompts you for the VPN host name of address in IPv4 or IPv6 format. For this lab activity, use the VPN host name. You may repeat this portion of the lab activity later using the IPv4 address and then the IPv6 address to observe the results.

Goodheart-Willcox Publisher

16. _____ The next dialog box to appear will prompt you for a user account name and password. You must have a user account on the VPN host. If not, create one now on the VPN host and then return to the VPN client to complete the connection. It is recommended not to select the **Remember this password** option because it is considered a security risk.

17. _____ You can verify a successful connection being established by opening the **Network and Sharing Center**. On the VPN host, the VPN connection will be indicated as **RAS (Dial-in) Interface**. The RAS connection will only appear after the VPN client has established a connection.

On the VPN client, the VPN connection will be indicated as **VPN Connection**.

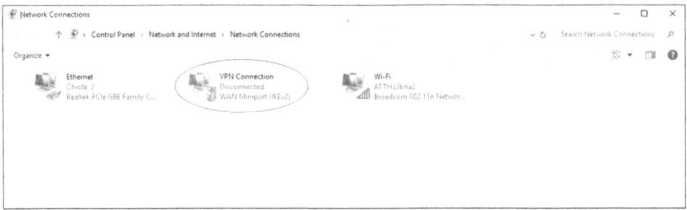

Goodheart-Willcox Publisher

If you move your mouse over the **Network** icon located in the notification area of the taskbar, you will see a dialog box similar to the one in the following screen capture.

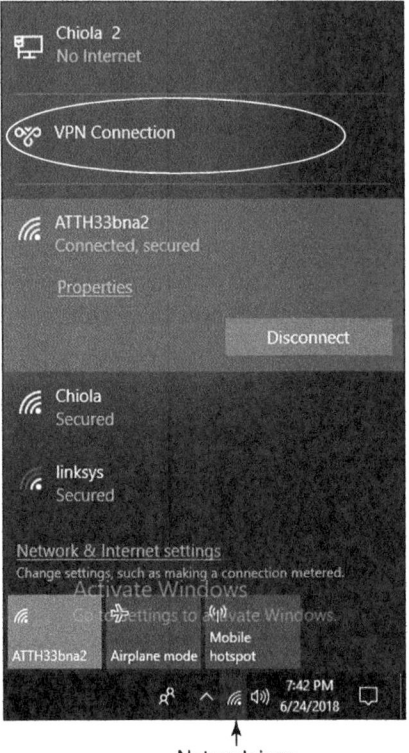

Network icon

Goodheart-Willcox Publisher

More than one VPN connection can be created. For example, you could configure a VPN client for multiple VPN connections, one for each company network in various cities. Each VPN configuration created will appear as a separate VPN connection option. You can simply click the option to start the existing VPN connection process.

18. _____ Call your instructor to inspect your VPN connection.

19. _____ If time permits, you may create another VPN connection, this time using the host IPv4 address or the Host IPv6 address.

20. _____ Return all materials to their proper storage area and then answer the review questions.

Review Questions

1. What are the two original tunneling protocols associated with VPN connections?

_____

_____

Name _____

2. What additional VPN protocols were introduced after the original two?
   _____
   _____

3. Which VPN protocol was developed by Microsoft to support and maintain wireless connections so they are not broken when passing from one wireless access point to another wireless access point?
   _____

4. Which VPN protocol utilizes Secure Sockets Layer (SSL) technology?
   _____

5. On which computer (VPN host or VPN client) must a user account and password be established before creating a VPN connection?
   _____
   _____

6. When does the VPN connection appear in the **View your active networks** section of the Network and Sharing Center?
   _____
   _____

7. Can you have more than one VPN connection configured on a client workstation?
   _____

Notes

Name _____ Date _____ Class _____

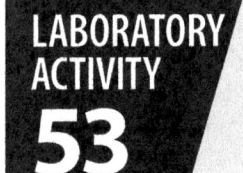

Observing VPN Activity with Wireshark

Outcomes

After completing this laboratory activity, you will be able to:
- Explain the basic connection process between a VPN client and host.
- Recall the role of the GRE protocol.
- Recall the role of the CHAP protocol as related to VPN.
- Recall the port numbers for PPTP, SSTP, and L2TP.

Introduction

In this laboratory activity, you will use Wireshark to view a sample capture containing a Virtual Private Network (VPN) communications. You will study the specific frames and data packets to see how VPN communicates. After studying the sample capture, you will generate your own capture and view its contents. Many of the protocols viewed in this lab activity will be better understood after completing Chapter 15—Network Security.

There are several tunneling protocols that can be used to support VPN connections. These protocols include Point-to-Point Tunneling Protocol (PTPP), Layer 2 Tunneling Protocol (L2TP), and Secure Socket Tunneling Protocol (SSTP). The particular network environment and the Windows operating system determine which protocol is used.

The Point-to-Point Tunneling Protocol (PPTP) will be viewed in this lab activity as well as other protocols related to a VPN. PPTP uses port 1723 to establish a connection between a VPN client and host. PPTP is an encapsulation protocol based on the Point-to-Point Protocol (PPP) and the Generic Routing Encapsulation (GRE) protocol. PPP was originally designed to encapsulate other protocols and transport them across a telephone connection. However, it does not offer any security.

Generic Routing Encapsulation (GRE) is designed to encapsulate a wide range of protocols beyond PPP. GRE encapsulates and encrypts the data carried inside a PPP packet. GRE does not encrypt IP header information, but rather hides it. The IP header contains the IP address of the destination and the source computers. The GRE header contains an alias IP address that is used in place of the assigned IP addresses. In this way, the original IP address is hidden during the tunneling operation. A tunnel is created, hiding not only the information inside the GRE packet, but also the "real" IP address of the destination and source. The GRE IP address is generally referred to as an *alias* or *virtual IP address*.

PPTP communication typically provides authentication through the Challenge Handshake Authentication Protocol (CHAP) or Microsoft Challenge Handshake Authentication Protocol (MS-CHAP). CHAP provides a mechanism for the verification of user passwords. The actual password is never exchanged inside packet contents; only a mathematical algorithm representing the password is exchanged. There will be more about CHAP in a later laboratory activity.

Please keep in mind that the term *Virtual Private Network* is generic in that it refers to any method of tunneling communications between two connections across a public or unsecured media. Other methods can be employed to accomplish the same task. For example, the Layer 2 Tunneling Protocol (L2TP) can be used, which incorporates all the same features as PPTP and also relies on the possession of a *certificate*. L2TP uses either port 500 or port 4500 to maintain a connection between a client and host. Port 500 is associated with the Internet Key Exchange (IKE) encryption method, and port 4500 is associated with Network Address Translation (NAT) when translating network IP addresses. An Internet Key Exchange (IKE) or Internet Protocol Security (IPSec) certificate is used with L2TP. The certificate verifies the identity of both the source and the destination. There will be more about certificates later while studying security. PPTP can be used on computers with Windows 2000 or later.

Secure Socket Tunneling Protocol (SSTP) is the latest tunneling protocol applied to Windows VPN connections. SSTP uses the SSL or HTTPS protocol over port 443. SSTP encapsulates PPP to create a VPN.

You will verify that PPTP is still used with Windows 10 and 11 even though newer VPN protocols have been introduced. You will also see where Windows 10 and 11 assign a temporary IPv6 address to be used with VPN connections but still relies on IPv4 as the default VPN protocol. There are options for the VPN configuration that will allow you to specify either IPv4 or IPv6 as the address mechanism, or both. The default is IPv4.

> **NOTE**
> Previously in a Windows XP VPN client, the DHCP server assigned an alias IPv4 address. This is no longer the case in Windows. Windows 10 and 11 generates a temporary IPv6 address and an IPv4 APIPA alias address, typically starting with 169.254 in the first two octets. You will identify this address using the **ipconfig** command during this laboratory activity.

Equipment and Materials

- Two Windows 10 or later computers configured as a peer-to-peer network. One computer must have the Wireshark program installed.
- Wireshark Sample 14 file

    Wireshark Sample 14 file location:

    _____

- Wireshark Sample 15 file

    Wireshark Sample 15 file location:

    _____

Procedure

1. _____ Report to your assigned workstation(s).

2. _____ Boot the Windows computers and verify they are in working order.

3. _____ One computer should be configured as a VPN host and the other as a VPN client. If they are not, configure them now and record the IPv4 address of each in the space provided.

    VPN host IPv4 address:

    _____

    VPN client IPv4 address:

    _____

4. _____ Start the Wireshark program and then open Wireshark Sample 14 file.

5. _____ Look at frames 1 through 7. Notice that the basic connection between the VPN host and client is being established using TCP and then PPTP. PPTP is used to configure the basic connection, such as identify the media (telephone line, network cable, etc.), operating system and revision, and other characteristics of the connection. You may expand the contents of the packets to examine them more closely.

6. _____ Look at frame 8. PPP is identified as the main protocol used for the packet. On closer examination, you will see that the frame is composed of not only PPP, but also GRE. GRE is encapsulating the PPP packet.

7. _____ Look at frames 18, 19, and 20. You will see the sequence of CHAP events. CHAP is used for authentication between the VPN host and client.

Name _____

8. _____ Now look at frame 37. The details of the packet contents should appear similar to the ones in the following screen capture.

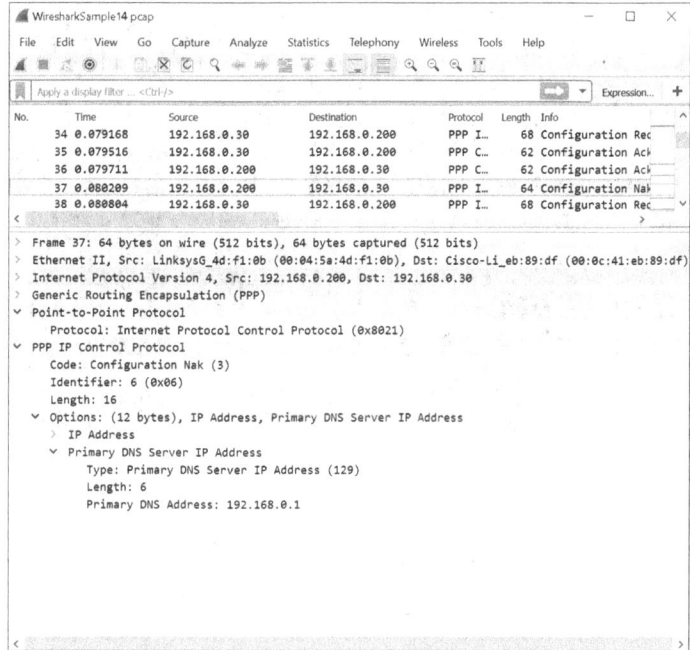

Goodheart-Willcox Publisher

Notice that the assigned destination and source IP addresses are indicated in the Internet Protocol packet header contents. The alias IP address and the DNS server IP addresses are indicated in the PPP IP Control Protocol packet. The alias IP address for the source (DNS server) IP address 192.168.000.200 is 192.168.0.1, and the alias IP address for the destination IP address 192.168.0.30 is 192.168.0.3. Notice that the contents are encapsulated inside the GRE packet.

9. _____ During most of the remaining frames in the sample, a series of GRE and PPP protocols are exchanged. You will notice that many of the frames have been identified as compressed data and encapsulated PPP. You will also see the common background activity frames associated with a peer-to-peer network.

10. _____ Look at frames 196 and 197 at the end of the sample capture. They are an echo-request and an echo-reply used to verify that the VPN connection still exists. In the second column labeled **Time**, the lapse time is approximately 59.9 seconds. Approximately every 60 seconds an echo-request and echo-response is exchanged. A VPN connection can last an undetermined amount of time, but it needs to incorporate a mechanism to detect an open circuit or if one of the computers disconnects for some reason, such as a power failure. The echo-request and echo-response is used for this purpose. This is similar to the ping echo-request, except that the ICMP protocol is not used.

11. _____ Open file **Wireshark Sample 15** and scan the protocols used to establish the PPTP connection. You will see that they are similar to the Windows XP sample capture. You will also notice that the VPN transactions using PPP and PPTP are carried out using IPv4 source and destination addresses even with a temporary IPv6 addresses being configured for the VPN.

12. _____ Close the sample capture and start your own capture of the VPN connection you have configured. Be sure that Wireshark is running before a connection is established. You may wish to wait a short period (one to two minutes) after booting the computers before starting Wireshark. This will keep a lot of activity from being included in the capture that is unrelated to the VPN connection when the computer is booted.

13. _____ After the VPN connection has been established, run the ipconfig command at each computer to inspect the assigned IP addresses. You will see a result similar to that in the following screen capture at the Windows 10 VPN client. Notice that the "PPP Adapter VPN Connection" section has two IPv6 addresses. One is the link-local address and the other is the default gateway address. These are only temporary IPv6 addresses that will be lost after breaking the VPN connection.

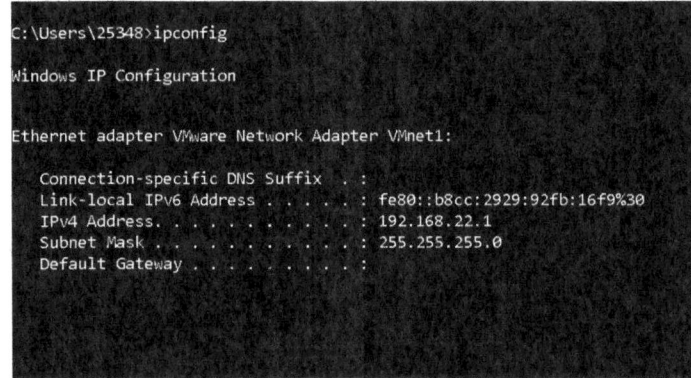

Goodheart-Willcox Publisher

Look at the following screen capture from the Windows 10 VPN host computer. Notice that the Windows 10 VPN host automatically generated an IPv4 address of **192.168.22.1** and an IPv6 address of **fe80::b8cc:2929:92fb:16f9%30** listed under the VMware Network Adapter VMnet1 section. The addresses are not DHCP assigned addresses. The Windows 10 computer automatically generated the IPv4 and IPv6 addresses.

Goodheart-Willcox Publisher

Read and record the assigned IPv6 addresses of the host and client and their corresponding aliases in the spaces provided.

Host assigned IPv4 address:

_____

Host assigned IPv6 address:

_____

Client assigned IPv4 address:

_____

Client assigned IPv6 address:

_____

Name _____

14. _____ Now, disconnect the VPN connection and then stop and view the contents of the Wireshark capture. Look for the key features discussed in the earlier steps of this laboratory activity. Notice that PPP and PPTP are still used to support VPN in Windows 10. Repeat the capture if necessary or until you are comfortable with the results.

15. _____ At the VPN client, use the **ipconfig** command to see if the PPP IPv6 temporary addresses have been lost since disconnecting the VPN connection.

16. _____ Return all materials to their proper storage areas and then answer the review questions.

Review Questions

1. Describe what happens when a basic connection between the VPN host and client is being established.

   _____
   _____
   _____

2. What is the role of the Generic Routing Encapsulation (GRE) protocol?

   _____
   _____

3. What protocol is used to authenticate the client and host?

   _____

4. What port number is associated with PPTP?

   _____

5. What port number is associated with SSTP?

   _____

6. What port numbers are associated with L2TP?

   _____

Notes

Name _____ Date _____ Class _____

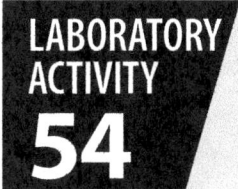

Microsoft Quick Assist

Outcomes

After completing this laboratory activity, you will be able to:
- Compare and contrast Remote Desktop and Quick Assist.
- Summarize the roles of expert and novice.
- Use Quick Assist to request help from an expert or helper.

Introduction

In this laboratory activity, you will configure and use the Windows 10 Quick Assist feature. The technology was introduced in Windows XP under the name Windows Remote Assistance. Windows 10 Quick Assist is much simpler to use than Windows Remote Assistance. Quick Assist is very useful for a technician performing network support. It allows a technician stationed at a help desk to access a user's computer, make changes to the system configuration, and perform other related repairs without leaving the help desk. Many repairs or modifications can be made from the help desk, thus eliminating the time it takes to go to the computer's location. The location of the computer can be as close as the same building or as far away as anywhere in the entire world.

Once Quick Assist is launched, a user has the option of getting assistance or giving assistance. Those providing assistance must have a Microsoft Online account. The person providing help is called an "expert" or "helper," while the person seeking help is referred to as a "novice."

The overall process of using Quick Assist is simple. A person providing help will select **Give assistance** from the main page in the Quick Assist tool. After the expert selects to give assistance, the software will automatically generate a user ID and security code for the session. Both users must enter these credentials in order for the remote connection to occur. The expert has the option of copying the code to the clipboard and can send the security code to the novice through e-mail. The novice will start the Quick Assist and click the **Get Assistance** option. From there, they must enter the security code provided by the expert and allow their screen to be shared.

The expert can chat with the novice through some form of videoconferencing software, and at the same time, view the computer system. The expert cannot take control of the other computer unless the novice gives permission. When the session is over, the connection is terminated.

The Quick Assist tool can be started by typing quick into the **Search** box located off the **Start** menu. Alternatively, a user can find it by opening **Start>Windows Accessories>Quick Assist**.

Both Quick Assist and Remote Desktop are based on the same Microsoft technology; however, they are very different. Look at the following table to compare Remote Assistance and Remote Desktop.

Quick Assist	Remote Desktop
Requires two people—one who needs assistance and one who provides assistance	Requires one person who accesses and controls a remote computer
The expert must be invited to help the novice	User can connect directly to the remote desktop without an invitation
Provides limited control over the novice computer	Provides complete control over the remote computer
Available in all Windows 10 versions with the Anniversary Update	Available only in Windows 10 Professional edition
Uses a user ID and security code to access	Uses computer name or IP address to identify the remote computer

> **NOTE**
> The network administrator might have Group Policy configured to prevent Quick Assist or other remote assistance features.

Equipment and Materials
- Two Windows 10 computers—one designated "novice," the other designated "expert"

> **NOTE**
> The computers may be connected as a peer-to-peer, but they must both have access to the Internet for this lab activity to work correctly.

Procedure

1. _____ Report to your assigned workstation(s).

2. _____ Boot the computers and verify they are in working order.

3. _____ At the designated expert computer, start the session by typing quick into the Search box located off the Start menu. Select Quick Assist from the results list. You should see a dialog box similar to the following screen capture.

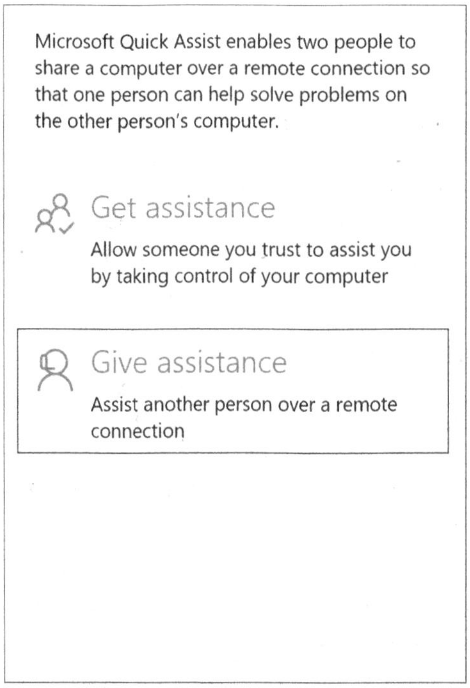

> Microsoft Quick Assist enables two people to share a computer over a remote connection so that one person can help solve problems on the other person's computer.
>
> **Get assistance**
> Allow someone you trust to assist you by taking control of your computer
>
> **Give assistance**
> Assist another person over a remote connection

Goodheart-Willcox Publisher

4. _____ Click on **Give Assistance** link and record the security code in the space provided.

   Security code: _____

Name _____

5. _____ At the designated novice computer, start the session by typing quick into the **Search** box located off the **Start** menu. Select **Quick Assist** from the results list, and choose the **Get Assistance** option.

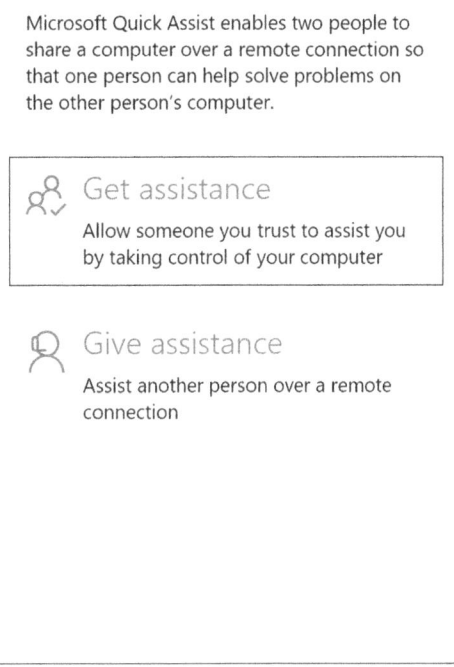

Goodheart-Willcox Publisher

6. _____ Enter the security code in the **Code** field of the dialog box.

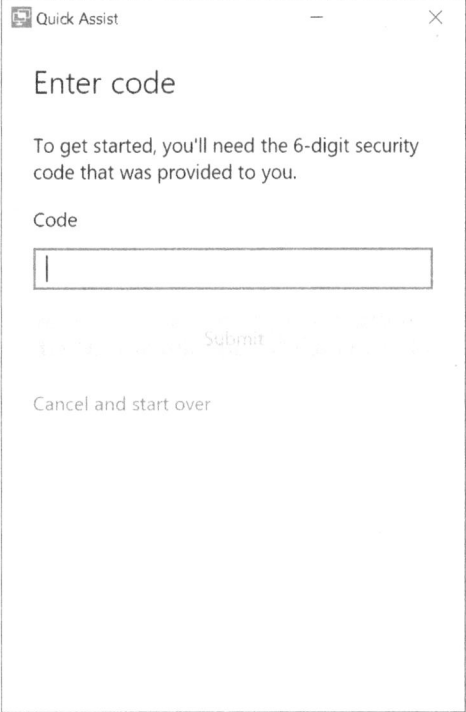

Goodheart-Willcox Publisher

7. _____ Click on **Allow** to grant access to the computer giving assistance.

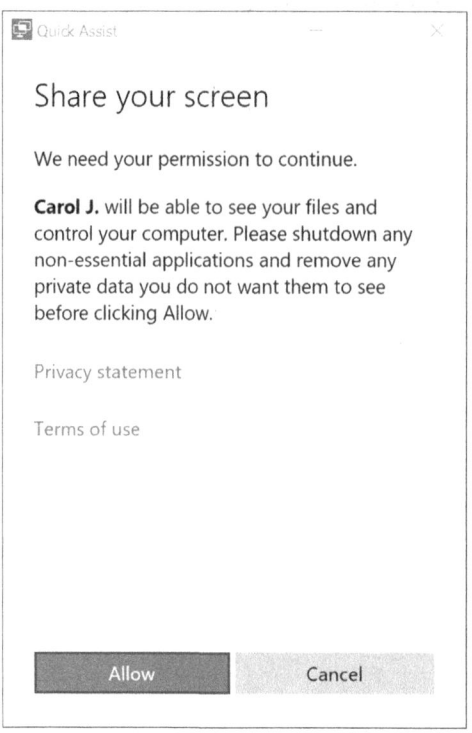

Goodheart-Willcox Publisher

Once permission is granted, the person giving assistance sees the novice computer screen on their own monitor. A toolbar with the following options is displayed.

- **Annotate**. Opens another toolbar with pen tools that can be used for freehand annotations
- **Actual Size**. Displays novice computer screen in native resolution, but will not fill entire expert screen
- **Restart**. Restarts the remote system
- **Task Manager**. Displays the utilities on the remote system
- **Pause**. Suspends session; either party can initiate
- **Resume**. Resumes session; appears in place of pause if **Pause** is selected
- **End**. Terminates connection
- **Reconnect**. Allows expert to reconnect with novice; appears only after session has ended, and novice must grant permission

8. _____ Use each of the previously mentioned tools to familiarize yourself with their functions and capabilities.

9. _____ Before closing the session, call your instructor to inspect your lab activity.

10. _____ Take a few minutes to repeat the lab activity, but reverse the roles of the computers.

11. _____ Return all materials to their proper storage area and then answer the review questions.

Review Questions

1. List several distinct differences between Quick Assist and Remote Desktop.

_____

_____

_____

_____

Name _____

2. The person who requests assistance is referred to as the _____.
   _____

3. The person who provides assistance is referred to as the _____ or _____.
   _____

4. How can the expert/helper and the novice exchange information?
   _____
   _____
   _____

5. How can Quick Assist help you as a network technician?
   _____
   _____
   _____

Notes

Name _____ Date _____ Class _____

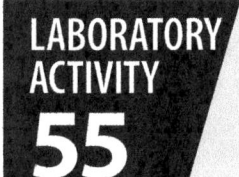

Using the Tracert and Pathping Commands

Outcomes

After completing this laboratory activity, you will be able to:
- Compare and contrast the **ping**, **tracert**, and **pathping** commands.
- Use the **ping**, **tracert**, and **pathping** commands to test a network route.
- Recall the function of commonly used switches associated with **tracert** and **pathping**.

Introduction

In this laboratory activity, you will use the **tracert** and **pathping** commands to verify the media route between a host and client. The **ping** command, which you are already familiar with at this point in the course, only verifies a complete path from source to destination and provides very limited information.

The **tracert** command displays the complete path from source to destination, listing the number of "hops" along the path. Each hop is an intermediate connection along the path from source to destination. The intermediate connection typically represents a router. The **tracert** command provides information such as the IP address, time taken to each hop displayed in milliseconds (1/1000), and sometimes, the name of each device encountered along the path.

The **pathping** command is an enhancement of the **ping** and **tracert** commands. Pathping first displays path information in a similar fashion as the **tracert** command. It then does an analysis of each hop along the path by sending a series of **ping** commands and performing calculations to display statistics about packet loss at each hop. The statistics can be used to identify problem areas along the path from source to destination. You can identify device failure along the intended path or areas of high traffic.

Look at the following screen captures which show a comparison of the **ping**, **tracert**, and **pathping** commands. In the following screen capture, a successful ping to www.comcast.net shows four successful echo request packets with the amount of time displayed in milliseconds for each.

Goodheart-Willcox Publisher

The next screen capture shows the results of the **tracert www.comcast.net** command. Notice that nine hops were encountered. The number of milliseconds for each echo request is shown along with the IP address of each hop.

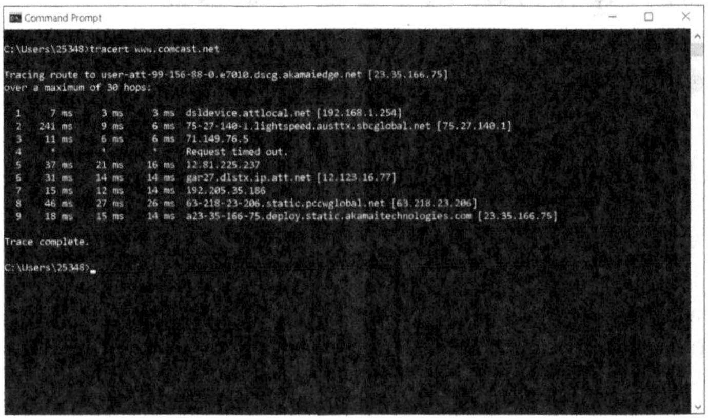

Goodheart-Willcox Publisher

The next screen capture shows the immediate results of issuing the **pathping www.microsoft.com** command. The immediate results contain a list of the nine hops but do not provide information about the amount of time to each hop. The information is not yet complete. As indicated in the screen capture, an additional 225 seconds (3 to 4 minutes) will be needed to perform additional echo requests so that a set of statistics about the route can be completed. The additional time is used to perform tests that calculate packet loss. These tests can indicate problems along the route, such as points of excessive network traffic.

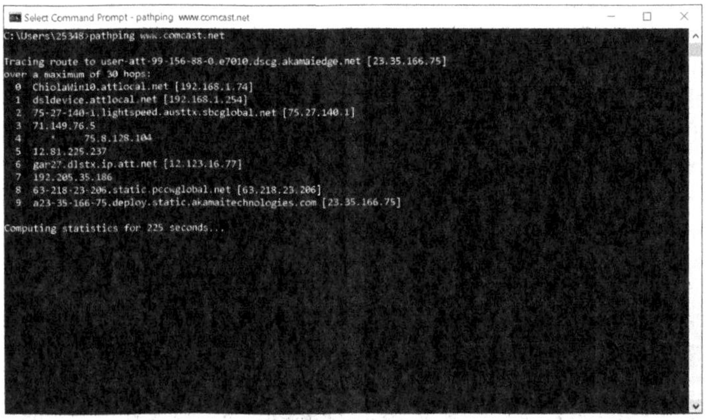

Goodheart-Willcox Publisher

The following screen capture shows the computed statistics for the **pathping** command. In this particular instance, there was no packet loss. Typically, problem areas along the route are indicated by short dashes in the **RTT** column and 100/100 in the **Lost/Sent** column. Packet loss is an indication of congestion usually caused by excessive traffic on the network. Be aware that many routers and firewalls are programmed to reject ICMP probes as a matter of security. This can also show packet loss.

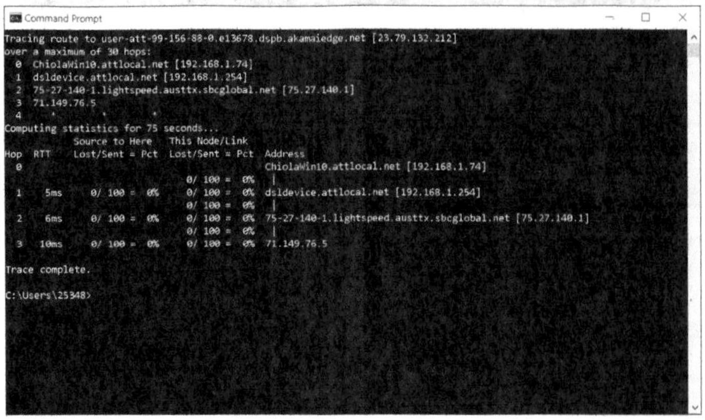

Goodheart-Willcox Publisher

Name _____

The **pathping** command is an excellent choice when testing a LAN consisting of a number of routers and you suspect that one or more are overloaded with network traffic. You could use the **pathping** command from the gateway to an internal workstation at the edge of the network to see the statistics generated on the local routers.

Commercial utilities are also available to perform a detailed analysis of routes between source and destination points. One such product is called *Ping Plotter* and is freely available at the time of this writing. You can conduct an Internet search for Ping Plotter and then add a copy to your software tool kit.

Ping, **tracert**, and **pathping** are encapsulated inside Internet Control Message Protocol (ICMP) packets. ICMP is a TCP/IP upper-layer protocol for transporting packets carrying error, control, and information messages.

The **ping** and **pathping** commands are also compatible with UNIX/Linux operating systems. The equivalent UNIX/Linux command for **tracert** is **traceroute**. These commands were developed to test TCP/IP-based communication systems; hence, any operating system that uses TCP/IP will also support the use of these commands.

Equipment and Materials
- Windows 10 computer with Internet access and Wireshark installed

Procedure

1. _____ Report to your assigned workstation.

2. _____ Boot the computer and verify that it is in working order.

3. _____ Access the command prompt and test the connection to one of the suggested Internet sites using the **ping** command. For example, **ping www.xfinity.com**.
   - www.xfinity.com
   - www.google.com
   - www.microsoft.com

4. _____ Use the **tracert** command to view the hops from your computer to the destination—for example, **tracert www.xfinity.com**. Answer the following question based on the result of the **tracert** command.

   How many hops were encountered?

   _____

5. _____ Use the **pathping** command to the same Internet site you used for the **tracert** command—for example, **pathping www.xfinity.com**. Answer the following question based on the result of the **pathping** command.

   How many hops were encountered along the route?

   _____

6. _____ Use the **/?** switch to answer the following questions about the **tracert** command.

   Which switch can be used to change the default number of hops?

   _____

7. _____ Which switch is used to force an IPv6 ping?

   _____

8. _____ Use the **/?** switch to answer the following questions about the **pathping** command.

   Which switch is used to change the default number of hops?

   _____

9. _____ Which switch is used to force the use of IPv6?

   _____

Use Wireshark to capture and study a set of packets generated by the **ping**, **tracert**, and **pathping** commands. This will provide insight into how the three commands are related and how they are different. After viewing the captured packets, look for the most common high-level protocol used. Also, take note of the number of packets used by each utility to carry out the command.

10. ____ After performing the Wireshark analysis, return all materials to their proper storage area.

11. ____ Answer the review questions.

Review Questions

1. Which command—**ping**, **tracert**, or **pathping**—provides the most detailed information about a connection path between a destination and a source?

2. Which command—**ping**, **tracert**, or **pathping**—requires the most amount of time to complete when gathering information about the route between the source and the destination?

3. Which command—**ping**, **tracert**, or **pathping**—should you use when you simply want to confirm a complete path exists between the destination and the source?

4. Which command—**ping**, **tracert**, or **pathping**—should you use if you want to confirm the number of hops between the source and destination quickly?

5. Which commands—**ping**, **tracert**, or **pathping**—are compatible with both Microsoft operating systems and Linux?

6. What UNIX/Linux command is comparable to **tracert**?

7. Which command is used to display packet losses at each hop?

8. Which command—**ping**, **tracert**, or **pathping**—simply sends out four echo request messages to verify route from source to destination?

9. Which TCP/IP upper-level protocol is designed to carry out the **ping**, **tracert**, and **pathping** echo request commands?

10. Which command—**ping**, **tracert**, or **pathping**—generates the most ICMP traffic when testing the path to the destination?

11. What switch is used to increase the number of hops for the **pathping** command?

12. Which command—**ping**, **tracert**, or **pathping**—would you use to locate a router suspected of causing packet exchange delays on your local network system?

Name _____ Date _____ Class _____

Observing the TCP/IP Three-Way Handshake

Outcomes

After completing this laboratory activity, you will be able to:
- Explain the packet exchange of a TCP/IP three-way handshake.
- Recall the role of a flag.
- Explain why TCP is considered a connection-oriented protocol.

Introduction

In this laboratory activity, you will capture and analyze a TCP/IP three-way handshake. TCP is a connection-oriented protocol, which means it establishes a connection between the source and the destination. UDP packets do not establish a connection between the source and destination. UDP is a "best effort" packet delivery system.

To establish a connection, the TCP protocol sends a series of three packets; hence, the name "three-way handshake," which is used to describe the action. During this process, no security information is exchanged. The following are the three steps of the three-way handshake process.

1. The source host sends a packet with the SYN (synchronize) flag set to on. Basically, it is requesting to make a connection with the destination host.

2. The destination host responds with both a SYN and an ACK (acknowledgment) flag set to on. This is an acceptance of the connection from the destination host to the source host.

3. The source host sends an ACK back to the destination host, and the three-way handshake is complete.

SYN and ACK are flags contained inside the TCP packet. *Flag* is a programming term. It refers to an assigned bit in a specific location that is used to identify a condition. Typically, a bit represented by a binary 1 represents a true condition, and a bit represented by a binary 0 represents a false condition. Look at the following screen capture to see an example of flag conditions in a captured packet.

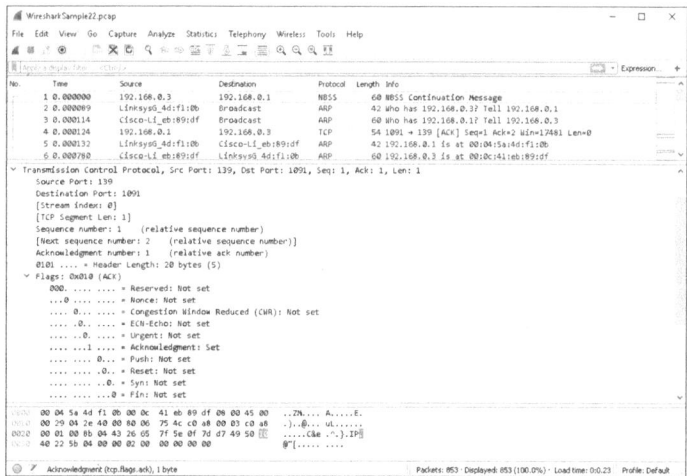

Goodheart-Willcox Publisher

The packet description section pane contains an area identified as **Flags**. Below the **Flags** heading, the binary position for acknowledgment is set to 1. This means the packet contains the acknowledgment flag required in the TCP handshake. The three-way TCP handshake is used whenever the TCP/IP protocol requires a connection to be maintained between two devices in a network.

In this laboratory activity, you will first open and view the contents of the sample Wireshark file. Then, you will make your own capture and examine it for the presence of the same three-way handshake.

Equipment and Materials

- Windows 10 computer with Internet access and Wireshark installed
- Wireshark Sample 16 file

    Wireshark Sample 16 file location:

    _____

- Wireshark Sample 17 file

    Wireshark Sample 17 file location:

    _____

Procedure

1. _____ Report to your assigned workstation.

2. _____ Boot the computer and verify that it is in working order.

3. _____ Open the **Wireshark Sample 16** file.

4. _____ Look at frames 18, 19, and 20. You will see that these frames contain the TCP three-way handshake used to establish a connection between a source host and destination host. The source host IP address is 192.168.0.101 and the destination host is 64.233.167.104.

5. _____ In frame 18, the first step in the process begins. Expand the contents of the packet and look at the flag. Notice that the SYN bit has been set to 1.

6. _____ In frame 19, you see the second step of the process in which the SYN and the ACK flag bits are set to 1.

7. _____ Frame 20 is the final or third step of the process. It contains the flag bit for ACK set to 1.

8. _____ Close the **Wireshark Sample 16** file.

9. _____ Open the **Wireshark Sample 17** file to see what the three-way handshake looks like in the IPv6 environment. The following screen capture shows the three frames of an IPv6 three-way handshake process.

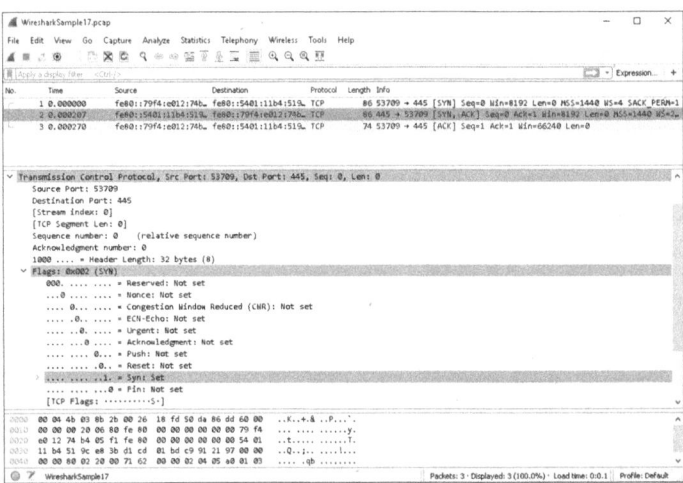

Goodheart-Willcox Publisher

Pay particular attention to the SYN and ACK series identified in the **Info** column. This is how you will locate the three-way handshake when you create your own Wireshark capture.

10. _____ Close the **Wireshark Sample 17** file.

11. _____ Start a Wireshark capture and then access the Internet using Internet Explorer and open any page. The default home page will be sufficient to generate the needed capture.

Name _____

12. _____ Stop the Wireshark capture and then search the capture for the TCP three-way handshake. When located, call your instructor to inspect your work.

13. _____ After your instructor views your capture, return the workstation to its original condition and return all materials to their proper storage area.

14. _____ Answer the review questions.

Review Questions

1. What is the purpose of the TCP three-way handshake?

2. Briefly describe the TCP three-way handshake process.

3. Which protocol is used for the TCP three-way handshake: TCP or UDP?

4. Which protocol is a "best effort" delivery protocol: TCP or UDP?

5. Why is TCP considered a connection-oriented protocol?

6. What is the purpose of a program flag?

7. True or False: The three-way handshake is only supported in IPv4.

Notes

Name _____ Date _____ Class _____

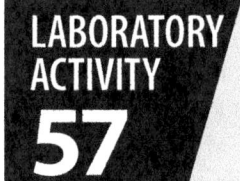

Wireless Encryption

Outcomes

After completing this laboratory activity, you will be able to:
- Summarize the security weaknesses related to wireless networks.
- Recall the purpose of a security key.
- Check if a wireless connection to an SSID has been made.

Introduction

Wireless media and devices are considered security risks because any wireless device within range may connect to a wireless network that is configured with default settings. The device default settings for the SSID and default administrator name and password can be commonly found by anyone who accesses the product information. This product information is typically available on the Internet or in the product information guide that accompanies the device when purchased. There are two things that you can do to increase the security of a wireless system dramatically:

- Change the default configuration.
- Enable encryption.

When using encryption, you must supply a security key also known as a *passphrase*. A security key is similar to a password. The security key must be the same for all wireless devices expected to connect to each other. By default, most wireless devices do not have any encryption enabled; thus, they are easily connected to by unauthorized persons. To provide good security, you must enable some type of encryption for the wireless devices.

This laboratory activity focuses on the WPA-Personal security type. Earlier wireless security was based on WEP, which is rarely encountered today except when using legacy hardware. Microsoft Windows 10 and most commonly encountered wireless devices support WPA-Personal security.

In this laboratory activity, you will configure encryption for the wireless devices on three computers. The three computers will be configured as an ad-hoc wireless network. When configuring the three computers, be sure to match the workgroup name, subnet mask, and network IP address. For example, all three computers should belong to the workgroup *Workgroup* and use the subnet mask 255.0.0.0 and one of the following IP addresses: 10.0.0.1, 10.0.0.2, or 10.0.0.3. Notice that the computers share the same network IP address: 10.

Each of the three computers must use the same SSID, encryption type, and security key. Using the same security key is referred to as *symmetric-key encryption*. The security key is a unique set of characters used to generate the encryption code that is used to encrypt the contents of the packets. The security key will be configured manually, but each computer must match. If the security key on a computer does not match the security key on the other computers, it will not be able to join the group. Security keys are typically made from ASCII or hexadecimal characters.

ASCII is represented by the entire alphabet *a–z* and *A–Z* and numbers *0–9*. The hexadecimal character set is limited to letters *a–f* and *A–F* and numbers *0–9*.

When making a connection to a wireless network using encryption, you may be required to provide the key when connecting for the first time. Providing a key is similar to providing a password when connecting to a shared network device for the first time.

> **NOTE**
> If this lab activity has been completed previously by another student using your assigned computer, the computer may already be configured for WPA-Personal and already have a wireless security key.

Before performing this laboratory activity, you may want to review your earlier lab experiences with wireless networking by rereading earlier wireless laboratory activities. This laboratory activity assumes that you can complete a default configuration of a wireless device.

A wireless device can be configured to connect to more than one SSID, but it can only connect to one SSID at a time. In other words, a wireless-enabled device such as a laptop can be configured for many different wireless networks, both encrypted and not encrypted. The wireless-enabled laptop can only be a part of one wireless network at one time.

Microsoft's version of WPA has two types of encryption available: Advanced Encryption Standard (AES) and Temporal Key Integrated Protocol (TKIP). You must match the encryption type for each computer.

> **NOTE**
> Windows uses AES by default, but other encryption types may be available for your configuration because of the drivers loaded during the installation of your wireless network adapter.

Wireless networks are extremely difficult to work with. They can be very frustrating because of the conflict between the Windows operating system's wireless configuration and the manufacturer's wireless configuration. For assistance, you may want to view the Microsoft TechNet Wireless Networking site. To access this site, you can conduct an online search using key terms such as Microsoft Windows 10 Wireless networking.

Equipment and Materials

- Three Windows 10 computers connected as a peer-to-peer network
- Three wireless devices: 802.11b, 802.11a, 802.11g, or 802.11n (The devices must match or be compatible; a USB wireless device is recommended for this laboratory activity, but is not required.)
- The following information provided by your instructor:

Account username:

_____

Account password:

_____

SSID name (Each group of three computers in should use a unique SSID.):

_____

WPA-Personal key (suggested: 8-character ASCII key, such as 12345678):

_____

Workgroup name (suggested: Workgroup):

_____

> **NOTE**
> Some legacy devices do not support WPA-Personal encryption. If you are using a legacy wireless network device, you must use WEP encryption.

> **NOTE**
> If the device you are using must be configured with the manufacturer's software, the dialog boxes in this activity may not match the laboratory activity screen captures. Also, be aware that wireless network device drivers and Windows service packs can introduce newer versions of security software and encryption types. Service packs and drivers can cause choices different from those in the laboratory activity. You can proceed with the laboratory activity using the steps as a general guide. All wireless devices will contain similar configuration settings even if they are not an exact match.

Name _____

Procedure

1. _____ Report to your assigned workstation(s).

2. _____ Boot the three computers and verify they are in working order.

3. _____ Label the three computers *Source*, *Destination*, and *Intruder*. This will help you while following the lab instructions.

4. _____ Each computer should have at least one matching user account. The username and password should be the same for each computer user account to ensure that each computer can access the others.

5. _____ Note that in a lab environment, configuration changes can often cause problems concerning accessibility. When a share is set up on a computer, check the share permissions for the user to ensure that the user has access. The permissions should match on all three computers using similar shares. Also, check that each of the three computers are configured for a workgroup, not a domain.

Consult the manufacturer's information before configuring the wireless devices. When the USB wireless device is first installed into a USB port, it will be detected automatically and the **Wireless Network Connection** icon will appear in the desktop notification area. The icon for the wireless device will be similar to the one in the following screen capture:

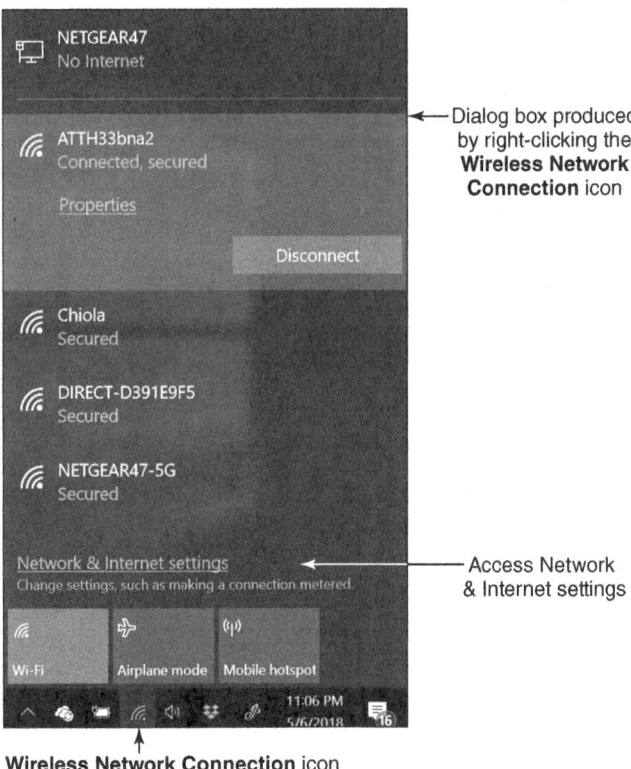

Goodheart-Willcox Publisher

6. _____ Notice that the **Wireless Network Connection** icon is represented by an image for a wireless signal. Clicking the icon will produce a dialog box similar to that in the previous screen capture. Notice that you can open the **Network & Internet settings** by selecting the link at the bottom of the dialog box.

Open the **Network and Sharing Center**. You should see information about the wireless connection similar to that in the following screen capture.

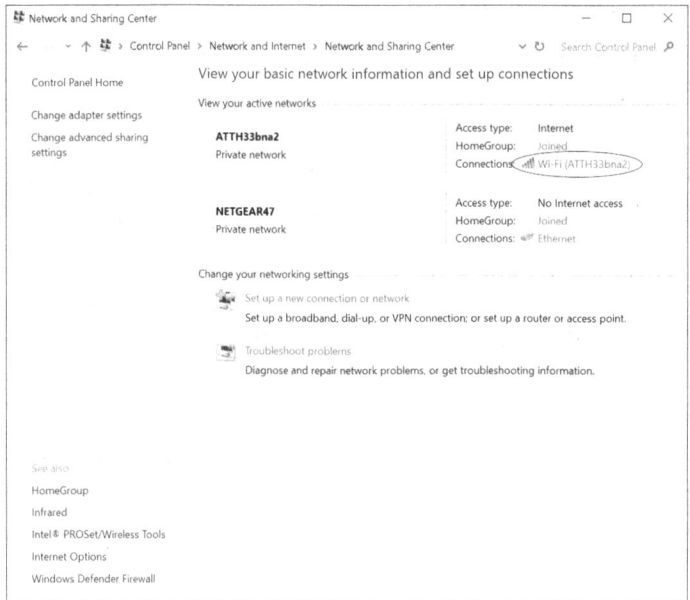

Goodheart-Willcox Publisher

To view the properties for the wireless network, select **Wi-Fi** followed by the name of the local network—for example, **Wi-Fi (ATTH33bna2)**.

7. ____ Do *not* select Local Area Connection, which is located immediately beneath the **Wi-Fi** connection.

After selecting **Wi-Fi**, a dialog box similar to the following will display.

Goodheart-Willcox Publisher

Name _____

Click the **Wireless Properties** button. A dialog box similar to the following will display.

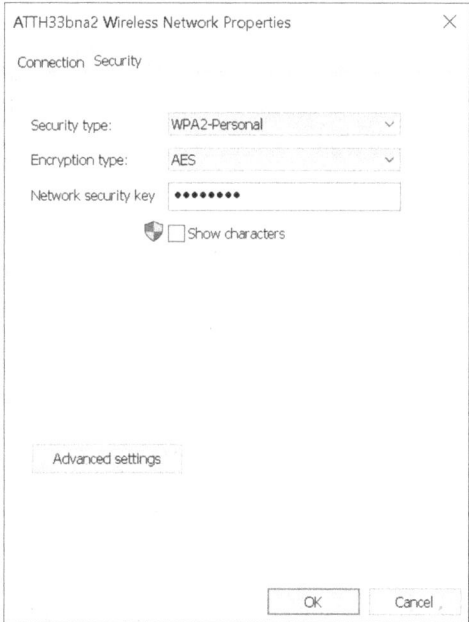

Goodheart-Willcox Publisher

8. _____ Under the **Security** tab is where you will select the security type, encryption type, and network security key. The network security key is also known as the *passphrase*.

9. _____ For each computer, select **WPA-Personal** for the security type and **AES** for the encryption type. Use **12345678** for the security key. This will make all of the computers capable of connecting to each other in ad-hoc mode.

10. _____ Check if all three computers are configured with a matching SSID and security type. To do this, click the **Wireless Network Connection** icon in the notification area and then move the cursor over the dialog box and let the cursor hover; do not click the connection. This will produce a box listing the connection information.

11. _____ After completing the configuration of all three computers, check if you can create a connection between the three computers.

12. _____ Call your instructor to inspect your laboratory activity thus far.

13. _____ Now, designate one of the computers as an intruder by changing the security key at the intruder computer so that it no longer matches the security key on the other two computers. For example, if you are using **12345678** as the security key, change the security key of one computer to **87654321**. Try to connect the intruder to one of the other two computers. You should not be able to connect successfully because the security key no longer matches. However, all three computers will be able to see each other in the list of wireless networks.

14. _____ Take a few minutes to explore the options available under the **Security** tab. Try configuring a different security and encryption type and observe the results.

15. _____ Return the computers to their original configurations and then answer the review questions.

Review Questions

1. What is a security key?

2. List two security weaknesses related to wireless networks.

3. What is the difference between an ASCII character set and a hexadecimal character set?

4. Must each of the following items match to support a wireless connection between computers? Indicate with either *Yes* or *No*.
   A. SSID_____
   B. Security type_____
   C. Encryption type_____
   D. Security key_____
   E. IPv4 address_____
   F. IPv6 address_____
   G. MAC number_____

5. True or False: You can only configure a wireless computer for one SSID.

6. True or False: You can connect to more than one SSID group simultaneously.

7. You can see the available wireless network computer in the Network browser and there are packets being exchanged as indicated in the **Wi-Fi Status** dialog box, but you cannot successfully connect to it. You have a user account on each wireless network computer. What is *most likely* the problem?

Name _____ Date _____ Class _____

NTFS Encrypting File System

Outcomes

After completing this laboratory activity, you will be able to:
- Use the **Advanced Attributes** dialog box to encrypt the contents of a file or folder.
- Identify which file types support file encryption.
- Summarize the effect on encryption when moving an encrypted file or folder.

Introduction

In this laboratory activity, you will encrypt an NTFS file or folder. File encryption is an essential part of data security. A computer can be compromised by unauthorized personnel. If a computer stores critical information, it is best to require a password for user log on and to encrypt the data. A computer may be accessed either directly or over a network. Files could be copied or opened by an intruder. A notebook computer containing customer lists, corporate information, sensitive e-mail information, bank account information, and other forms of sensitive information could be lost or stolen. A person might possibly open the files on the computer and reveal the contents.

The Windows Encrypting File System (EFS) requires NTFS to be installed on the partition where the file/folder is to be encrypted. EFS will not work on a FAT partition. Windows Home Edition does not support EFS. Only Windows Professional and Enterprise editions as well as Windows Server support EFS.

System files and compressed files cannot be encrypted. Do *not* encrypt files such as those with the EXE, DLL, and COM extensions. These file types are critical to other programs. You should only apply encryption to data files.

> **NOTE**
> Microsoft has an encryption method referred to as "Bitlocker," which was first introduced in Windows Vista. Bitlocker is designed to encrypt an entire disk drive, including hidden files and operating system files. Windows 7 introduced "Bitlocker To Go," which is designed to encrypt removable drives and smart cards. Bitlocker is only available for Windows 10 Professional and Enterprise operating systems. It is not enabled by default for Windows 10 Home edition.

To the user who encrypted the file/folder, encryption will be transparent. This means that the user will be able to open, modify, and copy an encrypted file/folder without having to decrypt the file/folder first. However, there are several copy rules concerning EFS files and folders to be aware of:

- When you copy or move an encrypted file/folder from one partition to another partition on the same computer and both partitions are NTFS, the file/folder remains encrypted.
- When you copy or move an encrypted file/folder from one partition to another partition and the destination partition is FAT32, the file/folder will no longer be encrypted.
- When you copy or move an encrypted file/folder to a NTFS partition on another computer, the file/folder remains encrypted.

It is important to note that the limited user will not be aware that there is an encrypted file/folder on the system. The encrypted file/folder will not appear in the limited user's GUI. A user with a user account equal to the user account that encrypted the file/folder will see that the file/folder is encrypted by its name appearing in green. However, the user will be denied access to the file/folder contents.

A command line encryption tool with the executable named **cipher.exe** can be run from the command prompt. The tool has been available since Windows 2000 but is seldom used today.

For more detailed information about using EFS, check the Microsoft TechNet support web site. Simply conduct an online search using the keywords Microsoft TechNet EFS. Look for "Microsoft" in the URL results. You can also find a lot of related information located in **Start>Help and Support**. When **Help and Support** opens, enter EFS into the **Search help** box.

Equipment and Materials

- Windows 10 Professional or Enterprise computer

Procedure

1. _____ Report to your assigned workstation.

2. _____ Boot the computer and verify that it is in working order. Be sure that at least two additional user accounts exist for this laboratory activity. One account should have access rights equal to your user account. The other account should have limited access. You may wish to use the account names AdminEqual and LimitedUser to help you identify the accounts.

3. _____ Create a new folder in the Documents folder called Secret Folder.

4. _____ Encrypt the folder by right-clicking Secret Folder and selecting **Properties** from the shortcut menu. The **Secret Folder Properties** dialog box will display. On the **General** tab, click **Advanced**. The **Advanced Attributes** dialog box will display. Under the **Compress or Encrypt attributes** section, select the **Encrypt contents to secure data** option. Click **OK**. Click **OK** again to close the **Secret Folder Properties** dialog box.

5. _____ Now, create a short memo with the contents, I have many secrets. Name the memo Secret Memo and save it to the Secret Folder directory.

6. _____ Use the two accounts you created and the Secret Memo file to experiment and answer the following questions. Record your answers in the spaces provided. Use the simple file-sharing mode for this series of tests.

7. _____ What color characters are used to represent the encrypted folder?

_____

8. _____ Can another equal user account view the contents of the encrypted file?

_____

9. _____ What happens when you drag or copy the encrypted memo into a different folder that is not encrypted? For example, what will happen if you drag or copy it into the Shared Documents folder?

_____

10. _____ What happens when you compress an encrypted file?

_____

11. _____ Can another equal user account send the encrypted document to the Recycle Bin?

_____

12. _____ When you have finished experimenting and answering the questions, answer the review questions.

13. _____ Return all materials to their proper storage areas and return the computer to its original condition. Be sure to remove the user accounts, test folder, and file.

Review Questions

1. What does the acronym EFS represent?

_____

2. What type of file should be encrypted?

_____

3. What color is a file or folder name displayed in after it is encrypted?

_____

Name _____

4. What happens when you move or copy an encrypted file to a folder that is not encrypted?
   _____
   _____

5. What happens when a limited account user attempts to access an encrypted file?
   _____
   _____

6. What happens when a user with an equal user account attempts to access another equal user's encrypted file or folder?
   _____

7. Can a user with an equal account to the user who encrypted a file remove or delete that user's encrypted file?
   _____

8. Who can restore a file from the Recycle Bin?
   _____

9. What type of files can you *not* encrypt?
   _____

10. What text command can be used to encrypt files?
    _____

Notes

Name _____ Date _____ Class _____

Configuring a Firewall

Outcomes
After completing this laboratory activity, you will be able to:
- Recall the role of Windows Firewall.
- Use the various options available to configure Windows Firewall.
- Identify the port number and protocol assignment of common TCP/IP services.
- Recall the function of the Windows Firewall security log.

Introduction
In this laboratory activity, you will become familiar with Windows Firewall, which was introduced with Windows XP and referred to as *Internet Connection Firewall*. In Windows XP service pack 2 and later, it was renamed to *Windows Firewall*. The workstation version of Windows Firewall is very similar to the server version.

A firewall is designed to prevent unauthorized access to or from a workstation through the Internet. It is a basic way of providing protection for a private network from Internet attacks.

> **NOTE**
> Originally, Microsoft recommended that the Windows Firewall should not be enabled on a workstation that is not serving as a gateway or as a stand-alone computer connected to the Internet. This was because Windows Firewall could create problems with network applications such as file sharing or VPN connections as well as with ICMP troubleshooting utilities such as **ping** and **tracert**. Today Microsoft has reversed the recommendation about using the Windows Firewall on individual workstations. Microsoft now recommends enabling Windows Firewall for all workstations in all types of settings such as Home, Public, and Domain. Windows Firewall is designed to automatically configure ports for most software applications and programs.

A firewall is designed to set restrictions for communication through the designated host or gateway. It can be configured to inspect each frame for the destination and source IP addresses, enable or disable services running on the host computer, create a log of network activities, and record items such as an attempted log on to the network.

A firewall will help to prevent attacks by malicious software, such as worm programs, but it does not provide full protection. Most malicious software, such as worm and Trojan horse programs, are spread by e-mail attachments. Since e-mail ports are typically left open for communication, an attachment containing malicious software can gain access to the computer or network system.

The firewall settings will automatically change according to the type of network environment (Home, Work, Public, or Domain) that is selected during the network configuration. For example, when a Public location is selected, most incoming ports will be blocked. Also, most software applications recognized by Microsoft are also automatically configured through the firewall during the configuration process. For example, the firewall will automatically unblock port 110 during the configuration process of e-mail that uses a POP3 e-mail client.

> **NOTE**
> Microsoft recommends that you disable the firewall when using a third-party firewall system.

Equipment and Materials
- Windows 10 computer

Procedure

1. _____ Report to your assigned workstation.

2. _____ Boot the computer and verify it is in working order.

3. _____ Open Windows Firewall by accessing **Control Panel>System and Security>Windows Defender Firewall**. You should see a dialog box similar to the one in the following screen capture.

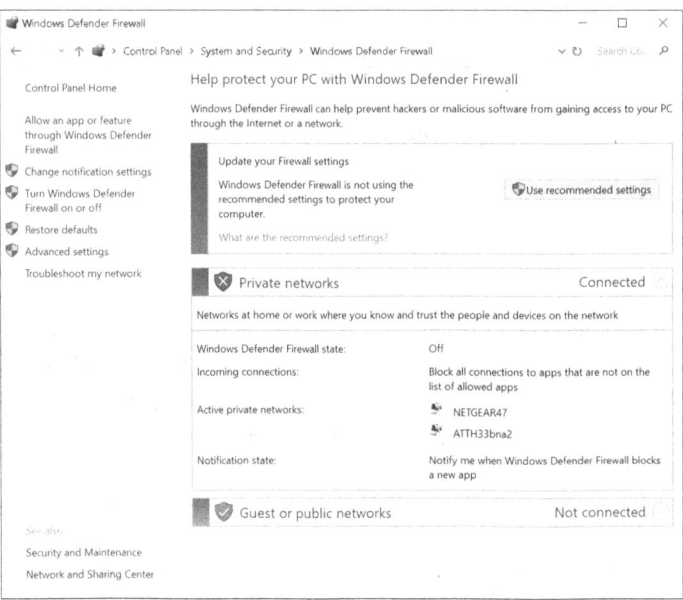

Goodheart-Willcox Publisher

You will see the two major firewall locations listed as **Private networks** (home or work) and **Guest or public networks**. Windows Firewall is automatically configured to match the type of network location and provide the best security for that location type without compromising functionality.

4. _____ In the left pane of Windows Defender Firewall, you will see the two options **Change notification settings** and **Turn Windows Firewall on and off**. Selecting either will produce a dialog box similar to the one in the following screen capture.

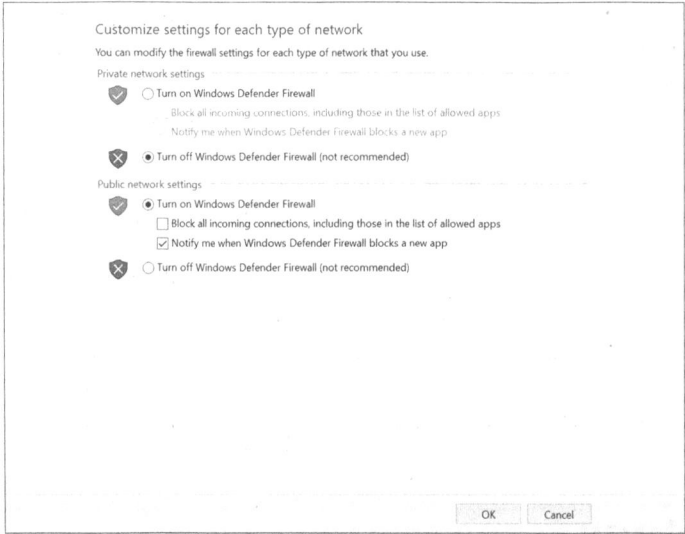

Goodheart-Willcox Publisher

Notice the options available in the dialog box. The first set of options correlate to a private network location. The second set correlates to a public type of location. The options for each are duplicated. This is where you turn the Windows Firewall on or off and also decide if you want to be notified when Windows blocks a new program.

Name _____

5. _____ Close the dialog box. Windows Firewall should still be in view.

6. _____ Notice the **Restore defaults** option in the left pane of Windows Firewall. Select this option to restore the default settings. Pay particular attention to the message that follows this action.

7. _____ Use the left arrow to return to Windows Defender Firewall or close the dialog box and open the Windows Firewall again.

8. _____ Select the **Advance settings** option. The **Windows Firewall with Advanced Security** console will display, similar to that in the following screen capture.

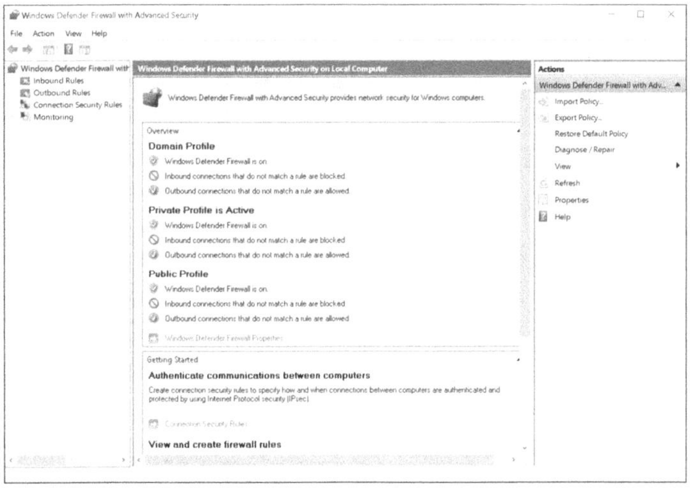

Goodheart-Willcox Publisher

9. _____ In the left pane, select **Inbound Rules**. This will produce a list of all rules configured for Windows Firewall.

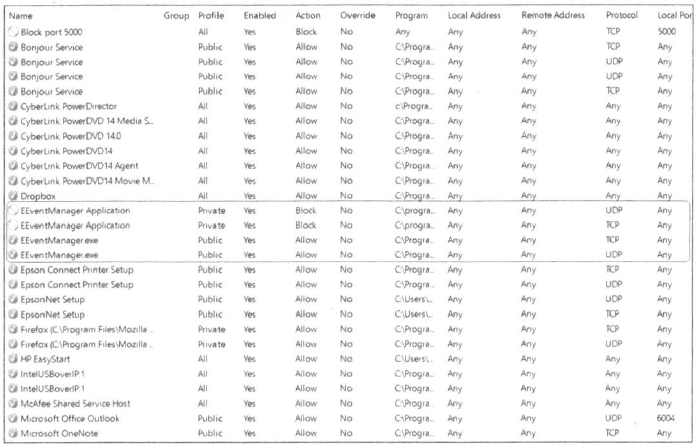

Goodheart-Willcox Publisher

Rules are the actions associated with a specific port, protocol, service, and more. In the circled area in the previous screen capture, EEventManager is listed four times—twice each for private and public type of network The location type is listed in the **Profile** column.

The **Enabled** column lists Yes or No indicating if the firewall is enabled for this feature. When the inbound rule is enabled, a check mark in a green circle will appear to the left of the **Name** column. If the firewall is not enabled for the feature, a check mark in a gray circle is used.

Notice that the port number assigned is located in the **Local Port** column. In the screen capture, port number 6004 is assigned to the three Microsoft Office Outlook entry. Most of the other entries are configured to use any available port.

10. _____ Take a minute and look at the column labels running from left to right across the chart of inbound rules. You can use the slide at the bottom to see any columns hidden from view.

11. _____ Locate the inbound rule **File and Printer Sharing (NB-Datagram-In)**. Open it by right-clicking it and selecting **Properties** from the shortcut menu or by double-clicking it. A **Properties** dialog box will appear similar to the one in the following screen capture.

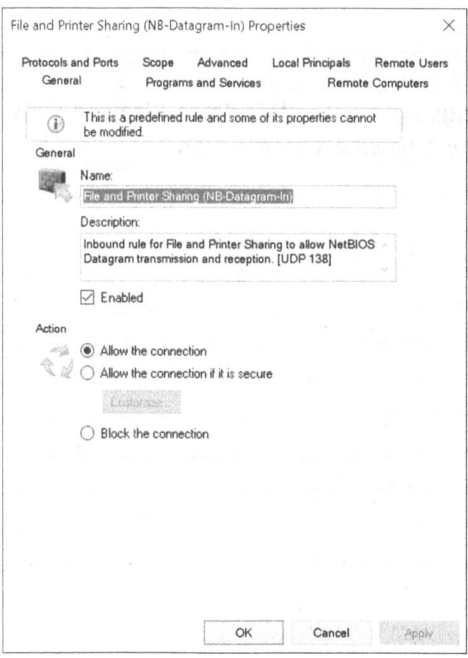

Goodheart-Willcox Publisher

Under the **General** tab, you will see the name of the inbound rule as well as a brief description and options for changing the configuration of the rule. For example, you can enable or disable the rule. You can also modify the action by selecting the **Allow the connection**, **Allow the connection if it is secure**, or **Block the connection** option.

Pay particular attention to the fact that some of the properties for this inbound rule cannot be modified as indicated by the message in the yellow textbox. This means that by Microsoft design, certain services must have specific configuration features to work properly, and therefore, cannot be changed.

12. _____ Select the **Advanced** tab. A dialog box similar to the following will display.

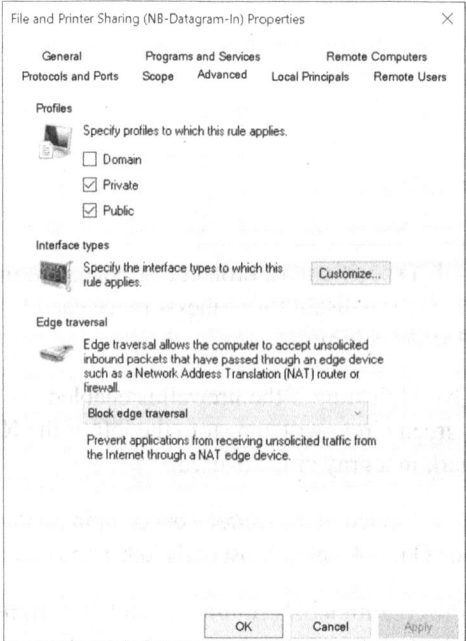

Goodheart-Willcox Publisher

Name _____

Notice how you can select the type of network location to enable for this rule. There is also an option that will allow you to select which interface type (network adapter) to apply this rule to when you have more than one network adapter installed.

The bottom section labeled **Edge traversal** allows you to configure how the rule should be applied when a network edge device is encountered on the network. An edge device is a NAT router or another firewall.

13. _____ Take a few minutes to explore the other tabs associated with the dialog box so that you can see the various ways the inbound rule can be configured. For example, you can configure the inbound rule for specific users, computers, IP addresses, programs, and services.

14. _____ Identify which port number or numbers are associated with the following inbound rules and outbound rules.

Inbound Rules
- File and Printer Sharing (SMB-In) _____
- File and Printer Sharing (NB-Name-In) _____
- Core Networking–Dynamic Host Configuration Protocol (DHCP-In) _____
- Core Networking–Dynamic Host Configuration Protocol for IPv6 (DHCPv6-In) _____
- FTP Server (FTP Traffic-In) _____
- Remote Desktop (TCP-In) _____
- World Wide Web Services (HTTP Traffic-In) _____
- Windows Peer-to-Peer Collaboration Foundation (PNRP-In) _____

Outbound Rules
- Core Networking–DNS (UDP-Out) _____
- Core Networking–Dynamic Host Configuration Protocol (DHCP-Out) _____
- Core Networking–Dynamic Host Configuration Protocol for IPv6 (DHCPv6-Out) _____
- File and Printer Sharing (LLMNR-UDP-Out) _____
- File and Printer Sharing (NB-Datagram-Out) _____
- File and Printer Sharing (SMB-Out) _____
- Network Discovery (SSDP-Out) _____
- SNMP Service (UDP-Out) _____

15. _____ Close all open dialog boxes and then access Windows Defender Firewall again.

16. _____ In the left pane, select **Allow an app or feature through Windows Defender Firewall**. A dialog box similar to the following will display.

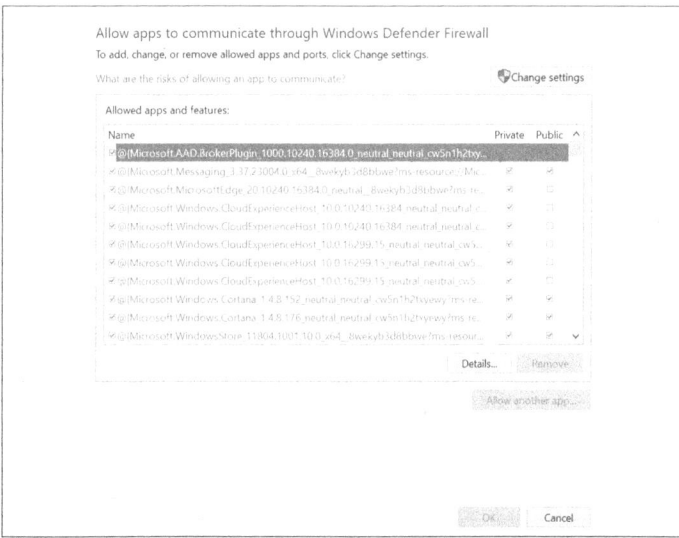

Goodheart-Willcox Publisher

When programs are installed on a computer, they are typically identified by Windows Defender Firewall and automatically configured to allow a connection to a remote port and to a local port. You will usually be prompted during the program installation and asked if you wish to permit the program to access the remote site or a local service. When allowed, the appropriate port numbers are assigned. The automatic configuration is not always successful, and you may need to configure a program manually. That is the purpose of the **Allow another app** button. This button will start a wizard that will allow you to configure a specific program or search for one using the **Browse** button. Click the **Allow another app** button and then take a minute to explore the **Add an app** dialog box that displays. Only explore this dialog box. Do *not* actually allow another program to have access through Windows Firewall at this time.

17. _____ Close all open dialog boxes and return all materials to their proper storage areas.

18. _____ Answer the review questions.

Review Questions

1. What is the purpose of a firewall?

2. Which two network locations turn Network Discovery on by default?

3. Which two port numbers are associated with Core Networking—Dynamic Host Configuration Protocol (DHCP-In)?

4. Which port number is associated with FTP Server (FTP Traffic-In)?

5. Which port number is associated with Remote Desktop (TCP-In)?

6. Which port number is associated with World Wide Web Services (HTTP Traffic-In)?

7. Which port number is associated with Core Networking–DNS (UDP-Out)?

8. Which two port numbers are associated with Core Networking—Dynamic Host Configuration Protocol (DHCP-Out)?

9. Which two port numbers are associated with Core Networking—Dynamic Host Configuration Protocol for IPv6 (DHCP-Out)?

Name _____

10. Which port number is associated with Network Discovery (SSDP-Out)?
_____

11. Why are some of the inbound and outbound rules repeated two or three times?
_____
_____
_____

Notes

Name _____ Date _____ Class _____

Digital Certificates

Outcomes

After completing this laboratory activity, you will be able to:
- Recall the purpose of a digital certificate.
- Identify sources of digital certificates.
- Use Certificate Manager to view digital certificates located on a computer.
- Use the Certificate Export Wizard to back up a digital certificate.

Introduction

Digital certificates are mainly used to establish identities prior to securely exchanging information. The typical uses of digital certificates are securing e-mail messages, securing remote server logons, verifying the integrity of a software program, and making a secure online purchase. There are several common sources of digital certificates found on a workstation or server. Some are loaded onto the computer when the operating system or software is installed. Some are loaded onto the computer during an SSL session on the Internet. Others have been purchased from a digital certificate company to be used for personal or company use.

Microsoft refers to the location of where certificates are stored as the *certificate store*. You can access the certificate store through the **Internet Properties** dialog box, which is accessed through **Control Panel>Network and Internet>Internet Options**. The **Internet Properties** dialog box will display. Select the **Content** tab and then click the **Certificates** button to access the certificate store. You can also access **Internet Properties** by entering Internet options in the **Search** box off of the **Start** menu.

Certificates on a workstation typically contain a public key that is used to exchange encrypted information with a company server that contains the private key. Certificates contain more than just a public encryption key. They usually contain the issuing authority name and validity dates.

In this laboratory activity, you will explore the certificate store and view information about the certificates. You will also back up a certificate.

Equipment and Materials
- Windows 10 computer
- USB flash drive for certificate backup

Procedure

1. _____ Report to your assigned workstation.

2. _____ Boot the computer and verify it is in working order.

3. _____ There are two common ways to access a dialog box to view digital certificate information. One way is to enter certmgr.msc into the **Search** box located off the **Start** menu. You must include the .msc file extension or the program will not appear in the search list results. The certmgr.msc program will appear at the top of the list under **Programs**. After selecting certmgr.msc from the list, you will see the Certificate Manager console similar to the one in the following screen capture.

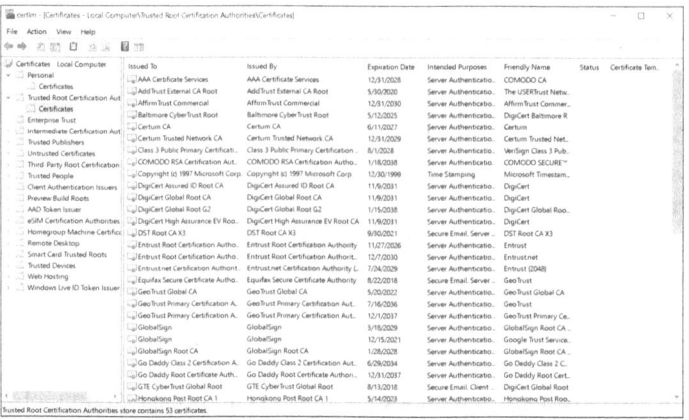

Goodheart-Willcox Publisher

The Certificate Manager console contains a list of all digital certificates installed on the computer. Notice that the tree directory in the left pane is arranged by classifications, such as **Personal**, **Trusted Root Certification Authorities**, and more. This provides a quick and easy way to locate digital certificates by function or classification.

4. _____ Close the Certificate Manager console.

5. _____ The second common way to access a dialog box to view digital certificate information is through the **Internet Properties** dialog box. The **Internet Properties** dialog box can be accessed through **Control Panel>Network and Internet>Internet Options**. You can also enter Internet into the **Search** box and then select **Internet Options** located under the **Control Panel** section of the **Search** results list. When the **Internet Properties** dialog box displays, select the **Content** tab and then click the **Certificates** button.

Goodheart-Willcox Publisher

Name _____

After clicking the **Certificates** button you will see the **Certificates** dialog box similar to that in the following screen capture.

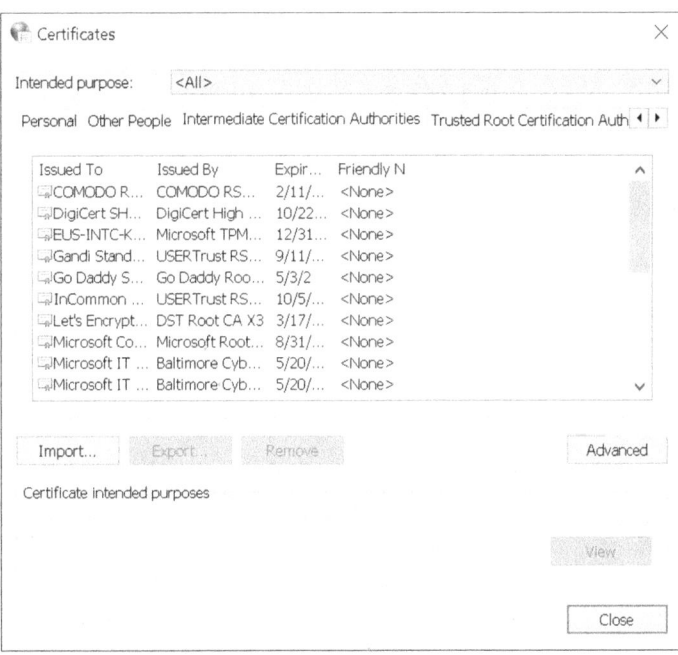

Goodheart-Willcox Publisher

The classification of certificate is grouped by the dialog box tab system. You can select the type of certificate by selecting the corresponding tab. For example, to view any personal certificates installed on the computer, you would select the **Personal** tab.

6. _____ After opening the **Certificates** dialog box, take a few minutes to view all the tabs: **Personal**, **Other People**, **Intermediate Certification Authorities**, **Trusted Root Certification Authorities**, **Trusted Publishers**, and **Untrusted Publishers**. You will need to use the arrows located at the right of the tabs to view the hidden tabs.

Personal certificates belong to the computer's owner. Other People certificates are obtained from other people, such as people you correspond with using e-mail. Trusted Root Certification Authorities and Immediate Certification Authorities require some explanation. A Trusted Root Certification Authority is a recognized self-certified source of certificate. For example, VeriSign is a company that creates certificates for other companies and individuals; hence, it is a "Root" Certificate Authority. It originated the certificate. An Intermediate Certification Authority is a company that uses certificates that were created by a root Certificate Authority such as VeriSign. Trusted Publishers and Untrusted Publishers are typically software publishers. Under the **Untrusted Publishers** tab, do not be surprised to see two certificates listed as Microsoft Corporation certificates. These are not true Microsoft certificates, but actual forgeries used to send out e-mail announcements. After being originally discovered, they were immediately revoked and, thus, pose no danger.

7. _____ Select the **Trusted Root Certification Authorities** tab. A dialog box similar to the following will display.

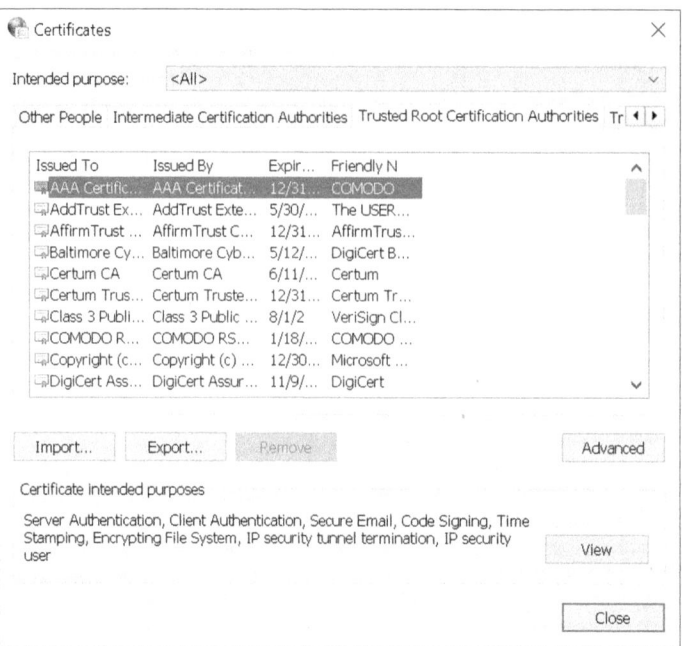

Goodheart-Willcox Publisher

8. _____ Click one of the items in the list and watch as the box labeled **Certificate intended purposes** located at the bottom of the dialog box changes.

9. _____ Select one of the certificates on the **Trusted Root Certification Authorities** tab and then click the **View** button. A dialog box that reveals details about that particular certificate will display.

Goodheart-Willcox Publisher

The purpose of the certificate is described and additional tabs are provided that allow you to view detailed information about the certificate. Take a few minutes to explore several certificates before moving on in the laboratory activity. When you are finished, close all open dialog boxes.

Name _____

10. _____ Open the **Certificates** dialog box again and then select the **Personal** tab. A dialog box similar to the following will display.

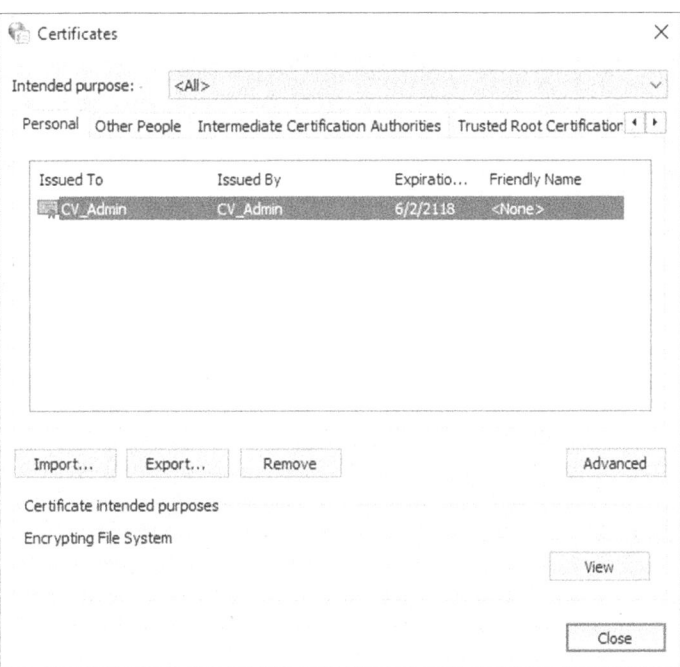

Goodheart-Willcox Publisher

The Personal certificates are the computer owner certificates that were automatically generated when certain configurations were made on the computer. The Personal certificates on your computer will not necessarily match the ones in the screen capture. The screen capture shows one Personal certificates. The certificate was created when a file or folder on the computer was encrypted. Take a minute to explore the Personal certificates on your computer. You should have Personal certificates created from prior laboratory activities. Explore one of the Personal certificates located on the computer and then answer the following questions.

What is the certificate used for? _____

When will the certificate expire? _____

How many bits are used for the encryption? _____

Does the certificate use a public key or a private key? _____

11. _____ To back up a digital certificate, double-click the digital certificate or highlight it and click the **View** button. The **Certificate** dialog box will open. Select the **Details** tab and then click the **Copy to File** button.

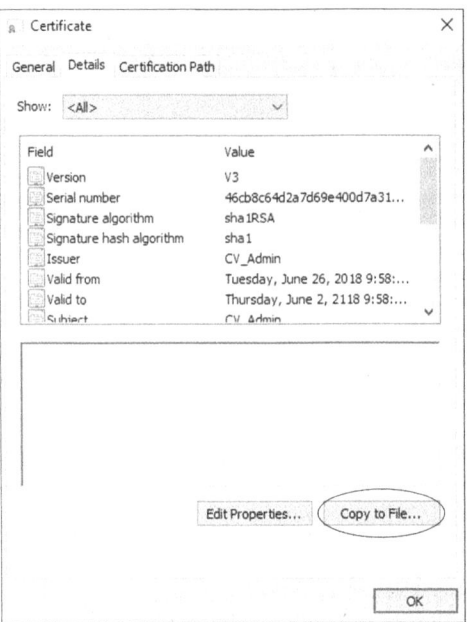

Goodheart-Willcox Publisher

The Certificate Export Wizard will open and look similar to that in the following screen capture.

Goodheart-Willcox Publisher

The wizard will prompt you with a series of dialog boxes asking for input concerning the backup of the certificate. Follow the wizard prompts and back up the Personal certificate to a USB drive. Call your instructor to inspect your work.

12. _____ Answer all review questions and then return all materials to their proper storage areas.

Name _____

Review Questions

1. What is the purpose of a digital certificate?

   _____
   _____
   _____

2. Where do certificates come from?

   _____
   _____
   _____

3. What is a certificate store?

   _____
   _____

4. Which type of key is typically stored on a workstation—public or private?

   _____

5. How do you make a backup of a certificate?

   _____
   _____
   _____

Notes

Name _____ Date _____ Class _____

SANS Organization

Outcomes
After completing this laboratory activity, you will be able to:
- Recall the purpose of the SANS organization.
- Summarize the web content located at www.SANS.org.

Introduction
This laboratory activity will familiarize you with the SANS organization website. The acronym SANS represents SysAdmin, Audit, Network, Security. SANS was first established in 1989 as a research and educational organization mainly concerned with information technology security. The SANS website, located at www.SANS.org, contains the most up-to-date and in-depth security materials and training. Some materials are free, and some require purchase. There is a security blog as well as newsletters and podcasts. There are step-by-step guides and security policy templates available and much more as you will see during this laboratory activity.

Equipment and Materials
- Windows 10 or later computer with Internet access

Procedure

1. _____ Report to your assigned workstation.

2. _____ Boot the computer and verify that it is in working order.

3. _____ Access the SANS organization website at www.SANS.org.

4. _____ On the home page, locate and then go to **About>SANS>Overview**. Answer the following questions. Record your answers in the spaces provided.

   What is the GIAC Certification Program?

   _____

   What cybersecurity courses are offered by SANS?

   _____

5. _____ Select the **Resources** link. You will see many of the resources available concerning security.

6. _____ **Resources>Overview** and select the **Security Policy Templates** link. Take a few minutes to explore the policy templates. The policy templates are outlines of policies that can be used by companies to create their own policy book for IT security. This is a fabulous resource for saving time when creating your own network security policy book.

7. _____ Enter the term **glossary** in the search bar to find the Glossary of Security terms. Answer the following questions. Record your answers in the spaces provided.

   How is the term *Kerberos* defined?
   _____

   How is the term *IP Spoofing* defined?
   _____

   How is the term *Public Key* defined?
   _____

8. _____ Go to **Resources>Overview** and select the **Internet Storm Center** link.
9. _____ What type of information is contained on the Internet Storm Center page?
   _____

10. _____ **Resources>Overview** and select the **CIS Controls v8** link.
11. _____ What information is contained on the CIS Controls v8 page?
    _____

12. _____ Navigate the website for a few minutes to explore your own interests.
13. _____ Answer the review questions.

Review Questions

1. What does the acronym SANS represent?
   _____

2. What is the primary function of the SANS organization?
   _____

Name _____ Date _____ Class _____

TCP/IP Filtering

Outcomes

After completing this laboratory activity, you will be able to:
- Recall the names of the three IANA port number ranges.
- Recall the role of port numbers in association with the TCP/IP suite.
- Use the New Inbound Rule Wizard to filter TCP/IP connections by port number.

Introduction

In an earlier laboratory activity, you used Windows Firewall to explore how port numbers are used to filter TCP/IP connections. In this laboratory activity, you will filter TCP, UDP, and IP port activity using the New Inbound Rule Wizard.

TCP/IP filtering is typically used as a security feature to prevent certain software programs from communicating with a computer by blocking all packets to a specific port number. For example, instant messaging has been identified as a potential security problem on private networks connected to the Internet. You could stop all instant messaging on your computer by blocking port number 1863.

The Internet Assigned Numbers Authority (IANA) is an organization responsible for overseeing the assigning of IP addresses, port numbers, and port number identification. You can see the complete set of port numbers identified by IANA at www.iana.org/assignments/port-numbers.

Packets contain address information, such as IP address and port number. The IP address is used to direct the packet to the correct host on the network, and the port number is used to identify which server or software program will receive the contents of the packet. Port numbers are used by the TCP/IP suite of protocols to establish connections for services and programs. A port number is used to match the software program or service to the information contained inside a network packet. For example, an HTTP packet uses port 80. This port number identifies that the contents are to be sent to the browser software program, such as Microsoft Edge or Google Chrome.

Port numbers are assigned by the IANA organization so that a standard for using port numbers can be maintained. For example, you would not want two different software vendors using the same port number for their software programs when communicating over a network using TCP/IP. If two vendors used the same software for different purposes, there would be a conflict. One of the software programs would fail to work. At times, two software packages can be assigned the same port number as long as a method to prevent interfering with other software programs has been incorporated into the software.

The port numbers are divided into three ranges: well-known ports, registered ports, and dynamic or private ports. Well-known ports range from 0 to 1023, registered ports range from 1024 to 49151, and dynamic or private ports range from 49152 to 65535.

The well-known port numbers are assigned by IANA and are used for specific core network processes such as FTP, echo request, time, DHCP, DNS, and HTTP. The registered port numbers are registered to specific companies and organizations to support their software packages. For example, the online-game portal Shockwave uses port 1626, and the game Half-Life uses port 27010 for online gaming. At times, port numbers can create a conflict between two programs causing one to fail.

The dynamic or private range is not assigned, but rather it is used to provide connectivity on a temporary basis when required. The dynamic or private port numbers can be used by any software program and are not regulated.

Equipment and Materials

- Windows 10 computer with Internet access

Procedure

1. _____ Report to your assigned workstation.

2. _____ Boot the computer and verify that it is in working order.

3. _____ Access **Start>Control Panel> Windows Firewall>Advanced Settings>Inbound Rules**. You will see a list of inbound rules similar to those in the following screen capture.

Goodheart-Willcox Publisher

4. _____ Select the **New Rule** option located in the right pane to start the New Inbound Rule Wizard. There are four rule types to choose from: **Program**, **Port**, **Predefined**, and **Custom**.

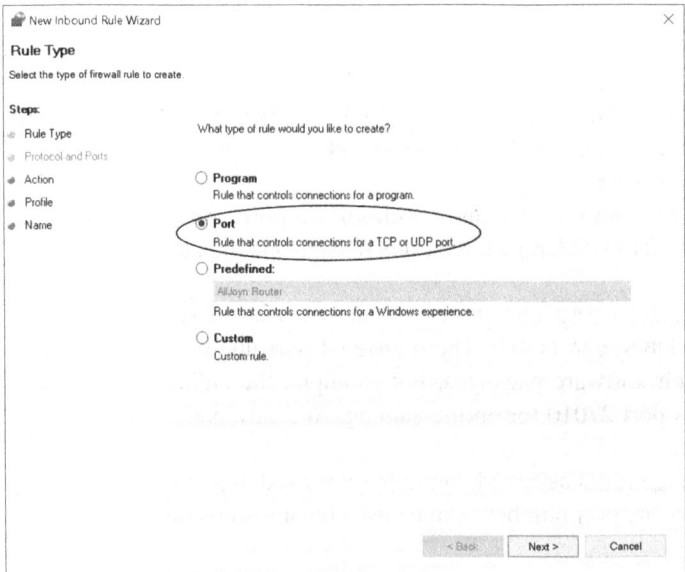

Goodheart-Willcox Publisher

The **Program** option refers to software programs located on the computer. The **Port** option refers to port numbers associated with programs and services. The **Predefined** option refers to predefined inbound rule configurations. The **Custom** option refers to an inbound rule for a program or service not covered by any of the three other options—for example, an undetected software application.

Name _____

5. _____ For this lab activity, select the **Port** option and then click **Next**. A dialog box similar to the following will display, prompting you to identify to which one of the two protocols, TCP or UDP, the rule should be applied. There is also an option to select all local ports and to specify a specific port or a range of ports.

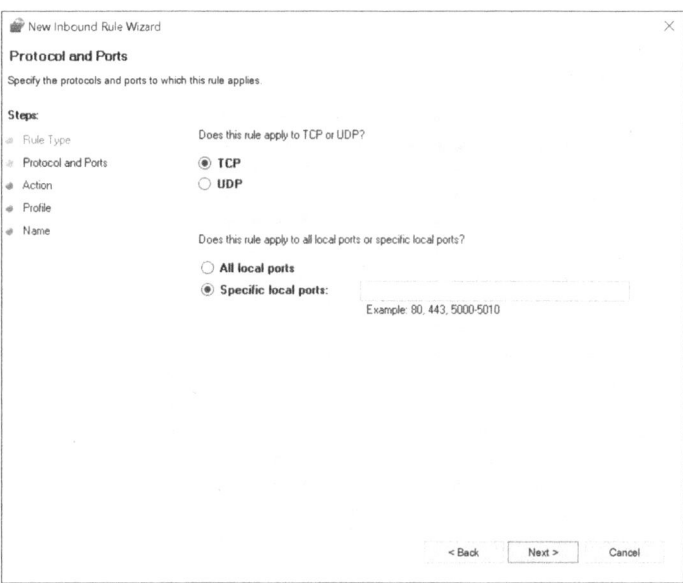

Goodheart-Willcox Publisher

6. _____ Select **TCP** and **Specific local ports**. Enter 5000 in the **Specific local ports** text box and then click **Next**. A dialog box will display, prompting you to select a type of action associated with the port. The options displayed are **Allow the connection**, **Allow the connection if it is secure**, and **Block the connection**.

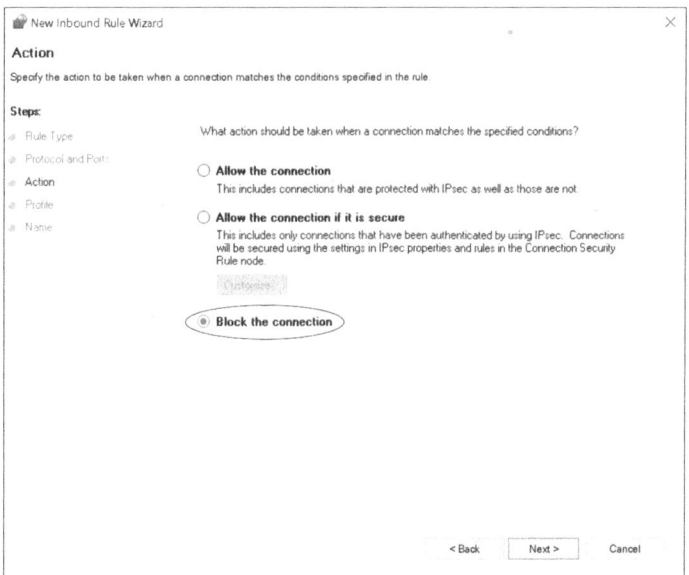

Goodheart-Willcox Publisher

7. _____ Select **Block the connection** and then click **Next**. The next dialog box presents three profile options that relate directly to the type of network location: **Domain**, **Private**, and **Public**.

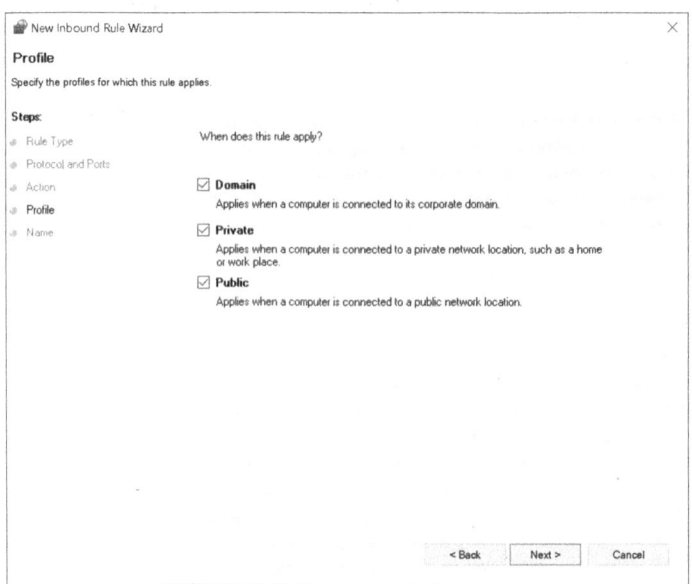

Goodheart-Willcox Publisher

Notice that the three profiles correspond to the three network location types that are encountered when first setting up or modifying a network location. You can apply this rule to any combination of location types.

8. _____ Select all three locations and then click **Next**. A dialog box similar to the following will display, prompting you to name and describe the inbound rule.

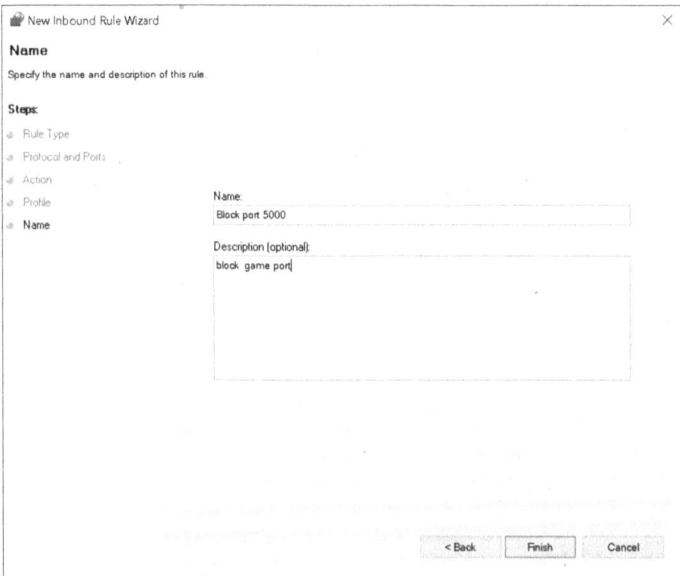

Goodheart-Willcox Publisher

9. _____ Name the rule Block port 5000 and use Block game port as the description. Click **Finish** to complete the inbound rule configuration.

Name _____

10. _____ Look at the list of inbound rules in Windows Firewall.

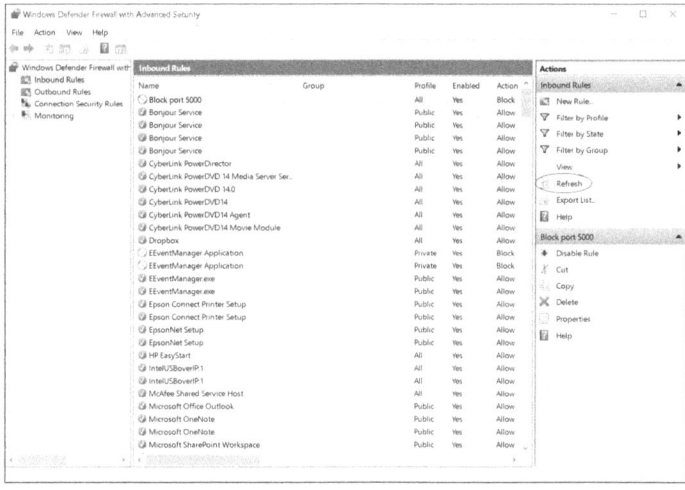

Goodheart-Willcox Publisher

At the top of the list you will see **Block port 5000**. If you closed and reopened Windows Firewall, the inbound rules will be listed alphabetically by default. You may need to scroll down the list to see the new rule you created. If the new inbound rule fails to appear in the list, select the **Refresh** option located in the right pane.

Note that the color of the icon for the inbound rule is red in contrast to the other inbound rules. A red icon indicates that the port is blocked, and green icon indicates that the port is open.

Using the slide control, you can view the hidden information about the rule, such as the actual assigned port number.

11. _____ Call your instructor to view the **Block port 5000** rule.

12. _____ Now, double-click the **Block port 5000** rule and then change the configuration to allow the port. Simply select the appropriate option corresponding to allow the connection.

13. _____ View the list of inbound rules once more. You should see that the **Block port 5000** rule has a green icon indicating that it is an allowed port connection.

14. _____ Remove the rule by right-clicking it and selecting **Delete** from the shortcut menu.

15. _____ Inspect the inbound rule list to verify the **Block port 5000** rule has been deleted.

16. _____ Return all materials to their proper storage areas and then answer the review questions.

Review Questions

1. Which two protocols are typically associated with port number filtering?

_____

2. What is the purpose of port filtering?

_____

_____

_____

3. List the names of the three major port number groups and their corresponding port number ranges.

_____

_____

_____

4. Which set of port numbers are not regulated?

_____

5. What role do port numbers play in support of the TCP/IP protocol suite?

_____

_____

6. What are the three profile options that can be assigned to the filtered port?

_____

7. Who is in charge of regulating port number assignments?

_____

8. What color icon is used to indicate that the port is blocked?

_____

9. What color icon is used to indicate that the port is open?

_____

Name _____ Date _____ Class _____

Downloading and Installing an Antivirus Program

Outcomes

After completing this laboratory activity, you will be able to:
- Test the antivirus software program using the EICAR test file.
- Use an antivirus program to scan a specific folder or file.

Introduction

In this laboratory activity, you will download and install a 30-day trial version of an antivirus program. You may also use one of the following websites from which to download and install a trial version of antivirus software. This laboratory activity is based on AVG Internet Security, but other antivirus software will produce similar results and closely match the laboratory activity.

- AVG: www.avg.com.
- Symantec: www.symantec.com.
- McAfee: www.mcafee.com.
- Kaspersky Lab: www.kaspersky.com.
- Sophos: www.sophos.com.

You will need a copy of the European for Computer Antivirus Research (EICAR) test files located at www.eicar.org. The EICAR test files are an industry standard used to test antivirus software configuration. The EICAR test files simulate an actual computer virus. You will use these files to test the antivirus software after it is installed and configured on your computer. The EICAR test files will be treated like a real threat to the computer or network.

The EICAR test files come in several versions. Each version represents a more difficult detection level starting with the eicar.com file—the easiest to detect—and progressing to the eicarcom2.zip—the hardest to detect. All virus scanners should be able to detect eicar.com.

Equipment and Materials

- Windows 10 computer with Internet access
- Downloaded copy of AVG Internet Security 30-day trial (Be sure you download the 30-day trial version; read the download page carefully.)
- Downloaded copy of the EICAR test files

> **NOTE**
> The computer may already have an antivirus software package installed. The antivirus software package, if installed, will detect the EICAR test files when you attempt to download them. If you have problems downloading the EICAR test files, you may need to temporarily disable the antivirus software on the computer or network. You must have your instructor's permission to disable the antivirus software, even if on a temporary basis.

Procedure

1. _____ Report to your assigned workstation.

2. _____ Boot the computer and verify that it is in working order.

3. _____ Download and install the 30-day trial version of AVG Internet Security located at www.avg.com. Be sure to download the AVG manual in PDF file format. The manual contains all the information you will need to install and configure this software package. It also has information about the EICAR test files.

4. _____ Create a folder on the desktop titled **EICAR**. You will use this folder for the downloaded copies of the EICAR test files.

5. _____ Navigate to the EICAR website at www.eicar.org. Select the **Download Anti-Malware Testfile** link at the bottom of the web page, then click the **Download** link. There are several formats available: TXT, COM, and ZIP. You may have difficulty downloading the COM file if your network or Internet access is protected by an antivirus software program. You may need to download the TXT file or the ZIP file instead. The COM file is detected by most antivirus programs as a malicious code. The antivirus program will block attempts to download this file. Be sure to read the information and instructions located at the EICAR website.

6. _____ Scan the EICAR folder on the desktop where you have installed the EICAR test files. Most antivirus software will perform a scan when you right-click the EICAR folder and select the scan option in the shortcut menu. The name of the scan option will vary according to the antivirus software program installed. The antivirus software should detect the test files. Do *not* delete or quarantine the EICAR test files until you call your instructor to inspect your antivirus configuration.

7. _____ Answer the review questions. You may use the download of the PDF version of the user manual for the antivirus program you installed, which is likely located on the antivirus website under a link titled Support or Documentation. Do *not* print a hard copy of the guide without first obtaining your instructor's permission.

8. _____ Return the computer to its original configuration.

Review Questions

1. What are the EICAR test files?

2. What is the default configuration setting in AVG Internet Security for handling an infected file when first detected?

3. Where does AVG Internet Security send an infected file that cannot be healed?

4. What are the scan options for AVG Internet Security?

5. What are the available options for an infected file once it is sent to the AVG Virus Vault?

6. Can you check e-mail with the AVG Internet Security program?

Name _____ Date _____ Class _____

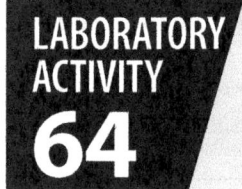

Obtaining Malware Information

Outcomes

After completing this laboratory activity, you will be able to:
- Use the Internet to obtain information about malware.
- Compare information about malware from different sources.
- Recall where you can find up-to-date information about the latest security threats.

Introduction

In this laboratory activity, you will obtain descriptions of several known types of malware. You will use a number of different sources so that you can compare information from each website. You will also locate a list of the most common threats at this time.

An excellent source for information is the website of the antivirus software you are using. Another excellent source of information is the www.sans.org website and organization. The SANS Institute has a listing of the latest threats to security. You should always check the SANS Institute website and antivirus vendor websites for information on the latest security threats. Microsoft also provides security information, which is located at http://technet.microsoft.com/en-us/security/default.aspx.

It is interesting to note that not all antivirus software manufacturers use the same name for a particular malicious software program. For example, one particular virus may have several names associated with it. Look at the following list of names that have been used by various software companies to identify the same virus. Multiple names can cause a great deal of confusion when researching information about a particular virus.

Software Company	Malware Identification Name
Computer Associates	Win32.DIWreck
Kaspersky	Trojan-Downloader.Win32.Vidlo.p
McAfee	Downloader-ACS
Sophos	Troj/Vidlo-P
Trend Micro	TROJ DLOADER.RY
CME	CME-402

Your assignment for this laboratory activity is to answer questions about various malicious software programs using the list of antivirus software vendors and the SANS Institute website.

Equipment and Materials
- Windows 10 computer with Internet access

Procedure

1. _____ Report to your assigned workstation.

2. _____ Boot the computer and verify that it is in working order.

3. _____ Use the Internet to research how each malicious software program listed in the following table is classified (Trojan, hoax, etc.), its characteristics, and how it is spread. Also, identify the source of your information.

Malicious Software	Classification	Characteristics	How it Spreads	Information Source
W32.Spacefam				
Backdoor.Cycbot				
Mal/GIFIframe-A				
Exploit.JS.Gumblar				

4. _____ Use the SANS Institute website and various antivirus websites to determine the top five current security threats. Record your answers in the space provided.

_____
_____
_____
_____
_____

Review Questions

1. Where can you find information about the latest threats to security?

_____
_____
_____

Name _____ Date _____ Class _____

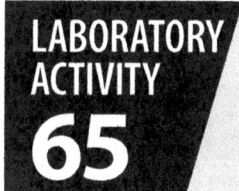

Reset Menu Options

Outcomes

After completing this laboratory activity, you will be able to:
- Recall the function of each Reset menu options.
- Use the Reset menu.
- Recall which programs and system features are accessible in safe mode.

Introduction

In this laboratory activity, you will explore the various options available from the **Reset** menu to recover your system. A successful startup of a Windows server or workstation is complete when the user successfully logs on to the system. Before a successful logon occurs, the system can fail for numerous reasons. One of the first tactics used to determine and correct the problem is to invoke the **Reset Options** menu by pressing and holding the [Shift] key at the sign-in screen and selecting **Power>Restart**. **Reset Options** can also be accessed by selecting **Start>Update & Security>Recovery**. Under the **Advanced startup** tab, select **Restart now**. Once the PC is restarted, you should see the **Choose an option** screen, as shown in the following capture.

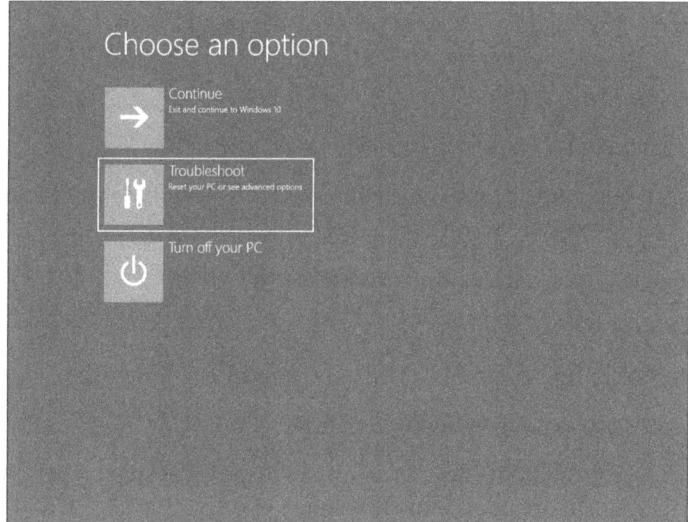

Goodheart-Willcox Publisher

Select **Troubleshoot>Advanced options>Startup Repair**. The system will restart, and you will be prompted to provide a username and password.

 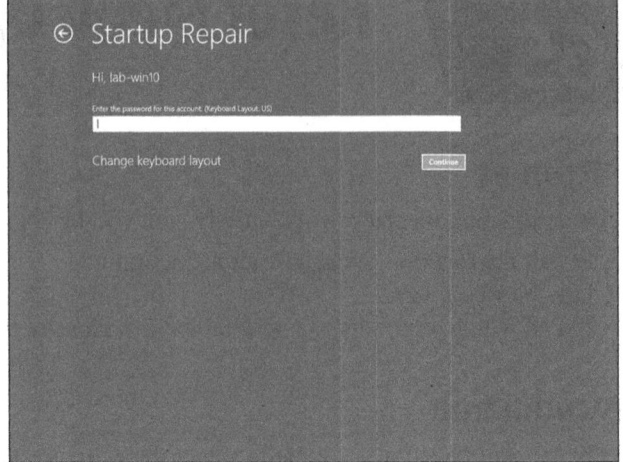

Goodheart-Willcox Publisher

Equipment and Materials

- Windows 10 or later computer

Procedure

1. ____ Report to your assigned workstation.
2. ____ Boot the computer and verify that it is in working order.
3. ____ Start the computer in safe mode by pressing and holding the [Shift] key and selecting **Power>Restart** at the logon screen. The system will restart and present the **Reset** menu.
4. ____ After the **Reset** menu appears, select the **Troubleshoot** option.
5. ____ Select **Advanced options**.
6. ____ Select **Startup Repair** to fix any problems that are preventing Windows from loading.
7. ____ Select the desired user account for Windows repair.
8. ____ Enter the password for the Windows account used in the previous step and click the **Continue** button. Windows will restart and attempt to fix any problems.
9. ____ Return the computer to its original configuration and then answer the review questions.

Review Questions

1. Which function key is used to access the **Reset** menu?

   _____

2. What determines a successful boot operation?

   _____

Name _____ Date _____ Class _____

Windows 10 Recovery Environment

Outcomes

After completing this laboratory activity, you will be able to:
- Recall how to access the Windows 10 or Windows 11 Recovery Environment.
- Summarize the function of each Windows 10/Windows 11 Recovery Environment option.
- Test the system memory with Windows Memory Diagnostic.
- Use the Windows 10 Recovery Environment command prompt.

Introduction

Windows XP and Windows Server 2003 were the last computer operating systems that supported the Microsoft Recovery Console. The Recovery Console provides a command prompt for accessing files and folders on a failed computer. It allows commands to be entered in an attempt to repair the system.

Now, Windows 10 uses the Windows 10 Recovery Environment (WinRE). Windows Recovery Environment has many recovery options. Look at the options in the following screen capture of the **Advanced Options** menu.

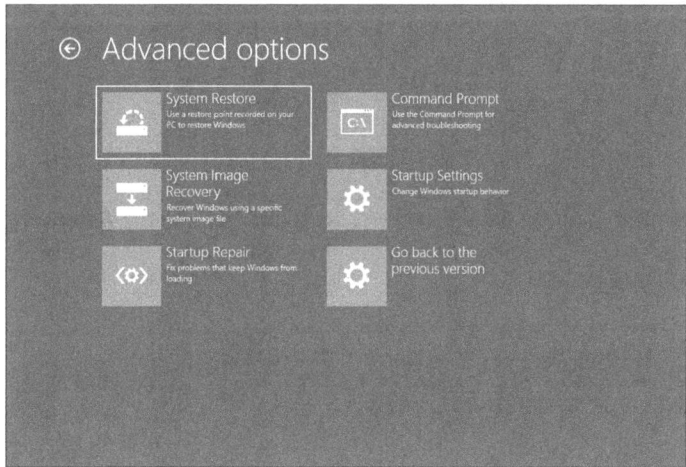

Goodheart-Willcox Publisher

Equipment and Materials

- Windows 10 computer

Procedure

1. _____ Report to your assigned workstation.

2. _____ Boot the computer and verify that it is in working order. Then, restart the computer.

3. _____ At the logon screen, hold down the [Shift] key and click the power icon to select **Restart**. When the computer restarts, select **Troubleshoot>Advanced Options** to open the **Advanced Options** menu, as seen in the previous screen capture.

> **NOTE**
> The **System Restore** option can be disabled on a networked computer by the system administrator. If this option fails to appear in the **Advanced Options** menu, call your instructor for assistance.

4. ____ Select **System Restore**. You will be prompted to select the language and then enter an administrator user account name and password.

The restore option can fix problems that prevent Windows 10 from loading. Follow the on-screen instructions to restore the system.

5. ____ Go back to the **Advanced Options** menu, and select the **System Image Recovery** option. You will again be prompted for an appropriate username and password. After the username and password have been entered, the **Systems Recovery Options** menu should appear similar to the one in the following screen capture.

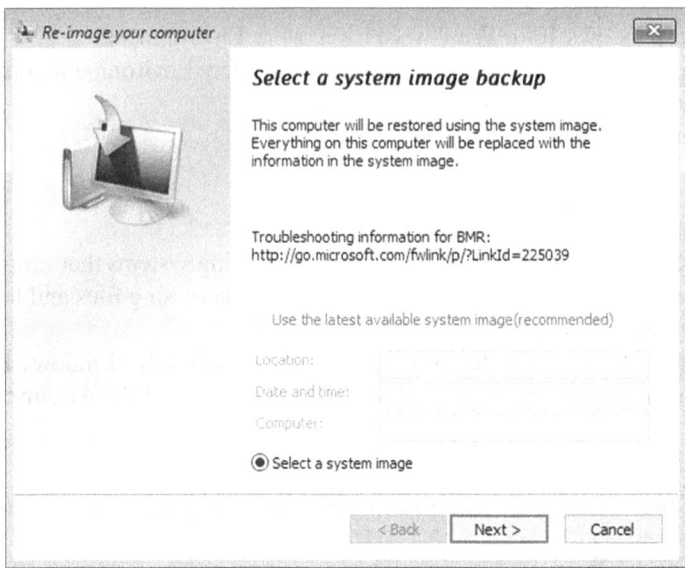

Goodheart-Willcox Publisher

Select the **Cancel** option after viewing the dialog box. Navigate back to the **Advanced Options** menu.

6. ____ Select the **Startup Repair** option. Now, you will try each of the options in the **System Recovery Options** menu.

Goodheart-Willcox Publisher

Simply follow the on-screen dialog boxes for each and observe the actions. Be aware that the memory test takes a long time. You may wish to cancel the test before it is completed.

Name _____

7. _____ Select the **Command** option. Run the following commands from the command prompt and observe the results: **dir**, **time**, **arp -a**, **tree**, **exit**. After entering the **exit** command, you will be returned to the **System Recovery Options** dialog box.

8. _____ Select the **Startup Settings** option. **Startup Settings** that could be modified include but not limited to the settings listed in the screen capture screen below.

Goodheart-Willcox Publisher

Click the **Restart** button to allow Windows to alter settings.

9. _____ Select the **Go back to the previous version** option. This option allows you to restore to the previous update with the hope of fixing the problem. This restore will not affect your personal files; however, you will lose all changes made to any applications and settings since your most recent update.

Goodheart-Willcox Publisher

Click the **Cancel** button to return to the previous window.

10. _____ Return all materials to the proper storage area and then answer the review questions.

Review Questions

1. How can the **Advanced Options** menu be accessed in Windows 10?

2. Which option in the **Advanced Options** menu restores your computer to an earlier time?

3. Which option in the **Advanced Options** menu automatically repairs damaged or missing required startup files?

4. What does WinRE represent?

5. What command closes the command prompt and returns you to the GUI?

Name _____ Date _____ Class _____

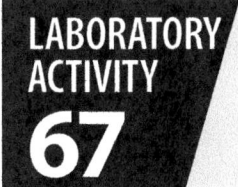

Create a Recovery Drive

Outcomes

After completing this laboratory activity, you will be able to:
- Recall the appropriate use of a recovery drive.
- Differentiate between a system image and a system recovery drive.
- Create a system recovery drive for Windows 10 or 11.
- Use a system recovery drive to recover an operating system that fails to boot because of corrupt or missing required files.

Introduction

In this laboratory activity, you will create a 64-bit Windows 10 or later system recovery drive. The Windows 10 system recovery drive is used to quickly repair a Windows 10 operating system that has failed to boot because of corrupt, damaged, or missing required files. The Windows 10 system recovery drive differs from a system image in that a system image contains all the files and folders contained on the disk drive, whereas the system recovery drive contains only the files necessary to recover the operating system boot process. The system recovery drive does not contain copies of any additional files such as documents, pictures, and music. It does not format the default system partition. The system recovery drive is the best choice for a quick recovery. Using a system image to recover a system could take a great deal of time.

You can create a 64-bit system recovery drive; however, the recovery drive type must match the computer system type. You may use either a recordable CD or DVD or USB drive to make the recovery drive, but know that an approximate minimum of 1Gb of space is required to make the recovery drive.

Equipment and Materials

- Windows 10 or later computer
- Recordable CD or DVD or USB drive

Procedure

1. _____ Report to your assigned workstation.

2. _____ Boot the computer and verify that it is in working order.

3. _____ Insert a recordable CD/DVD or USB drive into the appropriate drive.

4. _____ Access the **Create a recovery drive** wizard through **Start>Control Panel>System and Security**. From there, you can simply search by entering the phrase create recovery in the search bar and select **Recovery Drive** from the list of results.

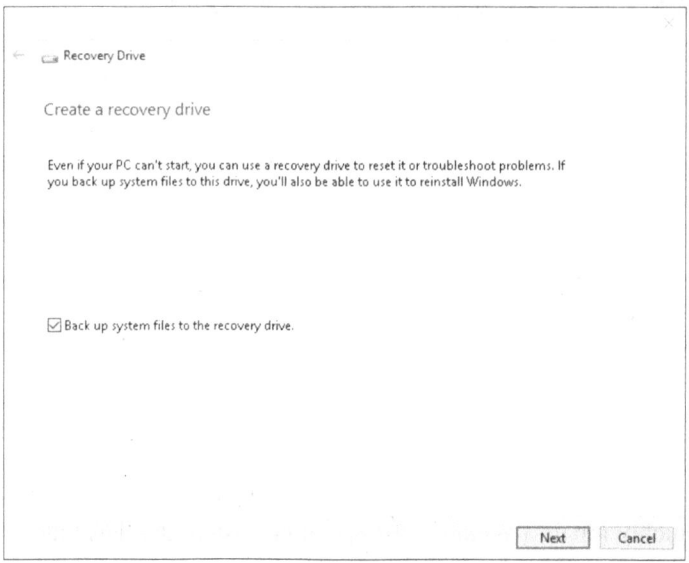

Goodheart-Willcox Publisher

5. _____ The first dialog box to appear requests that you select the appropriate drive to use for creating the recovery drive. Note that the data on the selected drive will be deleted. After selecting the appropriate drive, click **Next**.

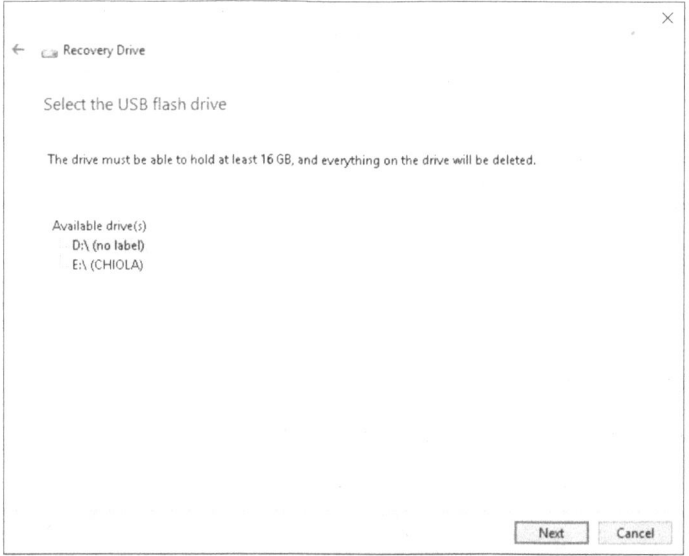

Goodheart-Willcox Publisher

Name _____

The next screen will again caution you to back up any personal files on the drive. After doing so, click the **Create** button.

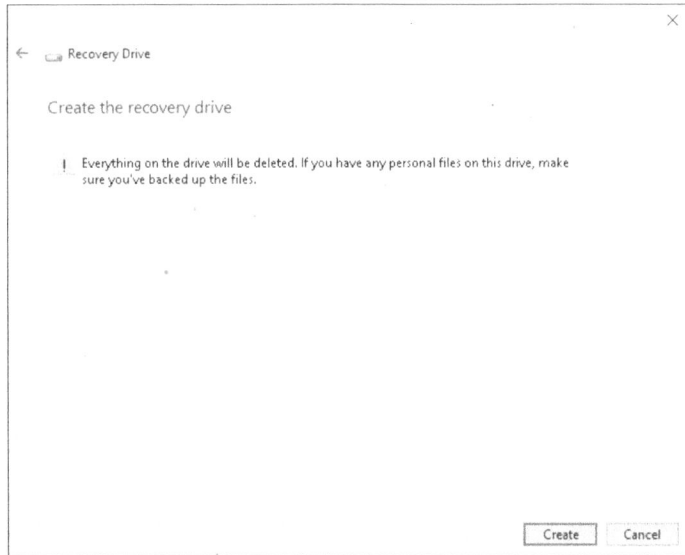

Goodheart-Willcox Publisher

The wizard will start and display the progress of the operation.

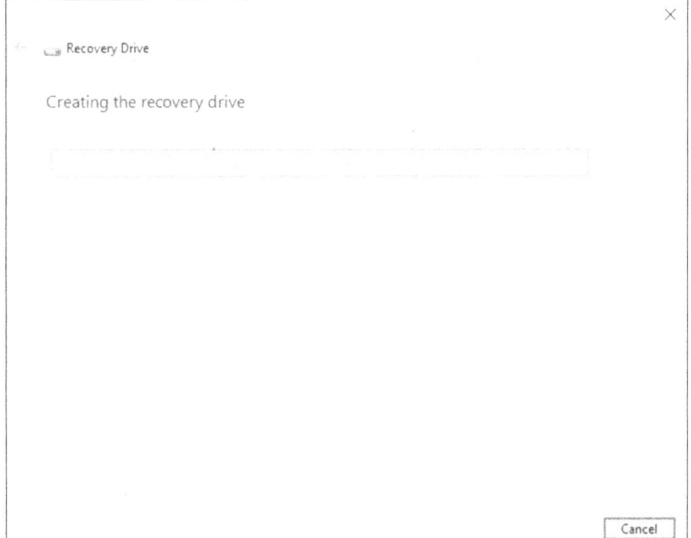

Goodheart-Willcox Publisher

6. _____ When the recovery drive is created, a dialog similar to the following will display, letting you know that the recovery drive is ready for use. Click the **Finish** button to close the dialog box.

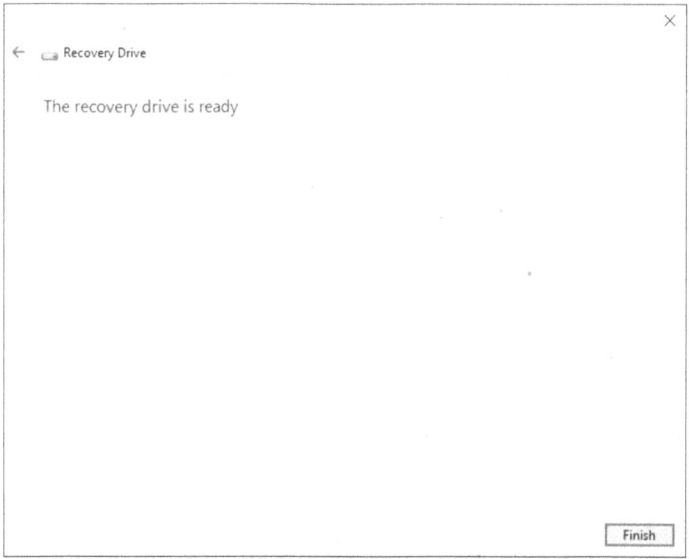

Goodheart-Willcox Publisher

7. _____ View the contents of the system repair disc with Windows Explorer. The contents should look similar to that in the following screen capture.

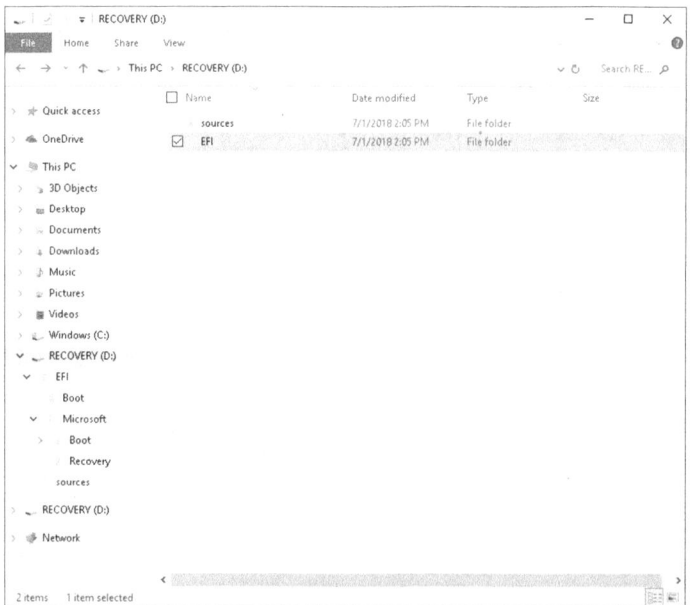

Goodheart-Willcox Publisher

There will be two main folders labeled **EFI** and **sources**. The recovery drive contains all the files necessary to repair the boot operation for Windows 10.

8. _____ With your instructor's permission, use the system repair disc to simulate repairing your computer. To do this, leave the system recovery drive in the computer. Reboot the computer and observe the process. You may need to change the boot order in the system BIOS so that the recovery drive is configured as the first boot device.

9. _____ Return all materials to their proper storage areas and then answer the review questions.

Name _____

Review Questions

1. What is the purpose of the Windows 10 recovery drive?

   _____
   _____

2. What is the difference between a system image and a system repair disc?

   _____
   _____
   _____

3. What is the complete path to **Create Recovery Drive** from the **Start** menu?

   _____
   _____

4. What type of storage media can be used to make a recovery drive?

   _____

5. _____ Choose the correct major section of Control Panel where the **Create a recovery drive** wizard is found.
   A. Hardware and Sound
   B. System and Security
   C. Programs
   D. Ease of Access

Notes

Name _____ Date _____ Class _____

System Configuration Utility

Outcomes

After completing this laboratory activity, you will be able to:
- Recall how to access the System Configuration utility.
- Carry out a selective startup troubleshooting procedure.

Introduction

In this laboratory activity, you will explore the function of the System Configuration utility. The System Configuration utility is an essential troubleshooting tool. It is very similar in operation for Windows 7–11 and Windows Server 2008–2019.

The System Configuration utility will help you solve many different problems usually caused by software programs, drivers, or corrupt configuration files. This utility uses the process of elimination to narrow down a list of all possible software, drivers, and configuration settings to find which is causing the problem.

The System Configuration utility can be started easily by typing System Configuration or msconfig.exe into the taskbar's search feature and selecting **System Configuration** from the results list. The **System Configuration** utility dialog box will look similar to the one in the following screen capture.

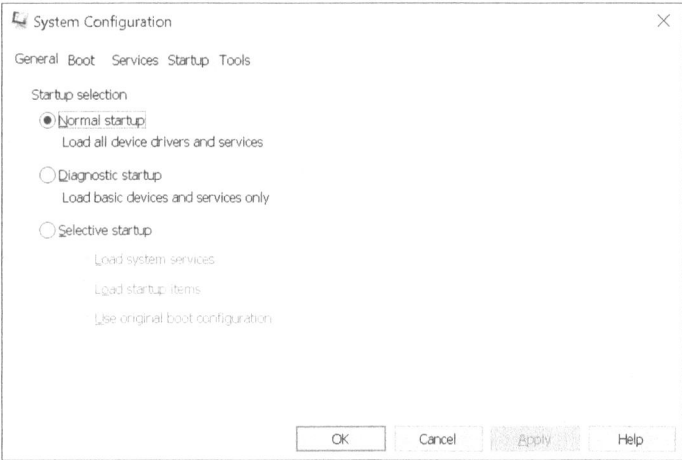

Goodheart-Willcox Publisher

The **General** tab provides a means to first eliminate all unnecessary items. The **Boot** tab lists different operating systems available and various boot options, such as **Safe Mode** and **No GUI Boot**. This tab also enables the user to set the timeout length. The **Services** and **Startup** tabs allow you to add items one at a time to the boot process. For example, you would normally select the **Diagnostic startup** option on the **General** tab. This will force the system to start in similar fashion as in safe mode. If you are able to reboot the system without the failure occurring, the problem is related to a system service or a program that is loading during startup. You can then select the **Selective startup** and **Load system services** options and reboot the system. If the failure reoccurs, the problem is related to a startup item. If the failure does not reoccur, the problem is related to a system service. Once you've determined the problem area, you can narrow down the cause of the system failure by adding items to the boot process one at a time from the **Services** page or **Startup** page and then rebooting. When the failure reoccurs after introducing a specific item to the boot process, you have found the problem service or startup item. The **Tools** tab essentially serves as a way to launch various utilities available in the operating system, such as Event Viewer, Windows Troubleshooting, and Computer Management.

Using the System Configuration Utility to troubleshoot a system failure can be a very time-consuming task, but it is well worth the effort if it prevents reformatting the disk drive, reinstalling the operating system, and adding files from the latest system backup.

Equipment and Materials

- Windows 10 or later computer

Procedure

1. _____ Report to your assigned workstation.

2. _____ Boot the computer and verify that it is in working order.

3. _____ Open the System Configuration utility by entering msconfig.exe into the **Search** box located off the **Start** menu.

4. _____ In the **System Configuration** dialog box, select the **Diagnostic startup** option to load only basic drivers and services required for the boot operation. Click the **Apply** button. You will be prompted to restart the computer for the change to take effect. Do so now.

5. _____ Re-open the System Configuration utility and select the **Selective startup** option and deselect **Load system services** and **Load startup items**. Reboot the system and observe the effect.

6. _____ Re-open the System Configuration utility and select **Load system services** or **Load startup items** and then reboot the system.

7. _____ For the option **Load system services** or **Load startup items** that you left deselected, go to its related page, **Services** or **Startup**, and reintroduce items to the boot process one at a time until all items have been selected.

8. _____ Return the System Configuration utility to a non-diagnostic mode by selecting the **Normal startup** option and rebooting the computer. Observe the effect.

9. _____ Now, explore the System Configuration tabs to see what type of files and configuration information is located under each.

10. _____ Select the **Tools** tab and then record in the space provided the tools that are available for troubleshooting.

_____

_____

_____

_____

_____

11. _____ Practice using the System Configuration utility until you feel comfortable with using it.

12. _____ Return all materials to their proper storage area. Be sure the computer is not left in diagnostic mode.

13. _____ Answer the review questions.

Name _____

Review Questions

1. Which options are available for a selective startup?

   _____

   _____

   _____

2. Explain how you would use the System Configuration utility to troubleshoot a startup problem.

   _____

   _____

   _____

   _____

   _____

3. Place an *X* by the tools that are available under the **Tools** tab.

   A. System Restore _____

   B. Internet Protocol Configuration _____

   C. Display Configuration _____

   D. Event Viewer _____

   E. Firewall Configuration _____

   F. Registry Editor _____

   G. Modem Configuration _____

   H. Task Manager _____

   I. Remote Assistance _____

   J. Remote Desktop _____

Notes

Name _____ Date _____ Class _____

Using the Nbtstat Command

Outcomes

After completing this laboratory activity, you will be able to:
- Use the **nbtstat** command for verifying NetBIOS name resolution.
- Recall the purpose of the **nbtstat** command.
- Recall the purpose of common command line switches used with the **nbtstat** command.
- Use the **net view** command to view a list of local area network computers.

Introduction

In this laboratory activity, you will explore the use of the **nbtstat** command. The **nbtstat** command is used to help troubleshoot NetBIOS name resolution problems. NetBIOS name resolution is still supported on current Windows operating systems in the effort to support legacy operating systems. NetBIOS names are used to support communication with an operating system that uses NetBIOS names such as Windows 98 or earlier and legacy hardware devices.

> **NOTE**
> Network computers and devices prior to Windows 2000 required NetBIOS names for communication. Starting with Windows 2000, NetBIOS names were only required to communicate with older operating systems.

Networks based on TCP/IP use a service called *NetBIOS over TCP/IP* to resolve NetBIOS names to IP addresses. Typically, a network device queries the WINS server through a broadcast to locate a NetBIOS named device. NetBIOS name resolution can also be achieved through the use of the lmhosts file, the host file, and DNS server queries. A quick way to see the NetBIOS names assigned to devices in a local area network is with the **nbtstat** command.

> **NOTE**
> TCP/IP networks use DNS names for device identification. IPv6 resolves computer names and IPv6 addresses automatically in a local area network.

The **net view** command will also be introduced during this lab activity. The **net view** command is used to display a list of local area network computers, domains, workgroups, and resources. To view a list of computers in the local network, simply enter net view at the command prompt.

The following screen capture shows the **net view** command used to list the computers on the local network. It also shows **nbtstat** with the **-n** switch. The **nbtstat -n** command lists the NetBIOS names that are associated with the local host adapter.

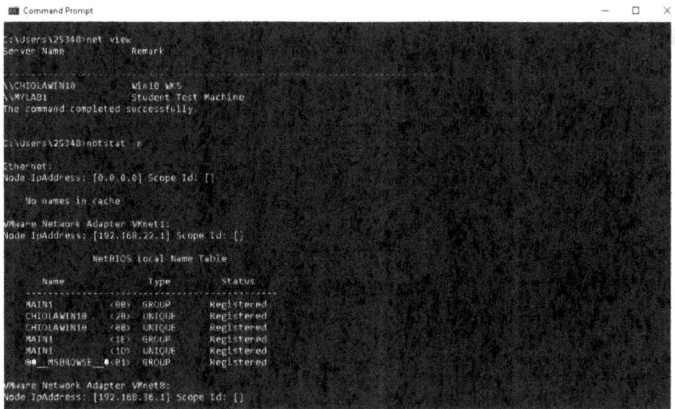

Goodheart-Willcox Publisher

Copyright Goodheart-Willcox Co., Inc.
May not be reproduced or posted to a publicly accessible website.

353

DNS names use 63 characters to identify network devices; NetBIOS uses 15 characters. When 63-character names are used and a NetBIOS name is required to provide compatibility with operating systems based on NetBIOS names, the 63-character names are automatically truncated.

> **NOTE**
> To view a complete list of NetBIOS suffixes, conduct an Internet search using the phrase Microsoft NetBIOS name suffix.

Look at the following screen capture of the **WINS** page of the **Advanced TCP/IP Settings** dialog box. Notice the options for LMHOSTS lookup and for NetBIOS settings.

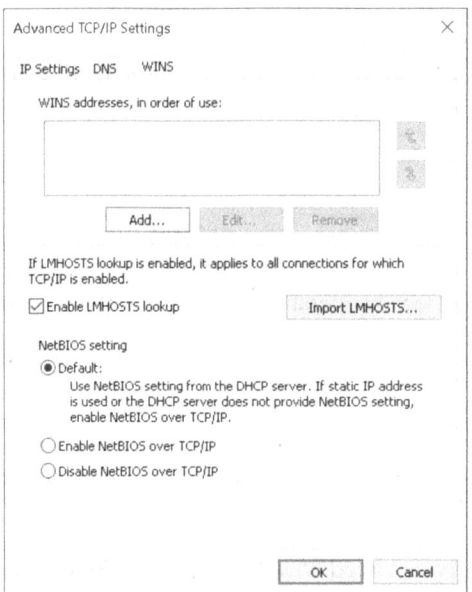

Goodheart-Willcox Publisher

Windows Internet Name Service (WINS) is based on NetBIOS names. NetBIOS names are fine for older operating systems that communicated only on local area networks, but they cannot be used to communicate over the Internet because they are not routable. Routers rely on IP addresses for routing packets across the Internet. To enable NetBIOS-named devices to be identified and routed over the Internet, they must be matched to IPv4 addresses. Look at the NetBIOS setting section of the **Advanced TCP/IP Settings** dialog box. The default setting uses the DHCP server to resolve NetBIOS names to IP addresses or enables NetBIOS over TCP/IP. When NetBIOS over TCP/IP is enabled or selected, the NetBIOS information is encapsulated and carried by the TCP/IP protocols.

You can disable NetBIOS over TCP/IP when using a server that supports DNS name registration and resolution. Disabling NetBIOS resolution reduces the number of NetBIOS broadcasts used to resolve device names on the local area network. If NetBIOS name resolution is required by the local area network, at least one network device must have NetBIOS over TCP/IP enabled.

Name _____

The **nbtstat** command is not case sensitive, but the switches are. Look at the **nbtstat** command syntax and command switches in the following screen capture. The **nbtstat** commands can be used to verify that the network adapter is indeed registering its NetBIOS name and that it is able to communicate with other computers using the NetBIOS name.

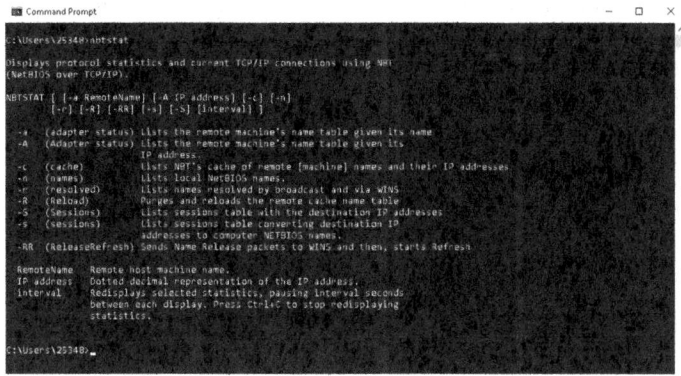

Goodheart-Willcox Publisher

NOTE
The **netstat** command is a test item on the CompTIA Network+ exam. Be sure you are familiar with the command and the display generated by the command. The **netstat** command questions can be very confusing, especially when compared to **nbtstat**. As a help, remember that **netstat** generates network statistics in relation to the TCP/IP protocol suite, and **nbtstat** generates information about the assigned NetBIOS names.

Equipment and Materials
- Two Windows 10 or later computers connected as a peer-to-peer network

Procedure

1. _____ Report to your assigned computer.

2. _____ Boot the computers and verify that they are in working order.

3. _____ Fill in the workgroup name, IPv4 address, and MAC address for each computer. This will help you better understand the information displayed by the commands and command switches.

   Workgroup name: _____

   Computer 1 name: _____

   IPv4 address: _____

   MAC address: _____

   Computer 2 name: _____

   IPv4 address: _____

   MAC address: _____

4. _____ Open a command prompt as the administrator by right-clicking the **Command Prompt** menu item and selecting **Run as administrator**.

5. _____ Enter the **net view** command to view all computers connected to and running on the local area network. You should see the name of both computers. If not, call your instructor for assistance.

6. _____ Enter **nbtstat** at the command prompt and observe the results.

7. _____ Enter the **nbtstat help** command and observe the results. You should see a list of information similar to that displayed by the **nbtstat** command.

8. _____ At one of the computers, enter the command nbtstat -A followed by the IP address assigned to that computer—for example, nbtstat -A 192.168.10.10. Then, enter the **nbtstat -A** command followed by the IP address assigned to the other computer. Enter the same commands at the other computer.

9. _____ At one of the computers, enter the command nbtstat -a followed by the computer name—for example, nbtstat -a Computer 1. At the other computer, do the same but using the name of that computer.

10. _____ Now, use the **nbtstat -n** command to display a list of all NetBIOS names for the local host adapter. For each entry, you should see a 15-character NetBIOS name followed by a 16th character, such as <00>, that identifies the device; the type of name, such as "unique" or "group"; and the status, such as "registered." If you do not see this information, call your instructor for assistance.

11. _____ Now use the **nbtstat -c** command to generate a list of NetBIOS names stored in the cache. If no names are displayed after issuing the command, use **net view**, **ping**, or the network browser to generate names in the cache. The names can remain in the cache typically up to 10 minutes. If you do not see the other computer name in the cache, call your instructor.

12. _____ After successfully seeing the list of names in the cache, you will purge the cache. Use the **nbtstat -R** command to purge the NetBIOS name cache. Use **the nbtstat -c** command to verify that the cache has been purged. No network computer names should appear in the display.

13. _____ Now use the **nbtstat -r** command to view all previous NetBIOS names resolved by broadcasts. You should see all the past names that were in the cache.

14. _____ Practice using the **nbtstat** command with the various switches until you are familiar with the purpose of each.

15. _____ Before shutting down the computers, answer the review questions.

Review Questions

1. What does the **net view** command display?

   _____

   _____

2. What information is revealed by the **nbtstat -n** command?

   _____

3. What command generated the following display?

Goodheart-Willcox Publisher

Name _____

4. What command generated the following display?

Goodheart-Willcox Publisher

5. What command generated the following display?

Goodheart-Willcox Publisher

6. Which **nbtstat** switch would you use to purge the NetBIOS name cache?

7. How would you fill the NetBIOS name cache with NetBIOS names if it were empty?

8. When is NetBIOS over TCP/IP required for a network adapter in a Windows XP computer?

9. How many characters are used in a NetBIOS name?

10. How many characters can be used in a DNS name for a device?

11. What does the acronym WINS represent?

12. What is the main difference between the **nbtstat** and **netstat** commands?

Notes

Name _____ Date _____ Class _____

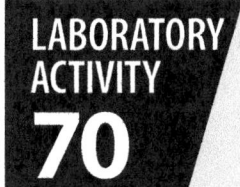

System Information

Outcomes

After completing this laboratory activity, you will be able to:
- Recall when to use the System Information utility.
- Use the System Information utility to identify system hardware and software configuration information.

Introduction

In this lab activity, you will explore the System Information utility, also known as *msinfo32.exe*. This utility is very handy for finding detailed information about a computer's hardware and software configuration. Look at the following screen capture of the System Information utility.

Goodheart-Willcox Publisher

In the left pane of the screen, three major categories of system information are listed: **Hardware Resources**, **Components**, and **Software Environment**. The right pane displays the details for these categories. In this laboratory activity, you will use the System Information utility to identify the system hardware and software configuration information on your lab computer.

Equipment and Materials

- Windows 10 or later computer

Procedure

1. _____ Report to your assigned workstation.
2. _____ Boot the computer and verify that it is in working order.

3. _____ Access the System Information utility by entering msinfo32 into the **Search** box located off the **Start** menu and selecting **msinfo32.exe** from the list. Look at the **System Summary** information and answer the following questions about the computer.

What operating system is installed? _____

What is the last service pack installed? _____

What is the system BIOS name and version? _____

Where is the /System directory located? _____

What is the size of the physical memory? _____

What is the size of the page file? _____

What is the size of the virtual memory? _____

4. _____ Now, look at the **Hardware Resources** information and answer the following question.

What is the assigned network adapter IRQ? _____

5. _____ Look at the **Components** information and answer the following questions.

What is the brand and model of the CD or DVD drive? _____

What is the brand of the display adapter? _____

To what resolution is the display set? _____

How many bits per pixel is the display set to? _____

6. _____ Look at the Network information listed under **Components**. Fill in the following information.

Adapter type (Probably Ethernet 802.3): _____

Adapter brand: _____

IP address: _____

Subnet: _____

DHCP enabled (*Yes* or *No*): _____

DHCP server IP address: _____

MAC address: _____

Gateway: _____

7. _____ Look at the **Software Environment** information and answer the following questions.

Approximately how many system drivers are installed? _____

Approximately how many drivers are signed? _____

Approximately how many services are running? _____

Approximately how many modules are loaded? _____

Approximately how many programs are loaded at startup? _____

What other Windows utility provides similar information about the software environment such as running programs and services?

_____

_____

Name _____

8. _____ Take a few minutes to explore the **Summary Information** utility and its menu items.

9. _____ Answer the review questions.

Review Questions

1. How is the **System Information** utility accessed?

   _____

   _____

2. When would you *most likely* use the **System Information** utility?

   _____

   _____

Notes

Name _____ Date _____ Class _____

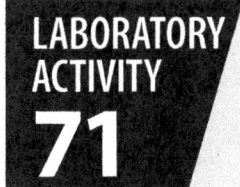

Online Help for Network Problems

Outcomes
After completing this laboratory activity, you will be able to:
- Identify sources for network troubleshooting information.
- Carry out Internet searches for network troubleshooting information related to a specific device, application, or operating system problem.
- Use network troubleshooting information found through Internet searches to solve network problems.

Introduction
This laboratory activity will familiarize you with various sources for network troubleshooting information. Many students and professionals spend too much time trying to solve a problem using trial and error. Chances are, you are not the first person to encounter the problem. Many users may have already experienced the problem, and a cause and a solution may have been posted on the Internet at the software or hardware provider's website or on other websites.

Before spending an extraordinary amount of time troubleshooting a network problem, you should conduct an online search based on the symptoms exhibited by the system. An hour or more spent on the same problem means you really need to conduct a search. However, the exact process of troubleshooting and the amount of time you spend troubleshooting will depend on your supervisor. Some organizations have a step-by-step procedure to follow. If the cause and solution to the problem are not determined through the procedure, the technician forwards the problem to a more experienced technician.

A good source of troubleshooting information is the operating system's or software product's website. For example, when troubleshooting Microsoft operating systems and software products, you would use the Microsoft website.

The Microsoft Support website has a wide range of resources for many Microsoft products. You can browse specific categories, or search for your issue. The support home page can be found at **https://support.microsoft.com/en-us**.

Goodheart-Willcox Publisher

For the SUSE Linux operating system, you should use the SUSE support web page. Conduct a search using the keywords **SUSE support**. You may also enter www.suse.com/support/kb/ into the address bar of your web browser. You may also find www.suse.com/support/kb/help/ to be useful.

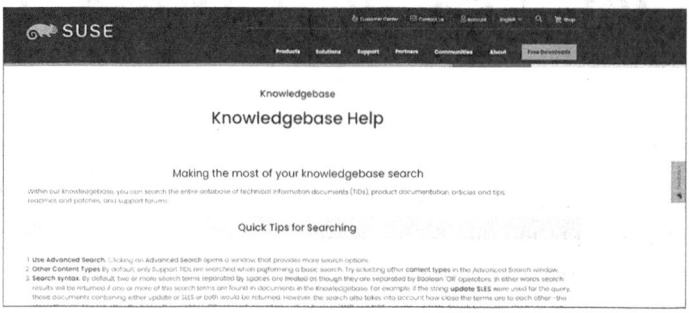

Goodheart-Willcox Publisher

You may find it difficult to describe the problem using terms that correctly identify the symptoms. Through experience, you may want to assemble a list of keywords to use in future searches.

You may also wish to review the Microsoft Knowledge Base article 242450: "How to Query the Microsoft Knowledge Base Key Words and Query Words." You may conduct a search using the key term **Microsoft 242450** to locate the article.

There are countless sources of information on the Internet. When conducting searches for troubleshooting problems, include the terms that relate directly to the manufacturer. For example, for a Microsoft operating system, include the term **Microsoft**, the operating system version, and the symptom.

Equipment and Materials

- Windows 10 computer with Internet access (Note: A Windows 11 computer is also acceptable.)

Procedure

1. _____ Report to your assigned workstation.
2. _____ Boot the computer and verify that it is in working order.
3. _____ Solve the following computer and network problems using the resources mentioned in this laboratory activity. Also, provide the source of the information.

Symptom:

A user complains that a workstation immediately reboots after shutting down. The workstation is running Windows 10 and is connected to a client/server network.

Problem and Solution:

_____

_____

Source:

_____

Symptom:

A user complains of a blue screen with a cryptic test message that reads, "A fatal exception 0D has occurred at 0028:c0038f07 in VXD VMCPD(01) + 00002DB."

Name _____

Problem and Solution:

_____

_____

Source:

_____

Symptom:

A user complains that they cannot play a media file that they received through e-mail. The error message reads, "The server could not be found. (Account: account name, POP server: 'mail', Error Number: 0x800ccc0d)." The user is using Windows 10 and Microsoft Outlook 2016.

Problem and Solution:

_____

_____

Source:

_____

Symptom:

When trying to activate Windows 10, the error "0xC004F061" occurs.

Problem and Solution:

_____

_____

Source:

_____

Review Questions

1. Why should you do an Internet search for a computer or network problem before spending an extraordinary amount of time troubleshooting the problem?

_____

_____

2. What is the Microsoft Support website and who is its intended audience?

_____

_____

Notes

Name _____ Date _____ Class _____

Establishing a Baseline

Outcomes

After completing this laboratory activity, you will be able to:
- Recall the reasons for establishing a network baseline.
- Use the Wireshark Network Protocol Analyzer to establish a baseline.
- Analyze statistical content commonly gathered in a baseline.

Introduction

In this laboratory activity, you will use Wireshark Protocol Analyzer to explore a network baseline and interpret statistics associated with a baseline. Establishing a baseline of network activity will prove to be a valuable network troubleshooting and maintenance tool.

A *baseline* is a reference of statistical information used to compare results and establish trends. The baseline is established for the first time after a network has been created. After the initial creation of a network system, a baseline is reestablished whenever a major change has taken place that might affect network performance. Changes that can affect network performance are the addition or replacement of workstations, new or replaced servers and equipment, new or modified network segments, and upgrading or replacing server and workstation operating systems.

A baseline should be established periodically to project a network's future needs. You can monitor network traffic and predict the need of additional segments, servers, data storage, and more.

Wireshark has an assortment of useful items under the **Statistics** menu for recording baseline information. Look at the following screen capture of the Wireshark **Statistics** menu.

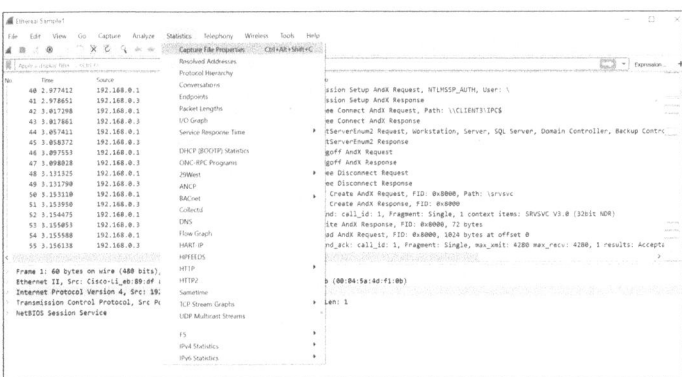

Goodheart-Willcox Publisher

The following table lists some of the common **Statistics** menu items you will explore during this laboratory activity. There is a great deal more detailed information in the Wireshark user guide available from the Wireshark website.

Statistics Menu Options	Description
Capture File Properties	General summary of network information and statistics during a specific time period
Protocol Hierarchy	Hierarchical display of all protocols captured during a specific time period
Conversions	Displays traffic between two end points
End Points	Displays traffic by addresses
I/O Graphs	Graphical display of the amount of traffic over a specific period of time

Equipment and Materials

- Windows 10 with Wireshark installed. (Note: Windows 11 is also acceptable.)
- Wireshark Sample 18 file

    Wireshark Sample 18 file location:

    _____

- Wireshark Sample 19 file

    Wireshark Sample 19 file location:

    _____

> **NOTE**
> The computer must be a part of a peer-to-peer or client/server network to generate network traffic.

Procedure

1. _____ Report to your assigned workstation.

2. _____ Boot the computer and verify that it is in working order.

3. _____ Start Wireshark and then open the sample Wireshark Sample 18 file. Look at the information in the **Summary** dialog box accessed through **Statistics>Capture File Properties**. The dialog box should look similar to the following.

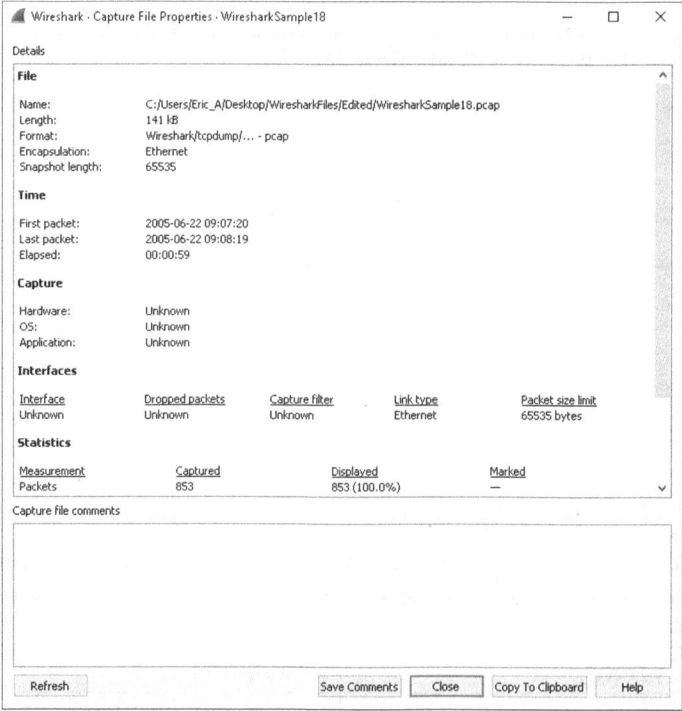

Goodheart-Willcox Publisher

Name _____

The **Capture File Properties** dialog box presents a summary of general network statistics such as the total time elapsed during the capture, total number of packets captured, average number of packets per second, average packet size, total number of bytes, average number of bytes per second, and average number of megabytes per second.

4. _____ Close the **Capture File Properties** dialog box.

5. _____ Access **Statistics>Protocol Hierarchy**. A dialog box similar to the following will display.

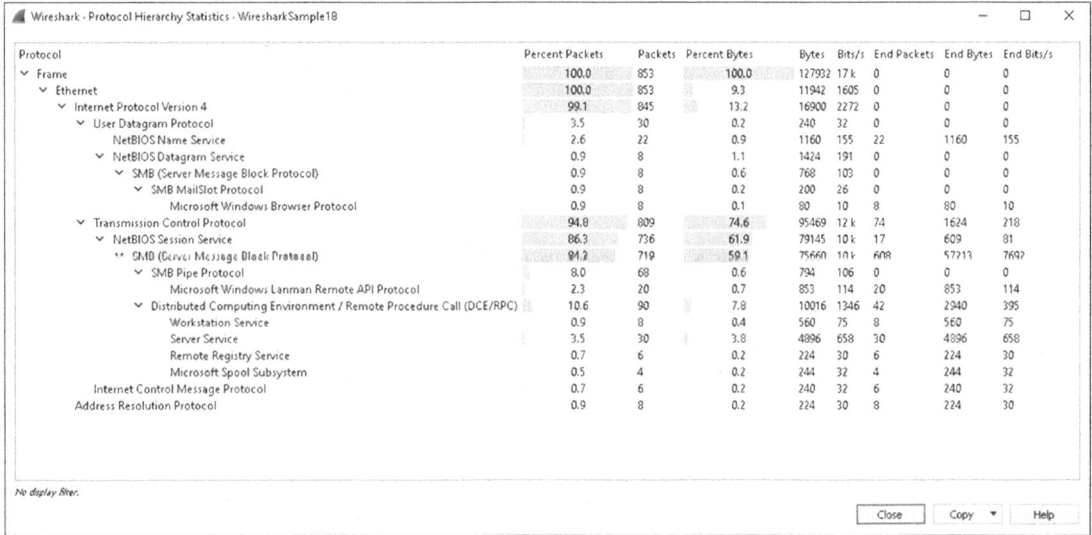

Goodheart-Willcox Publisher

You will see a detailed breakdown by protocol of all packets captured. The **Protocol Hierarchy** menu item can be used to identify network activity or to spot unusual or suspicious activity. For example, a high percentage of Address Resolution Protocol (ARP) requests could indicate an intruder probing the network for IPv4 and MAC addresses or indicate a defective hardware device or software program. In the Wireshark Sample 18 file, you will see that the total ARP percentage is less than 1% of the total packets. A low percentage of ARP requests is normal.

6. _____ Close the **Protocol Hierarchy Statistics** dialog box.

7. _____ Access **Statistics>Conversations**. Look at the following three screen captures. The first is of the **Conversations** dialog box with the **Name resolution** option disabled. The second screen capture shows the **Conversations** dialog box with **Name resolution** enabled. In the third screen capture, the **IPv4 6** tab is selected.

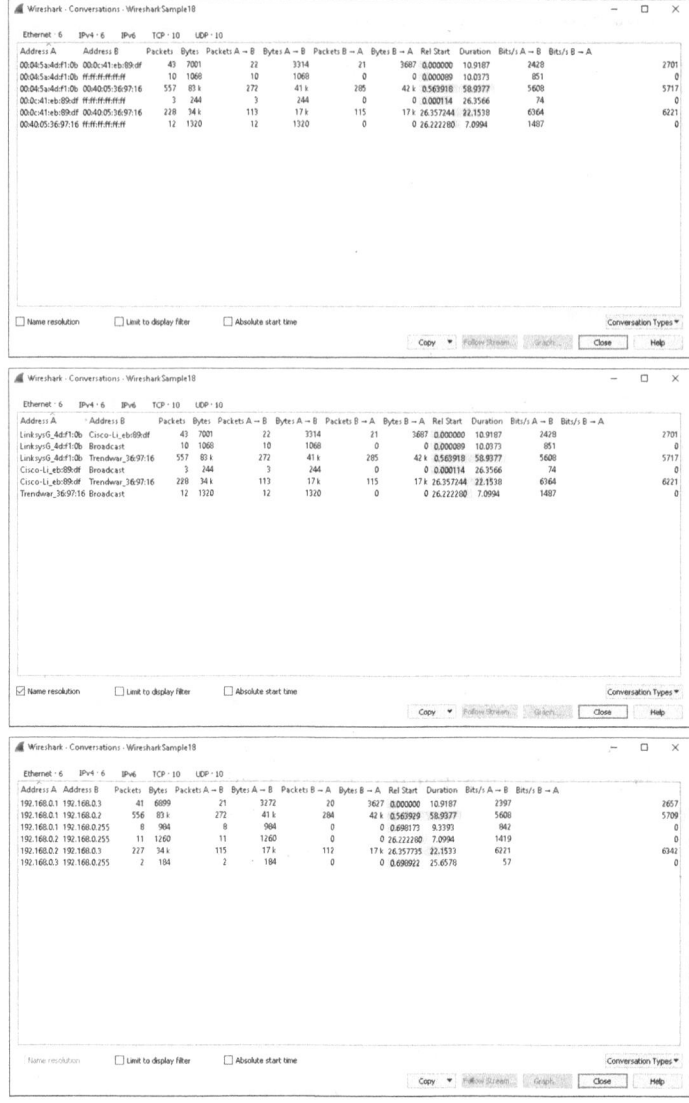

Goodheart-Willcox Publisher

The **Conversations** dialog box displays the traffic between various nodes on the network. The default tab selected is **Ethernet 6**. The number 6 indicates that six nodes are referenced by IP address. Source IP addresses are listed under column **Address A**, and destination addresses are listed under column **Address B**. Notice that broadcasts are considered IP addresses. Broadcasts are listed in the previous dialog box as 192.168.0.255.

The **Conversations** dialog box is very handy for locating an IP address that is sending an unusual amount of broadcast traffic. A high amount of broadcast traffic can indicate a problem such as a defective device, improper configuration, virus, or security breach. The **Conversations** and the **Endpoints** menu items allow you to display the information related to only Ethernet, IPv4, TCP, or UDP. Also, notice that in addition to these four protocols, traffic can be selected by additional protocols, such as Fibre Channel, FDDI, and IPX.

8. _____ Close the **Conversations** dialog box.

Name _____

9. _____ Access **Statistics>Endpoints**. The **Endpoints** dialog box will display and look similar to the following screen capture.

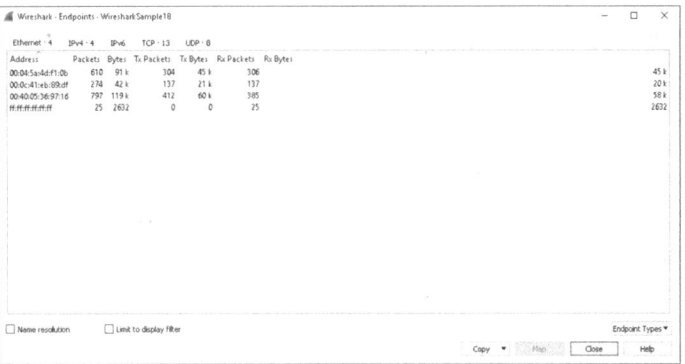

Goodheart-Willcox Publisher

The **Endpoints** dialog box displays network activity by each network device. This is an excellent way to determine where most of the network traffic is being generated. This can be helpful when identifying sources of high-volume traffic on the network. A switch can then be used to create segments to reduce the network traffic.

10. _____ Close the **Endpoints** dialog box.

11. _____ Access **Statistics>I/O Graph**. A dialog box similar to the following will display.

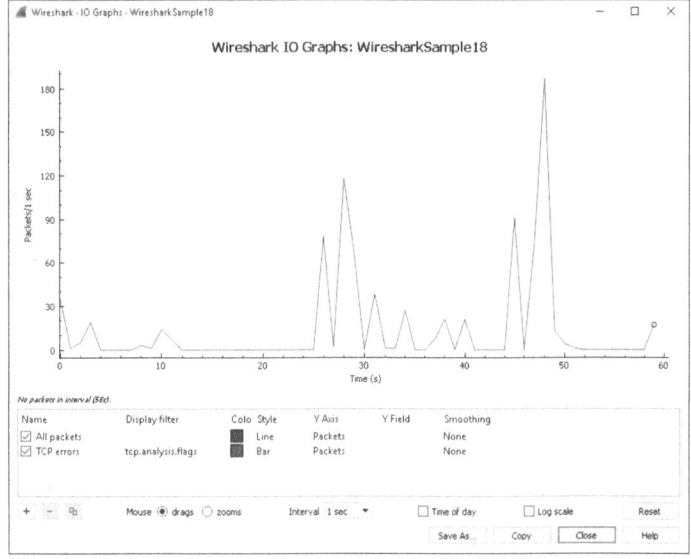

Goodheart-Willcox Publisher

The **I/O Graph** dialog box displays network traffic as a graph. You can make changes to the way the data appears in the graph by clicking and dragging the chart. The X axis is the horizontal axis and represents the time. You can modify the representation of time on the X axis by adjusting the time displayed in the **Interval** drop-down menu. The Y axis is the vertical axis and represents the network volume typically in packets or bytes. You can modify the display by filtering specific protocols and displaying them in a different color. This is controlled on the lower pane of the window. Double-clicking on a listed protocol will enable you to label the protocol in the graph, adjust the color used in the graph, or add and remove additional filters to and from the graph.

12. _____ Close the **I/O Graph** dialog box and Wireshark Sample 19 file.

13. _____ Open the Wireshark Sample 19 file and see if you can determine the network problem by looking at the statistics. Answer the following questions.

What type of protocol makes up the majority of the capture?

_____

Which network device address is generating the most broadcasts?

_____

What is the total lapse time of the capture?

_____

How many bytes per second were transmitted on average?

_____

Which are the top three devices generating traffic?

_____

What do you think is indicated by the statistics?

_____

14. _____ Create a capture over a time period of five minutes. Generate traffic conditions by accessing shares on another computer or by accessing the Internet and conducting a search or download. After five minutes have elapsed, stop the capture and prepare a report for your instructor. The report should list the network devices in the local area network and the amount of traffic generated by each protocol. Identify which device is generating the most traffic.

NOTE
A true baseline needs to gather information over a long period of time. In a typical lab setting, this is impossible. For this laboratory activity, you will limit the time to five minutes, unless instructed otherwise.

15. _____ After the report is complete, you may use the remaining time in the class period to experiment with the **Statistics** menu.

16. _____ Answer the review questions.

Review Questions

1. What is a baseline?

_____

_____

2. What changes may justify reestablishing a network baseline?

_____

_____

_____

3. Which Wireshark **Statistics** menu item will provide a listing of the amount of data exchanged between two devices in a network?

_____

4. Which Wireshark **Statistics** menu item will display a list of all devices on the network?

_____

Name _____ Date _____ Class _____

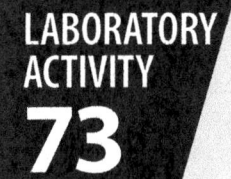

Laboratory Activity 73: Creating a CompTIA Network+ Certification Study Guide

Outcomes

After completing this laboratory activity, you will be able to:
- Use the Internet to locate and download a copy of the CompTIA Network+ certification objectives.
- Use the CompTIA Network+ certification objectives to create a study guide.

Introduction

In this laboratory activity, you will download a copy of the CompTIA Network+ certification exam objectives and then create your own study guide. After downloading a copy of the exam objectives in PDF format, you can save a copy of the objectives as a text file. This will allow you to manipulate the contents to copy sections of the original content and paste them into a Word document to create a student study guide. It also allows you to create ample space for notes pertaining to each topic.

You will complete the Network+ certification study guide using information from your textbook and laboratory manual, the Internet, and any other source you think is appropriate. Check with your instructor for additional sources.

There are many different Network+ certification study guides available commercially and for free. The problem with a ready-made study guide is that it typically does not help you actively learn the material. As a student, you are well aware that you learn a topic by reading, doing worksheets, writing reports, and doing other mental exercises that help you process and retain the information. You would most likely read a ready-made study guide once and then not review it. Your retention would be approximately equal to reading a text or a list of terms and definitions. To retain information, you must make some effort. For example, answering review questions and completing worksheets will better enable you to retain the information than if you simply read the information. A study guide that you prepare for yourself will better prepare you for the exam and will help you identify the areas for which you feel inadequately prepared.

Equipment and Materials

- Windows 10 computer with Internet and printer access and Microsoft Word

> **NOTE**
> A printer is not absolutely necessary for this laboratory activity. The finished product can be transferred to storage media such as a flash drive.

Procedure

1. _____ Report to your assigned workstation.
2. _____ Boot the computer and verify that it is in working order.
3. _____ Conduct a web search to locate the latest version of the Network+ certification exam objectives.
4. _____ Download a PDF version of the objectives. Also, download a copy of any sample test questions that might be available.

> **NOTE**
> Sample test questions are not always available for CompTIA certification exams on the CompTIA website.

5. _____ After successfully downloading a copy of the CompTIA Network+ certification exam objectives, take a minute to familiarize yourself with them.

6. _____ Open the PDF of the CompTIA Network+ certification exam objectives and then access **File>Save As Other>Text**.

7. _____ Open the CompTIA Network+ certification exam objectives text file in Notepad.

8. _____ After opening the text file of the CompTIA Network+ certification exam objectives, select the area of the file you wish to copy—for example, the Domain 1 section and all of its topics.

You can select the section of text you wish to copy by dragging the mouse pointer over the appropriate area while pressing the left mouse button. The selected area of text will be highlighted. Right-click the highlighted area and then select **Copy** from the shortcut menu.

9. _____ Open a new Microsoft Word document and paste the copied section into the new document by right-clicking a blank area and selecting **Paste** from the shortcut menu.

10. _____ Save the new document before making any changes. You might wish to name the file Firstname Lastname Network Study Guide Domain 1, replacing *Firstname Lastname* with your actual name. This will identify your work should your instructor want you to turn in a copy of your completed study guide for a grade.

11. _____ Now, you will format the text in the document to create a useful study guide. Create spaces for your notes or for drawings. Look at the example in the following screen capture.

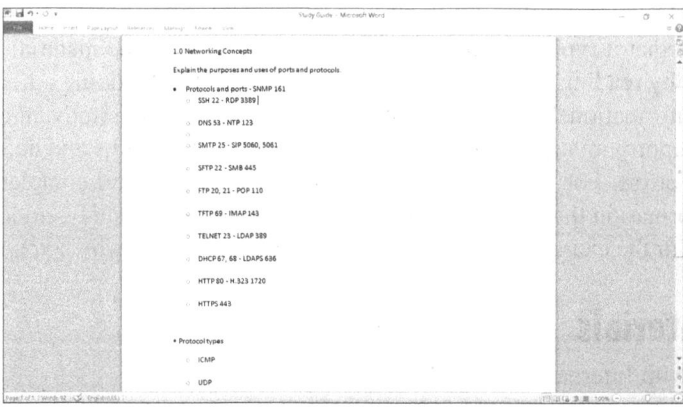

Goodheart-Willcox Publisher

Notice that spaces have been added. You can use the mouse and the [Enter] key to create spaces in the study guide. Save your study guide often when creating the spaces.

12. _____ When you are finished, call your instructor to inspect your work.

13. _____ When you receive your instructor's approval, you may print your study guide and begin filling in the blank areas with notes pertaining to the objectives.

Name _____ Date _____ Class _____

Writing a Résumé

Outcomes

After completing this laboratory activity, you will be able to:
- Create a résumé.
- Recall the headings to include in a résumé.
- Recall personal information you should *not* include as part of a résumé.

Introduction

In this laboratory activity, you will prepare a résumé. A résumé is a vital part of acquiring employment. Your résumé should contain the following headings and related information:
- Education
- Employment
- Job skills
- References

Before coming to class to perform this laboratory activity, gather information regarding your education, employment, job skills, and references. You will need to know the schools you have attended and the years you have attended them. List your education history as far back as high school. Include any special training you have had. Gather the names and addresses of the places at which you have worked and the dates of your employment there. Also, make note of the various job skills you have mastered.

> **NOTE**
> At a job interview, you should be prepared to provide a copy of any special training certificates, special recognitions, or degrees you have received.

At least four people should be selected as references. Be sure to obtain their permission before listing them on your résumé. Include contact information for each person, such as their name, phone number, e-mail address, and city and state of residence.

Depending on the version of Microsoft Word that you are using, specific résumé templates will be available. The templates can help you to format your résumé so it has a professional look and feel. The templates also contain sample information. In this laboratory activity, you will examine the sentence structure of the sample sentences before entering your own information. You will create sentences in a similar fashion. To enter your information, simply highlight the sample text and then replace it with your information.

When creating a résumé, do *not* list your Social Security number. You do not want your Social Security number and personal information on the same document. Your Social Security number will be requested after you are hired for a position. Do *not* include a copy of your driver's license number in the résumé for the same reason as the Social Security number. Your driver's license may be requested after you are hired. Do *not* post your résumé online at a website that charges fees. Do *not* post your résumé online at a nationally recognized website unless you are willing to relocate to another geographical area. If you plan to post your résumé to an online job board, make a second copy that does not list your physical address. Instead, use a general geographical area, such as Chicago or New York City.

Equipment and Materials
- Windows 10 computer with Internet access, printer access, and Microsoft Word or comparable word-processing software

Procedure

1. _____ Gather any notes you have made on references, employment, education, and job skills, and then report to your assigned workstation.
2. _____ Boot the computer and verify that it is in working order.
3. _____ Open Microsoft Word.
4. _____ Select **File>New**.
5. _____ Type resume into the search bar and press the [Enter] key.
6. _____ Choose a résumé template from the list shown. Be sure to select a résumé template, not a cover letter template. A preview of your chosen template will appear. Click the **Create** button to continue. The résumé will download, open, and contain instructional notes.
7. _____ Read through the sample information in the Experience section. Notice that the sentences are short and to the point, describing the most important tasks performed at the company. You will create similar sentences for your Employment section. Now look at the sentences under Education. Notice that the degree is listed followed by the title of the degree. Honors are listed below.
8. _____ Create the headings Education, Job Skills, Employment, and Reference by highlighting the sample headings and typing in the desired heading. Be sure to enter Education and Employment over the headings that contain fields for dates. For Job Skills and References, you can use the format of the heading styles such as Interests or Activities, or you can use the headings that contain fields for names and dates. You will be able to enter any information into the fields. Delete any unused headings along with sample information that is not used. Do not delete any of the sample information under your headings.
9. _____ Enter your information in the appropriate fields by highlighting the sample text and then typing in your information. List your employment and education history in descending order, from the most recent employment to your oldest employment. When entering your work experience, use action verbs such as managed, facilitated, oversaw, or developed. Remember to keep your sentences short.
10. _____ When you are finished, read through your résumé and spell check your work.
11. _____ If instructed to do so, print your document and give it to your instructor, or save your document to a storage device, such as a flash drive.
12. _____ Answer the review questions.

Review Questions

1. List four headings to include in a résumé.
   _____
   _____

2. What documentation should you be prepared to present at an interview?
   _____
   _____
   _____

3. What personal information should you *not* include as part of the résumé?
   _____
   _____
   _____

Name _____ Date _____ Class _____

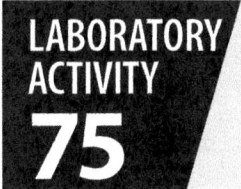

Conducting a Job Search

Outcomes

After completing this laboratory activity, you will be able to:
- Recall possible sources of job information.
- Execute a job search to locate an entry-level network technician position.

Introduction

In this laboratory activity, you will conduct a job search for an entry-level position as a network technician. You will collect information pertaining to at least three jobs in your local area or in close proximity to your hometown. Some possible sources of job information include:
- online job sites;
- governmental institutions; and
- large employers.

There are many job search sites on the Internet, such as www.indeed.com and www.moster.com. Access one of these sites and enter the keywords **network technician employment** or simply **employment**.

Governmental institutions, such as local school districts, colleges, and governmental offices, and large employers, such as local manufacturers and hospitals, typically post jobs on their website. You can also search a database of government jobs at www.usajobs.gov. Most jobs are acquired through acquaintances, such as other students, instructors, friends, neighbors, and business contacts.

While conducting your online search, gather information to turn in for this laboratory assignment. Print copies of possible job opportunities matching your skill set. Be prepared to turn in to your instructor a copy of each eligible job or the three best possibilities.

Equipment and Materials

- Windows 10 computer with Internet and printer access

Procedure

1. _____ Report to your assigned workstation.

2. _____ Boot the computer and verify it is in working order.

3. _____ Conduct a job search and identify at least three jobs for which you could apply. Use sources such as professional journals and the Internet.

4. _____ Submit to your instructor a copy of each job for which you may be eligible.

5. _____ Answer the review questions.

Review Questions

1. List three possible sources of job information.

2. List at least three examples of governmental institutions in which to find a job as an entry-level network technician.